IET PROFESSIONAL APPLICATIONS OF COMPUTING SERIES 35

Big Data Recommender Systems

IET Book Series on Big Data – Call for Authors

Editor-in-Chief: Professor Albert Y. Zomaya, University of Sydney, Australia

The topic of Big Data has emerged as a revolutionary theme that cuts across many technologies and application domains. This new book series brings together topics within the myriad research activities in many areas that analyse, compute, store, manage and transport massive amount of data, such as algorithm design, data mining and search, processor architectures, databases, infrastructure development, service and data discovery, networking and mobile computing, cloud computing, high-performance computing, privacy and security, storage and visualization.

Topics considered include (but not restricted to) IoT and Internet computing; cloud computing; peer-to-peer computing; autonomic computing; data centre computing; multi-core and many core computing; parallel, distributed and high-performance computing; scalable databases; mobile computing and sensor networking; green computing; service computing; networking infrastructures; cyberinfrastructures; e-Science; smart cities; analytics and data mining; Big Data applications and more.

Proposals for coherently integrated International co-edited or co-authored handbooks and research monographs will be considered for this book series. Each proposal will be reviewed by the editor-in-chief and some board members, with additional external reviews from independent reviewers. Please email your book proposal for the IET Book Series on Big Data to: Professor Albert Y. Zomaya at albert.zomaya@sydney.edu.au or to the IET at author_support@theiet.org.

Other volumes in this series:

Volume 1   **Knowledge Discovery and Data Mining** M.A. Bramer (Editor)
Volume 3   **Troubled IT Projects: Prevention and turnaround** J.M. Smith
Volume 4   **UML for Systems Engineering: Watching the wheels, 2nd Edition** J. Holt
Volume 5   **Intelligent Distributed Video Surveillance Systems** S.A. Velastin and
                P. Remagnino (Editors)
Volume 6   **Trusted Computing** C. Mitchell (Editor)
Volume 7   **SysML for Systems Engineering** J. Holt and S. Perry
Volume 8   **Modelling Enterprise Architectures** J. Holt and S. Perry
Volume 9   **Model-based Requirements Engineering** J. Holt, S. Perry and M. Bownsword
Volume 13 **Trusted Platform Modules: Why, when and how to use them** Ariel Segall
Volume 14 **Foundations for Model-based Systems Engineering: From patterns to models**
                J. Holt, S. Perry and M. Bownsword
Volume 15 **Big Data and Software Defined Networks** J. Taheri (Editor)
Volume 18 **Modeling and Simulation of Complex Communication** M.A. Niazi (Editor)
Volume 20 **SysML for Systems Engineering: A model-based approach, 3rd Edition** J. Holt
                and S. Perry
Volume 23 **Data as Infrastructure for Smart Cities** L. Suzuki and A. Finkelstein
Volume 24 **Ultrascale Computing Systems** J. Carretero, E. Jeannot and A. Zomaya

Big Data Recommender Systems

Volume 1: Algorithms, Architectures, Big Data, Security and Trust

Edited by
Osman Khalid, Samee U. Khan and Albert Y. Zomaya

The Institution of Engineering and Technology

Published by The Institution of Engineering and Technology, London, United Kingdom

The Institution of Engineering and Technology is registered as a Charity in England & Wales (no. 211014) and Scotland (no. SC038698).

© The Institution of Engineering and Technology 2019

First published 2019

The Institution of Engineering and Technology
Michael Faraday House
Six Hills Way, Stevenage
Herts, SG1 2AY, United Kingdom

www.theiet.org

British Library Cataloguing in Publication Data
A catalogue record for this product is available from the British Library

ISBN 981-1-78561-975-5 (Volume 1 hardback)
ISBN 981-1-78561-976-2 (Volume 1 PDF)
ISBN 978-1-78561-977-9 (Volume 2 hardback)
ISBN 978-1-78561-978-6 (Volume 2 PDF)
ISBN 978-1-78561-979-3 (2 volume set hardback)

Typeset in India by MPS Limited

Contents

Foreword   xv

1 Introduction to big data recommender systems—volume 1   1
Osman Khalid, Faisal Rehman, Samee U. Khan, and Albert Y. Zomaya

   1.1 Background   1
   1.2 About the book   3
   Acknowledgments   6
   References   6

2 Theoretical foundations for recommender systems   9
Mirza Zaeem Baig, Hasina Khatoon, Syeda Saleha Raza,
and Muhammad Qasim Pasta

   2.1 Introduction   9
      2.1.1 Definitions of RSs   10
      2.1.2 The need for an RS   10
   2.2 Applications of RSs   10
      2.2.1 Current use of RSs   11
      2.2.2 More areas for RSs   11
   2.3 Algorithms and theoretical foundations of RSs   12
      2.3.1 Phases of RSs   12
      2.3.2 Types of RSs   13
      2.3.3 Datasets for recommendations   20
   2.4 Problems related to RSs   21
      2.4.1 Data sparsity problem   21
      2.4.2 Cold start problem   22
      2.4.3 Scalability   22
      2.4.4 Overspecialization or diversity problem 22
      2.4.5 Vulnerable to attacks   22
   References   22

3 Benchmarking big data recommendation algorithms using Hadoop
or Apache Spark   27
Dinesh Kumar Saini, Kashif Zia, and Arshad Muhammad

   3.1 Introduction   28

3.2   Big data   28
    3.2.1   Hadoop   28
    3.2.2   Presenting the MapReduce model   30
    3.2.3   Hadoop input/output   30
    3.2.4   Apache Ambari and Ambari architecture   31
    3.2.5   Future of Hadoop   32
    3.2.6   How Hadoop works in social networking   32
3.3   Apache Spark   33
3.4   Recommender systems   33
    3.4.1   Design of recommender systems   34
    3.4.2   Collaborative recommendation and collaborative filtering   34
    3.4.3   Reducing the sparsity problem   35
    3.4.4   Content-based recommendation   35
    3.4.5   Visualization of recommendation   36
    3.4.6   Hybrid recommendation approaches   36
3.5   Systems based on nature-inspired algorithms   37
3.6   Benchmarking: big data benchmarking   37
3.7   Summary   38
References   38

4   Efficient and socio-aware recommendation approaches for bigdata networked systems   41
Vasileios Karyotis, Margarita Vitoropoulou, Nikos Kalatzis, Ioanna Roussaki, and Symeon Papavassiliou

4.1   Introduction   41
4.2   Background on recommendation systems and social network analysis   43
    4.2.1   Recommendation systems   43
    4.2.2   Social network analysis   46
4.3   Socio-aware recommendation systems   48
    4.3.1   Hyperbolic path-based recommendation system   48
    4.3.2   Probabilistic graphical models   50
    4.3.3   Information diffusion-aware recommendation approaches   55
    4.3.4   Context-based recommendations in pervasive systems 58
4.4   Qualitative comparison   65
4.5   Open problems and conclusion   66
References   66

5   Novel hybrid approaches for big data recommendations   71
Abdul Kader Saiod and Darelle van Greunen

5.1   Introduction   71
5.2   Context   72
5.3   The big data architecture   74

5.4 Different approaches to handle big data 76
  5.4.1 Approaches to detect and reduce data inconsistency 77
5.5 Complexity and issues of big DI 81
  5.5.1 Big data analysis and integration architecture 81
5.6 Big DI using HAs based on Fuzzy-Ontology 83
5.7 Developing approaches for the crisp ontology 84
5.8 Developing HAs for Fuzzy-Ontology 84
5.9 Extracting the big data key business functions for the proposed HAs based on Fuzzy-Ontology 86
5.10 Identify the specification for the purpose HIDAs for big data 87
5.11 Real-world project: hypertension-specific diagnosis based on HIDAs 88
  5.11.1 Data collection 88
  5.11.2 Step 1: HIDAs contrivance and excellence 90
  5.11.3 Step 2: determine and ascertain the necessity for fuzziness in hypertension diagnosis 91
  5.11.4 Step 3: specify fuzzy-associated elements in hypertension data 92
  5.11.5 Step 4: reusing the subsisting HIDAs resources 92
  5.11.6 Step 5: reusing the subsisting Fuzzy-Ontology resources elements 93
  5.11.7 Step 6: appropriate the subsisting of Fuzzy-Ontology elements 93
  5.11.8 Step 7: identify appropriate Fuzzy-Ontology elements 93
  5.11.9 Step 8: identify appropriate crisp ontology elements 95
  5.11.10 Step 9: formalisation 98
  5.11.11 Step 10: Fuzzy-Ontology result affirmation 98
  5.11.12 Step 11: documentation and notes 99
5.12 Mathematical simulation of hypertension diagnosis based on Markov chain probability model 99
5.13 Analysis of result 104
5.14 Conclusion 106
References 106

6 Deep generative models for recommender systems 111
Vineeth Rakesh, Suhang Wang, and Huan Liu

6.1 Introduction 111
6.2 Generative models 113
  6.2.1 Probabilistic matrix factorization 113
  6.2.2 Probabilistic latent semantic analysis 114
  6.2.3 Latent Dirichlet allocation 116
  6.2.4 Collaborative topic models 119
6.3 Deep learning for recommender systems 121
  6.3.1 Restricted Boltzmann-machine-based collaborative filtering 121

	6.3.2	Autoencoder for recommender systems	122
	6.3.3	Multilayer perceptron based recommender systems	124
	6.3.4	RNN/LSTM for recommendation	124
6.4	Deep generative models		125
	6.4.1	Collaborative denoising autoencoders	125
	6.4.2	Collaborative variational autoencoder	127
6.5	Summary		130
References			130

7   Recommendation algorithms for unstructured big data such as text, audio, image and video   133
Madjid Khalilian, Mahshid Alsadat Ehsaei, and Saloomeh TaheriFard

7.1	Recommender methods		134
	7.1.1	Content-based recommendations	134
	7.1.2	Collaborative recommendations	135
	7.1.3	Knowledge-based recommendations	137
	7.1.4	Demographic recommendations	138
	7.1.5	Hybrid recommendations	138
7.2	Big data analytic		139
	7.2.1	Text analytics	139
	7.2.2	Audio analytics	143
	7.2.3	Video analytics	152
	7.2.4	Image analytics	157
	7.2.5	Other recommender system	162
7.3	Recommender systems: challenges and limitations		163
7.4	Summary		164
References			165

8   Deep segregation of plastic (DSP): segregation of plastic and nonplastic using deep learning   169
K. Sreelakshmi, R. Vinayakumar, and K.P. Soman

8.1	Introduction		170
8.2	Related work		171
8.3	Deep learning		172
8.4	Scalable architecture		174
8.5	Software framework		176
8.6	Software and packages		176
	8.6.1	TensorFlow	176
	8.6.2	Keras	177
	8.6.3	OpenCV	177
8.7	Hardware components used		179
	8.7.1	Arduino UNO	179
	8.7.2	Windshield wiper motor	181

	8.7.3 Stepper motor	181
	8.7.4 Switching power supply	181
	8.7.5 ULN 2003	182
	8.7.6 Webcam	182
8.8	Hardware setup for segregation	183
8.9	Experiments and observation	185
	8.9.1 Training process	185
8.10	Conclusion and future work	188
Appendix A		188
Appendix B		189
Acknowledgments		189
References		189

9 Spatiotemporal recommendation with big geo-social networking data 193

Weiqing Wang and Hongzhi Yin

9.1	Introduction	193
9.2	Preliminaries about SAGE	197
9.3	Spatial–temporal SAGE model	197
	9.3.1 Problem definitions	197
	9.3.2 Model description	199
	9.3.3 Model inference	202
	9.3.4 Spatial smoothing	204
	9.3.5 Parallel implementation	205
9.4	Spatial item recommendation using ST-SAGE	208
9.5	Experiments	209
	9.5.1 Experimental settings	209
	9.5.2 Recommendation effectiveness	212
	9.5.3 Recommendation efficiency	215
9.6	Related work	217
9.7	Conclusion	219
References		219

10 Recommender system for predicting malicious Android applications 225

Tanya Gera, Jaiteg Singh, Deepak Thakur, and Rajinder Sandhu

10.1	Background	225
	10.1.1 Android operating system architecture	227
	10.1.2 Android application structure	229
	10.1.3 Application threats	230
10.2	The proposed recommender system for mobile application risk reduction	231
	10.2.1 Preprocessing	231

	10.2.2	Emulation and testing	232
	10.2.3	Features extraction	232
	10.2.4	Machine learning	232
	10.2.5	Dataset	233
10.3	Conclusion		233
References			233

11   Security threats and their mitigation in big data recommender systems   **235**
Madjid Khalilian, Maryam Fathi Ahmadsaraei, and Lida Farajpour

11.1	Introduction		235
11.2	Security issues and approaches in HDFS architecture		236
	11.2.1	Security issues in HDFS	237
	11.2.2	HDFS security methods	237
11.3	Big data recommender system attacks		239
	11.3.1	Attack tactics	239
	11.3.2	Probe attack strategy	239
	11.3.3	Ratings strategy	240
	11.3.4	Dimensions of attacks	240
	11.3.5	Models of attacks	241
11.4	Recommender algorithms		244
	11.4.1	Association rule mining	245
	11.4.2	Base algorithms	245
	11.4.3	k-Nearest neighbor	245
	11.4.4	k-Means clustering	246
	11.4.5	Probabilistic latent semantic analysis	246
	11.4.6	Recommender algorithms and evaluation metrics	246
	11.4.7	Profile classification	247
11.5	Attack response and system robustness		248
	11.5.1	Classification of attributes	248
	11.5.2	Enhanced hybrid collaborative recommender systems	249
	11.5.3	Defense against profile injection attacks	250
11.6	Conclusion		254
References			254

12   User's privacy in recommendation systems applying online social network data: a survey and taxonomy   **259**
Erfan Aghasian, Saurabh Garg, and James Montgomery

12.1	Introduction		259
12.2	Recommender systems and techniques: privacy of online social network data		260
	12.2.1	Privacy: definition	261

	12.2.2 Online social networks, classification, and privacy	262
12.3	Taxonomy of privacy	263
	12.3.1 Privacy concerns in social networks	263
	12.3.2 User-specific privacy risks and invasion	264
	12.3.3 Measuring privacy in online social networks	265
	12.3.4 Privacy-preserving approaches	271
	12.3.5 Privacy-preserving models	272
12.4	Privacy preservation in recommender systems	276
12.5	Conclusion and future directions	277
References		277

13 Private entity resolution for big data on Apache Spark using multiple phonetic codes **283**

Alexandros Karakasidis and Georgia Koloniari

13.1	Introduction	283
13.2	Related work	284
13.3	Problem formulation and background	286
	13.3.1 Problem formulation and notation used	286
	13.3.2 Phonetic algorithms for privacy preserving matching	287
	13.3.3 The Soundex algorithm	288
	13.3.4 The NYSIIS algorithm	289
	13.3.5 Apache Spark	289
13.4	A parallel privacy preserving phonetics matching protocol	290
	13.4.1 Multiple algorithms for phonetic matching	290
	13.4.2 Protocol operation	292
	13.4.3 Privacy discussion	294
13.5	Empirical evaluation	295
	13.5.1 Experimental setup	295
	13.5.2 Experimental results	296
13.6	Conclusions and future work	299
References		300

14 Deep learning architecture for big data analytics in detecting intrusions and malicious URL **303**

*N.B. Harikrishnan, R. Vinayakumar, K.P. Soman,
Prabaharan Poornachandran, B. Annappa, and Mamoun Alazab*

14.1	Introduction	304
14.2	Related works	305
	14.2.1 Network intrusion detection systems (NIDSs)	305
	14.2.2 Related works on phishing URL detection	307
14.3	Background	308
	14.3.1 Deep neural network	308
	14.3.2 Recurrent neural network	310
	14.3.3 Convolutional neural network	311

14.4	Intrusion detection	312
	14.4.1 Description of KDD-Cup-99 data set	312
	14.4.2 Description of Kyoto network intrusion detection (ID) data set	314
	14.4.3 Experiments on KDD-Cup-99	314
	14.4.4 Proposed architecture for KDD-Cup-99 data set	317
	14.4.5 Experiments on Kyoto network intrusion detection (ID) data set	318
	14.4.6 Proposed architecture for Kyoto	318
	14.4.7 Evaluation results for KDD-Cup-99	319
	14.4.8 Evaluation results for Kyoto	320
14.5	Intrusion detection (ID) using multidimensional zoom (M-ZOOM) framework	322
	14.5.1 Density measures	322
	14.5.2 Problem formulation	323
	14.5.3 Data set description	324
	14.5.4 Experiments and observations	324
14.6	Phishing URL detection	327
	14.6.1 Data set description of phishing URL detection	327
	14.6.2 URL representation	327
	14.6.3 Experiments	328
	14.6.4 Hyper-parameter tuning	328
	14.6.5 Proposed architecture for URL analysis	329
14.7	Proposed architecture for machine learning based cybersecurity	331
14.8	Conclusion and future work	332
	Acknowledgments	332
	References	332
Index		**337**

Foreword

The increase in the volumes of data creates new challenges that require novel and more efficient solutions to handle big data and scalability issues. Today we are witnessing advances in many areas that are dependent on recommender systems such as social networks, e-commerce websites, search engines, blogs, and sensor networks. Many of these advances are due to the many developments in algorithmics and analytics, wireless networking, Internet of things, high performance computing, and more.

Big Data Recommender Systems, 2 Volume Set, is an exciting and comprehensive reference that deals with a wide range of topical themes in the field. It is composed of two volumes that showcase the state of the art in recommender systems. Volume (1) *Big Data Recommender Systems: Algorithms, Architectures, Big Data, Security and Trust* covers aspects related to recommender systems preliminaries, algorithms, and architectures; recommendation approaches for big data; and trust and security measures for recommender systems. Volume (2) *Big Data Recommender Systems: Application Paradigms* presents a good overview of the many applications that show the richness of this field and its great potential.

This two-volume work will serve as a source of up-to-date and innovative research in this continuously evolving area. The books will provide an opportunity for researchers to explore the use of recommender system technologies and their impact on enhancing our capabilities to conduct more sophisticated studies. It will also be an ideal reference for graduate classes focusing on big data and recommender systems.

I believe that this book set is a great addition to the literature on the topic and should be well received by the research and development community.

Albert Y. Zomaya
Editor-in-Chief, *The IET Book Series on Big Data*

Chapter 1

Introduction to big data recommender systems—volume 1

Osman Khalid[1], Faisal Rehman[1], Samee U. Khan[2], and Albert Y. Zomaya[3]

1.1 Background

The past few years have seen significant evolution in Internet technologies that has allowed the deployment of a large number of web-based social networking and e-commerce applications. With 7.5% rise in global Internet population from 2016, the current users on the Internet have increased to 3.7 billion worldwide interacting with thousands of online applications such as Facebook, Twitter, Instagram, YouTube, Amazon, and FourSquare, to name a few [1]. This results in accumulation of huge volumes of data, also known as *big data*, on the daily basis in the form of images, videos, files, ratings, reviews, opinions, complaints, remarks, feedback, and comments for/about any item that may be a product, event, individual, and service. It has been reported in [2] that in just a single minute, the YouTube users upload 72 hours of new videos, Google receives 3,877,140 search queries, Facebook users share 2,460,000 pieces of content, Twitter users perform 473,400 tweets, Instagram users post 49,380 new photos, Yelp users post 26,380 reviews, and Pinterest users pin 3,472 images. Over 2.5 quintillion bytes of data are created every single day, and it is estimated that by the year 2020, 1.7 MB of data will be created every second [2].

Powerful and versatile tools are badly needed to automatically uncover hidden patterns and associations from tremendous amounts of big data and to transform such data into organized knowledge. The fields of information engineering and computational intelligence have made significant progress over the past decades. The potential ability to create intelligence from the analysis of raw data has been successfully applied to diverse areas, such as business, industry, sciences, social media, and e-commerce, to name a few. The overwhelming size of data has shifted the focus of research community from simple information extraction to filtering of pertinent information. Recommender systems were introduced in early 1990s as useful information

[1]Department of Computer Sciences, COMSATS University Islamabad, Abbottabad Campus, Pakistan
[2]Department of Computer Sciences, North Dakota State University, USA
[3]School of Information Technologies, University of Sydney, Australia

filtering tools for guiding users in a personalized way to discover products or services they might be interested in from a large space of possible options [3]. These systems apply various data mining and knowledge discovery techniques on users' contextual and historical data to extract personalized recommendations in the form of products, services, or information that closely match a user's preferences [4]. Recommender systems consider various factors such as stability, accuracy, disparity, and novelty to keep a balance of recommended items in context of a user's choices [3]. Nowadays, almost every e-commerce application has an integrated recommender system to boost business and to drive sales by converting targeted suggestions to purchases. For example, Netflix, an online movie hosting website, has a built-in movie recommender system. The chief production officer, Neil Hunt, of Netflix indicated that more than 80% of movies are watched through recommendations, and per year, 1 billion dollar is generated through recommended movies [5]. It is estimated in a Microsoft Research report that 30% of Amazon's page views are from recommendations [6,7]. The popular video hosting website YouTube reported in 2010 that recommended videos account for about 60% of all video clicks from home page [8]. Similarly, the coupling of online social networks, such as Facebook, with recommender systems created new opportunities for businesses that consider the social influence important for their product marketing. The social networks utilize recommendation engines to improve the user experience by personalizing the content that is provided to each user and enabling new connections.

The recommendation systems perform their computations on user-to-item interactions data that may be in the form of *explicit* ratings, in which a user selects numerical values from a specific evaluation system (e.g., five-star rating system), or *implicit* check-ins, that counts the number of user interactions with a particular item, venue, or content of interest [3]. Most online applications now also allow the users to write textual feedback about the item or service they interacted with. The basic idea of recommender systems is to utilize these various sources of data to infer customer interests. In mid-1990s, the traditional methods of recommendations were usually based on user-based collaborative filtering [7]. The first step in such techniques was to search across users that had interests similar to a given user, such as similar purchase patterns, and then recommend items of most similar users to the given user. Despite initial successes, the user-based collaborative filtering faced numerous challenges over the years in terms of scalability and recommendation quality with the gradual increase in volumes of data. In recent years, the term *big data* has evolved and is defined by four Vs: the Volume, Variety, Velocity, and Veracity [9]. Volume represents the amount of data in terabytes or petabytes, or more that is processed to compute recommendations. Variety represents the various types of data extracted from different sources like e-commerce sites or online social networks in any format like structured, unstructured, or semi-structured that should be handled by the system. Velocity means the speed with which data are generated on the Internet, e.g., large number of Amazon users giving feedback of thousands of items on daily basis. Finally, the Veracity means the reliability and trustworthiness of data. It is quite possible that reviews, opinions, or feedbacks are manipulated or sponsored by different stakeholders of online business for their personal interests [9].

Unfortunately, algorithms based on traditional user-based collaborative filtering have not evolved in capacity to handle this new volume of big data in real time or in an online modality. One major issue faced by traditional approaches is data sparseness and cold start [4]. Data sparseness occurs when we have insufficient entries of user interactions against items, resulting into loss of recommendation quality. Cold start results when a user is new to the system and does not have enough entries in the system to generate preferences. To address the issues (such as scalability) in traditional user-based collaborative recommendation algorithms, a variety of techniques have been developed over the years that attempt to reduce the dataset in a structured manner [7]. Such techniques apply various data preprocessing and refinement phases to omit the high- or low-frequency items, or to partition data by classifying various items. However, these models have their own limitations in dealing with data sparsity and cold start problems, while attempting to balance the recommendation qualities in terms of different evaluation metrics [10]. In recent years, numerous models based on item-based collaborative filtering, deep neural networks, and hybrid of user–item-based collaborative filtering have been proposed to address the challenges in the traditional recommendation approaches [3,4,10].

In current era, numerous research works are in progress to improve the scalability and recommendation quality of big data-based recommendation models. The parallel computing architectures, such as OpenMP [11], message passing interface (MPI) [12], MapReduce [13], and Spark [14], have been employed to boost up the recommendation computations. For instance, Hadoop [15] has its own file system called Hadoop Distributed File System (HDFS) where the data is deployed. Hadoop distributes the data in different clusters that perform the computations in parallel. However, the dependencies among data present further challenges to parallel computation operations.

In the past few years, numerous recommendation approaches have been proposed to address various challenges of recommender systems. However, there are still many open and unresolved issues that require novel and more efficient recommendation solutions to handle big data.

1.2 About the book

The book *Big Data Recommender Systems: Recent Trends and Advances* consists of two comprehensive volumes. Each volume consists of good quality chapters contributed by world renowned researchers and domain experts.

Volume 1 is aimed to cover the recent advances, issues, novel solutions, and theoretical research on big data recommender systems. The book encompasses original scientific contributions in the form of theoretical foundations, comparative analysis, surveys, case studies, techniques, and tools for recommender systems. A specific focus is devoted to emerging trends and the industry needs associated with utilizing recommender systems. Some of the topics covered in the Volume 1 include benchmarking of recommendation algorithms using Map Reduce, social recommendations, hybrid approaches (HAs), deep learning-based techniques, unstructured big data recommendations, machine learning (ML)-based models, and geo-social recommendations. A special section is included to cover the security and privacy concerns, cyberattacks on recommender systems, and their defensive measures.

Volume 2 is the collection of chapters written by world-leading researchers and scholars with a specific focus on *application domains* of recommender systems. The topics covered in Volume 2 include deep neural network-based algorithms, solutions to cold start problems, context-aware recommender systems, matrix factorization-based solutions, parallel processing, health-aware recommender models, big data processing and analytics, smart grid recommendation models, stream processing, Hadoop and Spark benchmarking, video recommendations, mood-sensitive recommendations, travel route recommendations, and models for point-of-interest-based recommendations.

In this book, Volume 1 aims to provide a platform for researchers, practitioners, and undergraduate/graduate students from engineering, computer sciences, knowledge engineering, data mining, and information systems. The book chapters are contributed by world-leading researchers and scholars who have been highly recognized in the field of big data, knowledge engineering, data mining, context awareness, opinion mining, parallel architectures, and large-scale data processing and recommendations. Expected readers include researchers, engineers, and IT professionals who work in the fields of knowledge engineering, big data, data mining, and recommender systems. The book could also be employed as the reference book for university students who study computer science. The book summarizes the latest research achievements and future research directions that will be of interest to practitioners and researchers alike in this dynamic and growing field. Volume 1 is organized into 14 chapters. A brief summary of the chapters is presented as follows.

Chapter 2: The chapter presents theoretical foundations of recommender systems. This begins with justifying the need of recommender systems in the current scenario of information overload and discusses various application areas where recommender systems can be useful and productive. It includes a discussion on both existing and possible future areas of applications. After a brief overview of the problems identified in the current recommender systems, some datasets are listed that may be useful for research and evaluation of various recommender system.

Chapter 3: The chapter presents a discussion on the benchmarking of big data recommendation algorithms using Hadoop and Apache Spark. The chapter explores big data issues specific to Hadoop, and the architecture of Hadoop is explained. Map Reduce process is illustrated, and the architecture of Apache Ambari and Apache spark is discussed in detail.

Chapter 4: The chapter investigates and summarizes some of the state-of-the-art approaches that exploit socio-related information for improving the performance of recommendation systems. Various types of social knowledge, such as information diffusion features and context awareness, are investigated, and it is demonstrated how they can be used to alleviate various problems of traditional and general purpose techniques.

Chapter 5: The chapter describes the applicability of the HA-based on Fuzzy-Ontology by illustrating its use in a hypothetical hypertension diagnosis project.

The proposed structure of Hybrid Integration Development Approaches based on Fuzzy-Ontology for big data is discussed in detail.

Chapter 6: The chapter presents some recent trends in generative and deep learning models for recommendation systems. The chapter discusses classic generative models such as probabilistic matrix factorization (PMF) and latent Dirichlet allocation (LDA) and explains the methodology of integrating PMF with LDA to create a hybrid model collaborative topic regression. A discussion on recommendation frameworks is provided that are purely based on deep learning, where the models such as restricted Boltzmann machine-based collaborative filtering (RBM-CF), Autoencoder-based recommendation (AutoRec), neural collaborative filtering, and Recurrent Recommender Network are discussed.

Chapter 7: The authors discuss various recommendation algorithms for unstructured big data, such as text, audio, image, and video. A detailed description of a music recommendation framework based on graph-based quality model is presented. The aforementioned framework is divided into two models: preference relation and graph-based quality model.

Chapter 8: A discussion on the contemporary research advances in ML for big data recommendations is presented. An evaluation of selected ML techniques is performed, and a few promising learning methods in latest research are highlighted. Some of the existing ML techniques are discussed in the context of recommender system.

Chapter 9: This chapter focuses on spatial item recommendation by exploiting both spatial and temporal information on geo-social networks. The authors propose a spatial–temporal sparse additive generative model (ST-SAGE) for spatial item recommendation, which effectively overcomes the challenges arising from travel locality and spatial–temporal dynamics of user behaviors. Specifically, to combat travel locality, ST-SAGE exploits both the co-occurrence patterns of spatial items and their content to infer and transfer user interests.

Chapter 10: The authors present a recommender system for predicting malicious Android applications. The concept of preprocessing, emulation and testing, and feature extraction has been used to identify malicious patterns. The proposed framework aims to automate the dynamic detection process by utilizing different systems: application instrumentation, imitating, testing, extraction, and ML.

Chapter 11: The chapter provides a discussion about the security issues of big data recommender systems. To enhance security, the proposed system intends to secure HDFS in Hadoop. The proposed approaches aim to combat attacks on the Name Node or Data Node. The authors have shown that the hybrid algorithms which are the combination of both user-based and item-based algorithms may present higher stability against attacks. The chapter also introduces different methods to discover attacks on recommender systems.

Chapter 12: The chapter surveys the main privacy concerns, measurements, and privacy-preserving techniques used in large-scale online social networks and recommender systems. It is based on historical works on security, privacy-preserving, statistical modeling, and datasets to provide an overview of the technical difficulties and problems associated with privacy preserving in online social networks.

Chapter 13: The chapter presents a cost-efficient parallel protocol for performing qualitative privacy preserving with the use of multiple phonetic encodings, combining the Soundex and the New York State Identification and Intelligence System (NYSIIS) phonetic algorithms. The first algorithm is proposed to encode the original text and the second one for decoding. The experiments using the Apache Spark platform show that the proposed algorithm efficiently handles large volumes of data while improving the quality of the matching process, and the results are compared to approaches using a single encoding algorithm.

Chapter 14: The chapter proposes a method to detect cyberattacks. The proposed method is an artificial intelligence-based hybrid architecture for an organization which provides supervised and unsupervised solutions to tackle intrusions, phishing, and URL detection. The prototype model uses various classical ML classifiers and deep learning architectures. The research specifically focuses on detecting and classifying intrusions and phishing URL detection.

Acknowledgments

We would like to express our sincere thanks to the authors of the chapters for reporting their thoughts and experiences related to their research and also for patiently addressing reviewers' comments and diligently adhering to the hectic deadlines to have the book sent to the publisher in a timely manner. We are indebted to the reviewers for providing insightful and thoughtful comments on the chapters which tremendously improved the quality of the chapters included in this book.

Our thanks are due to IET for publishing this book and for accommodating us at various stages of the publication process. We believe that this book is an important contribution to the community in assembling research work on big data recommender systems from various domains.

References

[1] "Data Never Sleeps 5.0," [Online]. Available: https://web-assets.domo.com/blog/wp-content/uploads/2017/07/17_domo_data-never-sleeps-5-01.png [accessed 15 October 2018].

[2] "Data Never Sleeps 6.0," [Online]. Available: https://www.domo.com/blog/data-never-sleeps-6/ [accessed 15 October 2018].

[3] J. Bobadilla, F. Ortega, A. Hernando, and A. GutiéRrez, "Recommender systems survey," *Knowledge-Based Systems*, vol. 46, pp. 109–132, 2013.

[4] O. Khalid, M.U.S. Khan, S.U. Khan, and A.Y. Zomaya, "OmniSuggest: a ubiquitous cloud based context aware recommendation system for mobile social networks," *IEEE Transactions on Services Computing*, vol. 7, no. 3, pp. 401–414, 2014.

[5] C.A. Gomez-Uribe and N. Hunt, "The Netflix recommender system: algorithms, business value, and innovation," *ACM Transactions on Management Information Systems*, vol. 6, no. 4, pp. 1–19, 2016.

[6]   A. Sharma, J.M. Hofman, and D.J. Watts, "Estimating the causal impact of recommendation systems from observational data," in *16th ACM Conference on Economics and Computation*, Portland, Oregon, USA, 2015.

[7]   B. Smith and G. Linden, "Two decades of recommender systems at Amazon.com," *IEEE Internet Computing*, vol. 21, no. 3, pp. 12–18, 2017.

[8]   J. Davidson, B. Liebald, J. Liu, *et al.*, "The YouTube video recommendation system," in *Proceedings of the Fourth ACM Conference on Recommender Systems*, Barcelona, Spain, 2010.

[9]   U. Sivarajah, M.M. Kamal, and Z. Irani, "Critical analysis of big data challenges and analytical methods," *Journal of Business Research*, vol. 70, pp. 263–286, 2017.

[10]   F. Rehman, O. Khalid, and S.A. Madani, "A comparative study of location-based recommendation system," *Knowledge Engineering Review*, vol. 32, no. 7, 2017.

[11]   "OpenMP," [Online]. Available: https://www.openmp.org/ [accessed 15 October 2018].

[12]   B. Barney, "Message passing interface," [Online]. Available: https://computing.llnl. gov/tutorials/mpi/ [accessed 15 October 2018].

[13]   "Apache MapReduce," [Online]. Available: https://www.ibm.com/analytics/hadoop/mapreduce [accessed 15 October 2018].

[14]   "Apache Spark," [Online]. Available: https://spark.apache.org/ [accessed 15 October 2018].

[15]   "Apache Hadoop," [Online]. Available: https://hadoop.apache.org/ [accessed 15 October 2018].

Chapter 2
Theoretical foundations for recommender systems

Mirza Zaeem Baig[1], Hasina Khatoon[1], Syeda Saleha Raza[2], and Muhammad Qasim Pasta[3]

2.1 Introduction

Recommender system (RS) is software that provides suggestions to a user in decision-making process. The decision-making may be for commercial purpose (What things to buy?), for personalized applications (What movie to watch and which music to listen to?), or simple information retrieval (What are the most relevant papers for the topic?). These systems have become an important component of almost all applications that relate to some form of information retrieval and processing by using various search techniques. This chapter provides the background to the theoretical foundations of RSs. We start with a traditional approach and discuss some commonly used definitions of RSs. After justifying the need for such systems in the current scenario of information overload, application areas where RSs can be useful and productive are discussed. It includes the discussion on both existing and possible future areas of applications. The list presented is not exhaustive, as many areas have opted to add value to their applications by integrating with some form of RS. The next section gives a brief overview of the phases through which RS passes in order to perform its function. The types of RSs are discussed giving their advantages and disadvantages, and content-based recommenders, collaborative filtering (CF)-based recommenders, hybrid recommenders, image-based recommenders, and graph database (GDB)-based recommenders are discussed in detail. After a brief overview of the problems identified with the current RSs, some datasets are listed that may be used for research and evaluation of various RSs. The chapter ends with the cited references.

[1]Department of Computer Science, National University of Computer and Emerging Sciences (FAST-NU), Pakistan
[2]Dhanani School of Science & Engineering, Habib University, Pakistan
[3]Department of Computer Science, Usman Institute of Technology, Pakistan

2.1.1   Definitions of RSs

There are many definitions of RSs found in literature. RSs are defined as a decision-making strategy in the presence of a large, complex set of information [1]. It allows for listing of personalized contents and services with prioritization and personalization. In the current scenario of information overload from the Internet, it makes possible the timely access to important information. It is also referred to as information filtering system that deals with the problem of information overload [2]. The purpose of RSs is to provide support to users in terms of additional knowledge in the form of recommendations and to provide hints about products and systems.

A good definition from [3] states that the RSs are systems that, based on information about the past patterns and consumption patterns in general, recommend new items to the user. It is a subclass of information filtering system that seeks to predict the 'rating' or 'preference' that a user would give to an item [4]. According to Seroussi [5], discovery assistance is a better term for such systems and he argues that the RSs are systems that help users discover items they may like.

2.1.2   The need for an RS

In this era of web marketing, these systems play an important role. The goal of RS is to generate meaningful recommendations to users for items or products that might interest them. It fetches more revenue for product providers and adds value to products and services.

The rising trend towards the use of the Internet for an ever-growing set of applications has forced users to use a number of search engines. A search engine is helpful in finding out about an object and results in the form of listing of all possible sources of information from all over the world. For every query made to a search engine, there are thousands of links suggested to the user. The amount of information obtained is very large and a user can find it difficult to filter and narrow down the search to explore further. Moreover, a large amount of irrelevant information is also obtained as a result of the search. This is because the search engine relies on pattern matching and finding similarities. This problem of information overload from the Internet can be alleviated with the use of RSs. Using various filtering techniques, a recommendation system narrows down the information on the basis of the behaviour and inclination of the user.

2.2   Applications of RSs

There are a number of areas where RSs are applied and used. Some of these have been in use since the arrival of the Internet. There are a number of other areas where the deployment of RSs can be useful as this is also expected to increase the efficiency of the underlying applications. The following subsections cover these areas. The presented applications may not be an exhaustive list, because many more areas of applications are adding RSs to explore their benefits and usefulness.

2.2.1 Current use of RSs

2.2.1.1 Product recommendation (e-commerce)

These RSs are meant mostly for commercial applications. For example, if we show the intention to buy a book having a title/author/area, the result would be accompanied with recommendations for similar titles or other books from the same author or other books from the same area. In addition, information is also provided about other buyers who bought the same book and also some of the additional book suggestions in the same area or companion books which others purchased. Online marketing of apparels and clothes also increases their sales by adding RSs.

2.2.1.2 Movie or music recommendation (entertainment)

These RSs are personalized according to the user's likes and previous accesses. Such systems should have a profile of the user or similar users to give a better and more accurate recommendation. It may have a commercial aspect from the sellers/distributors of the genre of movie or music.

2.2.1.3 Scholarly search and news articles

These RSs ease the search process by profiling the user and other users who search from the same area or are involved in the same area of research. Political inclinations and the regional environment are also considered for personalized newsletters and news services.

2.2.1.4 Services

These RSs are built to provide recommendations for travelling, consultation, most suitable shopping malls, hospitals, etc.

2.2.2 More areas for RSs

Most of the time, we associate RSs with online retail trade, but there are many emerging areas where RSs have found their use. Designers of various applications find value addition to their products by adding an RS. Decision-making is therefore made easier in these applications. Some of the emerging areas are discussed in the following.

2.2.2.1 Recommend courses for students

On an online registration system for students of a university, this system would return a list of courses (based on the past courses and grades) where the student has the potential to do well. This would work as the advisory service that would include the past pattern for the same academic programme.

2.2.2.2 Perform career counselling

Based on the academic background and the social status of the user, proper career counselling can be performed by the system. In addition, the current trends towards a particular field gathered by analysing users would help in the decision-making process.

Besides the above, many non-traditional areas have started using RSs. Some of these areas are tourist guides, financial investments, matchmaking, acquiring of property, etc.

The next section of the chapter describes algorithms and types of RSs. It discusses about the phases of RS and then discusses in detail about different ways RSs could be implemented and used.

2.3 Algorithms and theoretical foundations of RSs

Work in the domain of RSs has been continuing since the mid-1990s [6]. Since then, various useful studies on RSs have been done. Some have surveyed the field of RSs [6,7,8,9], some have described different approaches to recommendations [6,10,11,12,13,14], some have thrown light on the advantages, disadvantages, and problems related to different approaches [6,8,15], while others have tried to overcome these issues. In this section, we will provide comprehensive detail of RSs, along with the description of the broad categories that encompasses the RSs.

RS can be defined as the system that predict and recommend most suitable items to the users based on their characteristics. In order to do so, the RS goes through a set of phases. These phases are described in the next subsection.

2.3.1 Phases of RSs

RSs go through the set of the following phases to provide recommendations.

2.3.1.1 Information collection

In this phase, information related to user is collected. Using this information, a user profile is constructed. This profile is essential for the RSs in order to provide efficient predictions. There are different ways of collecting such information including implicit, explicit, and hybrid feedback from the user. Implicit feedback does not need user's input; rather the RS implicitly collects information through different techniques like user's behaviour on the system, pages visited, products clicked, etc. Explicit feedback requires user's input to collect information and construct the profile. Generally, this is done through developing a user profile by letting the user fill different web forms that collect the information and stores it. Hybrid feedback combines both implicit and explicit information collection techniques [16].

2.3.1.2 Learning phase

In this phase, user's features are filtered out and the relevant ones are extracted, which could be used in the prediction phase.

2.3.1.3 Prediction/recommendation phase

In this phase, the prediction or recommendation is made as to which items the user may prefer. The prediction could be made solely by using the user's profile, or it may use other techniques to provide recommendations like item similarity measures, machine learning techniques, Bayesian techniques, and decision trees.

2.3.2 Types of RSs

Although RSs can be categorized into various categories, we have classified them into five broader ones based on the approach they follow to provide recommendations to the users. These categories are described in detail in the following.

2.3.2.1 Content-based recommenders

Introduction
This type of RSs provides recommendations of items to a user based on the description of item and user's interest. For example, if the user has liked a particular type of clothing item – which has a feature or description like 'cotton jeans' – in the past, the system would recommend to this user the items that have the similar features or description.

Discussion
In content-based systems, an item profile and a user profile are constructed. Item profile is a collection of records that represent different characteristics of the item. For example, particular clothing item would have its size, colour, price, fabric, etc., as the specific records of its item profile. Similarly, a user profile contains certain information of the user that is useful for the RS to produce recommendations. User profile can be constructed through explicit information collection from the user or implicit methods for information collection about the user as discussed above. RSs that produce user profiles implicitly are more preferred over the ones that require users to provide explicit information because most of the time users do not prefer to provide information, or the information they provide is not authentic and/or accurate [6,17].

Once the item and user profiles are constructed, the RS then combines this information to generate recommendations for a particular user. A recommendation of an item 'T_i' for a user 'U_i' is generated by considering ratings '$R (U_i, t)$' given by user 'U_i' to the items 't', where $t \in T$ (T is the set of items) and are similar to item 'T_i' based on the item profile. Similarity among the items can be computed by using any similarity measures such as cosine distance and/or Jaccard distance [17].

Recommendations in such cases could also be generated through classification algorithms, where the probability that a user would like an item could be estimated. These algorithms also help in generating top N list of recommendations for a particular user. Other methods for producing content-based recommendations are Bayesian classifiers and machine learning techniques like clustering, K-nearest neighbours, decision trees, and neural networks [6].

Content-based RSs have several advantages, and some of these are described by Poonam *et al.* in [8]:

i.   Explicit rating system in this approach provides users an independence and way to develop their own user profile in the system.
ii. They can still recommend items that are not yet seen by any user. This is advantageous in the case when a new user joins the system.

Table 2.1   Example utility matrix

	P1	P2	P3	P4	P5	P6	P7
User A	4			5	1		
User B	5	5	4				
User C				2	4	5	
User D		3					3

iii. They provide transparency to the user by giving explanation about how this RS works.

iv.   They do not need a large amount of memory to store data and compute recommendations.

Poonam *et al.* [8] also discussed the disadvantages that a content-based RS could have. They are as follows:

i.   It is difficult to extract item features in certain domains.
ii.   They work on the item similarity approach so it suffers from overspecialization problem (later discussed in Section 2.4 of this chapter).
iii. It is hard to acquire feedback from the user about a particular recommendation. Therefore, it is not possible to determine if the recommendation made is correct or not.
iv.   It is harder to construct user profiles, as users do not provide information about them explicitly or easily.

2.3.2.2   CF recommenders

Introduction

CF recommenders are the most popular among other recommendation approaches [8]. They recommend items to the user based on the ratings given to the items by certain similar users. For example, let us consider User A is similar to User B. So, if User B has liked Item A, then it is likely that User A would also like Item A. In this way, CF recommenders construct a utility matrix of users and items which represents which user likes what items. This utility matrix is then used to compute similarity among users and predict ratings of unrated items by a certain user. Table 2.1 shows an example utility matrix. In this matrix, Users A–D have rated products P1–P7 on a rating scale of 1–5. Notice that, from this utility matrix, we can infer the similarity of users by seeing what ratings they have given to certain products. As an illustration, see User A and User B, they seem to like similar products like 'P1'. So, they could be said similar to each other. Now, see User A and User C, they seem to give opposite ratings to products P4 and P5. So, they could be said dissimilar to each other.

However, we do not usually infer the ratings directly by looking at the table. The CF recommenders use different similarity measures to compute similarity among users and items, which we would discuss in the upcoming subsections.

Discussion

CF process works through the utility matrix as in Table 2.1. The focus here is to predict the ratings for the unrated items based on the available data in the matrix, and producing recommendations later on. The following process is followed [6]:

1. Each entry say 'T_{ij}' represents a rating given by user 'i' to the item 'j' in the matrix. The rating is numeric, and it can also be 0, which means that the item 'j' is not yet rated by the user 'i'.
2. The missing ratings are predicted by first computing the similarity between items and users. So, the most similar 'N' users to the user 'i' are found and similarly most similar 'N' items to the item 'j' are found.
3. Using the similarities calculated in Step 2, the output is generated. The output consists of the *prediction* of the value 'T_{ij}' and a list of top N recommended items for the user.

CF could be done through two major techniques:

1. **Memory based**

    In memory-based techniques, the entire or a sample of data from the utility matrix is used. In this approach, unknown ratings are predicted and similarities among users and items are calculated using the rating information in the utility matrix, and a list of 'N' items to be recommended to a particular user is generated.

    The memory-based approach is classified into two types [6]:

    i.   **User based:** In the user-based approach, similarity between users is computed and then the rating of user 'i' for an item 'j' is predicted based on what average rating has been given to this item by the similar 'N' users.

    ii. **Item based:** In item-based approach similarity between items is computed and then the rating of user 'i' for an item 'j' is predicted based on what average rating the user 'i' has given to the 'N' similar items.

    Similarity Measures: There are different similarity measures that could be used to compute the similarity between users and items. Some commonly used are the following [6]:

    i.   cosine similarity
    ii.   correlation-based similarity
    iii. Pearson correlation
    iv.   cosine vector similarity
    v.   adjust cosine vector similarity
    vi.   Spearman correlation
    vii. Gaussian kernel.

2. **Model based**

    In model-based approaches, recommendations are provided by constructing statistical models for predicting the ratings. Not all of the data and information is used in this approach. Some of the model-based approaches for estimating the probability of ratings are the following [6]:

    i.   cluster-based models
    ii. Bayesian networks

iii.   latent factor and matrix factorization.

CF scheme has its own advantages that are explained by Poonam *et al*. in [8]:

i.   Implementation of RSs is made easy through memory-based CF technique.
ii.   Data addition is made easy and incremental in memory-based CF technique.
iii. Prediction performance and accuracy is improved through model-based CF technique.

CF scheme has its disadvantages as well. Some researchers have discussed them as follows [8,18]:

i.   CF recommenders require huge amount of data to make recommendations.
ii.   CF recommenders require a huge amount of computation power to compute the results.
iii. In CF recommenders, the utility matrix often gets sparse, which affects the quality of recommendations.

2.3.2.3   Hybrid recommenders

Introduction

The type of recommenders where multiple recommendation techniques are combined together to produce a single unified recommendation system is called hybrid recommenders [6]. The basic idea behind this approach is to overcome the drawbacks of individual recommendation techniques by combining the advantageous features of different techniques together, and hence producing a unified recommender [8]. Hybrid RSs can be implemented in various ways, and some of them are discussed by [6] and [8] as follows:

- Implement different recommendation techniques individually and combine their predictions and recommendations.
- Consolidate some features of content-based technique into the other one.
- Consolidate some features of CF technique into the other one.
- Develop a unified RS combining multiple techniques together.

Discussion

The hybrid RSs are classified into seven classes that are explained by [8] and [15]:

i.   **Weighted:** Scores from multiple techniques are combined together to produce a single recommendation.
ii.   **Switching:** Based on the context, the RS switches between the available recommendation techniques to produce a recommendation.
iii. **Mixed:** Recommendations from a combination of different recommendation techniques are combined and produced at the same time.
iv.   **Feature combination:** Features from several different recommendation data sources are combined together in a single recommendation algorithm.
v.   **Cascade:** One recommender with higher priority refines the results produced by the lower priority recommenders and produces the final recommendation.
vi.   **Feature augmentation:** One recommender's output is used as an input to the other recommender.
vii. **Meta Level:** One recommender's model learned is used as an input to the other recommender.

Table 2.2 An overview of image-based recommendation systems

Research paper	Scenario	Approach
Dey *et al*. [19]	Smartphone-based image recommendations	SVMs
Saxena *et al*. [20]	Shoe recommendations	Developed own filtering-based algorithm focusing on unsupervised learning
Wang *et al*. [21]	Handbag recommendations	Joint learning of attribute project and SVM
McAuley *et al.* [22]	Complimentary objects recommendation	Convolutional neural networks along with some other approaches
Bell and Bala [23]	Interior design and product recommendations	Convolutional neural networks

2.3.2.4 Image-based recommenders

Introduction

This type of RSs provides recommendations to the users based on the similarity between the images of the products. The similarity is computed by focusing on different features of the product like style, colour, size, shape, and texture.

Discussion

There are different approaches that are being followed to develop image-based RSs. These approaches are commonly based on different machine learning techniques encompassing supervised and unsupervised learning approaches. Some of the used techniques involve simple feed-forward neural networks, convolutional neural networks, support vector machines (SVMs), etc. Table 2.2 provides an overview of different approaches being used in different scenarios for image-based recommendations.

2.3.2.5 RSs using GDBs

The goal of recommendation systems is to generate meaningful recommendations to enhance the user experience in the context of choosing a possibility. This is usually done by predicting the interest of a user based on various types of information [24,25,26]. The usage of graphs in recommendation systems is not something new and the people working in domain of recommendation systems have been using graphs in different ways since early days of recommendation systems [25,27,28]. Aggarwal *et al.* used an approach based on graph algorithms for content-based filtering [27]. Silva *et al.* used graph to represent the social network in order to recommend friends in a social network based on the topology of the network graphs [29]. Huang *et al.* used a two-layer graph approach for a digital library recommendation system [25]. An attempt to produce a hybrid CF- and content filtering-based online newspaper recommender using graphs is discussed in [28].

There has been tremendous work done in last decade to develop new approaches for recommendation systems. The performance of a recommendation system is heavily dependent on the processing of a lot of users' historical data [30]. GDBs have introduced new perspective to deal with interconnected data in huge sizes.

Despite being fairly new, GDBs provide opportunity to improve the performance of applications dealing with huge amount of interconnected data and recommendation systems are one such example.

Introduction

A graph (data structure to hold connected data) is a collection of edges and vertices. These vertices, also known as nodes, are used to represent entities in a domain such as a person, an actor, a place, or an item. The edges represent the relationship among vertices such as friendship relationship between two persons, or purchase relationship between an item and a customer [31]. The vertices and edges may also have properties to show further details about them. In case of vertices, examples of such properties could be age of a person or price of an item whereas in case of edges, it could be date of purchase of an item by a customer [32].

GDBs, usually categorized as not only structured query language (NoSQL) databases, are aiming to resolve everything using graphs. They focus on entities (vertices or nodes) and the relationships (edges) between them. A GDB stores data in the graph format in which vertices (nodes) and edges (relationships) are the building blocks. GDBs are optimized for highly connected data and can become an effective tool for modelling interconnected data. Due to diversification in structure, the GDB has been adapted in various domains such as social networks, geographic information systems [33], e-commerce [34,35,36], and recommendation systems [37,38,39].

Since GDBs are optimized for highly connected data, they give performance advantage over relational databases, as relational databases provide limited capability to capture the semantics. In today's era of big data, where we have huge data to process and analyse, the handling of such complex data of interactions becomes next to impossible in conventional databases. In schema-based databases, such as relational databases, the schema itself puts a limitation on how the information could be stored, and change in the schema requires a manual process in order to adapt new data. This is quite infeasible when we are exploring new kind of data on daily basis [26]. Therefore, it has been considered that relational databases are not suitable for storing relationship-based data [24]. It is also important to mention that all traversals in GDBs are localized and not required to explore unrelated data, which is a problem with Structured Query Language (SQL) [40]. GDBs such as, Neo4j, InfoGrid, CosmosDB, and Infinite are popular in the market these days.

In GDBs, we can model almost anything by defining entities as vertices and the relationship among these entities as edges. Different GDBs support different types of structures that can be modelled, but most common type supported by most of the GDBs is Property Graph which is a multi-graph consisting of attributed, labelled, and directed vertices and edges. Here, attributed means that an entity or relationship may have different attributes associated with them such as age and price. Labelling allows grouping similar entities together.

Discussion

Broadly, we can divide recommendation systems into two basic parts: Pattern Discovery and Pattern Application. As the name suggests, in Pattern Discovery, the system discovers the potential patterns that can be helpful in recommendation for a user.

Such patterns can be discovered through an algorithmic approach in which a dataset is processed using machine learning algorithms to identify the patterns which were not identified earlier. This is the area which got primary focus in the last decade [41,42,43]. Another mechanism which can help to identify the patterns in the data is visual analytics, in which domain experts identify the hidden patterns by using graph visualization [44,45,46]. Yet another way to learn the patterns is through business experts who understand and know the business in detail, because of their experience in the domain [47].

Once a pattern has been found either by using machine learning algorithms or through business experts, the next step is to implement these patterns in business applications in order to generate recommendations for users. The success of a recommendation is not only dependent on how effectively it can identify the patterns, but also dependent on the ability to apply identified patterns in the business application. We may have to apply these patterns offline when recommendations are not time critical, e.g. in case of generating recommendations for an e-mail campaign or identifying potentials friends for a person. Such jobs can be performed in a batch mode, and extensive algorithms can be used, in which it may be required to perform multiple iterations on the data.

However, there are applications in which recommendations need to be generated between a web request and a web response. Recommending another restaurant while a user is viewing any specific restaurant or recommending an item while user requests to view a specific item are examples of such cases. For such cases, we need systems that can generate recommendations within milliseconds which may include execution of complex queries on a huge data in order to match certain patterns. GDBs are appropriate candidates for such cases, as they are optimized to deal with interrelated data, and hence find patterns quite efficiently as compared to other database models.

Content-based filtering and CF are naturally supported by GDBs. We can calculate recommendation using graph in a similar fashion as we do in other recommendation systems. We can define a similarity function to compare set of nodes. This similarity function can be used to find most similar nodes which can be returned to a user as recommendations. Property Graph model allows us to store pre-calculated similarity as a property on the edges. We can use numerous already available methods to calculate similarity between two nodes such as cosine similarity, Pearson correlation, or any other method which calculates items' frequency [24,48].

The fundamental operation to retrieve information from the graph is traversal, which is walking along the elements of a graph [31]. In graph, traversal is a localized operation unlike relational databases. It means that in order to travel from one node to another node, we do not need any global information and each node and edge act as mini-index in the graph. The absence of need of global indexes for traversal means that GDBs have no performance impact on the size of the graph, which is quite a contrast from the case of SQL [26].

Unfortunately, no standardization has been made for traversal-based languages which results in different implementation of languages and frameworks for this purpose. The most common implementations are Cypher Query Language for Neo4j GDB [49], GraphQL developed by Facebook [50], Gremlin which can work with different GDBs including Neo4j [51], and SPARQL which is used for resource description framework (RDF)-based databases [52].

The next subsection gives an overview of popular datasets that have been used for evaluating and comparing RSs.

2.3.3   Datasets for recommendations

This subsection describes some publicly available datasets to evaluate recommendation systems. Some of these datasets contain only user–item rating data and, therefore, are suitable for CF techniques, while others also contain product catalogue information which can be used to make content-based or hybrid recommendations. A brief description of these datasets is given in the following.

2.3.3.1   MovieLens

MovieLens dataset [53] is one of the most popular datasets used for recommendations. This dataset is compiled and made available by GroupLens, a research laboratory in the Department of Computer Science and Engineering at the University of Minnesota. The dataset was gathered through the MovieLens website, where users specify their preferences for movies in the form of five-star ratings. The data is in a typical user–item rating format and contains 20 million ratings of 27,000 movies by 138,000 users. In this dataset, each user is represented by an ID and no demographic information of the user is available. However, the published dataset contains only those users that have rated at least 20 movies. For movies, in addition to IDs, their titles and genre are also available. This dataset is most suitable for the CF technique.

2.3.3.2   Jester

Jester [54] is a research project of UC Berkeley laboratory for Automation, Science and Engineering, to study social information filtering. The data are collected from Jester online joke recommendation website [55] and contains continuous ratings of jokes by anonymous users on a scale of -10 to $+10$. Multiple datasets have been collected over different time spans and are available on Jester's website. The largest among them is the size of 4.1 million ratings of 100 jokes by 73,421 users. This dataset is also well-suited for CF in scenarios where a large number of users have rated a small number of items.

2.3.3.3   BookCrossing

BookCrossing dataset [56] dataset has been gathered through a four-week crawl from BookCrossing website [57]. The dataset contains 1,157,112 ratings of 271,379 distinct ISBNs, rated by 278,858 members of BookCrossing. The ratings are both implicit and explicit with explicit ratings expressed on a scale of 1–10 and implicit ratings represented by zero. The dataset also contains some demographic information of users in the form of their Age and Location. Moreover, some content-based information of books, including book title, author, year of publication, and publisher, is gathered from Amazon website and is incorporated into this dataset. This dataset can, therefore, be used for both content-based and CF techniques of recommendation.

2.3.3.4 Amazon product data

Amazon product data [58] is an extensive dataset gathered from Amazon website. The dataset contains 143.7 million product reviews and ratings, and metadata of products in the form of product name, categories, price, brand, and image feature. Moreover, this dataset also contains information of other items purchased and other links viewed by the same user. Some visual features of products have also been extracted from product images using deep convolutional networks and have been made available in the dataset.

2.3.3.5 Yahoo Webscope datasets

Yahoo Webscope [59] is a library of several datasets that have been made available by Yahoo for noncommercial purposes. Some of these datasets specifically address the areas of recommendations and classifications. A brief description of some such datasets is given as follows:

- Yahoo! Music rating
  This dataset contains preferences of Yahoo music community and contains over 717 million ratings of 136,000 songs given by 1.8 million users. The details of songs including artist, album, and genre are also available in the dataset.
- Yahoo Delicious
  Delicious is a bookmarking website for storing online bookmarks. Yahoo Delicious dataset contains 100,000 URLs that were bookmarked on Delicious website by its users. Each URL has been bookmarked at least 100 times.
- Yahoo! Movies rating
  This dataset contains movie preferences of Yahoo users, rated on a scale of A+ to F. Users in this dataset are anonymous. However, detailed information is available about movies that include cast, crew, synopsis, genre, average ratings, and awards. This dataset is a good candidate for both CF and content-based filtering.

The next section ends the chapter with a brief overview about the problems and challenges that the RSs face nowadays.

2.4   Problems related to RSs

Although RSs are extremely powerful tools on the web these days, yet they have some problems and challenges which they face every now and then. These challenges are discussed in detail by [8], [6], [60], and [61] and have been summarized in the following subsections.

2.4.1 Data sparsity problem

Data sparsity problem arises in RSs as time progresses. This problem is caused by a drastic increase in the number of users and items. As not many of the users are rating the items very frequently, the utility matrix becomes sparse, which results in degradation of recommendation quality.

2.4.2   Cold start problem

When a new user or item is entered into the system, the cold start problem arises. In this case, it is not easy to provide recommendations as there is not much information available regarding the new user or new item. Therefore, useful recommendations are not produced. There are three kinds of cold start problems: new user problem, new item problem, and new system problem.

2.4.3   Scalability

As the number of users and the size of data increases rapidly, RSs suffer from scalability problem and thus could produce inaccurate or inefficient results. In fact, the users demand timely recommendations, and to overcome this challenge, RSs require high computational resources.

2.4.4   Overspecialization or diversity problem

This problem restricts the user to get already known recommendations or recommendations that are very specific to their profile, which does not allow them to discover newly added items into the system or other available options.

2.4.5   Vulnerable to attacks

Many hackers try to promote certain items on the web by hacking the RSs, which makes them vulnerable to attacks. This makes it one of the major challenges faced by the developer of any RS.

References

[1]   A.M. Rashid, I. Albert, D. Cosley, *et al.* 'Getting to know you: learning new user preferences in recommender systems'. *Proceedings of International Conference on Intelligent User Interfaces*; Jan 13–16, San Francisco, CA, 2002. New York, NY: ACM Press, pp 127–134.

[2]   J.A. Konstan and J. Reidel. 'Recommendation systems: from algorithms to user experience'. *User Model User-Adapt Interact* 2012, 22:101–123.

[3]   F.O. Isinkaye, Y.O. Folajimi, and B.A. Ojoko. 'Recommendation systems: principles, methods and evaluation'. *Egyptian Informatics Journal* 2015, 16:261–273.

[4]   F. Ricci, L. Rokach, and B. Shapira. 'Introduction to recommender systems handbook' In F. Ricci, L. Rokach, B. Shapira and P.B. Kantor (eds.), *Recommender Systems Handbook*. Boston, MA: Springer; 2011, pp. 1–35.

[5]   Y. Seroussi. 'The wonderful world of recommender systems'. Article at Yasirseroussi.com 2015

[6]   M. Sharma and S. Mann. 'A survey of recommender systems: approaches and limitations'. *International Journal of Innovations in Engineering and Technology* 2013, 2(2):8–14.

[7]   F. Ricci, L. Rokach, B. Shapira and P.B. Kantor (eds.). *Recommender Systems Handbook*. Boston, MA: Springer; 2011.

[8]   P. B. Thorat, R.M. Goudar, and S. Barve. 'Survey on collaborative filtering, content-based filtering and hybrid recommendation system'. *International Journal of Computer Applications* 2015, 110(4): 31–36.

[9]   M. Elahi, F. Ricci, and N. Rubens. 'A survey of active learning in collaborative filtering recommender systems'. *Computer Science Review* 2 Jun 2016.

[10]   G. Linden, B. Smith and J. York. 'Amazon.com recommendations item-to-item collaborative filtering'. *IEEE Internet Computing* 2003, 7(1):76–80.

[11]   Y. Koren. *The Bellkor Solution to the Netflix Grand Prize*. Netflix prize documentation, 81, 2009.

[12]   R.J. Mooney and L. Roy. 'Content-based book recommending using learning for text categorization'. *Proc. ACM SIGIR'99 Workshop Recommender Systems: Algorithms and Evaluation*; New York, NY: ACM Press, 1999, pp. 36–43.

[13]   G.D. Linden, J.A. Jacobi and E.A. Benson. *Collaborative Recommendations Using Item-to-Item Similarity Mappings*; U.S. Patent No. 6,266,649, July 24, 2001.

[14]   L.M. de Campos, J.M. Fernández-Luna, J.F. Huete, and M.A. Rueda-Morales. 'Combining content-based and collaborative recommendations: a hybrid approach based on Bayesian networks'. *Int. J. Approx. Reason.* 2010, 51(7):785–799.

[15]   N. Pereira and S.K. Varma. 'Survey on content-based recommendation system'. *International Journal of Computer Science and Information Technologies* 2016, 7(1):281–284.

[16]   F.O. Isinkaye, Y.O. Folajimi, and B.A. Ojokoh. 'recommendation systems: principles methods and evaluation'. *Egyptian Informatics Journal* 2015, 16: 261–273.

[17]   J. Leskovec, A. Rajaraman, and J.D. Ullman. *Mining of Massive Datasets*. Cambridge, UK: Cambridge University Press; 2014, Chapter 9.

[18]   H.-N. Kim, A. El-Saddik, and G.-S. Jo. 'Collaborative error-reflected models for cold-start recommender systems. *Decision Support Systems* 2011, 51(3):519–531.

[19]   S. Dey, S. Sonwane, and D. Muneshwar. 'A survey paper on image recommender system for smartphone'. *International Journal of Advance Foundation and Research in Science & Engineering* 2014, 1(5):69–72.

[20]   A. Saxena, N. Khosla, V. Venkataraman, N. Khosla and V. Venkataraman. *Building an Image-Based Shoe Recommendation System*; In: CS229n course project reports (2015), Stanford University, Stanford, USA.

[21]   Y. Wang, S. Li, and A.C. Kot. 'Joint learning for image-based handbag recommendation'. *2015 IEEE International Conference on Multimedia and Expo (ICME)*. IEEE, 2015.

[22]   J. McAuley, C. Targett, J. Shi, and A. Van Den Hengel. 'Image-based recommendations on styles and substitutes'. *SIGIR'15*, 2015.

[23]   S. Bell and K. Bala. 'Learning visual similarity for product design with con-volutional neural networks'. *ACM Transactions on Graphics* 2015, 34(4):98: 1–98:10.

[24]   J. Skrasek. 'Social network recommendation using graph databases'. PhD thesis, Masaryk University Faculty of Informatics, 2015.

[25]   Z. Huang, W. Chung, T. Ong, and H. Chen. 'A graph-based recommender system for digital library'. *Proceedings of the 2 ACM/IEEE-CS Joint Confer-ence on Digital Libraries*, Portland, Oregon, USA; 2002. New York, NY: ACM Press; pp. 65–73.

[26]   J.J. Miller. 'Graph database applications and concepts with neo4j'. *Proceedings of the Southern Association for Information Systems Conference*, Atlanta, GA, USA; vol. 2324. Atlanta, GA: Association for Information Systems; 2013.

[27]   C.C. Aggarwal, J.L. Wolf, K.-L. Wu, and P.S. Yu. 'Horting hatches an egg: a new graph-theoretic approach to collaborative filtering'. *Proceedings of the Fifth ACM SIGKDD International Conference on Knowledge Discovery and Data Mining*, San Diego, CA, USA, Aug. 1999. New York, NY: ACM; 1999.

[28]   M. Claypool, A. Gokhale, T. Miranda, P. Murnikov, D. Netes, and M. Sartin. 'Combining content-based and collaborative filters in an online newspaper'. *Proceedings of the ACM SIGIR'99 Workshop Recommender Systems: Algo-rithms and Evaluation*, Berkeley, CA, Aug. 1999. New York, NY: ACM; 1999.

[29]   N.B. Silva, I.-R. Tsang, G.D.C. Cavalcanti, and I.-J. Tsang. 'A graph-based friend recommendation system using genetic algorithm'. *Proceedings of the 2010 IEEE Congress on Evolutionary Computation*, Barcelona, Spain. July 2010; IEEE; pp. 1–7.

[30]   H. Lee and J. Kwon. 'Efficient recommender system-based on graph data for multimedia application'. *International Journal of Multimedia & Ubiquitous Engineering* 2013, 8(4):247–256.

[31]   M.A. Rodriguez and P. Neubauer. 'Constructions from dots and lines'. *Bulletin of the American Society for Information Science and Technology* 2010, 36(6): 35–41.

[32]   I. Robinson, J. Webber, and E. Eifrem. *Graph Databases*. O'Reilly Media, Incorporated, 2013.

[33]   J. Daltio and C.B. Medeiros. 'HydroGraph: exploring geographic data in graph databases'. *Proceedings of the Brazilian Symposium on GeoInformatics*; Brazil, 2015. Brazil: Ministry of Science, Technology, Innovation and Communication/National Institute for Space Research; pp. 44–55.

[34]   E. Zimeo, G. Oliva, F. Baldi, and A. Caracciolo. 'Designing a scalable social e-commerce application'. *Scalable Computing: Practice and Experience* 2013, 14(2):131–141.

[35]   A. Anthony, Y.-K. Shih, R. Jin, and Y. Xiang. 'Leveraging a graph-powered, real-time recommendation engine to create rapid business value'. *Proceed-ings of the 10th ACM Conference on Recommender Systems*; ACM, 2016, pp. 385–386.

[36]   Z. Fu, Z. Wu, H. Li, *et al.* 'Geabase: a high-performance distributed graph database for industry-scale applications'. In *Advanced Cloud and Big Data (CBD), 2017 Fifth International Conference on*; IEEE, 2017, pp. 170–175.

[37]   F. Zarrinkamal, M. Kahani, and S. Paydhar. 'Using graph database for file recommendation in PAD social network'. *Seventh International Symposium on Telecommunications (ST)*; 2014. IEEE; pp. 470–475.

[38]   M. Fröhlich. 'Case study of a graph database system that supports ideation and writing process'. Working Paper, 2017. Available: https://www.researchgate. net/profile/Moritz_Froehlich/publication/318641886_Case_Study_of_a_ Graph_Database_System_that_Supports_Ideation_and_Writing_Process/links/ 5a7b3dc6458515c95de421fe/Case-Study-of-a-Graph-Database-System-that-Supports-Ideation-and-Writing-Process.pdf

[39]   J. Cordeiro, B. Antunes, and P. Gomes. 'Context-based recommendation to support problem solving in software development'. *Proc. 3rd Workshop Recommendation Syst. Soft. Eng*; 2012. Piscataway, NJ: IEEE Press; pp. 85–89.

[40]   M.A. Rodriguez and P. Neubauer. 'The graph traversal pattern' CoRR, vol. abs/1004.1001, 2010.

[41]   S. Xiaoyuan and T.M. Khoshgoftaar. 'A survey of collaborative filtering techniques'. *Adv. Artif. Intell.*, vol. 2009, 2009.

[42]   C. Desrosiers and G. Karypis. 'A comprehensive survey of neighborhood-based recommendation methods'. *Recommender Systems Handbook*; 2011, pp. 107–144. [Online]. Available: http://www.springerlink.com/index/N3JQ 77686228781N.pdf.

[43]   J. Liu and C. Wu. 'Deep learning-based recommendation: a survey'. In *International Conference on Information Science and Applications*; Macau, China; March 20–23, 2017. Singapore: Springer, 2017, pp. 451–458.

[44]   S. Chen, X. Yuan, Z. Wang, *et al.* 'Interactive visual discovering of movement patterns from sparsely sampled geo-tagged social media data'. *IEEE Trans. Vis. Comput. Graph.* 2016, 22(1):270–279.

[45]   H. Zhao, H. Zhang, Y. Liu, Y. Zhang, and X. L. Zhang. 'Pattern discovery: a progressive visual analytic design to support categorical data analysis'. *Journal of Visual Languages & Computing* 2017, 43:42–49.

[46]   T.H. Lee, K. Levinski, W.S. Tang, and L. Zhu. *Visualization of Graphical Representations of Log Files*. US Patent 9,684,707, June 20, 2017.

[47]   R. Van Bruggen. *Learning Neo4j*. Birmingham: Packt Publishing Ltd.; 2014.

[48]   S. Sawant. 'Collaborative filtering using weighted bipartite graph projection: a recommendation system for yelp'. *Proceedings of the CS224W: Social and Information Network Analysis Conference*, December 2013. Stanford, CA: Stanford University; 2013. Available: http://snap.stanford. edu/class/cs224w-2013/projects.html

[49]   N. Team. *Cypher Query Language*, 2013.

[50]   H. He and A. Singh. *GraphQL: Query Language and Access Methods for Graph Databases*. Technical report, Department of Computer Science at University of California, Santa Barbara, 2007.

[51]   M.A. Rodriguez. 'The Gremlin graph traversal machine and language (invited talk)'. *Proc. 15th Symp. Database Program. Languages*; 2015. New York, NY: ACM; pp. 1–10.

[52]   E. Prud'hommeaux and A. Seaborne. *SPARQL Query Language for RDF*, 2006.

[53]   F.M. Harper and J.A. Konstan. 'The MovieLens datasets: history and context'. *ACM Transaction on Interactive Intelligent Systems*. 2015, 5(4):19:1–19:19.

[54]   K. Goldberg, T. Roeder, D. Gupta, and C. Perkins. 'Eigentaste: a constant time collaborative filtering algorithm'. *Information Retrieval* 2001, 4(2): 133–151.

[55]   Jester online joke recommendation website [Online]. Available: http://eigentaste.berkeley.edu [Accessed: August, 2018].

[56]   C.-N. Ziegler, S.M. McNee, J.A. Konstan, and G. Lausen. 'Improving recommendation lists through topic diversification'. *Proceedings of the 14th International Conference on World Wide Web*, New York, NY, USA, 2005. 2005. New York, NY: ACM; pp. 22–32.

[57]   Book crossing website [Online]. Available: http://www.bookcrossing.com [accessed: August 2018].

[58]   'Amazon review data' [Online]. Available: http://jmcauley.ucsd.edu/data/amazon/links.html [accessed: 31 August 2017].

[59]   'Webscope | Yahoo Labs.' [Online]. Available: https://webscope.sandbox.yahoo.com/catalog.php?datatype=r [accessed: 31 August 2017].

[60]   L. Lü, M. Medo, C.H. Yeung, Y.-C. Zhang, Z.-K. Zhang, and T. Zhou. *Recommender Systems. Physics Reports*. 2012, 519(1):1–49.

[61]   Y. Chen, C. Wu, M. Xie, and X. Guo. 'Solving the sparsity problem in recommender systems using association retrieval'. *Journal of Computers* 2011, 6(9):1896–1902.

Chapter 3
Benchmarking big data recommendation algorithms using Hadoop or Apache Spark

Dinesh Kumar Saini[1], Kashif Zia[1], and Arshad Muhammad[1]

Recommender or recommendation systems have gained popularity in recent years, and big data is the driving force behind recommendation systems. Recommendation systems changed the way websites communicate with the users by providing a recommendation based on users history such as purchases and searches. Recommendation systems are used in a variety of areas such as movies, music, research articles and social tags. For example, recommendation system in Facebook "People you may know," Netflix "Because you watched" and YouTube "Recommend for you." These systems usually produce a list of recommendations in two ways: collaborative and content-based (CB) filtering. Collaborative filtering (CF) is based on a model of prior user behavior, which can be constructed from sole user's action or from the actions of other users who have similar behaviors, while content-based filtering constructs a recommendation on user's behavior such as by using historical browsing information. Apart from these, the hybrid approach can be used by combining two models. While designing, such systems require compute function values at several thousand points and thus are computationally quite extensive. These systems need parallel computations to speed up the search for an acceptable solution that can be recommended through nature-inspired computation. There are many factors that are essential while designing accurate recommendation algorithms. Some of these factors are diversity, recommender persistence, privacy, user demographics, trust and labeling. Recommendation system cannot perform its job without data, and big data supplies the amount of user's data such as past purchase history, browsing history [1,2]. In fact, efficient recommendation system requires big data. The best solution is Hadoop; it is a platform used to store, generate, manage and distribute big data easily around several large server nodes [3–5]. Hadoop offers Hadoop distributed file system (HDFS), which distributes all the data in different clusters and performs parallel operations. This chapter will explore big data issues and specific in Hadoop and HDFS.

[1]Faculty of Computing and Information Technology, Sohar University, Oman

3.1 Introduction

A recommender or a recommendation system classifies the subclass of information filtering system, which predicts the rating or preference of a user that he/she would give an item. Indeed, recommendation systems are critical in today's big data world, and many recommendation algorithms are available [6,7]. Such system has gained popularity in recent years and used in many areas, such as movies, music, news and social tags. Recommender systems usually produce a list of recommendations in two ways; collaborative [8,9] and content-based filtering [7,10]. CF is based on a model of prior user behavior, which can be constructed from sole user's behavior or from the behavior of other users who have similar behaviors, while content-based filtering constructs a recommendation on user's behavior such as by using historical browsing information. Apart from these, a hybrid approach can be used by combining two models. The main advantage of the collaborative approach is that it does not rely on machine-analyzable content and can accurately recommend complex items, such as movies. The collaborative approach assumes that users who agreed in the past will agree in future as well, i.e., the users who like the similar kind of products/items in the past will like in future as well. One of the examples of CF is item-to-item CF used by Amazon.com. Other examples include famous social websites such as Facebook, Myspace and LinkedIn. CF usually has three problems such as cold start, scalability and sparsity. Content-based filtering is based on the description of an item and user's preferences. Content-based system uses keywords to describe the items and building user profiles to identify types of items that user may like. To abstract the features of the items, an item presentation algorithm is applied, such as vector space representation. These systems are a good alternative for search engines in contrast, as they allow users to discover items, which may not be found with search algorithms. Such systems use search engines indexing.

3.2 Big data

The main concept revolves around the idea that any dataset cannot be processed on a single machine to meet the mandatory service-level agreements [11]. The essential part of this meaning is fundamental; it is likely to process almost any rule of data on one machine. Even the data that could not be stored on one computer can be carried into another machine by analyzing it from common storage such as a network attached storage medium. On the other hand, the amount of time it takes to process this whole data will be too long in comparison to the available time during which it can process this entire data [12].

3.2.1 Hadoop

Gouge Cutting and Mike Cafarella created Hadoop (Highly Archived Distributed Object Oriented Programming) in 2005. However, MapReduce, based on Google published in 2004, was developed for helping a distributed analysis and search Engine Project. The best feature is that it is an open-source-based Java Framework technology, which allows storing, managing, generating access and affecting vast resources and determines the flexible high degree of fault possibility and high expandability from big data and for less cost. Hadoop controls a large number of dataset and generates a huge dataset from different platform systems such as videos and audios, folders, images, files, software and email chats. All these extensions and formats are stored in a Hadoop designed by clustering, and without schema, it leads to collecting from any systems which could be different.

Moreover, there are many structures and components found in Hadoop, for instance, Avro, Chukwa, Flume and so on. The Hadoop install or bundle provides us with several features such as source code, planning and work arrangement. Hadoop cluster covers one Master node and many Slave nodes. The Master node involves Data node, Name node, Job Tracker and Task Tracker everyplace slave node items as together a Task Tracker and Data node, which grips compute first and data only worker node as shown in Figure 3.1. The Business Tracker manages the business schedule. Hadoop contains two fragments: HDFS and MapReduce. HDFS runs storage of data and generates MapReduce to provide an exploration of data in the collected environment. The design of Hadoop architecture is explained in Figure 3.1.

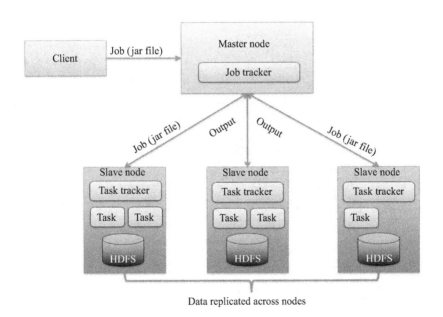

Figure 3.1   Hadoop architecture [13]

3.2.2   Presenting the MapReduce model

Hadoop helps the MapReduce model, developed by Google. This model has two steps, together of which are practice and user can define them, which are aimed at an application:

- Map: A primary digestion and conversion step in which separate input records can parallelly be processed.
- Reduce: An accumulation or summarization stage in which totally connected records need to be managed composed through a single entity.

The fundamental theory of MapReduce in Hadoop is that job is usually divided into independent chunks, processed by the map tasks in parallel. The outputs of the maps input to the reduce tasks both input and output of the job stored in the file-system. Figure 3.2 explains the mechanism of the MapReduce model [14].

3.2.3   Hadoop input/output

I/O is an expensive operation in some MapReduce program, and then everything that can decrease the I/O to disk or complete the network is satisfied with a better overall amount. The Hadoop framework allows one to compress output from the Mapper in addition to the Reducer. On the other hand, there is a trade-off: compression is CPU intensive and puts away CPU cycles. Any CPU cycles recycled for compression are mislaid for other processes, for instance, the Mapper, Reducer, Partitioned, Combiner,

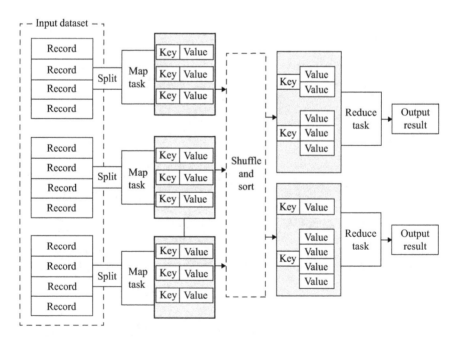

Figure 3.2   MapReduce Mode [14]

Category plus Shuffle, Ext. Similar to the maximum choices in Hadoop, and this one contains resource trade-offs that can necessarily be occupied entirely during the design period.

3.2.4   Apache Ambari and Ambari architecture

Horton mechanism has established the open source Apache Ambari invention, which stands for the software that allows Hadoop organization by supportive activities for instance provisioning, handling and observing Hadoop clusters [15]. An Ambari customs Ganglia, Nagios and Hadoop-based APIs and runs a very native web–user interface that lets administrators achieve Hadoop clusters. The Hadoop platform chains some data warehousing results, totaling Apache Hive, Impala and Shark. All these results are abstractly comparable to interpersonal databases at a far bigger scale but with the change in their application and custom model as shown in Figure 3.3. Interactive databases are frequently used in transactional structures in which only row SQL language inserts, updates and deletes need to be achieved atomically. Competent indexing and referential honesty with primary/foreign keys let current interactive databases to discover records speedily and secure that all data still is a severe schema. Moreover, relational databases attempt to escape full table tests when likely since the I/O bandwidth is partial and inclines to designate the block in these structures. Data warehousing results are designed to solve many problems. Hadoop system solutions accomplish their presentation via using a cluster of several networked nodes in which the I/O bandwidth is significantly advanced. The main advantage of clusters is the ability toward scaling to actual huge datasets where conservative interactive databases fail to complete. High-speed minute processes are challenging to implement in the current distributed system; thus cluster-based results do not provision relations or smooth only one-row inserts/updates/deletes. Data warehousing results are chosen

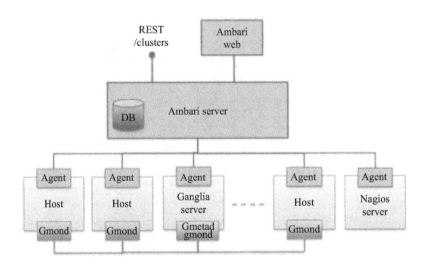

Figure 3.3   Ambari architecture [16]

for those analytics who have completed the same huge datasets. Also, in these custom models, occupied table shots are shared.

3.2.5   Future of Hadoop

Hadoop has "Expressed gap" as a framework for initial adopters, from developers and technology supporters to a planned data platform contained by original Chief Technical Officers and Chief Information Officers across typical enterprises. In these, people, who need progress toward the act of their businesses and solve original commercial chances, appreciate that with Apache Hadoop as acutely combined addition to their present data design suggestions for the fastest route to success as per their aims while exploiting their current money. Working advancing, Horton works besides the Apache Hadoop communal resolve stay to focus on growing the easiness with which enterprises organize and custom Hadoop, and on growing the platform's interoperability by the bigger data network. This contains creation positive, as it is dependable, established, and more profoundly, readily aimed at several enterprise capabilities.

3.2.6   How Hadoop works in social networking

A social networking site, for example, Facebook consumes TBs of data. No doubt, a user needs to retrieve the families or friends list of a user; the answer period is likely to be constant by what users of a shared classification consume come to assume. Tens of millions of users with more than one billion page views every day—Facebook ends to accumulate vast amounts of data. One of the challenges faced, since the early days, is developing a scalable method for the storage, and processing of all these bytes using this historical data is of very part of the way in which we can improve the user experience on Facebook. It can only be done by enabling engineers and analysts with our easy-to-use tools for mines and manipulation in the large datasets. Figure 3.4 shows how big data is generated from various sources.

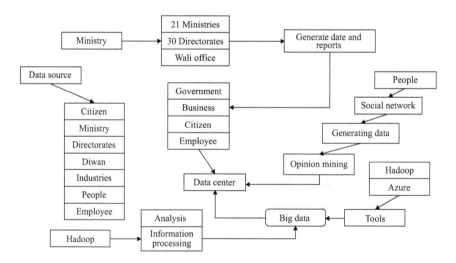

Figure 3.4   Hadoop and social networking data

3.3 Apache Spark

Apache Spark is developed by UC Berkeley AMP lab, and it is an open source. It is more powerful in terms of functionality from Hadoop and MapReduce [17]. It uses Resilient Distributed Dataset 2 that is immutable in nature and is a collection of distributed objects. There are two primary variables in the Spark, which are broadcast variable and accumulators. Because of Lazy Evaluation, actions are evaluated, and transformations are stored for further execution. Apache Hadoop and Spark process the massive amount of data based on MapReduce technique, which uses mining and machine-learning algorithms in different domains. Spark Mlib is also designed based on machine-learning algorithms. Data presentation, processing, storage, analysis can be done in Mlib. Apache Spark is much better compared to others in terms of performance, analysis and versatility. Some issues like architectural-fit, skill set development, adoption and measurement of business benefits still need to be fixed in Spark, as it seems very promising.

3.4 Recommender systems

Some of the computation methods that can be used while designing recommender are as follows:

- Differential evolution algorithm
- Ant colony optimization algorithm
- Particle swarm optimization algorithm
- Direct search methods
- Genetic algorithms.

In this chapter, we reviewed and studied all the recommender systems till date developed for the learning content management systems. Both types of recommender systems structured and nonstructured are analyzed, and all the recommender systems based on user access are also reviewed in the chapter. An attempt has been made to propose the method for reducing the sparsity in the recommendation systems. Content-based recommendation systems are studied in detail, and comparison is formed in the chapter. A framework is proposed in the chapter for the recommender system. Nature-inspired soft computing algorithms are suggested for the recommender system. The demand for ubiquitous learning environments by the learner communities at various levels of education has enhanced the research in the domain of web-based educational systems that has grown exponentially in the last years [18]. Learning systems can be designed based on recommendations' recommender systems, Semantic web-based information filtering system that takes the inputs from learner profiles and then aggregates the inputs to provide recommendations for the learners in their learning objects and service selection choices. Recommender systems [19] are information extraction systems that can filter unseen information and can predict whether a user would like a given item. Given a new item, recommender systems can predict whether a user would be this item or not, based on the user preferences ("likes" positive examples and "dislikes" negative samples), observed behavior and information. Learner groups often depend on recommendations that fit the group's learning preferences and knowledge levels [20]. Recommender-based learning management systems look for the particular group's learning patterns and assist the learners in fetching the best suited learning materials for their learning requirements. Data used in designing the recommender systems can be of two types:

- Structured ratings/rankings
- Unstructured textual comments.

Types of recommender system:

- Single user recommender systems
- Group recommender systems.

Design of recommender systems—Two main approaches for recommendation systems can be taken based on CF [21–23], based on learner's profiles or view/rating data collected. Collectively deriving user learning object profiling, which uses this knowledge for learning objects recommendations. The techniques include learner rating matrix, convolutional neural network (CNN), correlation.

First, characteristics of a learner are profiled, and then the content-based individual learner profiles are built. Recommendations are made if there are similarities found in the item attributes. Techniques include soft computing techniques like decision trees, artificial neural networks (ANN), Bayesian classifiers or we can use nature-inspired recommender techniques. The disadvantage of these types of recommender techniques is that, they require vast amount of historical data. Content filtering is based on specifications/characteristics of learning objects (not just their ratings).

3.4.1   Design of recommender systems

Recommender systems are designed for a variety of tasks that require clustering items of similar interest with learners in a group in the way that allows similarity matching to rank items in the recommender system based on their similarity indices. Most algorithms like the K-nearest neighbor or the Pearson correlation coefficient or the cosine distance and recently nature-inspired algorithms have been used to devise the similarity of these items to cluster them and assemble them for user related. The majority of recommender systems use the distance calculation methods such as Pearson correlation, cosine vector similarity, adjusted cosine, vector similarity, mean-squared difference and Spearman correlation to evaluate the similarity of existing items [24–27]. Figure 3.5 shows the design of recommender systems for driving the recommendations.

3.4.2   Collaborative recommendation and collaborative filtering

In specific domains, the CF-based recommendation system depends on user behavior, user characteristics and their activity logs or background. CF has been developed and improved over the past decade to the point where a wide variety of algorithms exists to

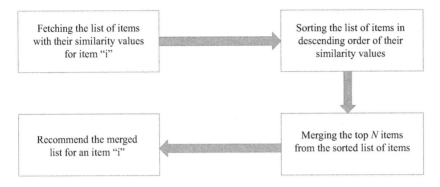

Figure 3.5   Driving recommendations

generate recommendations [28–30]. They can be classified into two groups: memory based and model based. A recommender predicts the next recommended item for the user. This prediction is based on memory-based CF. It uses a similarity measure between pairs of users to build a prediction, typically through a weighted average. The chosen similarity measure determines the accuracy of the prediction [31–33].

3.4.3   Reducing the sparsity problem

CF-based personalized recommendation algorithm works on the parameters of the user and the item attribute data. Recommendations are generated by the values of similarity in user ratings and user preference and other characteristic similarity ratings. The hybrid CF method employs the user attribute and item attribute; this can alleviate the sparsity issue in the recommender systems; such a consistency between two users is then used as a trust metric in CF methods that select neighbors based on the metric. Only a small number of neighbors are required to stabilize the recommendation quality. Recommendation quality is also excellent. Furthermore, trust (consistency) propagation reduces the severity of the sparsity problem intrinsic to CF methods.

3.4.4   Content-based recommendation

A CB-based learning management system as shown in Figure 3.6 uses learning material, and it has semantic similarity between them. The user ratings derived from previous interactions of the learner with the system are stored for evaluating the learning object or objects with which the learner has interacted. A weight is assigned to the learning object based on these ratings. A content-based recommendation method seeks to learn objects that can be grouped under already evaluated learning objects depending on the characteristics of these learning products. The usefulness of others' experiences often depends on recommender's personality and task. If there are no other users similar to them, making use of user profile can be an answer.

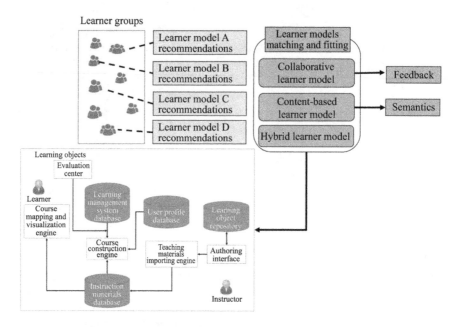

Figure 3.6   Framework for recommender-based learning management systems

3.4.5   Visualization of recommendation

Recently the focus on motivation to use recommender systems has resulted in the following desired characteristics for these recommender systems. Users need to develop trust in the system to try the recommendations and depend on the ratings for future searches. User's preference for detailed information in the recommendations is suggested to them. As these lead the way to inform decision-making and use the explanations to help make decisions pertaining to them to choose the ideal item that matches the learning preference analogous to the e-commerce discussed in the chapters [34–36]. Further, users feel that the explanations help them understand the recommendations better and make choices that are better than their current mood or interests. Provide a more detailed review of research on explanations in recommender systems. Research in this domain is now dealing with enhancing the abilities of recommender systems and important decision-making activities and the importance of visualization of these explanations for improving the dependability and suitability of these systems. Table 3.1 shows the comparison among different recommender approaches.

3.4.6   Hybrid recommendation approaches

Recommender systems apply machine-learning and data-mining techniques for filtering unseen information and can predict the fit between the users' preferences and the learning content. In Tertiary education, the learning process can be tedious in spite of the availability of several online research databases, e-book collection. The challenge

Table 3.1   Comparison recommender approaches

Approach(es)	Benefit(s)	Limitation(s)
Content-based filtering	No domain information required	Cold-start, over specialization
Collaborative filtering	No domain information required	Cold-start, sparsity
Hybrid filtering	Improve item-user	Slow performance, time

Table 3.2   Examples of modern recommender systems

System name	Year	Domain
X-Learn [1]	2007	Learning
MONERS [40]	2017	Mobile news recommender system
The CYCLADES system [21]	2008	Digital archives recommender system
Multifunctional integrated learning environment [22]	2011	Recommender for integrated learning environment
Community commands [23]	2013	Command recommender for software applications
ANTSREC [41]	2014	Semantic recommender for e-commerce

is in integrating the contents of all learning resources into a single learning channel capable of administering a learning path to learners of a particular module.

3.5   Systems based on nature-inspired algorithms

Recent research on recommender systems is based on nature-inspired algorithms. Swarm intelligence is the basis for understanding the collective learning styles/preferences of learners with approximate similarity in learning. Swarm-based approach recommends learning scenarios in learning environments. Style-based ant colony system is an extension of the ant colony system, and the learning path problem is described. In [37–39], the authors discuss the creation of improved learner communities based on the concept of ant colony system to create an optimal composition of learning groups. Table 3.2 lists some of the modern recommender systems in the domains of archiving, software application, learning and software application development.

3.6   Benchmarking: big data benchmarking

MapReduce, NoSQL Databases, Graph Databases, Hadoop and relational databases have emerged as the platforms while benchmarking structured parts of current TPC

DS can be considered. Parallel data generation frameworks can also be used for semistructured or unstructured data models. Performance is the primary benchmark component in Teradata Aster DBMS in cluster environments, which help in establishing concurrent benchmarking models. Link Bench is also a benchmarking tool used for social graph models, based on real-world database workload for social applications like Facebook. All benchmarking tools are characterized big datasets.

3.7 Summary

We provided a discussion on the benchmarking of big data recommendation algorithms using Hadoop and Apache Spark. The chapter explores big data issues specific to Hadoop, and the architecture of Hadoop is explained. MapReduce process is illustrated and architecture of Apache Ambari and Apache spark is discussed in detail.

References

[1]   De Mauro A, Greco M, Grimaldi M. A formal definition of big data based on its essential features. Library Review. 2016;65(3):122–135.

[2]   Schroeder R. Big data and the brave new world of social media research. Big Data & Society. 2014;1(2):1–11.

[3]   Hilbert M, López P. The world's technological capacity to store, communicate, and compute information. Science. 2011;332(6025):60–65.

[4]   Shvachko K, Kuang H, Radia S, *et al.* The Hadoop distributed file system. In: Mass storage systems and technologies (MSST), 2010 IEEE 26th symposium on. IEEE; 2010. p. 1–10.

[5]   Jiang J, Lu J, Zhang G, *et al.* Scaling-up item-based collaborative filtering recommendation algorithm based on Hadoop. In: Services (SERVICES), 2011 IEEE World Congress on. IEEE; 2011. p. 490–497.

[6]   De Meo P, Garro A, Terracina G, *et al.* Personalizing learning programs with X-Learn, an XML-based, "user-device" adaptive multi-agent system. Information Sciences. 2007;177(8):1729–1770.

[7]   Herlocker JL, Konstan JA, Terveen LG, *et al.* Evaluating collaborative filtering recommender systems. ACM Transactions on Information Systems (TOIS). 2004;22(1):5–53.

[8]   Zafar M, Zia K, Muhammad A, *et al.* An agent-based model of crowd evacuation integrating agent perception and proximity pressure. In: Proceedings of the 14th international conference on advances in mobile computing and multi media. ACM; 2016. p. 12–19.

[9]   Zafar M, Zia K, Saini DK, *et al.* Modeling human factors influencing herding during evacuation. International Journal of Pervasive Computing and Communications. 2017;13(2):211–234.

[10] Vesin B, Klašnja-Milićević A, Ivanović M, *et al.* Applying recommender systems and adaptive hypermedia for e-learning personalization. Computing and Informatics. 2013;32(3):629–659.

[11] Muhammad A, Saini DK, Zia K, *et al.* Educational aspects of service orientation: Smart home design issues and technologies. TEM Journal. 2017;6(2):250.

[12] Labrinidis A, Jagadish HV. Challenges and opportunities with big data. Proceedings of the VLDB Endowment. 2012;5(12):2032–2033.

[13] White T. Hadoop: The definitive guide. Cambridge, Yahoo Press; 2012.

[14] Alham NK, Li M, Liu Y, *et al.* A MapReduce-based distributed SVM ensemble for scalable image classification and annotation. Computers & Mathematics with Applications. 2013;66(10):1920–1934.

[15] Inoubli W, Aridhi S, Mezni H, *et al.* An experimental survey on big data frameworks. Future Generation Computer Systems. 2018;86:546–564.

[16] Murthy AC, Vavilapalli VK, Eadline D. Apache Hadoop YARN: Moving beyond MapReduce and batch processing with Apache Hadoop 2. Boston, MA: Pearson Education; 2013.

[17] Ortega F, Bobadilla J, Hernando A, *et al.* Using hierarchical graph maps to explain collaborative filtering recommendations. International Journal of Intelligent Systems. 2014;29(5):462–477.

[18] Wang SL, Wu CY. Application of context-aware and personalized recommendation to implement an adaptive ubiquitous learning system. Expert Systems with Applications. 2011;38(9):10831–10838.

[19] Yang HL, Wang CS. Recommender system for software project planning one application of revised CBR algorithm. Expert Systems with Applications. 2009;36(5):8938–8945.

[20] Burke R. Hybrid web recommender systems. In: The adaptive web. Berlin, Heidelberg: Springer; 2007. p. 377–408.

[21] Billings SA. Nonlinear system identification: NARMAX methods in the time, frequency, and spatio-temporal domains. New York, NY: John Wiley & Sons; 2013.

[22] Srivastava DK. Big challenges in big data research. Data Mining and Knowledge Engineering. 2014;6(7):282–286.

[23] Kalnis P, Mamoulis N, Bakiras S. On discovering moving clusters in spatio-temporal data. In: International Symposium on Spatial and Temporal Databases. Springer; 2005. p. 364–381.

[24] Gong S. Employing user attribute and item attribute to enhance the collaborative filtering recommendation. Journal of Social Work. 2009;4(8):883–890.

[25] Do Kim H. Applying consistency-based trust definition to collaborative filtering. KSII Transactions on Internet and Information Systems (TIIS). 2009;3(4):366–375.

[26] Al-Taie MZ, Kadry S. Visualization of explanations in recommender systems. Journal of Advanced Management Science. 2014;2(2):140–144.

[27] Verbert K, Parra D, Brusilovsky P, *et al.* Visualizing recommendations to support exploration, transparency and controllability. In: Proceedings of the

2013 international conference on Intelligent user interfaces. ACM; 2013. p. 351–362.

[28]   Prakash LS, Saini DK, Kutti NS. Integrating EduLearn learning content management system (LCMS) with cooperating learning object repositories (LORs) in a peer to peer (P2P) architectural framework. ACM SIGSOFT Software Engineering Notes. 2009;34(3):1–7.

[29]   Saini DK, Prakash LS. Plagiarism detection in web based learning management systems and intellectual property rights in the academic environment. International Journal of Computer Applications. 2012;57(14):6–11.

[30]   Tintarev N, Masthoff J. Designing and evaluating explanations for recommender systems. In: Recommender systems handbook. Berlin, Heidelberg: Springer; 2011. p. 479–510.

[31]   Konstan JA, Miller BN, Maltz D, *et al.* GroupLens: Applying collaborative filtering to Usenet news. Communications of the ACM. 1997;40(3):77–87.

[32]   Shardanand U, Maes P. Social information filtering: Algorithms for automating "word of mouth". In: Proceedings of the SIGCHI conference on Human factors in computing systems. ACM Press/Addison-Wesley Publishing Co.; 1995. p. 210–217.

[33]   Leng Y, Lu Q, Liang C. A collaborative filtering similarity measure based on potential field. Kybernetes. 2016;45(3):434–445.

[34]   Li W, Matejka J, Grossman T, *et al.* Design and evaluation of a command recommendation system for software applications. ACM Transactions on Computer-Human Interaction (TOCHI). 2011;18(2):6.

[35]   Salehi M, Fathi A, Abdali-Mohammadi F. ANTSREC: A semantic recommender system based on ant colony meta-heuristic in electronic commerce. International Journal of Advanced Science and Technology. 2013;56:119–130.

[36]   Kurilovas E, Zilinskiene I, Dagiene V. Recommending suitable learning paths according to learners' preferences: Experimental research results. Computers in Human Behavior. 2015;51:945–951.

[37]   Vig J, Sen S, Riedl J. Navigating the tag genome. In: Proceedings of the 16th international conference on Intelligent user interfaces. ACM; 2011. p. 93–102.

[38]   Wang TI, Wang KT, Huang YM. Using a style-based ant colony system for adaptive learning. Expert Systems with Applications. 2008;34(4):2449–2464.

[39]   Lee HJ, Park SJ. MONERS: A news recommender for the mobile web. Expert Systems with Applications. 2007;32(1):143–150.

[40]   Wilson DC, Smyth B, Sullivan DO. Sparsity reduction in collaborative recommendation: A case-based approach. International Journal of Pattern Recognition and Artificial Intelligence. 2003;17(05):863–884.

[41]   Hu H, Wen Y, Chua TS, *et al.* Toward scalable systems for big data analytics: A technology tutorial. IEEE Access. 2014;2:652–687.

Chapter 4

Efficient and socio-aware recommendation approaches for bigdata networked systems

Vasileios Karyotis[1], Margarita Vitoropoulou[1],
Nikos Kalatzis[1], Ioanna Roussaki[1],
and Symeon Papavassiliou[1]

In this chapter, we present several approaches designed for providing efficient recommendations in large web systems characterized by bigdata scales. The key feature of the considered approaches is that they all rely on different elements and properties of social/complex network analysis for addressing various deficiencies of legacy and current recommendation systems when very large operational scales emerge. The main challenges of recommendations addressed by the presented approaches are the diversity (novelty) of recommendations, the cold-start problem, scalability and noise filtering issues, as well as the efficiency of developing these approaches and integrating them in operational systems. This chapter aspires to provide an educated overview, leading to a solid fundamental background on how social/complex network analysis can be exploited for more effective recommendations in stringent environments characterized by large scales of users, items and associated data, cumulatively referred to as big network data. Furthermore, our work aims at highlighting the design principles that are more interesting for enabling the extension of the presented approaches and their combination with other current state-of-the-art techniques, thus leading to more socio-aware and efficient recommendation approaches in the near and longer term future.

4.1 Introduction

The proliferation of network infrastructures, user devices and software technologies have enabled the development of very large interconnected systems offering diverse products and services, even enabling social activities, with characteristic examples including among others Amazon, Google, Facebook and Twitter. The number of users in such systems has grown rapidly, reaching the order of billion users in many cases, while for each user several data is maintained regarding his/her profile, activity, behavior and other information relevant to marketing or system-maintenance

---

[1]School of Electrical and Computer Engineering, National Technical University of Athens, Greece

purposes. Examples of these data may include demographic data, preferences, interactions/relations with other users, interactions with the available "items,"[1] social activity information and others.

The data volume collected today regarding items or users is already exceeding the computational scales offered by the state-of-the-art processing algorithms [1]. This volume is expected to further increase in the future, since far more data sources will become available. For instance, in the anticipated dawn of the era of Internet of Things (IoT) and smart homes/buildings, multiple, diverse information regarding the daily routine of human users will become available, and potentially exploited by online systems for customized, cheaper and more efficient services/items provided [2] (e.g., a smart fridge monitoring the inventory of goods and suggesting online order of those reaching low quantities and found at discount). Within the existing and future systems characterized by bigdata scales, several operations or computations will need modification or even reinventing them in order to cope with the anticipated scales of operation.

In all the aforementioned web systems, and many more, it is often necessary to employ various forms of recommendation systems (RSs) to increase the efficiency of marketing and create added-value services for the users [3,4]. The term RS characterizes generically the techniques and software tools that generate effective suggestions about new or existing items for particular users or classes of users. The main goal of an RS is to increase the number of items sold and eventually the corresponding financial revenue, while potentially suggest diverse items, e.g., promote unpopular items in a movie database that some users may eventually find interesting. Other functions include the creation of a more satisfying experience for users and increasing user fidelity (which asserts that the longer the user interacts with a system, the more refined the user activity model can become, and thus, the more probable to increase the revenue generated by a more customized experience). By aiming at predicting users' preferences for items not already considered, an RS reduces the transaction[2] costs of finding and selecting items in the online shopping environments, and thus the associated operational costs. The basic concept behind an RS is a well-designed decision-making strategy under a complex information environment [3,4]. The latter consists of an information-processing system that persistently collects data (actively or passively) on the three main entities involved: *items*, *users* and *transactions* (relations between items–users or users–users, etc.).

The success of an RS is typically evaluated according to metrics such as prediction accuracy,[3] credibility and filtering efficiency [3]. Traditional recommendation

---

[1]The term "item" refers to specific products sold in e-shops, services offered by cloud or other online systems and, in general, to all objects that can be sold to potential customers–users of the described systems.

[2]The term "transaction" denotes various iterations between the online system and the user. These transactions are required in order to pose to the user several iterative inquires, using the response of each iteration to create and refine an accurate user profile.

[3]A metric indicating the difference between the ratings predicted by the RS for a user and the actual ratings provided by the users.

approaches have succeeded in yielding good indices with respect to the above and other metrics until now. However, as we delve deeper into the bigdata era, even simple tasks, such as search and matching can become very challenging and demand significant resources in order to complete successfully. Traditional problems faced by RS, such as the long-tail problem [1] (which is explained in detail in the forthcoming sections), become more prominent in bigdata environments due to the larger datasets (data regarding users and/or items) involved.

The purpose of this chapter is to contribute to the reconsideration of traditional recommendation methodologies and fill in missing gaps in the literature of socio-aware RS approaches. The chapter collects and presents some of the latest state-of-the-art methods, which are especially designed to address several of the aforementioned challenges faced by RS in bigdata environments via the use of features and tools from social network (SN) analysis (SNA). We aspire to show that the approaches presented demonstrate the usefulness of considering elements/tools from SNA for improving RS and aid in maintaining the efficiency, scalability and accuracy of RS in very large environments characterized by bigdata scales.

The rest of this chapter is structured as follows. Section 4.2 provides a working background on RSs and SNA, while Section 4.3 presents the approaches of interest in the considered environment. More specifically, Section 4.3.1 presents hyperbolic network embedding based RSs, Section 4.3.2 provides recommendation approaches based on probabilistic graphical models, Section 4.3.3 describes information diffusion-aware recommendation techniques and Section 4.3.4 presents approaches exploiting social context information. Finally, Section 4.4 includes a qualitative comparison of the presented techniques, while Section 4.5 recapitulates the contributions of this chapter and provides some indicative directions for future work.

4.2 Background on recommendation systems and social network analysis

4.2.1 Recommendation systems

In this subsection, we provide some background on RSs, starting with a cumulative definition. One of the most popularly employed definitions nowadays is that presented in [3], and it is based on the notion of utility function denoting the usefulness of an item for a user.

Definition 4.1. (Recommendation problem). *Given a user $u \in U$, where U is the set of all users, and an item $i \in I$, where I is the set of all recommendable items, let $f(u, i)$ be a utility function that measures the usefulness of item i to user u, $f : U \times I \rightarrow R$, where R is a totally ordered set of non-negative real numbers or integers. The goal of the recommendation problem is to find for each user $u \in U$ the item $i' \in I$ over all items in I that maximizes the expected utility for this specific user u, namely an item such that $\forall u \in U : i'_u = \underset{i \in I}{\arg\max}\, f(u, i)$.*

	Item 1	Item 2	Item 3	Item 4	Item 5	...	Item m − 1	Item m
User 1	$r_{1,1}$	?	?	?	?		?	?
User 2	?	$r_{2,2}$	$r_{2,3}$	?	?		$r_{2,m-1}$	?
User 3	$r_{3,1}$	?	$r_{3,3}$	$r_{3,4}$	?		?	$r_{3,m}$
...								
User n − 1	?	$r_{n-1,2}$	?	$r_{n-1,4}$	?		?	$r_{n-1,m}$
User n	$r_{n,1}$	?	?	?	$r_{n,5}$		$r_{n,m-1}$	?

Figure 4.1   Example of a user–item utility matrix. Question marks correspond to unrated items to be estimated by the RS

In the above definition, the objective is to find the item that maximizes the utility function for the specific user. In different applications, different forms of these functions allow quantifying different utilities for the involved users.

The two fundamental entities of an RS, i.e., the users and the items, form two distinct spaces (sets), the user space (set) and the item space (set), respectively. Elements in both user and item space have various attributes (properties). These features are typically represented by the components of associated feature vectors, namely, the user feature vector and the item feature vector. The utility function measures the value that an item has for a user, in the form of a user rating. User ratings are defined on a subset of space $U \times I$, and thus, the main challenge in a recommendation problem is to predict the missing values of f in the corresponding user–item utility matrix [3], as shown in Figure 4.1. In contrast to this approach, which estimates the numerical values of user ratings (they are typically referred to as rating-based approach), other approaches denoted as preference-based techniques formulate the recommendation problem with the objective to predict the users' relative preference ordering between items, as implied by past rating values. A couple of characteristic examples of such approaches are presented in Section 4.3.2. It is evident that the utility matrix can grow significantly in modern web systems, as the number of users and involved items increases drastically.

Recommender systems appear quite diverse in terms of their function, varying in terms of their application domain, the knowledge used and the computational model adopted [4]. For this reason, several classifications have emerged, with the most widely accepted to be the one that uses the model of numerical user ratings for the existing items as the underlying substrate for computing recommendations. According to this substrate, given explicit (user ratings) or implicit user feedback (inference of user's preference derived from the online user behaviors), a learning algorithm is applied to filter the user's attributes and use them to perform an educated prediction of recommendation options for each user. Regarding the numerical-rating-based approach, recommendation techniques can be classified into two broad categories: *content-based* and *collaborative filtering (CF)*. Combining these two approaches leads to hybrid filtering, which is elaborated upon later in this subsection. It should be stressed once more that in these steps outlined above, bigdata scales emerge in modern systems, where recommendations need to be provided for possibly millions of users and over millions-to-billions of items, further complicating the involved technical challenges.

Content-based approaches originated from the field of information retrieval [5]. In general, they focus on the creation of user profiles by analyzing the features of the items that a user has rated in the past. Most frequently, these features are textual descriptions of items, e.g., if the item is a film, it could be genre, duration, production year, while for a clothing item, it could be fabric, size, etc., in the form of annotations accompanying the item. Assuming some known utilities $f(u, i_j)$ of items $i_j \in I$ assigned by user u, the utility $f(u, i')$ of item i', which is similar to items i_j, can be estimated. Methods in this category suggest different ways of performing these estimations.

Contrary to content-based methods which are centered around item–item similarity, CF techniques rely on users' ratings similarity (according to measures such as cosine or Jaccard distance [6]), in order to predict the utility of an item for a particular user. More specifically, the utility $f(u, i)$ of item i to user u is computed by the utilities $f(u_j, i)$, where $u_j \in U$ are the users who are similar to user u. Collaborative recommendations can be either *neighborhood based* or *model based*. In neighborhood-based recommendations, sometimes referred to as memory based, the user–item ratings, represented algebraically by a matrix (see user-item utility matrix in Figure 4.1), are directly used to estimate ratings for unrated items. Similarity-based neighborhoods are defined either between the users (user-based) or between the items (item-based), and a weighted average of the corresponding ratings is calculated [7]. Model-based approaches, in contrast to the neighborhood-based, exploit the user–item rating patterns to build a predictive model of ratings with the use of data mining and machine-learning techniques (Bayesian network, clustering, association analysis) [7].

To summarize roughly the difference between the above two approaches, the content-based aims at recommending items similar to items that a user has already chosen, while on the other hand, CF approaches provide recommendations by suggesting to a user items that similar users have selected before.

We should note that both of the aforementioned families of approaches have several limitations, a summary of which can be found in [6,7], along with more extensive explanations. In general, a content-based system is highly dependent on the availability of the descriptive data (limited content analysis). In addition, it is susceptible to over-specialization and exhibits the users' cold-start problem [3], which also appears as a main drawback along with sparsity and scalability issues in collaborative systems. In particular, rating data characteristics such as the size and shape of the rating space which is defined to be the ratio of the number of users to the number of items, as well as the rating density which is the proportion of known ratings among all possible ratings, are shown in [8] to have a significant impact on collaborative systems' predictive accuracy. Finally, CF systems fail to categorize users who have common preferences with more than one group of similar users (they belong to the intersection of the different clusters of users) and by extension fail to output accurate recommendations, a problem known as the gray sheep problem [9]. Hybrid methods are

Weaknesses	Content-based	Collaborative Filtering
Users' cold start problem	◊	◊
Items' cold start problem		◊
Data sparsity	◊	◊
Over-specialization	◊	◊
Limited Content Analysis	◊	
Gray sheep problem		◊

Figure 4.2   Summary of weaknesses of traditional recommendation systems

introduced to overcome these constraints (for a summary of weaknesses of traditional RS approaches see Figure 4.2) and improve prediction performance in multiple ways: either by combining the outputs of individual recommender approaches (weighted and mixed hybrid systems) or by switching between the two techniques depending on their performance's scores (switching hybrid systems), or by incorporating content-based features to collaborative methods and vice versa (feature augmentation and feature combination hybrid systems).

Recently, a new type of RS is introduced, referred to as social RSs (SRS) [5,6], which is based on the bilateral relation between RS and SNs. The former leverage the structural nature (properties and features of the entities that constitute the network, as well as the interactions between network nodes) and mechanisms of SNs, quantified by appropriate SNA metrics (briefly presented in the next subsection), in order to produce more accurate and efficient results. Conversely, SRSs contribute to the formation and evolution of SNs through recommendations of individuals or groups.

Contrary to traditional RSs, SRS can also take into consideration different relations among users, e.g., in the form of *trust* [6,7] (defined as the subjective expectation of one's future behavior [10]), or *influence* (which is described as the importance of each user in propagating information), using either structural analysis (location-based SNA) or behavioral analysis (interaction-based SNA) [11]. The correlation between ratings and social structure of recommendations is obtained by quantifying the above features. This results in the definition of new, social-based similarity measures, which alleviate the problems of sparsity and cold-start [12]. Trust relationships increase RS coverage when the application of traditional similarity measures is impossible (e.g., Pearson correlation coefficient (PCC) can only be applied to users with high overlap in items' ratings [13]), while users with no previous ratings may receive accurate recommendations by connecting to a "trusted" or "influential" user of the network. Context is also another form of user–item developing relations, which will be analyzed in more detail in Section 4.3.4.

4.2.2   Social network analysis

Lately, SNA has been widely employed in information and communication technologies, aiming at more targeted and efficient per case solutions, e.g., better communications, efficient coverage and tracking [14,15]. Characteristic features of SNA that are typically exploited in various solutions include the properties of the emerging complex network topologies (e.g., random, small-world (SW), scale-free) which, together with the features indicated by various SNA metrics (e.g., the clustering coefficient and centrality metrics such as degree and betweenness centrality), play an important role in identifying the key actors of a network known in the literature as mediators, ambassadors or experts [5], as well as in measuring the importance of each node in propagating information (detection of the most influential nodes).

A *random graph* (RG) model over a set of N nodes postulates that any two randomly selected nodes can be connected with a fixed probability p (relational character of network). There exist several RG models. The most commonly employed (Gilbert model) is $\mathcal{G}(N, p)$, in which every possible edge occurs independently with probability $0 < p < 1$. In the Erdős–Rényi (ER) model, $\mathcal{G}(N, E)$, a graph is chosen uniformly at random from the collection of all graphs that have N nodes and E edges. *Scale-free* (SF) is a type of network whose degree distribution follows a power-law, at least asymptotically. That is, the fraction $P(k)$ of nodes in the network having k connections to other nodes scales for large values of k as $P(k) \sim k^{-\gamma}$, where γ is a parameter whose value is typically in the range $2 < \gamma < 3$, although occasionally it may lie outside of these bounds [14,15]. *SW* networks correspond to complex systems where most nodes are not neighbors of one another, but most nodes can be reached from every other by a small number of hops or steps. Thus, an SW network [14,15] is defined as a network where the typical distance L between two randomly chosen nodes grows proportionally to the logarithm of the number of nodes N, i.e., $L \propto \log N$. Practically, this means that nodes of the network are linked by a small number of local neighbors. However, the average distance between nodes remains small.

The most notable metrics in SNA which are adopted by RSs can be divided into three broad categories [16]: The first focuses on the network **connections** via the metric of homophily, which measures the tendency of network users to connect to the ones they consider similar to them (based on, e.g., demographic criteria). Centrality metrics (degree, betweenness, closeness, eigenvector) measure each one of them from a different perspective, the importance of each node in the network, and they form a subclass of local measures of the second category of **distribution**-centered metrics along with the global measure of density, which characterizes networks to be dense when the number of edges is close to the maximal number of edges, or else, sparse. Another metric of this type, the average path length, is defined as the expected distance between a random selection of a pair of nodes in the network, according to the chosen distance measure (hop-count, Euclidean distance) for shortest paths computation [14]. Last, the **segmentation**-based category includes a set of metrics that identify networks' structure both at node and network level with the most common ones to be the structural cohesion, which relates to networks' connectivity and the clustering coefficient that reveals the extent of triadic closure in the network.

A popular topic in SNA is the one of community detection. The goal of community detection in networks is to identify the groups of vertices, known as modules, that share common properties within the network as well as their hierarchical order [17]. In the case of RS, communities are mostly formed based on users' profile and their strength of ties, and are used as input to neighborhood-based collaborative filtering (CF) [5]. Identifying changes in networks' structure (addition/deletion of edges), known as link prediction [5], and inferring missing links in partially observed networks are another two closely related SNA tasks, which can be potentially integrated in RSs with similarity-oriented techniques. In the latter, the process of items' recommendation can be considered as a link prediction problem in user–item bipartite networks [18].

4.3   Socio-aware recommendation systems

In this section, we present each of the family of socio-aware approaches that adopt elements from SNA for improving the performance, scalability, or other factors of RS operation. We refer to them cumulatively as "socio-aware," even though the use of social features can be different, e.g., social structure, social properties and context information.

4.3.1   *Hyperbolic path-based recommendation system*

Nowadays, in many online systems, it is required to add diversity in the recommendations provided to the users, in order to increase the potential of promoting items with less popularity. This is especially required in very large-scale systems, characterized by bigdata order of magnitude, where the quantity of items available is prohibitive for detailed inspections, and the thematic areas of the items are voluminous and diverse as well. The approach presented in this subsection aims at addressing this aspect of socio-aware recommendations in big network data environments.

The main concept in this approach, which we refer to as hyperbolic path-based recommendations (HPR), and it is depicted in Figure 4.3, is to cast the recommendation problem as a (path) routing problem over the item graph, after the latter has been embedded in the hyperbolic space.[4] A fundamental assumption is that knowledge on the interactions among items and users can be represented in graph form. Items correspond to the nodes of the item graph and users to the edges of the user graph. Links between pairs of users are determined according to a similarity function, which may correspond to any type of social, marketing, or other possible associations developing between users and could be of potential interest/use in the recommendation of items. Similarly, links between pairs of items are determined according to a different similarity function, which also indicates some type of association of items with respect to users and their preferences. A characteristic example of this association is the co-view metric employed for videos, defined as the ratio of number of times that two videos have been jointly viewed by a user over the product of times each video has been viewed independently and indicates the tendency that two videos will be both selected for viewing by a user. Links connecting items with users can be defined and represent the times a user has selected a specific item, thus creating a two-layer

---

[4] **Hyperbolic network embedding** consists of the assignment to each node of a graph with coordinates in the hyperbolic space denoting its location, so that distances of node pairs in the hyperbolic space approximate the corresponding node distances measured in hops in the original graph [19]. From this mapping, the shortest path geometric distances between the nodes can be calculated more efficiently based on the hyperbolic coordinates, rather than computing shortest paths in the original graph.

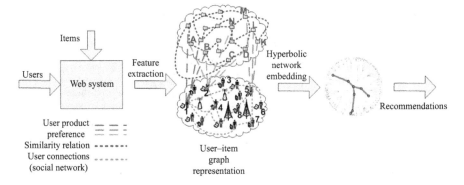

Figure 4.3   Overview of hyperbolic path-based recommendation approach

item–user graph hierarchy that represents the available knowledge of the system, as well as knowledge to be inferred by the recommendation problem.

The hyperbolic recommendation-known destination (HRKD) algorithm is a simple in concept approach in the class of HPR [20]. It begins with an already selected item by a user, sets a specific item goal, which corresponds to a marketing goal that the RS wishes to promote, and attempts to find a path starting with the item-source in the item graph. The item-product graph has been embedded in the hyperbolic space, which allows for very efficient discovery of the desired path via greedy routing over the hyperbolic coordinates. Thus, in this case, the path discovery does not take place with the traditional computationally demanding shortest path search algorithms, but rather neighboring nodes are discovered efficiently by comparing distances of hyperbolic coordinates (Figure 4.3). The details of HRKD algorithm are described in [20], where the operation, complexity analysis and some implementation features are presented. Furthermore, performance results over a simulated system can be found in [20].

In addition, [20] presents hyperbolic recommendation-unknown destination (HRUD), which is an extension of the previous approach, with the objective to lead the recommendation path to any of a set of desired items, rather than to a very specific one. This serves the goal of promoting a whole set of items to different users, by leading them progressively toward the specific groups of items and having them selecting any of them. In this case, where more recommendation diversity is desired, social features from the user graph can be exploited to increase the efficiency of the recommendation. Rather than using an item source already chosen by a specific user, or in absence of such an item (when a user just enters the system), the recommendation path can start with an item already chosen by a neighbor (in the user graph) of the user under consideration. Starting with such an item and dictated by social association, the recommendation path is again determined via greedy routing, selecting neighboring items in the item graph, until one of the destination items is accepted by the user. If no such item is reached or no such item is accepted by the user, the recommendation is determined unsuccessful.

Performance evaluation for both HRKD and HRUD can be found in [20], where five-user classes and ten-item classes have been considered. The number of features was assumed to be fixed and equal to 100 for both items–users. For a pair of target user and recommended item, the inner product between their feature vectors was employed for accepting the item with probability proportional to this inner product. Thus, a user was more likely to select products similar to his/her profile, while in order to reduce biases, there was always a chance of selecting irrelevant products in place of relevant ones, as it is expected in reality. The item and user graphs were considered to have the power-law form, as it is the case for many online SNs of users and also for the associations developing between a few popular and many unpopular items of an online electronic shop. The details of the evaluations and the performance results for various densities of the user–item graphs can be found in [20]. The performance metrics employed for the evaluation were the success rate/percentage, the average minimum hyperbolic distance to the destination (which indicates how far away from the goal item the recommendation path stopped in case of failure to reach the goal) and the average recommendation precision (defined as the number of recommendations that the target user has chosen over a recommendation round divided by all recommendations made by HRKD or HRUD for a recommendation round), which are all typical evaluation metrics for analogous recommendation approaches.

Already identified directions for future work include the implementation and evaluation of the proposed approaches in an operational system with real users signifying the practical merit of HRKD and HRUD. Another interesting direction will aim at extending the framework to provide recommendations of common target items to pairs of users possibly bearing different and diverse interests, e.g., lead a married couple with totally different hobbies/interests to a joint item such as a summer cruise vacation by locating rendezvous points of greedy paths starting from different items already chosen by each one of them.

4.3.2 Probabilistic graphical models

A different category of RSs aims at predicting the score that a user would assign to an item (rating prediction) and suggest to the user a list of ranked, most relevant items (top-N recommendation task) according to the rating predictions. There are several approaches to achieve these tasks, but lately a family of probabilistic graphical models has emerged [21–24] employing the concept of Markov random fields (RFs) (MRFs) for the representation of information dependencies and solution of the corresponding problems. This family will be presented in this section, after briefly describing the notion of MRFs. It is worth noting that in general, most of these approaches belong to the class of CF or hybrid methodologies, with a greater tendency toward the second.

Considering a finite set $S, |S| = N$ with elements $s \in S$ referred to as sites (i.e., graph nodes corresponding to items or users) and a phase space Λ be the set of possible states of each $s \in S$, a collection $X = \{X_s, \forall s \in S\}$ of random variables with values in Λ is called an RF on S with phases in Λ. A configuration $\mathbf{x} = \{x_s, \forall s \in S, x_s \in \Lambda\}$, corresponds to one of all possible states of the system. Assuming $\mathcal{N}_s$ is the neighborhood of site (node) s, the RF X is called an MRF with respect to a neighborhood system $\mathcal{N}$ of all $\mathcal{N}_s$, if for every site $s \in S$,

$$\mathbb{P}(X_s = x_s \mid X_r = x_r, r \neq s) = \mathbb{P}(X_s = x_s \mid X_r = x_r, r \in \mathcal{N}_s) \tag{4.1}$$

A RF X is called a Gibbs RF if it satisfies $\mathbb{P}(X = \mathbf{x}) = (1/Z)e^{-(U(\mathbf{x})/T)}$, where $Z := \sum_{\mathbf{x} \in \Lambda^n} e^{-(U(\mathbf{x})/T)}$ is called the partition function and T is called the temperature of the system. $U(\mathbf{x})$ is called the potential function and represents an "energy" metric of configuration x. The potential function is not unique. However, a very useful class of potential functions is one in which $U(x)$ is decomposed into a sum of clique (maximally connected subgraph) potentials, $U(x) = \sum_{c \in C_s} \Phi_c(x)$, where C_s is the set of cliques of nodes formed in the topology. Each clique potential depends only on the states of the cliques formed by the sites of the MRF. The clique-based representation of $U(\mathbf{x})$ is very useful in various applications of MRFs, e.g., in the modeling of malware propagation in computer/communication networks when malware is transmitted through direct neighbor interactions [25], a process resembling considerably the spreading of rumors and marketing trends in an SN.

4.3.2.1 Pairwise recommendation MRFs

One of the first approaches employing the concept of MRF for recommendations is the one presented in [21], where the belief propagation (BP) approach is employed for computing the marginal probability distributions of a pairwise-MRF (PMRF) modeling the similarity associations between various items. Assuming M users and N items, the objective is to predict the numerical value (typically in the discrete range of 1–5) of the collection of variables $S_z = \{r_{zi} : i \in I \setminus I_z\}$, where r_{zi} is the recommendation score of user z for item i, I is the set of items and I_z denotes the set of rated items by user z. The employed PMRF consists of a hidden (item rating to be predicted) and an observed layer of sites (Figure 4.4). The observed sites correspond to known local evidence, i.e., average item rating from other users, weighted by user similarities with the user for which the rating is estimated: $y_i = \bar{r}_z + ((\sum_{v \in \hat{U}_i} s_{zv}(r_{vi} - \bar{r}_v))/\sum_{v \in \hat{U}_i |s_{zv}|})$, where $\hat{U}_i$ denotes a set of K_z users most similar to user z among users that rated item i, Figure 4.4. Similarity can be computed with any of the similarity measures mentioned before. Two items are connected if their similarity is above a predefined threshold, or if at least one is among the K most similar items of the other, or both. K is a fixed parameter. A local evidence function $\phi(r_{zi})$ represents how one item should be rated according to the local evidence y_i and a compatibility function between two

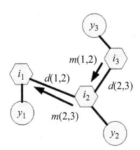

Figure 4.4 Example of a PMRF: Observed (circles), hidden (hexagons) layers, and exchange of messages. Functions d(·,·) denote dependence relations determined between site pairs of the PMRF

connected items i_a, i_b is defined as $\psi_{ab}(r_{z_{i_a}}, r_{z_{i_b}}) = (1/Z_{ab})\exp(-((r_{z_{i_a}} - r_{z_{i_b}})^2/\sigma_{ab}^2))$, where σ_{ab}^2 is adjusted according to item similarity, penalizing the incompatible rating from connected items if they deviate from each other. The authors employ a probabilistic message passing (in the form of BP) algorithm over the defined PMRF and the obtained beliefs (expectations of the marginal probability distributions) corresponding to the desired rating predictions are exact if the PMRF has no loops, otherwise they constitute approximations of the desired ratings (Figure 4.4). The approach was evaluated in [21] on the 100K MovieLens dataset according to the mean absolute error and root mean square error metrics, demonstrating comparative performance with the state of the art at the time and linear complexity per active user. Further, it can update the recommendations for each active user instantaneously, using the most recent rating, without the need to solve the marginal distributions for all users. The results indicate that such approaches can scale well in bigdata environments and efficient implementations.

4.3.2.2   Preference networks

The work in [22] suggests preference networks (PNs), a probabilistic model for combining content-based with CF into a single conditional MRF. Thus, it is a hybrid recommendation approach. The goal of PNs is again to estimate the missing user to item ratings of the utility (preference) matrix for only a limited set of items for each user (top-N ranking), as a user is typically interested in a moderate number of items.

In PNs, each vertex of the underlying undirected graph $G(V, E)$ corresponds to a rating r_{ui} of user u for item i and each edge captures a relation between two ratings, either of item–item or user–item nature. Specifically, there is an edge between any two ratings by the same user, and an edge between two ratings on the same item (Figure 4.5). The resulting network is typically very densely connected. The PN is a conditional MRF that defines a distribution over the graph, $P(X|\mathbf{o}) = (1/\mathbf{Z}(\mathbf{o}))\cdot\Psi(X, \mathbf{o})$, where $\Psi(X, \mathbf{o}) = \prod_{t \in V} \psi_t(\mathbf{r_t}, \mathbf{o}) \prod_{(t,t') \in E} \psi_{t,t'}(\mathbf{r_t}, \mathbf{r_{t'}}, \mathbf{o})$, where $\mathbf{o}$ is the vector of all user and item features combined, X the set of item rankings to be estimated, $Z(\mathbf{o})$ is the normalization constant and ψ the potential function, where $\psi_t(r_t, \mathbf{o})$ encodes information associated with rating r_t and $\psi_{t,t'}$ captures correlations between two

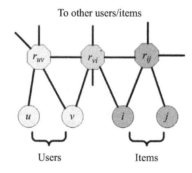

Figure 4.5   Example of a preference network, where the associations between user–user, item–item and user–item are shown

different ratings. The approach first estimates the parameters of the model, which are then used for preference (rating) prediction, and then top-N recommendation is ensured by ordering the obtained preferences.

In the following, we briefly outline parameter selection and preference prediction. Due to the density of the obtained network, standard log-likelihood methods are not applicable, mainly due to complexity issues. The authors resort to a simple pseudo-likelihood learning method, where the log-likelihood is replaced by the regularized sum of log local likelihoods. Maximizing the emerging function yields efficient estimation of the parameters, and supervised learning can be employed for finding a unique maximum (the pseudo-likelihood function attains a concave form on the vector of estimated parameters). To optimize the parameters, a stochastic gradient ascent method is used, updating the parameters by passing the set of ratings by each user, and 2–3 passes of all data is sufficient. Once the model has been estimated, new ratings, in addition to the known ones employed for the training, can be added. As the size of new data is typically small compared to the existing ones (those employed for training), it can be assumed that model parameters do not change. The prediction of the rating r_{ui} is given as $\hat{r}_{ui} = \text{argmax}_{r_{ui}} P(r_{ui}|N(u,i),\mathbf{o})$, where $N(u,i)$ is the set of neighbor rating connected to r_{ui}.

It may appear non-obvious that a prediction may depend on unknown ratings (other predictions to be made), but this is the advantage of the Markov networks. For instance, consider the recommendation of a relatively new item i to a set of promising users. One can make joint predictions $\hat{r}_i = \text{argmax}_{r_i} P(r_i|N(i),\mathbf{o})$. Based on the evaluations provided in [22], PNs have competitive performance against both the well-known item-based and user-based CF methods in the rating prediction task, and against the user-based method in the top-N recommendation task at the time of the study.

4.3.2.3 Ordinal random fields

An interesting observation for RSs, in general, is that while users are not good at making consistent quantitative judgment, namely, they are not consistent at providing the same numerical rating for the same item at different times, ordinal preferences, i.e., relative orders between items, such as which item is best, second best, among a set of items, are considered to be more consistent across like-minded users. Ordinal matrix factorization (OMF) [26] has been suggested as an effective relevant method in the past. In contrast to numerical-ranking-based methods, OMF needs weaker assumptions since user preferences now represent the ordering of items. The two graphical-based approaches presented before, namely, the PMRF and PNs, both considered numerical user preferences.

The work in [23] develops a unified model, denoted as ordinal RFs (ORF) combining elements from OMF and previous MRF-based techniques. ORF model can employ any OMF representation and focuses on the local structure of the system, namely, on the second order interactions between similar users or items, also used in neighborhood-based collaborative filtering. At the same time, it can capture the global structure as well, i.e., the weaker but higher order interactions among all users and items. In general, the OMF aims at obtaining the ordinal distribution $Q(r_{ui}|u,i)$

over all possible rating values for each user/item pair. Predicting the rating of user u on item i is then equivalent to identifying the rating with the greatest mass in the ordinal distribution $Q(r_{ui}|u, i)$.

In the MRF model considered, a vertex represents a preference r_{ui} of user u on item i and each edge captures a relation between two preferences by the same user, similarly to the previously presented MRF based-models. This standard MRF model captures the local structure between item–item correlations. The ORF combines such item–item correlations with the point-wise ordinal distribution: $P(\mathbf{r_u}) = \Psi_u(\mathbf{r_u}) \prod_{r_{ui} \in r_u} Q(\mathbf{r_{ui}}|\mathbf{u}, \mathbf{i})$, where $\Psi_u(\mathbf{r_u})$ is the potential function capturing the interaction among items and $\mathbf{r_u}$ is the set of preferences from user u. The potential function can be decomposed into pairwise potentials: $\Psi_u(\mathbf{r_u}) = \exp\left(\sum_{r_{ui}, r_{uj} \in r_u} \mathbf{w_{ij}} \mathbf{f_{ij}}(\mathbf{r_{ui}}, \mathbf{r_{uj}}) \right)$, where $f_{ij}(\cdot)$ is the correlation feature between items i, j and w_{ij} is a weight that controls the relative importance of each correlation feature to ordinal distribution. The feature function captures the item–item correlation in the form $f(r_{ui}, r_{uj}) = g(|(r_{ui} - \bar{r}_i) - (r_{uj} - \bar{r}_j)|)$, where $g(t) = 1/(1 + e^{-t})$ and $\bar{r}_i$, $\bar{r}_j$ are the average ratings for items i and j, respectively. This function captures the intuition that correlated items should receive similar ratings by the same user after offsetting the goodness of each item. User–user correlations can be determined analogously and also the bias with identity features for item–users can be designed. The decomposition of the potential function in pairwise potentials allows proper scaling in bigdata environments and distributed operation.

The work in [23] provides more details on parameter estimation of the model based on a pseudo-likelihood approach, by maximizing the regularized sum of log local likelihoods. Following the estimation of model parameters, rating prediction is straightforward, by identifying the rating with the greatest mass in local likelihood $\hat{r}_{ui} = \text{argmax}_{r_{ui}} P(r_{ui}|\mathbf{r_u})$. The local likelihood in this case serves as a confidence measure. For predictions of scalar values, the expectation $\hat{r}_{ui} = \sum_{r_{ui}=1}^{L} r_{ui} P(r_{ui}|\mathbf{r_u})$ can be handily used. The authors in [23] compare the performance of the ORF approach with K-nearest neighbors and OMF approaches, verifying the effectiveness of their approach.

4.3.2.4 Preference Markov random fields

As far as the second and higher order interactions among users and items are concerned in preference relation models, the work in [24] is the first to address them both via an MRF-based model approach. The preference relation is a kind of relative preference, and it is invariant to irrelevant factors, e.g., the user's mood. It encodes user preference in the form of pairwise ordering between items, as π_{uij}, indicating the strength of user's u preference relation for the ordered item pair (i, j). A higher π_{uij} indicates a stronger preference on the first item over the second. Assuming $\pi_{uij} \in [0, 1]$, it may be defined that u prefers i over j if $\pi_{uij} \in ((2/3), 1]$, j over i if $\pi_{uij} \in [0, 1/3)$, or else i, j are equally preferable to u. The user-wise preference can be defined as $p_{ui} = ((\sum_{j \in I_u} \pi_{uij} > (2/3) - \sum_{j \in I_u} \pi_{uij} < (1/3))/|\Pi_{ui}|)$, where Π_{ui} is the set of user u's preference relation related to item i.

The task of preference-relation based systems is to take the preference relation as input and output top-N recommendations. The goal is to estimate the value of each unknown $\pi_{uij} \in \Pi_{\text{unknown}}$, such that $\hat{\pi}_{uij} = \text{argmax}_{\hat{\pi}_{uij} \in [0,1]} (|\pi_{uij} - \hat{\pi}_{uij}|)$. In practice, it may be easier to estimate $\hat{\pi}_{uij}$ by the difference between the two user-wise preferences, $\hat{\pi}_{uij} = \phi(\hat{p}_{ui} - \hat{p}_{uj})$, where $\phi(\cdot)$ is a function that bounds the value into $[0,1]$ and ensures $\phi(0) = 0.5$, e.g., the inverse-logit function. The optimization problem then becomes $(\hat{p}_{ui}, \hat{p}_{uj}) = \text{argmax}_{\hat{p}_{ui}, \hat{p}_{uj}} (|\pi_{uij} - \phi(\hat{p}_{ui} - \hat{p}_{uj})|)$.

The preference MRF uniquely combines preference relations with local and global structure features, providing as output item rankings. In the MRF employed, each user u has a graph G_u, where each vertex represents a preference (rating) p_{ui} of user u on item i, and each edge represents an item–item relation. An edge connects two preferences co-rated by the same user. The edges correspond to item pair regardless of users, so that the edge between p_{ui}–p_{uj} and the edge between p_{vi}–p_{vj} correspond to the same item–item correlation ψ_{ij} of item pair i, j. If I_u denotes the set of items evaluated by user u and $\mathbf{p_u} = \{p_{ui} | i \in I_u\}$ denotes the joint set of preference expressed by user u, then the MRF defines the distribution $P(\mathbf{p_u}) = (1/Z_u) \mathbf{R} \Psi(\mathbf{p_u})$, where Z_u is a normalization constant and $\Psi(\mathbf{p_u}) = \prod_{(ui,uj) \in E_u} \psi_{ij}(p_{ui}, p_{uj})$. The potential $\psi_{ij}(p_{ui}, p_{uj}) = \exp\{w_{ij} f_{ij}(p_{ui}, p_{uj})\}$ captures the correlation between i and j, f_{ij} is the correlation feature function and w_{ij} is a weight factor realizing the importance of each correlation feature (weights are estimated from real data). The unknown preference can be predicted as $\hat{p}_{ui} = \text{argmax}_{p_{ui} \in [-1,1]} P(p_{ui} | \mathbf{p_u})$, where $P(p_{ui} | \mathbf{p_u})$ measures the confidence of the prediction.

In this form, the MRF captures the item–item correlations; thus, it needs to include ordinal distributions capturing global structure, e.g., user-wise preferences, such as $P(\mathbf{p_u}) = \Psi_u(\mathbf{p_u}) \prod_{p_{ui} \in \mathbf{p_u}} \mathbf{Q}(p_{ui} | \mathbf{u}, \mathbf{i})$, where the potential Ψ_u captures the interactions among items evaluated by user u. The potentials can be further factorized as exponential terms of weighted sums of the feature functions mentioned above. Feature design can take place as with ORFs, and the parameter estimation of the approach can be similarly based on the maximization of a regularized sum of log local likelihoods, as explained in more detail in [24]. The latter contains experimental analysis and comparison with relevant approaches, which can be used by the interested reader for comparison with the rest of graphical models presented in this section.

4.3.3 *Information diffusion-aware recommendation approaches*

Another aspect of socio-awareness that can be exploited for improving the performance of RSs is information diffusion, or features of this process as it evolves over an SN of users. In general, one can observe growing interest by the research and industrial communities in integrating the sharing mechanism of information diffusion processes in recommender techniques for SNs [27,28]. The main reason for this is twofold: information propagates *rapidly* through social connections and reaches *targeted* users. With respect to the latter, the models presented in this subsection attempt to tackle key problems of previous RSs, e.g., the long-tail effect (explained in more detail in the following), information overload and increase system efficiency in bigdata environments by combining the similarity-based predictions of traditional recommendation methods with the social-based predictions developed for the information propagation mechanisms.

Initially, we provide some necessary fundamental concepts regarding information diffusion in SNs. Formally, information diffusion is defined as *the process by which information is communicated through certain channels among the users of an SN* [29]. The main factors influencing information diffusion are the network structure (density, centrality, clustering, connectivity) and the strength of ties (frequency of interactions, strength of influence) [27,28]. A significant aspect of SNA refers to the modeling of information diffusion, which can be coarsely classified as explanatory or predictive [30]. The goal of explanatory models is to infer the underlying network over which information propagates, given the times the users learn a piece of information. In contrast, in predictive models, the main concept is to predict the outcome of a specific diffusion process based on temporal or spatial network characteristics [30]. Widely used predictive graph-based models of information diffusion are the sender-oriented independent cascade probabilistic model in which node u at time t becomes active (receives information from the diffusion process) and has one single chance of activating each inactive neighbor v at time $t + 1$, with a probability p_{uv}. The process continues until no more activations can take place. The receiver-oriented linear threshold model is the most popular of the threshold models used in studying diffusion in networks. In these models, *a threshold value or a set of threshold values are used to distinguish ranges of values where the behavior predicted by the model varies significantly* [29]. Each edge uv of the network is affiliated with a weight w_{uv}, and each node v has a threshold t_v. Node v is activated if the fraction of its active neighbors exceeds t_v [29]. In the case of RSs, both explanatory and predictive modeling approaches are employed in order to strengthen their performance.

We segregate recently proposed approaches on information diffusion-aware RS into three categories according to the incorporation of the diffusion mechanism in recommender systems. First, a noteworthy issue which comes as a consequence of the power-law distribution of product sales in online commerce, such as Amazon and Netflix [31], is the *long-tail problem*: although a small set of products are extremely popular (hits/blockbusters), the less common products (niche products) exceed in aggregate the market share of the former [31,32]. Therefore, it is essential for an RS to provide suggestions of long-tail products. This serves not only retailers, who experience greater profit from sales of otherwise unpopular items, but also individuals, who have access to more diverse products, which in turn increases their engagement to the online platforms. Until now, due to data sparsity, RS weakly enhance item diversity. From the perspective of information diffusion, estimating users' influence (influential users of RSs are modeled in the literature with temporal criteria as initial/early adopters [33] but can also be considered as the ones who exhibit high similarity to a great portion of users, having at the same time high out-degree in the SN) and inferring how influence propagates in the network may address the long-tail problem in RS, as follows: recommending long-tail items to the most influential users of the network leads to the wide adoption of the former through the diffusion mechanism. In [33], a collaborative innovation diffusion-aware recommendation mechanism is proposed to improve novel knowledge sharing (innovation diffusion) between the users of a corporate portal, where 80% of the total traffic comes from 2% of unique pages. Recommendation of long-tail information to a portal user u who visits a page p is obtained based on the browsing behavior, during a specific time period, of a small portion of users (reference users) who are the first to access page p before user u. The preferences of the reference users and user's u browsing history are conjoined and evaluated with the metrics of *precision* and *long-tail precision*, which is defined as a measure of the novelty of webpages, and then sorted in order to suggest to user u the highest ranked ones.

The second category includes the methodologies that tackle the problem of information overload. The exponential growth of information in online systems, accompanied by the limited processing ability of users, impacts decision-making and increases the need for mechanisms of relevant information retrieval and delivery. Traditional RSs handle this problem by filtering large volume of generated data according to users' similar preferences, disregarding users' social relations in a network. From this point of view, different models of information diffusion serve either as an alternative [34] or an extension [35,36] of the filtering mechanism in RS, adding social criteria (influence, trust, homophily) in recommendations. In [36] the correlation between information diffusion modeling and CF is highlighted with a joint ranking-oriented model of recommendations, where the authors assume that both mechanisms make predictions of users' preferences from a different perspective. Using a latent factor model and assuming that users are highly influenced by their friends, the latent factor of user u who adopts item i will be very close to the ones who have adopted item i in the past. The predicting score of ratings, $\hat{y}_{u,i}$, is computed by taking into consideration users' similarity and the linear combination of several temporal and structural features of information cascades as follows: $\hat{y}_{u,i} = \sum_j b_j \gamma_j^d + (p_u^T + \sum_{s \in C_i} a_s p_s^T)((1/Z) \sum_{w_j \in T_i} q_{wj} + a d_{p(i)})$, where b is a weight parameter vector, γ^d is a diffusion attribute, C_i is the cascade of item i, p_s is the latent factor for each user in C_i, q_i is a latent factor for item i, a_s is the weight parameter of each user in C_i and $d_{p(i)}$ is a latent factor for the user that starts the cascade of item i. Vahabi *et al.* [35], present a graph-based model of recommended items' expected diffusion in a network where conflicting suggestions between RS and social diffusion are predicted and withheld in order to optimize recommendation and avoid information overload. The diffusion process models the set of users who receive reposting information. Based on the latter, the authors present the resulting diffusion network with a *neighborhoodness graph* where an edge (i,j) is formed if all posts generated by user i will arrive at user j through the diffusion mechanism; thus, these posts should not be included in recommendations to user j (redundant information). This is formally defined as follows: given an SN $G(V,E)$, a neighborhood graph $G_n(V_n, E_n)$ and a set of posts S, the authors aim to find the optimal value $\mathbf{x}^* = \text{argmax}_x \sum_{i=1}^{N} \sum_{t \in S} E_{it} x_{it}$, subject to $\sum_{t \in S} x_{it} = K$, and $x_{it} + x_{jt} \leq 1, \forall (i,j) \in E_n, \forall t$, where E_{it} is defined as a measure of the engagement potential of item t when recommended to user i,

$$x_{it} = \begin{cases} 1, & \text{if post } t \text{ is a recommendation to user } i \\ 0, & \textit{otherwise} \end{cases}$$, $\mathbf{x}$ is a $(N \times |S|)$-dimensional vector. This problem, which is equivalent to the maximum-weighted independent set problem, is proved to be NP-hard [35] and the authors propose a heuristic greedy algorithm for its solution. The work in [34] considers a recommendation task as an

information diffusion problem which aims to maximize cascade size and minimize cascade time, thus optimizing recommendations. Ulah *et al.* [34], assume that the popularity of users impacts recommendations in their neighborhood of similar users. They counteract the information overload challenge with the control of the diffusion process by formulating a model of users' influence with multiple criteria (spatial, demographic, opinion similarity), ranking users based on their influence score, which is defined as a convex combination of the above features and the network structure, and finally selecting the most highly rated ones to initiate the temporal process of diffusion. The rank of a node u in a directed network is given by the equation $Rank_{directed}(u) = \sum_{x \in U} I(u,x) + \sum_{x \in U} \sum_{z \in X \cap z \notin U} I(u,x)I(x,z)$, where $I(u,x)$ is the influence of user u on user x, U is the neighbor set of u, x is a neighbor of u and X is the neighbor set of x. In the case of an undirected network, the rank of node u is given by $Rank_{undirected}(u) = \sum_{x \in U} e_{ux} + \sum_{x \in U} \sum_{z \in X \cap z \notin U} e_{xz}$, where e is an edge between two users.

Until now, we presented methods that overcome existing weaknesses of traditional RSs, but few can achieve high efficiency in terms of accuracy and user commitment to the RS. The contribution of information diffusion modeling to efficient CF in terms of improved precision and recall is underlined in [37], where two diffusion networks are constructed according to users' time and subject-related adoption patterns instead of the similarity networks of traditional RSs. Given the initial adopters, three probabilistic models of information propagation are proposed to predict how information will spread on the defined information flow networks. Another approach presented in [38] proposes a stochastic model for information diffusion which takes into consideration the strength of users' ties, W_{ij}, and based on the former, the authors quantify and study the trade-off of users' benefit from social interactions, which is quantified by the discrepancy in ratings between strongly tied users (e.g., friends) and it is calculated by the formula $D_i = (\ell/l) \sum_k ((\sum_j W_{i,j} |R_{j,k} - R_{i,k}|)/\sum_j W_{i,j})$, where ℓ is the number of items of interest (in this study, items are businesses and users' ratings are reviews), $R_{i,k}$ is the rating of item k by user i versus networks' ability of time-effective recommendations' propagation measured with the average waiting time for a user to rate an item, given by $\bar{H} = (1/n(n-1)) \sum_{i,j=1}^{n} H_{i,j}$, where $H_{i,j}$ is the time needed for user i to be informed of an item which was initially rated by user j (hitting time). They consider an efficient RS to be the one that optimizes both the utilities described above and provide an algorithm for its construction.

4.3.4   Context-based recommendations in pervasive systems

It was already mentioned that context information can be used as another form of socio-awareness, and it can be exploited for providing more efficient recommendations. In this section, we present such approaches for RSs that adopt elements from pervasive computing, context-aware/personalized services and SNs in support of intelligent and more accurate recommendations.

4.3.4.1   Context-aware recommendation systems

Contextual information has been proved useful in increasing the accuracy of predictions in various application domains including RSs [3]. RS can be considered as

Context 1	Item 1	Item 2	Item 3	...	Item m-1	Item m
User 1	$r_{1,1,1}$	$r_{1,2,1}$	?		$r_{1,m-1,1}$	$r_{1,m,1}$

Context 2	Item 1	Item 2	Item 3	...	Item m-1	Item m
User 1	$r_{1,1,2}$	?	$r_{1,3,2}$		$r_{1,m-1,2}$	$r_{1,m,2}$

Context 3	Item 1	Item 2	Item 3	...	Item m-1	Item m
User 1	$r_{1,1,3}$	?	$r_{1,3,3}$		$r_{1,m-1,3}$	$r_{1,m,3}$
User 2	?	$r_{2,2,3}$	?		$r_{2,m-1,3}$	?
User 3	$r_{3,1,3}$	?	$r_{3,3,3}$		?	$r_{3,m,3}$
...						
User n-1	?	$r_{n-1,2,3}$	?		?	$r_{n-1,m,3}$
User n	$r_{n,1,3}$	?	?		?	?

Figure 4.6   Example of a user–item–context utility matrix, modified in the case of context-related information. Question marks correspond to unrated items to be estimated

decision-support mechanisms that offer users personalized suggestions for products and other services. An important subclass of RS are the context-aware RSs (CARS) that take into account the context in which an item or a service will be consumed or experienced, [39]. The main difference of traditional RS and CARS is depicted in the factorization of the context information in the computation of recommendation (Figure 4.6).

Traditional RS: Users × Items → Ratings.

Context-Aware RS: Users × Items × Contexts → Ratings.

According to [39], there are three main approaches in designing context-aware recommendation algorithms: (a) *prefiltering*, where context-dependent criteria are applied to the list of items, selecting those appropriate to a given context and then considering the filtered ones for recommendation; (b) *post-filtering*, where the filters are applied after recommendations have been computed; and (c) *contextual modeling*, where contextual considerations are embedded with the recommendation algorithm itself.

Context data can be obtained in several ways, such as by explicitly gathering from relevant users/items, by implicitly deriving from data or environment, or by inference techniques using statistical methods and/or data-mining mechanisms. In pervasive computing environments, only the last two options have been considered. In order to identify context types that have impact in the recommendation mechanism, it is a common practice to preprocess recorded contextual data through statistical methods [40].

Application of CARS is especially attractive for the cases where users access the system with mobile devices. The proliferation of evermore powerful mobile devices (e.g., smart phones, tablets) along with the recent advances in mobile computing research and wireless network technologies allow the migration of RSs to mobile platforms [41].

Such environments allow access to RSs at anytime and anywhere (ubiquity), while at the same time, measurements from built-in sensor devices are able to describe user's dynamically changing situation. Sensors are acting as contextual sources providing information referring to user's geolocation, motion and environmental conditions. For example, CARS are redefining the way physical shopping is performed through the support to individual customers in order to make more informed decisions about where to eat, shop, relax, etc. Since such sensors will be increasing dramatically in number, the anticipated environments where these approaches will need to operate are those of bigdata systems.

There are various research efforts where recommendation algorithms utilize contextual data in support of personalized output. Research efforts presented in [42,43] are indicative early attempts of CARS, that are leveraging tensor factorization techniques in order to estimate latent features for items–users–context, in spaces that include more than the traditional two-dimensional items–users model. In a similar manner, in systems presented in [44,45] user/device "location" is utilized as one of the most obvious context for improving CARS estimations. In work presented in [4,46], the utilization of sensors available on smart phones allow the exploitation of additional contextual data (current user's location, time, weather conditions) in support of user behavior classification and user's next activity recommendation. In [47], a comprehensive survey and analysis of the state-of-the-art on time-aware RSs (TARS) is presented. These approaches are exploiting temporal context and time dimension in user modeling and recommendation strategies in order to improve overall recommendations performance. The review mainly focus on reported results and conclusions about how to incorporate and exploit time information within the recommendation processes and provides a comprehensive classification of evaluation protocols for TARS. The authors in [48] present a survey on CARSs based on computational intelligence (CI) techniques. The approaches presented are exploiting CI techniques that not only improve recommendations accuracy but also tackle issues such as sparsity, cold-start and scalability. The authors introduce a taxonomy of CI techniques utilized in CARS where the prevailing approaches are fuzzy sets, artificial neural networks, evolutionary computing, swarm intelligence and artificial immune systems. Finally, in the CARS survey presented in [49], the authors are comparing the various approaches based on the prefiltering, post-filtering and contextual modeling classification. The presented review aims to identify which method outperforms the others and under which circumstances, in an attempt to provide practical suggestions on how to select a good approach in order to improve the performance of a CARS.

As it is indicated in [50], among the main challenges that most of the modern CARS have to overcome is that they are not generic and flexible enough to be utilized across different application domains. Existing CARS are not able to be easily adapted to the specificities of each domain which results in a situation of several different frameworks following customized context modeling and management approaches that are hard to be integrated. In addition, a common weakness that is anticipated in

CARS [50] is that incorporated contexts are not enough for tailoring personalized services to users as only few context data types are utilized. In addition, existing frameworks and research efforts that are available in literature reviews lack of real life evaluation as most of them follow an offline evaluation strategy and/or user studies. Although these evaluation approaches are effective during the design and development of a system, the expected results are often contradicting when CARS is applied in real life application domains [51].

4.3.4.2   Context-aware recommendation systems in IoT ecosystem

In IoT ecosystems, modern embedded systems can exploit the advantages offered by context-aware and profile-driven recommendations. In fact, using data from IoT sensors as a context-aware computation and CARS are areas of increased research. It should be noted that the IoT architecture creates all the properties of a bigdata environment, namely, volume, velocity, variety and veracity, called the 4 Vs. Thus, data management and knowledge extraction requirements imposed by bigdata environments should also be considered when designing CARS that will be utilized in IoT ecosystems. Most RSs follow a request–response approach in which the recommendations are provided to the user upon his request. However, authors in [52] introduce a proactive RS that recommendations are pushed to the user when the current situation seems appropriate, without explicit user request. The authors present a framework of a CARS that recommends different types of items proactively under the IoT paradigm. A major part of the design is the context aware management system which utilized a neural network that realizes the reasoning of the context to determine whether to push a recommendation or not and what type of items to recommend. The authors in [53] present a novel CARS which is based on a multi-agent system (MAS) solution for generating personalized recommendations on mobile devices with the use of contextual data acquired from an IoT environment. A server-side MAS architecture for bigdata processing is used in order to anticipate the mass data processing required for the personalization model preparation. Context-aware recommendations for very sparse input data, based on different sensors and IoT information, are delivered with the usage of a factorization technique entitled CARS2. In [54], the authors propose a mechanism for providing venue recommendations combining information sources from IoT ecosystems as well as Web Services and applications. The proposed algorithm considers qualitative attributes and semantic information of the venues (e.g., price and atmosphere), the profile and habits of the user for whom the recommendation is generated and the opinions of the user's influencers. CARS that attempt to leverage on IoT frameworks have to face various challenges imposed by the existing weaknesses of the current IoT landscape. Given that IoT technology companies are developing solutions independently of each other and that are utilizing different platforms, frameworks and protocols results in many different IoT devices that cannot easily be integrated. Beside the data and platform interoperability challenge in IoT ecosystems, there is a lack of standards for authentication and authorization of IoT edge devices something that is particularly important when services are handling information about user's behavior and personal preferences.

4.3.4.3   Context-aware recommendation systems and social networks

User context and SN data have recently attracted much attention as it has been proven to be a valuable combination of information for improving accuracy of RSs. However, understanding user context and emerging user community structures through knowledge extraction approaches is often a complicated task as relevant collections of raw data are of unprecedented growth, noise, uncertainties and complexities. As it is already stated in Section 4.3.4.1, CF approaches aim to leverage similarities on the behavior of users that share common characteristics. One of the first approaches that enhanced CF RSs with context information is presented in [55]. The system was able to predict a user's preference in various context situations based on past experiences of other like-minded users that have performed various actions in similar context. The system was able to automatically evaluate the influence of context on an activity, while an adaptation of Pearson's correlation coefficient was used to measure the correlation between two different context variables with respect to their user ratings.

The authors in [56] propose a CARS that incorporates processed SN information. Context is handled through the application of random decision trees, in order to partition the original user–item-rating matrix and group ratings with similar contexts. Predictions of a user's missing preference for an item are realized though matrix factorization. SN information is incorporated through an additional social regularization term to that allows to constrain taste difference between a user and his/her friend and to take into higher consideration (with an increased weight) friends with similar tastes. Similarity between the user and his/her friends is measured based on friends past rating patterns, i.e., characteristics of the items that both users have commonly rated. The PCC [57] is utilized for similarity evaluation as it has been proven to be more accurate than other similarity evaluation approaches. Similarity of user u_j and his/her friend u_f is calculated based on

$$S(j,f) = \frac{\sum_{v \in V(j) \cap V(f)} (R_{j,v} - \bar{R}_j)(R_{f,v} - \bar{R}_f)}{\sqrt{\sum_{v \in V(j) \cap V(f)} (R_{j,v} - \bar{R}_j)^2} \sqrt{\sum_{v \in V(j) \cap V(f)} (R_{f,v} - \bar{R}_f)^2}}, \tag{4.2}$$

where $v \in V(j) \cap V(f)$ is the set of items that u_j and u_f have commonly rated, and R_j, R_f are the average ratings of u_j and u_f, respectively. Similarity calculation is enhanced with contextual information through a context-aware version of PCC:

$$S_c(j,f) = \frac{\sum_{v \in V(j) \cap V(f)} w_v(R_{j,v} - \bar{R}_j)(R_{f,v} - \bar{R}_f)}{\sqrt{\sum_{v \in V(j) \cap V(f)} w_v(R_{j,v} - \bar{R}_j)^2} \sqrt{\sum_{v \in V(j) \cap V(f)} w_v(R_{f,v} - \bar{R}_f)^2}}, \tag{4.3}$$

and the weight w_v of each item V_v is calculated based on

$$w_v = \frac{N(pcc_v)}{\sum_{v' \in V(j) \cap V(f)} N(pcc_{v'})}, \tag{4.4}$$

where the function $N(\cdot)$ normalizes the given value to the range [0,1], and pcc_v represents the PCC between u_j's rating R_j, v and u_f's rating R_f, v on the same item V_v.

In a similar manner, authors in [58] propose a context-aware CF RS, for m-commerce environments, that aims to identify and exploit influence-based hierarchies among users. The authors claim that in any SN, there are some individuals who have some inspirational power over the others leading them to influence their decisions and behaviors. Reasoning on SN data, the system identifies "impressive" users and uses their profile information in an attempt to achieve more accurate recommendations and to resolve the cold-start problem.

In [59] a Simultaneous Extraction of Context and Community (SECC) model applicable on user contexts and group structures in pervasive computing environments is presented. As authors claim, the model can be utilized in many cases, including community-detection and CARSs. The proposed approach allows the seamless and simultaneous discover of user context latent patterns and user communities. The SECC model employees reasoning on user context and user interactions in order to identify communities of users that have similar behaviors. This information is then exploited for providing recommendations based on user profile and/or historical context behaviors. The SECC model adapts the theory of nested Dirichlet process theory, which allows a nested structure to be built in order to summarize data at multiple levels.

The authors in [60] introduce the notion of pervasive communities, called Community Interaction Spaces, that aims to bring together pervasive computing systems and social media, in order to enhance interactions among users, communities, resources and smart environments. The proposed framework supports the formation of dynamic physical or virtual pervasive communities of users that demonstrate commonalities for a nontrivial period. The formulated communities are exploited, among others, in support of mobile services proactive adaptation through the provision of personalized, context-aware recommendations. The system is able to build context-aware prediction models of user–service interactions context-aware community intent models through data-mining techniques applied on recorded user-services interaction histories of individuals that may belong to specific communities. A community member can then benefit from the community knowledge—captured in the community behavior model—through recommendations for estimating future user–device interactions and providing the respective recommendations. Each recommendation is accompanied by a confidence level that acts as an indicator for further handling of prediction by users or services. The triggering factor for initiating a recommendation can be either a performed user–service interaction or a user situation update. The framework utilizes a hybrid approach for building the prediction model that allows the extraction and modeling of both sequential patterns of user–service interactions and situation/context-based patterns of interactions. For the first discrete time, variable order Markov chains (VOMC) are employed, while for the second, an adaptation of Naive Bayes (NB) statistical model is utilized.

In more details, the history of recorded user–service interactions is modeled as a^{t_k} at time of observation t_k $(k = 1, 2, \ldots, K)$, while the respective user situation is modeled as $s^{t_k} = \{c_1^{t_k}, c_2^{t_k}, \ldots, c_n^{t_k}\}$, where $c_i^{t_k}$ is the value of context information of type $i, (i = 1, 2, \ldots, n)$. Given a sequence of actions $d : \{a^{t_{k-1}}, a^{t_{k-2}}, \ldots, a^{t_{k-\ell}}\}$ where

ℓ is the sequence length, the most probable next action is identified based on VOMC by maximizing the respective probability:

$$a_{\text{seq}}^{t_k} = \underset{a_{\text{seq}}^{t_k} \in A}{\text{argmax}} \{P[a^{t_k}|d]\} = \underset{a_{\text{seq}}^{t_k} \in A}{\text{argmax}} \left\{ \frac{N(a^{t_k} \cdots a^{t_{k-\ell}})}{N(a^{k-1} \cdots a^{t_{k-\ell}})} \right\} \tag{4.5}$$

Given an update of user's situation, the most probable user interaction in a current situation snapshot described by $s^{t_k} = \{c_j^{t_k}\}, j = 1, \ldots, n$ is estimated based on the NB model through the maximization of the respective probability:

$$a_{\text{sit}}^{t_k} = \underset{a^{t_k} \in A}{\text{argmax}} \{P[a^{t_k}|s^{t_k}]\} = \underset{a^{t_k} \in A}{\text{argmax}} \left\{ P(a^{t_k}) \times \frac{\prod_{j=1}^{n} P(c_j^{t_k}|a^{t_k})}{P(s^{t_k})} \right\}. \tag{4.6}$$

Combining the two approaches, each outcome is weighted based on the number of occurrences contributed in probability calculation. The interaction predicted based on both inputs is estimated by

$$\alpha_{\text{comb}}^{t_k} = \underset{a^{t_k} \in A}{\text{argmax}} \{w_{\text{sit}} \cdot P[a^{t_k}|s^{t_k}] + w_{\text{seq}} \cdot P[a^{t_k}|d]\}, \tag{4.7}$$

where w_{sit} and w_{seq} reflect the amount of history records used for the situation and sequence based user service interaction prediction. As it is described in [60], evaluation of the proposed approach with real datasets delivered satisfactory results especially in cases where users with no previous interaction histories were utilizing the community's history log with the hybrid prediction mechanism in support of their personal predictions.

Combining social media information along with context for improving recommendations is a promising approach; however, it imposes various challenges. One important aspect that is often neglected is the issue of protecting the privacy of the users. Collecting and processing interactions not only from the online behavior of the users (e.g., social media) but also from real life activities (e.g., context types such as user's location, physical activities, mood) poses serious threats on users' privacy. Applying the appropriate privacy protection mechanisms often increases the complexity of the CARS approaches and adds a significant but necessary overhead to the overall functionality. Beyond user privacy risks, recommender systems are also vulnerable to various security threats. For example, although application of CARS has been proved effective in e-commerce services, at the same time it introduces vulnerabilities to malicious profile injection attacks, also known as "shilling attacks" [61]. The attacker (e.g., malicious users, competing vendors) attempt to insert fake profiles into the user–item matrices aiming to alter the predicted ratings on behalf of their advantages. Although, there are various approaches to detect and confront this kind of attacks, such security challenges should be considered during the design of CARS rather than trying to apply possible protection mechanisms on top of the service.

4.4 Qualitative comparison

In this section, we present an overall qualitative comparison of the presented approaches, based on the operational characteristics of each technique. Figures 4.7 and 4.8 provide a summary of the strengths and weaknesses exhibited by the presented methods. The symbol employed denotes that the corresponding family of approaches contains at least one specific approach exhibiting the corresponding strengths/weaknesses, while absence of the symbol can be interpreted as absence of the corresponding feature, or that it was impossible to conclude at the moment definitely on the existence/absence of the corresponding feature.

According to Figures 4.7 and 4.8 and taking into account the corresponding challenges posed by traditional recommender systems (Figure 4.8), it can be observed that all four presented families of approaches have several strengths, addressing many of the challenges imposed on traditional RS especially under bigdata environments. However, they exhibit several weaknesses as well, even though far less than their advantages. Most of them have to do mainly with the verification over operational, realistic conditions and privacy/security problems. Working toward the first direction will enable adopting these approaches in large-scale application scenarios as well, while working toward the second is a secondary step, which will ensure the integrity of the provided results and increase the trust over such schemes.

Strengths	HPRS	PGM	IDARS	CARS
Adaptive		◊		◊
Improved performance (recommendation accuracy)	◊	◊	◊	◊
Addresses efficiently the users' *cold start* problem	◊	◊		◊
Addresses efficiently the items' *cold start* problem		◊		
Handles efficiently information overload		◊	◊	
Addresses efficiently the long-tail problem	◊	◊	◊	
Applicable to popular emerging paradigms			◊	◊
Increases user engagement to platform (user fidelity)	◊		◊	
Addresses efficiently the *grey sheep* problem	◊			◊

Figure 4.7 Comparison of strengths of the presented approaches

Weaknesses	HPRS	PGM	IDARS	CARS
Cannot scale up to unprecedented growth of data, noise, uncertainties and complexities			◊	◊
Cannot address the cold start problem		◊		
Lack of real (operational) evaluation	◊			◊
Sensitivity to user data privacy		◊		◊
Vulnerability to security threats	◊			◊
Interoperability issues (data and platform)	◊		◊	◊
Application domain specific design		◊	◊	◊

Figure 4.8 Comparison of weaknesses of the presented approaches

4.5   Open problems and conclusion

In this chapter, we investigated and summarized some of the state-of-the-art approaches that exploit socio-related information for improving the performance of RSs. Various types of social knowledge, such as information diffusion features and context-awareness, were investigated, and it was demonstrated how they can be used to alleviate various problems of traditional and general purpose techniques. In addition, different approaches based on, e.g., hyperbolic network embedding and MRFs were presented as alternative solutions to addressing diverse problems of RSs, such as diversity of recommendations and cold start. Overall, all the presented approaches can be useful and especially handy in addressing various aspects of RSs in very large-scale environments, dynamic conditions and hard decision-making constraints, thus making them very promising for all such cases.

Several directions for future research can be identified. First, studying all the previous approaches and in general the recommendation problem under dynamic and time-constrained conditions of the online networked system under consideration, is a very challenging endeavor by itself with numerous potential benefits.

Furthermore, from the approaches presented above, it becomes evident that the success of any good RS is based on a comprehensive consideration set of the information sources available, their representation and approach for exploiting (using in decision-making) this information. The kind of information source used has a great impact on the recommendation quality. Therefore, with the advent of web 3.0, context-aware information (e.g., geo-social information) and information from a variety of sensors (e.g., sensors for measuring various health data) along with the above information would be incorporated, it seems that the future of RSs could lie in the exploitation of socio-awareness, derived from diverse sources, e.g., IoT systems.

Another aspect to be addressed is privacy. It is an important issue because online systems that exploit information from social networking sites are prone to misbehavior by malicious behaviors of some of these users. Ensuring the privacy of legitimate users and the integrity of the collected results is essential, and significant work needs to be done in the corresponding field.

References

[1]   J. Leskovec, A. Rajaraman, J. Ullman, "Mining of Massive Datasets", Cambridge: Cambridge University Press, 2nd Ed., Dec. 2014.

[2]   P. P. Gaikwad, J. P. Gabhane, S. S. Golait, "A Survey based on Smart Homes System using Internet-of-Things", *Proc. Int'l Conf. on Computation of Power, Energy Information and Communication (ICCPEIC)*, Sep. 2015.

[3]   G. Adomavicius, A. Tuzhilin, "Toward the Next Generation of Recommender Systems: A Survey of the State-of-the-Art and Possible Extensions", *IEEE Transactions on Knowledge & Data Engineering.*, Vol. 17, No. 6, pp. 734–749, 2005.

[4]   F. Ricci, L. Rokach, B. Shapira, P. B. Kantor, "Recommender Systems Handbook", *Springer Science+Business Media, LLC, 233 Spring Street*, New York, NY 10013, USA, 2011.

[5]   J. Stan, F. Muhlenbach, C. Largeron, "Recommender Systems Using Social Network Analysis: Challenges and Future Trends", *Encyclopedia of Social Network Analysis and Mining*, Springer, New York, NY, pp. 1522–1532, 2014.

[6]   A. K. Falahi, N. Mavridis, Y. Atif, "Social Networks and Recommender Systems: A World of Current and Future Synergies", *Computational Social Networks: Tools, Perspectives and Applications*, Springer, London, pp. 445–465, 2012.

[7]   F. O. Isinkaye, Y. O. Folajimi, B. A. Ojokoh, "Recommendation Systems: Principles, Methods and Evaluation", *Egyptian Informatics Journal*, Vol. 16, No. 3, pp. 261–273, 2015.

[8]   G. Adomavicius, J. Zhang, "Impact of Data Characteristics on Recommender Systems Performance", *ACM Transactions on Management Information Systems*, Vol. 3, No. 1, pp. 1–17, Article 3, 2012.

[9]   R. Burke, "Hybrid Recommender Systems: Survey and Experiments", *User Modeling and User-Adapted Interaction*, Vol. 12, pp. 331–370, 2002.

[10] W. Sherchan, S. Nepal, C. Paris, "A Survey of Trust in Social Networks", *ACM Computing Surveys*, Vol. 45, No. 4, pp. 1–33, 2013.

[11] B. Hajian, T. White, "Modelling Influence in a Social Network: Metrics and Evaluation", *2011 IEEE Third Int'l Conf. on Privacy, Security, Risk and Trust and 2011 IEEE Third International Conference on Social Computing*, pp. 497–500, 2011.

[12] P. Massa, B. Bhattacharjee, "Using Trust in Recommender Systems: An Experimental Analysis", *Trust Management: Second International Conference, iTrust 2004, Oxford, UK, Mar. 29–Apr. 1, 2004. Proceedings*, Springer, Berlin, Heidelberg, pp. 221–235, 2004.

[13] P. Massa, P. Avesani, "Trust-Aware Collaborative Filtering for Recommender Systems", *On the Move to Meaningful Internet Systems 2004: CoopIS, DOA, and ODBASE: OTM Confederated International Conferences, CoopIS, DOA, and ODBASE 2004, Ayia Napa, Cyprus, Oct. 25–29, 2004. Proceedings, Part I*, Springer, Berlin, Heidelberg, pp. 492–508, 2004.

[14] V. Karyotis, E. Stai, S. Papavassiliou, "Evolutionary Dynamics of Complex Communications Networks", *CRC Press – Taylor & Francis Group*, Boca Raton, FL, USA, Oct. 2013.

[15] R. Albert, A.-L. Barabasi, "Statistical Mechanics of Complex Networks", *Reviews of Modern Physics*, Vol. 74, No. 1, pp. 47–97, 2002.

[16] E. Otte, R. Rousseau, "Social Network Analysis: A Powerful Strategy, Also for the Information Sciences", *Journal of Information Science*, Vol. 28, No. 6, pp. 441–453, 2002.

[17] S. Fortunato, "Community Detection in Graphs", *Physics Reports*, Vol. 486, No. 3–5, pp. 75–174, 2010.

[18] L. Lu, T. Zhou, "Link Prediction in Complex Networks: A Survey", *Physica A: Statistical Mechanics and Its Applications*, Vol. 390, No. 6, pp. 1150–1170, 2011.

[19] E. Stai, V. Karyotis, S. Papavassiliou, "A Hyperbolic Space Analytics Framework for Big Network Data and Their Applications", *IEEE Communications Magazine*, Vol. 30, No. 1, pp. 11–17, 2016.

[20]   N. Papadis, E. Stai, V. Karyotis, "A Path-based Recommendations Approach for Online Systems via Hyperbolic Network Embedding", *IEEE ISCC*, Jul. 2017.

[21]   E. Ayday, J. Zou, A. Einolghozati, F. Fekri, "A Recommender System Based on Belief Propagation over Pairwise Markov Random Fields", *50th Annual Allerton Conference*, Oct. 2012.

[22]   T. Tran, D. Phung, S. Venkatesh, "Preference Networks: Probabilistic Models for Recommendation Systems", In Proc. of 6th Australasian Data Mining Conference (AusDM), Gold Coast, Australia, pp. 195–202, 2007.

[23]   S. Liu, T. Tran, G. Li, Y. Jiang, "Ordinal Random Fields for Recommender Systems", *Proceedings of the Sixth Asian Conference on Machine Learning*, Vol. 39, pp. 283–298, Nov 2015.

[24]   S. Liu, G. Li, T. Tran, Y. Jiang, "Preference Relation-based Markov Random Fields for Recommender Systems", Vol. 106, No. 4, pp. 523–546, 2017.

[25]   V. Karyotis, "A Markov Random Field Framework for Modeling Malware Propagation in Complex Communications Networks", *IEEE Transactions on Dependable & Secure Computing*, 2017, accepted for publication, DOI: 10.1109/TDSC.2017.2703622.

[26]   Y. Koren, J. Sill, "OrdRec: An Ordinal Model for Predicting Personalized Item Rating Distributions", *Proceedings of the ACM RecSys'11*, pp. 117–124, 2011.

[27]   S.-M. Cheng, V. Karyotis, P.-Y. Chen, K.-C. Chen, S. Papavassiliou, "Diffusion Models for Information Dissemination Dynamics in Wireless Complex Communication Networks", *Hindawi Journal of Complex Systems*, Vol. 2013, 13 pages, Article ID 972352, 2013.

[28]   E. Stai, V. Karyotis, A.-C. Mpitsaki, S. Papavassiliou, "Strategy Evolution of Information Diffusion under Time-Varying User Behavior in Generalized Networks", *Elsevier Computer Communications*, Vol. 100, pp. 91–103, 2017.

[29]   H. Zhang, S. Mishra, M.T. Thai, "Recent Advances in Information Diffusion and Influence Maximization of Complex Social Networks", *Opportunistic Mobile Social Networks*, CRC Press – Taylor & Francis Group, Boca Raton, FL, USA, pp. 37–69, 2015.

[30]   A. Guille, H. Hacid, C. Favre, D. A. Zighed, "Information Diffusion in Online Social Networks: A Survey", *SIGMOD*, Vol. 42, No. 2, pp. 17–28, 2013.

[31]   H. Yin, B. Cui, J. Li, J. Yao, C. Chen, "Challenging the Long Tail Recommendation", *Proceeding of the VLDB Endowment*, Vol. 5, No. 9, pp. 896–907, 2012.

[32]   C. Anderson, "The Long Tail: Why the Future of Business Is Selling Less of More", *Hyperion*, New York, NY, 2006.

[33]   M. Ishikawa, P. Geczy, N. Izumi, T. Yamaguchi, "Long Tail Recommender Utilizing Information Diffusion Theory", *2008 IEEE/WIC/ACM International Conference on Web Intelligence and Intelligent Agent Technology*, pp. 785–788, 2008.

[34]   F. Ulah, S. Lee, "Social Content Recommendation Based on Spatial-Temporal Aware Diffusion Modelling in Social Networks", *MDPI Symmetry*, Vol. 8, No. 9, 18 pp., 2016.

[35] H. Vahabi, I. Koutsopoulos, F. Gullo, M. Halkidi, "DifRec: A Social-Diffusion-aware Recommender System", *Proc. of 24th ACM International on Conference on Information and Knowledge Management (CIKM '15)*, pp. 1481–1490, 2015.

[36] Y. Pan, F. Cong, K. Chen, Y. Yu, "Diffusion-aware Personalized Social Update Recommendation", *Proc. of the 7th ACM conference on Recommender systems (RecSys '13)*, ACM, New York, NY, USA, pp. 69–76, 2013.

[37] X. Song, B. L. Tseng, C. Y. Lin, M. T. Sun, "Personalized Recommendation Driven By Information Flow", *Proc. of 29th Annual International ACM SIGIR Conference on Research and Development in Information Retrieval*, Aug. 2006.

[38] F. M. F. Wong, Z. Liu, M. Chiang, "On the Efficiency of Social Recommender Networks", *IEEE Conference on Computer Communications (INFOCOM)*, pp. 2317–2325, 2015.

[39] G. Adomavicius, B. Mobasher, F. Ricci, A. Tuzhilin. "Context-aware Recommender Systems", *AI Magazine*, Vol. 32, No. 3, pp. 67–80, 2011.

[40] B. Xu, J. Bu, C. Chen, D. Cai. "An Exploration of Improving Collaborative Recommender Systems via User-item Subgroups", *Proc. of 21st International Conference on World Wide Web*, 2012.

[41] L. O. Colombo-Mendoza, R. Valencia-Garcia, G. Alor-Hernandez, P. Bellavista, "Special Issue on Context-aware Mobile Recommender Systems", *Pervasive and Mobile Computing*, Vol. 38, pp. 444–445, 2017.

[42] D. Koller, M. Sahami. "Toward Optimal Feature Selection", *Proc. of 13th International Conference on Machine Learning (ICML)*, 1996.

[43] Y. Koren, R. Bell, C. Volinsky, "Matrix Factorization Techniques for Recommender Systems", *Computer*, Vol. 42, No. 8, pp. 30–37, 2009.

[44] H. Ma, D. Zhou, C. Liu, M. R. Lyu, I. King, "Recommender Systems with Social Regularization", *Proc. of 4th ACM International Conference on Web Search and Data Mining*, 2011.

[45] C. Palmisano, A. Tuzhilin, M. Gorgoglione. "Using Context to Improve Predictive Modelling of Customers in Personalization Applications", *IEEE Transactions on Knowledge and Data Engineering*, Vol. 20, No. 11, pp. 1535–1549, 2008.

[46] D. Gavalas, M. Kenteris, "A Web-based Pervasive Recommendation System for Mobile Tourist Guides", *Personal and Ubiquitous Computing*, Vol. 15, No. 7, pp. 759–770, 2011.

[47] P.G. Campos, F. Díez, I. Cantador, "Time-aware Recommender Systems: A Comprehensive Survey and Analysis of Existing Evaluation Protocols", *The Journal of Personalization Research*, Springer, Vol. 24, No. 1–2, pp. 67–119, 2014.

[48] A. Abbas, L. Zhang, S.U. Khan, "A Survey on Context-aware Recommender Systems based on Computational Intelligence Techniques", *Computing*, Vol. 97, No. 7, pp. 667–690, 2015.

[49] U. Panniello, M. Gorgoglione, "Incorporating Context into Recommender Systems: An Empirical Comparison of Context-based Approaches", *Electronic Commerce Research*, Vol. 12, No. 1, pp. 1–30, 2012.

[50]   K. Haruna, M. Akmar Ismail, S. Suhendroyono, *et al.*, "Context-Aware Recommender System: A Review of Recent Developmental Process and Future Research Direction", *MDPI Applied Sciences*, Vol. 7, No. 1211, 25 pp., 2017.

[51]   Y. Zheng, B. Mobasher, R. Burke, A. Carskit, "A Java-based Context-aware Recommendation Engine". *In Proceedings of the 2015 IEEE International Conference on Data Mining Workshop*, Atlantic City, NJ, USA, pp. 1668–1671, 14–17 Nov. 2015.

[52]   Y. Salman, A. Abu-Issa, I. Tumar, Y. Hassouneh, "A Proactive Multi-type Context-Aware Recommender System in the Environment of Internet of Things", *IEEE International Conference on Ubiquitous Computing and Communications (CIT/IUCC/DASC/PICOM)*, Liverpool, UK, Oct. 2015.

[53]   B. Twardowski, D. Ryzko, "IoT and Context-Aware Mobile Recommendations Using Multi-agent Systems", *IEEE/WIC/ACM International Conference on Web Intelligence and Intelligent Agent Technology (WI-IAT)*, pp. 6–9, Dec. 2015.

[54]   D. Margaris, C. Vassilakis, "Exploiting Internet of Things Information to Enhance Venues' Recommendation Accuracy", *Journal of Service Oriented Computing and Applications*, Vol. 11, No. 4, pp. 393–409, 2017.

[55]   A. Chen, "Context-Aware Collaborative Filtering System: Predicting the User's Preference in the Ubiquitous Computing Environment", *International Symposium on Location- and Context-Awareness, LoCA 2005: Location- and Context-Awareness*, pp. 244–253, 2005. Part of the Lecture Notes in Computer Science book series (LNCS, volume 3479).

[56]   X. Liu, K. Aberer, "SoCo: A Social Network Aided Context-aware Recommender System", *Proc. of 22nd ACM International Conference on World Wide Web (WWW '13)*, New York, NY, USA, pp. 781–802, 2013.

[57]   J. Breese, D. Heckerman, C. Kadie, "Empirical Analysis of Predictive Algorithms for Collaborative Filtering", *Proc. of UAI*, 1998.

[58]   G. Assadat, A. Boroujeni, S. A. H. Golpayegani, "Improving Context Aware Recommendation Performance by Using Social Networks", *Journal of Information Technology Research (JITR)*, Vol. 7, No. 3, pp. 1–14, 2014.

[59]   T. Nguyen, V. Nguyen, F. D. Salim, D. V. Le, D. Phung, "A Simultaneous Extraction of Context and Community from Pervasive Signals Using Nested Dirichlet Process", *Pervasive and Mobile Computing*, Vol. 38, pp. 396–417, 2017.

[60]   N. Kalatzis, N. Liampotis, I. Roussaki, *et al.*, "Cross-community context management in Cooperating Smart Spaces", *Personal and Ubiquitous Computing*, Vol. 18, No. 2, pp. 427–443, 2014.

[61]   I. Gunes, C. Kaleli, A. Bilge, H. Polat, "Shilling Attacks Against Recommender Systems: A Comprehensive Survey", *Artificial Intelligence Review*, Vol. 42, No. 4, pp. 767–799, 2014.

Chapter 5

Novel hybrid approaches for big data recommendations

Abdul Kader Saiod[1] and Darelle van Greunen[1]

Hybrid approaches (HAs) based on Fuzzy-Ontology are one of the core functions to efficiently handle and process massive dataset from diverse heterogeneous sources (DHS). HAs are becoming a noticeable trend in recent times due to its wide range of functionality to tackle all types of problem spaces. HAs are in the high demand for organisations to run their daily business operations as increasing numbers of numerous dataset occur every day. Therefore, big data communications are challenging in the traditional approaches to satisfy the needs of the consumer, as data are often not capturing into the database management systems (DBMS) in a seasonably enough fashion to enable their use subsequently. In addition, big data plays a vital role in containing a plenty of treasures for all the fields in the DBMS. However, one of the main challenges of HAs for the big data integration (DI) system is the inherent difficulty to coherently manage data from DHS, as different data sources have several standards and different major systems. It is practically challenging to integrate diverse data into a global schema to attain what looked forward to. The efficient management of HAs using an existing DBMS presents a challenge because of incompatibility and sometimes inconsistency of data structures. As a result, no common methodological approach is currently in existence to effectively solve every DI problem. The challenges of HAs raise the need to find a better way to efficiently integrate voluminous data from DHS. To handle and align massive dataset efficiently, the HAs algorithm with the logical combination of Fuzzy-Ontology along with big data analysis platform has shown the results in term of improved accuracy. The proposed novel HAs will combine the promising features of Fuzzy-Ontology to search, extract, filter, clean and integrate data to ensure that users can coherently create new consistent of datasets.

5.1 Introduction

Hybrid approaches (HAs) have become an exciting research and commercial interest in the big data management fields. The term HAs refers to applications that offer

[1]Faculty of Engineering, Nelson Mandela University (NMU), The Built Environment and Information Technology, Port Elizabeth, South Africa

complete full trust solution through various combination approaches. HAs are considered as innovative heuristic solution package and essential mechanism that can tackle heterogeneous task deployed with multiple solutions in big database management systems (DBMS). Today, the large-scale databases (LSDB) are experiencing the massive voluminous datasets from every possible domain like information communication terminology (ICT), electronic health records (EHRs), cloud computing, social media, chain management, with the continuous applications of local area network (LAN), wide-area network (WAN), wireless, sensors, mobile and cloud technologies transmission, etc. Big data is defined as so voluminous and complex unstructured, semi-structured and structured dataset that traditional data processing software applications are inadequate to deal with them. However, one of the main challenges in big data is the inherent difficulty to coherently manage incompatible and sometimes inconsistent data structures from diverse heterogeneous sources (DHS) [1]. Traditional approaches integrate well for comparatively small data domain but fail when they are being applied to unstructured, semi-structured and massive datasets. The efficient logical combination and existing approaches preserve the traditional approaches for the interoperability. The HAs with its logical functions including efficient sensitivity can easily handle big data integration (DI) process and with the efficient algorithmic logic address the data quality (DQ), data accuracy, inconsistency, etc. Most of the existing approaches such as peer-to-peer data warehouses, middleware, data grid, data mining, semantic and ontology actually establish semantic connections between heterogeneous data sources. Although these approaches offer advantages in some aspects, but they do not provide a coherent mechanism to solve every DI problem. In addition, none of them pays strong attention to data inconsistency which has been a long-standing challenge in database environments [2–4]. This implies that big data can show inconsistency because different organisations have several standards and different major systems, which have emerged as critical issues and practical challenges [5–7]. The challenges become even more important when implementing any big data domain including an exponential increase of data, particular infrastructure need, need for a skilled workforce, need interoperable data standards, privacy and security, and the need to include people, processes and policies to ensure their adoption. This implies the efficient approach to address this task is to formation the original algorithm with respect to big data domain, so as to integrate big data. Such HAs that league dexterous performance along with big data domain to preserve the generic data accuracy for the DI approach are proposed in the chapter. In particular, the chapter focuses on the novel HAs based on Fuzzy-Ontology for big data communication of smart interfaces and perfect data mapping in traditional data as well as global and wide area network, mobile and wireless network and cloud computing, etc.

5.2 Context

Often big data has heterogeneous sources with different characteristics and standards including the diverse velocity, frequency and volume. There are many ways to handle, process, acquired, store and analyse the big data. It is important to understand the big data execution process and storing model as additional dimension always comes into play the vital key role, such as data standard, data security, data governance and data policies. Selecting an approach or developing an appropriate approach for big DI solution is challenging because there are too many factorial issues have to be taken in the approach account. In the big DI processes, many unstructured free text data composed and collected with the uncertain incident may cause the inconsistency. For instance, the web domain is largely composed of pages with text paragraphs. Other examples of document collections with this structure are text notes, book collections, scholarly published articles, archives, and news. Using the information retrieval systems, in well-managed domain majority of these types of unstructured and structured large textual data are indexed contents, so the consumer can easily express their information that they are looking for. However, using non-text data to index these large textual data may lead the structure of LSDB to effective way accessing data. The four well-known latest approaches that exist to detect and reduce data inconsistency are the following [8]: (1) rough set theory, (2) logic analysis of inconsistent data approach, (3) corresponding relational variables of functional dependencies and (4) fuzzy multi-attribute theory. An approach for reducing data inconsistency has to be combined with an approach for DI to coherently solve the data inconsistency and the DI issues simultaneously. The domain ontology may effectively combine data from DHS for DI [8].

The development of the purpose that HAs based on Fuzzy-Ontology for big data communication as proposed above takes into account the data inconsistency challenge that specific big data initiatives will play in addressing the DQ issues in LSDB, the business interoperability requirements and its priorities. A mathematical modelling approach based on HAs based on Fuzzy-Ontology which was initially explored in for DI [9–13] is nominated. This provides a strong theoretical and practical framework to work with heterogeneous, complex, conflicting and automatic consensus approaches for big DI.

Fuzzy logic and fuzzy set theory concept can be represented in the classic ontology to imprecise the expression concept and data relationship [14–16]. Ontology is one of the effective feasible concept and commonly used approach to efficiently conceptualise the semantic online applications. The hybrid combination of Fuzzy-Ontology can easily address the data uncertainty and reduce the data inconsistency. Fuzzy logic is defined as a form of probabilistic approximate methodological logic to deal and define between the fixed and exact values. For instance, the web domain is largely composed of pages with text paragraphs. Other examples of document collections with this structure are text notes, book collections, scholarly published articles, archives, and news. It is one of the biggest advantages of fuzzy logic that it can handle the concept of partial truth to extended information to deal with vagueness where the concept range could be exactly false or exactly true.

The concept of ontology is defined as to provide a generic and explicit requirement [17] to represent information which becomes the most adapted domain today. One of the major advantages of HA is the incremental academic interest to demonstrate the knowledge base applications, such as data scalability, shareability, machine reliability including readability and data stability. The classical ontology also refers to a crisp ontology that effectively deals with vague and imprecise information which is initially undeniable on traditional ontology [18,19]. To deal with vague data needs to standardise data to knowledge base representation value to structurally quantify and represent.

The efficient combination of fuzzy logic and theory appropriate to deal with vagueness addresses the DQ in big data integration. The combination of two approaches, namely Fuzzy-Ontology introducing that functionality into crisp ontology was invented in the early 2000s [6]. This concept summarised that encasing the fuzzy sets theory, Fuzzy-Ontology can associate the architect data which has a vague and imprecise concept of truth degree in another word a belief of the world.

5.3   The big data architecture

Big data becomes relevant for more and more organisations and move to new fields of applications where massive volumes of data are automatically generating continuously from diverse data sources and applications. When dealing with big datasets, organisations face difficulties in being able to create, manipulate and manage the big data. Big data is particularly a problem in business analytics because traditional approaches and procedures are not designed to search and analyse massive datasets. Existing literature shows that several techniques, software, applications and major approaches currently exist to deal with the big data, which historically have faced DBMS. After a profound analysis of various cutting-edge commercial accomplishment existing on the software market and an intensive review of the literature, it appears there are still some limitations to practical approaches for big DI [8]. Big data architectures typically consist of three segments [21]: (1) storage systems, (2) handling and (3) analysis (see Figure 5.1). Big data architecture is premised on a skilled approach for developing reliable, scalable and completely automated data pipelines.

Integration is the exchange between different organisations and other important players that brings big data or functions from one data platform to another. Integration is important because when we look at the quantity and diversity of data involved in the big data domain systems, it would be virtually impossible to process or analyse without breaking through the data silos. Like traditional information technology systems, the big data utilises completely different technical and semantic standards to depict and manage data, making it extremely difficult to correctly and simply integrate data from various conflicting systems. Big data stores in a linear record of each data info. It includes data types, pattern, length, demographics, progress notes, vital signs, history, indexes, etc. By offering HAs, it helps automate and streamline their workflow. Given a large part of the picture exists within the big data, we would have expected integrating into and out DBMS would have been easier for other sources. However, for the majority of commercial organisations (COs), it requires a skilled team of experts to bring the idea to fruition. This team typically includes project manager, operational owner, systems administrator/network engineer, interface engine analyst, big data/application interface analyst, big data web service analyst, big data analyst,

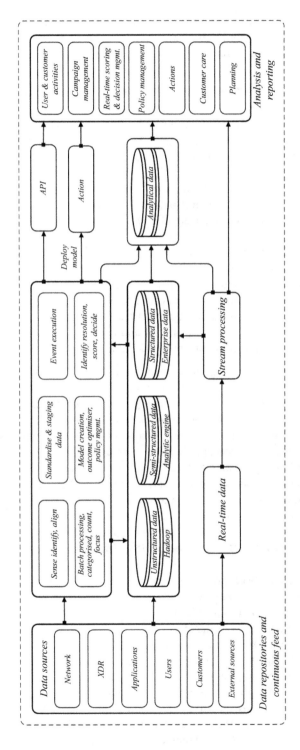

Figure 5.1   Big data advanced analytic platform architecture

support staff, etc. In addition to orchestrating all of the involved parties, it is also important to make sure the COs are meeting all of the electronic data standards interpretations. Despite its complexity, there is a linear list to follow for the project initiative.

1. *Planning and paperwork*: Prepare contracts, business associate agreements and kick off meetings.
2. *Gather Requirements*: Sample Health Level-7 or HL7 Messages, sample Extensible Markup Language (XML), sample JavaScript Object Notation (JSON), data dictionaries, Application Programming Interfaces (APIs) and associated documentation;
3. *Infrastructure/Virtual Private Network (VPN)*: Infrastructure should be spun up with the VPN creation and verification;
4. *Setup interface*: Make sure the front end of an organisation's endpoints are set up, including interface.
5. *Testing*: Use the sample notes/messages collected previously to review and acknowledge with inbound and outbound to resolve any potential issues.
6. *Go live*: Migrate to production and deploy. Data feeds are opened and the integration will allow other sources to populate the system.
7. *Ongoing support*: Unfortunately, this is not a set it or forget it situation. Make sure the support staff is alert, well trained and ready to tackle all of the issues that will inevitably arise from this implementation.

With all of the hands that have to go into creating and maintaining this integration, it can serve as a major bottleneck for domain systems. The big data complexity can fall into three main buckets: (1) custom data mappings, (2) security of data connectors and (3) projects requiring different degrees of project management. Many organisations feel forced to limit the data they integrate because of the lack of understanding of what is possible. These issues become worse and more complicated with LSDB, the total opposite of what organisation actually needs. In such cases, HAs with different approaches combination and techniques could be the efficient solution to tackle and manage big DI process for the complete integration.

5.4   Different approaches to handle big data

Many researchers and software providers across the world have undertaken initiatives aimed at handling and addressing the big data issues in LSDB to meet the interoperability need to the organisations. It is important to examine the approaches that have been taken by these organisations that can be learned. Publicly available documentation on the approaches taken by these organisations that have integrated big data to support the interoperability of information systems (ISs) was reviewed. The number of publications reviewed was constrained by the limited number of documents available in the public domain. Enormous amounts of big data are becoming increasingly accessible through the LSDB adoption of ISs. DI and interoperability have started to play a key role in COs to run their business process. Much of this can be attributed to business data transitioning from a volume-based incentive model to a value-based model. With how COs are set up today, providing value-based business logic is largely unsustainable. COs have had to alter priorities from business expectation to customer. Big data is a significant resource for data and business workflows. However, because many big data domains are unable to talk to each other or talk to applications outside of their own silos, data within the big data remain largely inoperable.

5.4.1 Approaches to detect and reduce data inconsistency

Data inconsistency detection and reduction are the central issues for the DQ. However, it becomes far more challenging when data are centralised and distributed, in which inconsistency detection often necessarily requires integrating data from DHS in LSDB. In order to provide quality service in COs, the big DI systems must be able to prevent dirty data from heterogeneous data source. Inconsistent data are one of the dirty data that occur because of the data structures from different organisations' data sources that are different and have different standards. Generally, factual dependencies are among the heterogeneous sources in the big data value and characterise the same objects, which are defined as inconsistency in the data value level. If the information is no longer reliable in the DBMS and consumes more cost and efforts, then the issues rise up and identify as data inconsistency. The rapid development of big data technology currently has transformed most data sources from paper and manual base to electronics base. Basically, in big data integration the heterogeneous data conflict between each other in the source level at the schema, representation and value level. DQ is recognised as one of the most important issues for big DI systems. Detecting and identifying the inconsistency is one of the central technical issues for the DQ concerns to successful big data implementation. This challenge raised the need for a DQ tool that is effective in interoperability – the tool has automatic and efficient inconsistency detection approaches. There are four latest approaches discussed in Section 5.2 to identify and address data inconsistency have been determined; they are the following:

1. *Rough set theory*: Rough set theory [22] is defined as a mathematical methodology that partial consciousness (i.e. to vagueness or imprecision) concerned with the analysis and modelling of classification and decision issues involving vague, imprecise, uncertain or incomplete information. The rough set concept can be defined by means of topological operations, interior and closure, called approximations. In this approach, vagueness is expressed by a boundary region of a set. The concept of the rough set was originally proposed by Pawlak in 1982 as a mathematical tool to deal with vagueness and uncertainty in the classification of objects in a set. Rough set is defined as a formal approximation of a crisp set in terms of a pair of sets which give the lower and the upper approximation of the original set. Its philosophy is based on the assumption that to every object of the universal set, we associate some information. Objects characterised by some information are indiscernible in view of the available information about them. In the standard version of the rough set theory [23], the lower- and upper-approximation sets are crisp sets, but in other variations, the approximating sets may be fuzzy sets. Rough sets have been proposed for a variety of applications, including artificial intelligence and cognitive sciences, especially machine learning, knowledge discovery, data mining, expert systems, approximate reasoning

and pattern recognition. Its philosophy is based on the assumption that to every object of the universal set, we associate some information. Objects characterised by some information are indiscernible in view of the available information about them. The indiscernibility relation generated in this way is the mathematical basis of rough set theory.

2. *Logic analysis of inconsistence data*: Quality data is appropriate for use and presupposed for analyses; big data is used and the value of the big data guaranteed. Data consistency refers to whether the logical relationship between correlated data is correct and complete. In the field of databases [24], it usually means that the same data that are located in different storage areas should be considered to be equivalent. Equivalency means that the data have equal value and the same meaning or are essentially the same. Data synchronisation is the process of making data equal.

3. *Functional dependencies corresponding relational variables*: Detecting inconsistencies in distributed data is recognised as one of the most important issues for DQ [25]. There are given a database D and a set Σ of dependencies as DQ rules, to identify tuples in D that violate some rules in Σ. When D is a centralised database, there have been effective Structured Query Language (SQL) based techniques for finding violations. It is, however, far more challenging when the data in D are distributed, in which inconsistency detection often necessarily requires exchanging data from one site to another. A central technical issue for DQ concerns inconsistency detection, to identify errors in the data. More specifically, given a database D and a set Σ of dependencies serving as DQ rules, the detection problem is to find all the violations of Σ in D, i.e. all the tuples in D that violate some rules in Σ. For a DQ tool to be effective in practice, it is a must to support automated and efficient inconsistency identification approaches. The issue identifier becomes easier if the database D is centralised, but it makes very difficult when heterogeneous data sources.

4. *Fuzzy multi-attribute theory*: Comparing to other approaches, the fuzzy multi-attribute is one of the simpler and widely implemented. Fuzzy multi-attribute is expanded to achieve the fuzzy exposition when data are uncompleted and vagueness. Today, the multi-attribute decision-making (MADM) is the most central segment in modern decision science, the theory and approach of which have been widely applied in the fields of medical science, engineering design, social life, investment decision-making and project evaluation. Regarding the MADM problem, both the attribute value and attribute weight of a scheme are exponential fuzzy numbers. In recent years, research on fuzzy numbers has attracted attention from scholars and experts and has been widely used in the field of MADM issues [26]. The MADM problem is of profound theoretical significance and has a wide practical application background in various industries. Therefore, research on MADM issues has always been a key subject for people. In real life, the uncertainty of decision information is regularly caused due to complex object environments and the fuzziness of human thinking. In solving such a class of issues, fuzzy numbers such as interval numbers, triangular fuzzy numbers and

trapezoidal fuzzy numbers are usually adopted to express such uncertainty of decision-making information.

Lakshmana *et al.* [27] proposed and discussed a new approach for the sequencing of an interval-valued intuitionistic fuzzy set, stated this approach by the way of calculation example analysis and made a comparison with other approaches as well. Park *et al.* [28] extended the TOPSIS (Technique for Order Preference by Similarity to Ideal Solution) approach in order to solve the issues of multi-attribute group decision-making in interval-valued intuitionistic fuzzy circumstances, in which all preferential information provided by decision-makers would be indicated by an interval-valued intuitionistic fuzzy decision matrix. Xu [29] proposed an ideal approach to solving the problem with interval-valued intuitionistic fuzzy MADM with the attribute weight not completely known or completely unknown. Wang *et al.* [30] and Wei [31] established an objective programming model based on the distance measure and difference maximum, respectively, and proposed an MADM approach where the attribute weight information is incomplete and the attribute value is an interval-valued intuitionistic fuzzy number.

Problem description: Regarding a fuzzy MADM problem, suppose $A = \{A_1, A_2, \ldots, A_m\}$ is the scheme set, $C = \{C_1, C_2, \ldots, C_n\}$ is the attribute set, and $R = (\tilde{a}_{ij})_{m \times n}$ the fuzzy decision-making matrix, where $\tilde{a}_{ij} = (c_{ij}, \sigma_{ij}, \tau_{ij})$ represents the exponential fuzzy number attribute value of the jth attribute C_j of the ith scheme, $1 \leq i \leq m, 1 \leq j \leq n$. In addition, the attribute weight is still given in the form of an exponential fuzzy number, i.e. the attribute weight vector $W = \tilde{\omega}_1, \tilde{\omega}_2, \ldots, \tilde{\omega}_n$, where $\tilde{\omega}_j = (C_{\omega j}, \sigma_{\omega j}, \tau_{\omega j})$ represents the weight of the jth attribute C_j. Try to sort and prioritise schemes according to the fuzzy decision-making matrix and attribute weight information [32].

Decision-making phases: Steps of such a decision-making approaches are listed as follows:

Phase 1: Construct a fuzzy decision-making matrix R according to the attribute value of each scheme.

Phase 2: Standardised processing of the decision-making matrix. Since the attribute values of schemes in the decision-making matrix R have different units of measurement and are subjected to different measurement criteria, in order to achieve unified processing the following equations can be employed for the standardised processing, so as to obtain the standardised decision-making matrix $R' = (\tilde{R}_{ij})_{m \times n'}$ where $\tilde{R}_{ij} = (\tilde{c}_{ij}, \tilde{\sigma}_{ij}, \tilde{\tau}_{ij})$. In the MADM problem, the benefit-oriented attribute and cost-oriented attribute are two major attribute types.

For the benefit-oriented attribute, there is

$$\tilde{C}_{ij} = \frac{C_{ij}}{\Sigma_{i=1}^{m} C_{ij}}, \tilde{\sigma}_{ij} = \frac{\max C_{ij}}{\Sigma_{i=1}^{m} C_{ij}} \sigma_{ij}, \tilde{\tau}_{ij} = \frac{\max C_{ij}}{\Sigma_{i=1}^{m} C_{ij}} \tau_{ij} \qquad (5.1)$$

For the cost-oriented attribute, there is

$$\tilde{C}_{ij} = \frac{\frac{1}{C_{ij}}}{\frac{1}{\Sigma_{i=1}^{m} C_{ij}}}, \tilde{\sigma}_{ij} = \frac{\min \frac{1}{C_{ij}}}{\Sigma_{i=1}^{m} C_{ij}} \sigma_{ij}, \tilde{\tau}_{ij} = \frac{\min \frac{1}{C_{ij}}}{\Sigma_{i=1}^{m} C_{ij}} \tau_{ij} \qquad (5.2)$$

Phase 3: Determination of positive ideal scheme A^+ and negative ideal scheme A^- of the fuzzy MADM problem.

Positive ideal scheme:

$$A^+ = \left[A_1^+, A_2^+, \ldots, A_n^+\right], \ A_j^+ = (C_j^+, \sigma_j^+, \tau_j^+) = ({}_i^{\min}\tilde{c}_{ij}, {}_i^{\min}\tilde{\sigma}_{ij}, {}_i^{\min}\tilde{\tau}_{ij}). \tag{5.3}$$

Negative ideal scheme:

$$A^- = \left[A_1^-, A_2^-, \ldots, A_n^-\right], \ A_j^- = [c_1^-, \sigma_2^-, \tau_n^-] = ({}_i^{\min}\tilde{c}_{ij}, {}_i^{\min}\tilde{\sigma}_{ij}, {}_i^{\min}\tilde{\tau}_{ij}) \tag{5.4}$$

where $j = 1, 2, \ldots, n$.

Phase 4: Determination of the weights of the attributes. The weight information of the attribute is given in the form of an exponential fuzzy number, i.e. the attribute weight vector.

$$W = (\tilde{w}_1, \tilde{w}_2, \ldots, \tilde{w}_n) = \{(c_{w1}, \sigma_{w1}, \tau_{w1}), (c_{w2}, \sigma_{w2}, \tau_{w2}), \ldots, (c_{wn}, \sigma_{wn}, \tau_{wn})\} \tag{5.5}$$

Calculate the score value of each attribute using, suppose exponential fuzzy number. $\tilde{a} = (c, \sigma, \tau)$; the score function is

$$p(\tilde{w}_j) = \frac{\phi E(\tilde{w}_j)}{(1 - \phi)Var(\tilde{w}_j)} \tag{5.6}$$

where $\tilde{w}_j$ represents the weight of the jth attribute C_j and represents the decision-maker's attitude preference on the expected value of the decision-making information and variance. Therefore, the accurate weight of each attribute can be obtained as

$$W_j = \frac{P(\tilde{w}_j)}{\sum_{j=1}^{n} P(\tilde{w}_j)} \tag{5.7}$$

Phase 5: Calculate the weighted distance between each scheme and the positive/negative ideal scheme. The weighted distance between scheme A_i and the positive ideal scheme:

$$D_i^+(A_i, A^+) = \sum_{j=1}^{n} w_j D(A_{ij}, A_i^+) \tag{5.8}$$

The weighted distance between scheme A_i and the negative ideal scheme:

$$D_i^-(A_i, A^-) = \sum_{j=1}^{n} w_j D(A_{ij}, A_i^-) \tag{5.9}$$

Phase 6: Calculate the relative closeness ε_i of each scheme and sort schemes according to the value of relative closeness; a larger ε_i value represents a more optimal scheme.

$$\varepsilon_i = \frac{D_i^-\left(A_i, A^-\right)}{D_i^+\left(A_i, A^+\right) + D_i^-\left(A_i, A^-\right)} \tag{5.10}$$

According to the definitions of expectation and variance in probability theory, and by comprehensively considering the attitude preference of the decision-maker, this approach can realise the accurate treatment of attribute weight. Subsequently, based on the distance measure between exponential fuzzy numbers, the distance between each scheme and the positive/negative ideal schemes was calculated, respectively, so as to obtain the relative closeness of each scheme. Finally, the feasibility and effectiveness of the approaches were verified through case analysis. The decision-making approach is superior for clear logic, a simple decision-making process and ease of being understood. In addition, such an approach has excellent application value and practical decision-making value, providing a scientific and practical decision-making reference for solving fuzzy MADM issues.

5.5   Complexity and issues of big DI

Big DIs are the combination of technical and business processes used to combine data from disparate sources into meaningful and valuable information. A complete big data solution approach delivers trusted data from DHS and term referring to the requirement to combine the data from multiple separate business systems into a single unified view, often called a single view of the truth. There are three primary components of DQ as follows: (1) data profiling, (2) data correction and (3) data monitoring (see Figure 5.2). In addition, it is the process of retrieving data from multiple source systems and combining it in such a way that it can yield consistent, comprehensive, current and correct information for the business work process, report and analysis. The objective of big DI becomes even more important in the case of merging systems of different similar organisations [5,33]. One of the key knowledge from literature is that big data initiatives, especially at the integration level, should take into account business logic system needs and challenges. It should also take into account the data inconsistency challenge that specific big data initiatives will play in addressing the DQ issues in LSDB, the COs interoperability requirements and its priorities.

5.5.1   Big data analysis and integration architecture

The amount of big data being collected and stored in the LSDB is a highly unprecedented rate. The management and processing of massive datasets are time-consuming, costly and a hindrance to analyse. So, the process to store, manage, analyse and extract meaningful value from the vast volume of data is a big challenge. HAs based on Fuzzy-Ontology is a decision support system (DSS) technology that allows extracting, grouping and analysing historical data from heterogeneous sources in order to discover information relevant to decision-making. The following are the typical big data analysis:

1.   *Policy analysis*: Gaining insights into patient populations and service patterns to identify new policy initiatives
2.   *Target population identification and stratification*: Using cross-agency service and outcome patterns to identify new targeting approaches, refine intervention strategies and develop differential treatment protocols
3.   *Utilisation analysis*: Analysing cross-agency service utilisation patterns to optimally allocate scarce programmatic and fiscal resources.

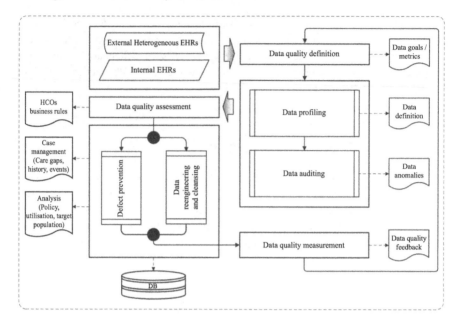

Figure 5.2   The DQ process model

The HAs deployment requires a number of design and implementation issues to be addressed, such as where integrated data would be stored, how the data would be moved from the administrative data sources to the destination database, what approaches would be used to match and link data about clients and service providers across data systems and what technologies would be used to deliver data to the decision makers. Successful DI approaches should address data architecture, data matching and mapping, data retrieval/delivery, data security, technologies and tools and data governance process. The hybrid architectures combine the architectural approaches to the third-party data transaction for incident governance purposes whereas statistics data is used to meet the real-time requirements.

5.5.1.1   Combine two figures at work

HAs integration architecture for policy and population analytics: The charter for the DQ management identifies stakeholders and processes for monitoring, measuring and controlling the accuracy, timeliness, consistency and reliability of data. Effective governance of DQ would set expectations, priorities and metrics for data collection and management practices for specific data categories. Cross-programme governance of DQ establishes multidisciplinary efforts for data stewardship, data reconciliations, etc.

Heterogeneity is the norm for both data sources and targets since these are various standards of applications, database brands, file types, and so on. All these have different data models, so the data must be transformed in the middle of the process, and the transforms, themselves, vary widely. Then there are the interfaces that connect these pieces, which are equally diverse. And the data does not flow uninterrupted or in a straight line, so need data staging areas. Simply put, that's a ton of complex and diverse stuff that have to organise into a DI solution. Goals of DI architecture imposes order on the chaos of complexity to achieve certain goals.

5.5.1.2 Architectural patterns as development standards

Most components of DI approaches fall into one of three broad categories: (1) servers, (2) interfaces and (3) data transformations. DI architecture is simply the pattern made when servers relate through interfaces. The point of an architectural pattern is to provide a holistic view of both infrastructure and the implementations built atop it so that people can wrap their heads around these and have a common vision for collaboration. Also, when inheriting someone else's work, get up to speed faster when they have followed development standards and established patterns. Well-run organisations have development standards, and architectural patterns should be among those.

- *Simplicity for reuse and consistency*: As development standards and architectural patterns are applied to multiple DI projects, the result is simplicity, which fosters the reuse of DI development artefacts (like jobs, routines, data transforms, interfaces), which in turn increases consistency in the handling of data.
- *Harmony between common infrastructure and individual solutions*: For a solution (like a data flow or a project) to be organised in a preferred architecture, the infrastructure (especially the DI production server and the interfaces it supports) must enable that architecture.

5.6 Big DI using HAs based on Fuzzy-Ontology

As an example, information in big data is being promoted for use in clinical decision support, patient registers, measurement and improvement of integration and quality of care, and translational research. To do this big data-derived data product, creators need to logically integrate patient data with information and knowledge from diverse sources and contexts. The proposed HAs based on Fuzzy-Ontology alignment framework with two core features:

1. *the use of background knowledge and the ability to handle vagueness in the matching process and*
2. *the resulting concept alignments to improve the DQ in big data.*

The procedure is based on the use of a generic reference linguistic, which is used for fuzzifying the ontologies to be matched. Generally, the choice of this linguistic is problem-dependent. In the first step of our approach, each domain concept is represented as a fuzzy set of reference concepts. In the next step, the fuzzified domain concepts are matched to one another, resulting in fuzzy descriptions of the matches of the original concepts. Based on these concept matches, we consider an algorithm that produces a merged Fuzzy-Ontology that captures what is common to the source ontologies. The undertaken Fuzzy-Ontology approach has been compared to a crisp ontology purpose and scope as well as Fuzzy-Ontology.

5.7   Developing approaches for the crisp ontology

It is widely accepted that there is no common single existing methodological approach that can solve every DI problem. Aiming to provide good guidelines for crisp ontology constructions, various ontology development approaches have been presented. An ontology development approach provides a formalisation for scheduling activities or tasks that should be followed and performed during the design process. Workflows proposed by different approaches might fare better or worse regarding efficiency, ease of use, comprehensiveness and rationality. A well-organised schedule of activities proposed by ontology development approaches can provide methodological supports for ontology professionals. The most well-known ontology approaches proposed in current literature are METHONTOLOGY [34], NeOn [35], DILIGENT [36], On-To-Knowledge [37], HCOME [38] and DOGMA [10]. In addition, Noy and McGuiness [39] presented a very descriptive yet simple guide to creating crisp ontologies. A set of survey papers, such as Jarrar and Meersman [10], are also available providing good references to existing ontology development approaches and their features. To conclude, a considerable amount of approaches can come in handy for developing crisp ontologies. However, these approaches dedicated to crisp ontologies cannot be directly applied to construct Fuzzy-Ontologies due to major differences between Fuzzy-Ontologies and crisp ones. In order to develop Fuzzy-Ontologies, additional procedures, such as including fuzzy logic to approximate vagueness and conceptualising the fuzzified vagueness, have considered in the development process.

5.8   Developing HAs for Fuzzy-Ontology

HAs based on Fuzzy-Ontologies mainly focuses on dealing with conceptual formalisms. In other words, how to represent Fuzzy-Ontologies in a formalised language is the most active work. Using the Fuzzy-Ontologies in a standard and effective way is the main contribution to address the DQ issues in big data. As an example, the IKARUS-Onto (Imprecise Knowledge Acquisition Representation and Use) methodology [40] is an approach for Fuzzy-Ontology development. It focuses on the provision of a methodological guideline for the conversion from crisp ontologies into fuzzy ones. It consists of five formal stepsthat are (1) including acquiring crisp ontology, (2) establishing the need for fuzziness, (3) defining Fuzzy-Ontology elements, (4) formalising fuzzy elements and (5) validating fuzzy ontology. The proposed structure of Hybrid Integration Development Approaches (HIDAs) based on Fuzzy-Ontology for big data is shown in Figure 5.3.

The IKARUS-Onto approach represents a comprehensive guidance for fuzzifying the crisp ontologies. Thus, it is suitable to be used to develop Fuzzy-Ontologies in domains with the existence of crisp ontologies. Similarly, the fuzzy ontomethodology proposed by Ghorbel *et al.* [41] also emphasises on formalising the activities for developing fuzzy extensions based on available crisp ontologies. The fuzzy ontomethodology consists of three steps: (1) including the conceptualisation, (2) providing the ontologisation and (3) providing the operationalisation. Processes grouped in each step are too ambiguous to be understood and used in practice. In addition, the

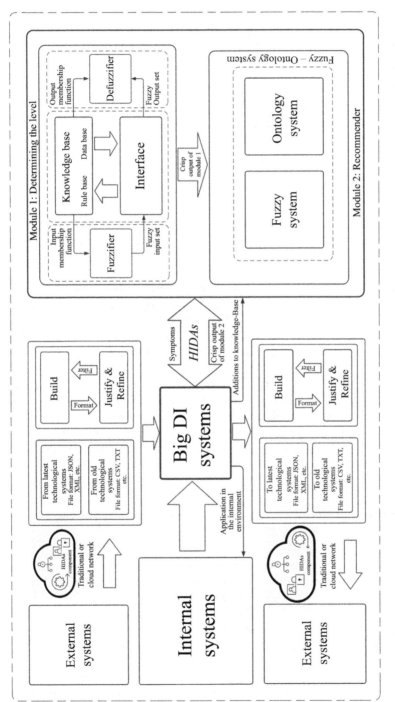

Figure 5.3 The complete Hybrid Integration Development Approaches (HIDAs) structure based on Fuzzy-Ontology for big data integration systems

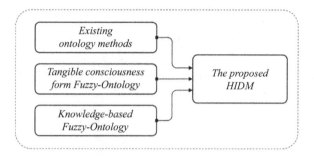

Figure 5.4   Inputs inspiring to conceive the HIDAs

fuzzy ontomethodology is devoted to providing guidelines for building ontologies for semantic web search. Reusing fuzzy elements (e.g. fuzzy concepts, fuzzy sets, fuzzy relationships or fuzzy data types) that have been defined in existing Fuzzy-Ontology can enhance the interoperability and shareability in the ontology community as well as guaranteeing less workload. The propose mythology considers to reusing the existing Fuzzy-Ontology elements, in the development process to efficiently integrate the big data. While attempting to model knowledge in domains where no existing crisp ontologies are available, the development of big data Fuzzy-Ontology should be guided in a formal way. The existing Fuzzy-Ontology approaches rely on the existence of crisp ontologies. Ontologies should be built following a methodological guideline in order to better model imprecise and vague information. To this end, this chapter presents HAs based on Fuzzy-Ontology development approaches which could provide well-defined professional principles to improve the development and building of Fuzzy-Ontology from scratch. This proposed approach could enable good treatments and utilisations of inconsistence big data resolution in terms of generality, completeness, accuracy, reusability, efficiency and shareability.

5.9   Extracting the big data key business functions for the proposed HAs based on Fuzzy-Ontology

This section presents the evaluation footstep of the generic HAs based on Fuzzy-Ontology. This footstep introduces a novel modification into the Fuzzy-Ontology development process. Remaining the original concept, the proposed HAs approach will integrate bid data and address data inconsistency and other related issues simultaneously, which means that the proposed approach will not reconstruct the entire Fuzzy-Ontology methodological concept. Figure 5.4 Inputs inspiring to conceive the Hybrid Integration Development Approaches (HIDAs).

Eventually, the HIDAs development will consider some extra fuzzy-associated intention on the existing Fuzzy-Ontology methodological approaches. As illustrated in Figure 5.4, the proposed HIDAs for big DI to address DQ issues are settled on the three fundamental interpretation keys. All these knowledge resources are inspiring to create the new HIDAs for big data to address the DQ.

1. *Introducing the subsistence proposed HIDAs for constructing the crisp ontology*: In nature, the development of Fuzzy-Ontologies would not completely reform the crisp ontology development process. Instead, the general flow to construct Fuzzy-Ontologies should be compliant with conventional crisp ontology development approaches. Nevertheless, new changes will be introduced into conventional approaches with additional fuzzy considerations. Thus, conventional crisp ontology development approaches are selected as the starting point to create the new HIDAs. It is worth noting that each crisp ontology development approaches fare better or worse in terms of some specific evaluation considerations, such as consideration for reusing existing ontologies. Hence, several approaches, including NeOn, are comprehensively studied so that strengths of each method can be correctly collected and applied in the new HIDAs. In addition, the IKARUS-Onto approaches and the fuzzy ontomethodology are also taken as valuable references to the proposed HIDAs.
2. *Introducing tangible consciousness to developing the HIDAs*: Though different ontology experts have different preferences to design Fuzzy-Ontologies, an initial group of informal steps could be abstracted from their practical experiences. These informal steps could provide a preliminary foundation which could afterward be formalised as formal methodological activities or processes.
3. *Introducing knowledge base from Fuzzy-Ontology objective tools*: Various Fuzzy-Ontology software tools, here particularly referring to Fuzzy-Ontology editors, have been created and been off-the-shelf. The Fuzzy-Ontology Generation Framework (FOGA) [42] provides support for automatically generating Fuzzy-Ontologies. The fuzzy OWL2 plug-in [19] enables ontology professionals to define fuzzy-related knowledge by means of OWL2 annotations in a very visualised and easy way. By practising with Fuzzy-Ontology design tools, especially referred to fuzzy OWL2, lessons can be learned, such as the way a conceptual model is implemented by editors. The practice with Fuzzy-Ontology tools can imply an informal workflow, which is the default process specified in those tools, to develop Fuzzy-Ontologies.

5.10 Identify the specification for the purpose HIDAs for big data

The aim of the proposed HIDAs is to provide a formal abstraction of activities that need to be done throughout the development process. The proposed approaches are dedicated to presenting the first methodological approach to build Fuzzy-Ontologies from scratch, rather than converting existing crisp ontologies into fuzzy ones. The whole workflow of the proposed HIDAs can be viewed in Figure 5.4. In general, all the activities or tasks are grouped into 11 phases to form the entire lifecycle of building a Fuzzy-Ontology. Each phase and its associated purposes and activities are elaborated in the following subsections.

5.11 Real-world project: hypertension-specific diagnosis based on HIDAs

This section describes the applicability and interoperability of the proposed HIDAs. This is a simple hypothetical use case real-world hypertension diagnosis which aimed to explore the specific Fuzzy-Ontology hypertension architecture. Hypertension diagnosis can get information about the different stage of blood pressure ranges such as optimal stage, normal stage, high normal stage, Stage 1 (mid), Stage 2 (moderate) and Stage 3 (severe). Input parameters for Fuzzy-Ontology decision-making knowledge systems are age, body mass index (BMI), systolic and diastolic and one output parameter is hypertension risk. The intention of generating the hypertension diagnosis is to help providers to characterise and identify the exact hypertension level to make better decisions for their patients. The diagnosis result will clearly identify the specific hypertension risk level which is going to be overlooked. It will represent a formal linguistic input and output (risk level and stage) parameters which will provide clinicians to acquire a general understanding hypertension diagnosis.

Hypertension is defined as blood pressure enhanced to unhealthy and dangerous levels. The blood pressure measurement takes into account how quickly blood is passing through veins and the amount of resistance the blood meets while it's pumping. Although hypertension has been associated with factors such as alcohol consumption, smoking, high BMI and inadequate exercise, research has suggested that the degree of association between socioeconomic status and hypertension varies between males and females. Data on hypertension prevalence for the country are available from the 1998 South African DHS, which show a prevalence of 21% for both males and females using the 140/90 mmHg threshold.

N.B.: *The architecting use case project has considered only the hypertension ramifications instead of complete EHRs.*

5.11.1 Data collection

This sub-step is to prepare for the formularisation of proposed HIDAs. A hypertension diagnosis risk-level-specific Fuzzy-Ontology will formularise in the following steps. The subset of data collection is divided into two groups: male and female. All patients age between 18 and 60 years old. The parameter subsets were considered as gender, age, BMI, heart rate and blood pressure. Some other information was also undertaken into account like patient's lifestyle, working background and medical history. This additional information was included in the parameter subjects that knowledge gained from the distributed questionnaire.

To collect the BMI information, traditional scale and tools were used to measure the weights and heights. BMI is defined as the patient's individual body weight divided by the patient's height squared. This is a universal method and widely used globally. The unit of measure is considered as international standard $\frac{kg}{m^2}$. Three different BMI category ranges were considered: (1) first category range between 19 to 25 is considered a healthy weight, (2) second category range between 16 to 18 are considered as underweight and (3) third category range between 25 to 30 are considered as overweight (Tables 5.1–5.4).

Table 5.1   According to various BMI category range around adult South African males (18–60 years) distribution of blood pressure (systolic and diastolic)

Blood Pressure	Male				Female			
	SBP (mmHg)		DBP (mmHg)		SBP (mmHg)		DBP (mmHg)	
	Percentage	Number	Percentage	Number	Percentage	Number	Percentage	Number
Normal	17.25	250	23.12	272	60.25	750	45.05	584
Prehypertension	81.2	950	49.45	584	38.25	256	45.24	560
Hypertension	2.56	300	30.01	352	2.49	320	8.97	120

SBP and gender chi-square = 49.44*** ($p < 0.001$); DBP and gender chi-square = 23.23*** ($p < 0.001$).

Table 5.2   According to various BMI category range around adult South African female (18–60 years) distribution of blood pressure (systolic and diastolic)

BMI	SBP				DBP			
	Normal	Prehypertension	Stage 1	Stage 2	Normal	Prehypertension	Stage 1	Stage 2
Underweight	73.1	26.9	0	0	65.4	26.9	7.7	0
Normal	54.4	43.4	0	2.2	45.6	41.2	13.2	0
Overweight	23.6	73.6	0.9	1.8	17.3	52.7	27.3	2.7

SBP chi-square = 43.24*** ($p < 0.001$) and DBP chi-square = 45.44*** ($p < 0.001$).

Table 5.3   Adult South African male's (18–60 years) distribution blood pressure (systolic and diastolic) where BMI is the risk factor

BMI Classification	Odds ratio SBP			Odds ratio DBP		
	Prehypertension	Stage 1	Stage 2	Prehypertension	Stage 1	Stage 2
Underweight	0.45	0.59	1.15	0.53	0.42	0.53
Normal	NC	NC	NC	NC	NC	NC
Overweight	1.77		1.48	2.82	2.65	8.98

NC = reference category/normal category.

Table 5.4   *Adult South African female's (18–60 years) distribution blood pressure (systolic and diastolic) where BMI is the risk factor*

BMI Classification	Odds ratio SBP			Odds ratio DBP		
	Prehypertension	Stage 1	Stage 2	Prehypertension	Stage 1	Stage 2
Underweight	0.56	0.61		0.54	0.63	1.1
Normal	NC	NC	NC	NC	NC	NC
Overweight	0.56	2.28	0.98	2.75	3.74	8.8

NC = reference category/normal category.

5.11.2   Step 1: HIDAs contrivance and excellence

To ontology description as the target domain, the dictation is to formularise into different properties of a hypertension risk level to demonstrate a semantically efficient diagnosis for clinicians and providers. This approach will also enable to use a hypertension alert execution treatment service process and carry out into machine learning language database to reuse in knowledge base approaches. For the efficient indication, a list of indicators has been delineated. Answer of these indications has used to delaminate the proposed HIDAs contrivance and excellence in our close-bodied process.

1. *Question*: What type of outcome is expected from the HIDAs?
    Answer: Hypertension risk level that is going to be inspected are different SBP (systolic blood pressure), DBP (diastolic blood pressure), age and BMI (BMI) as major factors which affect the blood pressure.
2. *Question*: Are the HIDAs used as an appropriate solution technology upon other approaches exempli gratia principle solution?
    Answer: This specific HIDAs conceptualisation is one of the most promising solution architectures for machine learning technology. The HIDAs is dictated to achieve efficient hypertension diagnosis by using formularised linguistic variable expression for specific hypertension and measure its interoperability.
3. *Question*: What architect ramifications will be the desired HIDAs?
    Answer: Due to the motivated contrivances, the aim of the desire HIDAs architecture will limit to specific hypertension diagnosis only instead of complete EHR systems. The hypertension diagnosis ramification model contrivance logic will store into machine learning technology database to reuse or inherit to similar related hypertension diagnosis applications, so that schematic hypertension diagnosis will be characterised as a domain-specific HIDA.
4. *Question*: Who will be the stakeholders and what will be their roles during the HIDAs development process?
    Answer: HIDAs professional will be the main stakeholders while clinicians and providers will provide their knowledge and patients will be the participants as data sources.

5. *Question*: How to ensure the successful HIDAs development and implementation when different types of stakeholders engaged in the development process?

   Answer: The HIDAs development process will be controlled, managed and maintained by only HIDAs professionals and they will collect knowledge and data from secondary (clinicians and providers) and third party (patients) stakeholders. The conceptualisation knowledge will use to build the model framework architecture and data will use to test the approach. All stakeholders will actively engage during the development process, such as refinement and correction, to ensure the interoperability.

All indication and answer described above declared that the HIDAs development process will follow the specific HIDAs model architecture and will use the appropriate hypertension data.

5.11.3 Step 2: determine and ascertain the necessity for fuzziness in hypertension diagnosis

Fuzzy-Ontology is defined as to handle vagueness, uncertainness, inaccurateness and impreciseness. The objective of this section is to determine and ascertain the necessity for fuzziness in hypertension diagnosis. The eventual destination of this section is to ascertain what kind of approach is needed to build: Fuzzy-Ontology or crisp ontology. In this step, the primary and secondary stakeholders should decide to ascertain if there are any needs of fuzziness in the hypertension diagnosis. To delaminate the proper decision, a list of operations need to perform:

1. *Understand the data*: It's needed to provide a proper investigation over the target domain. First of all, there is need to analyse raw hypertension data to gain complete understanding of the data and all types of incidents and ascertain if there are any needs of fuzziness. Determine and note if any vague or similar incident presents.

2. *Implement the fuzziness where needed*: The secondary stakeholders will decide whether fuzziness will include into the HIDAs architecture, before the appearance of the Fuzzy-Ontology approaches. The crisp ontology is capable to handle general vague data and is widely implemented. But, crisp ontology often failed in case of complex vague data and inaccurate, uncertain and inconsistent data. The crisp ontology is unable to deal when the expectation is high according to the degree of vagueness and its complexity. But Fuzzy-Ontology is capable to deal with these incidents where crisp ontology fails. So, the secondary stakeholder justifies the incident and asks if HIDAs expert should extend the fuzziness.

3. *Determine the type of fuzziness*: According to Fuzzy-Ontology definition, the fuzziness might already present in the ontology elements. So, it is important to determine if any fuzziness exists and if it exists then what kind of fuzziness in individual or blurry concept.

The determination of each and the specific fuzzy element may not be possible but should be sufficient enough in the fuzzy set. This issue may partially solve when reusing the Fuzzy-Ontology. Once the necessity of fuzziness can be determined and ascertained, it's needed to implement the logic to obtain a special type of fuzzy elements that exist in the semantic ontology. In EHRs as the target domain, there are two types of important features in hypertension diagnosis that are involved in modelling data: (1) diagnosis and (2) measure. So all certain elements could be handled by the crisp ontology. But the patient would like to hear the hypertension level in linguistic specification rather than numeric quantification. As linguistic specification often exposes vagueness, it is not easy to map efficiently hypertension explicit numeric measure to linguistic specification. For instance, the hypertension diagnosis level determines in three level: mid, moderate and severe. The interval between different levels is blurry and could be overlapped to the other level. According to this investigation, to manage and handle this blurry vagueness is implicit to patient's age and BMI needs to apply on fuzziness. This analysis summarised that Fuzzy-Ontology will be more efficiently manage and handle the hypertension diagnosis domain than the crisp ontology along.

5.11.4   Step 3: specify fuzzy-associated elements in hypertension data

As Fuzzy-Ontology associated with the model architecture for the proposed hypertension diagnosis in EHRs domain, it is essential to establish solid cooperation between HIDAs professionals and healthcare providers. Section 5.2 described that to specify the fuzzy associated elements, these need to be established by the healthcare professionals. To provide accurate hypertension diagnosis and establish the boundary between fuzzy-associated elements and particular data, HIDAs professional must collect the wisdom and recommendation from healthcare professional as follows:

- *Appropriate the accurate data*: The patient's raw data, such as various ages and BMI, can be apparently specified by the appropriate hypertension risk level. Those characteristics are directly affecting the patient's blood pressure. Different level of hypertension diagnosis with numerical representation can be calculated apparently to illustrate the patient's age and BMI category.
- *Fuzzy-associated elements*: The linguistic representation of hypertension diagnosis such as *mid, moderate* and *severe* contains vague meanings because age and BMI could be described as *severe* to some extent while it could also be labelled as *moderate* with a probability. The definitions for linguistic classifications for the level of hypertension diagnosis should be fuzzified to meet the EHRs domain needs.

The knowledge base of the EHRs domain is accurately divided into two parts: (1) precise information and (2) fuzzy-related information. Afterwards, they can be modelled with different treatments and healthcare services.

5.11.5   Step 4: reusing the subsisting HIDAs resources

The aim of the EHRs domain and excellence is the desire Fuzzy-Ontology, subsisting HIDAs resources. It is concernment to check resources in online projects, publications, etc., to reuse them. The resource found could be not only the fuzzy elements or crisp ontology, but also the Fuzzy-Ontology to reuse them in potential approach.

After the profound analysis and search for the resources in online projects and open publications, there are some elements that have been identified to reuse them, such as hypertension, hypertension levels and hypertension specification. We have found an approach called clinical DSSs (CDSSs) that build to assist the healthcare professional to diagnose their patients and to provide relief to the provider from some support together with the diagnosis. The CDSSs ontology comprises a classification of conceptual wisdom including the relay upon practical experiences in the case and rule-based logic accordingly. Several model functions and classes for hypertension diagnosis involve inappropriate implementation as a part of the diagnosis.

5.11.6   Step 5: reusing the subsisting Fuzzy-Ontology resources elements

Since the CDSSs ontology, which is selected as the ontology candidate to be reused from Phase 4, is a crisp ontology, then a conclusion, that only crisp ontology elements could be reused, can be drawn in this phase. Specifically, CDSSs are tools which are designed to assist clinicians for better clinical decision-making with knowledge and relevant clinical data of the patient, intelligently filtered and presented, to enhance health and health care ontology; these are selected to be reused as follows:

1. *Category specification*: Represent appropriate hypertension risk level and status, when these specific data are captured. For hypertension, diagnosis specification could represent the level of hypertension of the particular patient.
2. *Diagnosis*: Define the category specification that was diagnosed in the specific occurrence of hypertension.
3. *Contribution*: Define the specification of the latest result or diagnosis that could achieve from the proposed approach. The result will be the patient hypertension status after diagnosis.

5.11.7   Step 6: appropriate the subsisting of Fuzzy-Ontology elements

As we will not reuse any subsisting of hypertension Fuzzy-Ontology elements, we will skip this section.

5.11.8   Step 7: identify appropriate Fuzzy-Ontology elements

This section is to represent how to identify appropriate and various Fuzzy-Ontology elements to illustrate uncertain and vague data. We will convert here all hypertension-related numeric representation to linguistic specification. The determination of fuzzy data type of the blood pressure level and its breakdown that ensures the fuzzy description logic, are shown in Table 5.5.

Fuzzy data types determined and identified in the hypertension fuzzy description logic are represented in Table 5.6.

The determination of appropriate fuzzy concepts in the hypertension-specific diagnosis is demonstrated in Table 5.7.

The Fuzzy Description Logics (FuzzyDL) [18] syntaxes are followed by the fuzzy concept expressions. The fuzzy data type is defined as the essential goal to standardise

Table 5.5   Determination of fuzzy data type of the blood pressure level and its breakdown that ensure the fuzzy description logic [43]

Category	Systolic		Diastolic
Hypertension	<90 mmHg	And/or	<60 mmHg
Optimal	<120 mmHg	And	<80 mmHg
Normal	120–129 mmHg	And/or	80–84 mmHg
High normal	130–139 mmHg	And/or	85–89 mmHg
Level one (Mid)	140–159 mmHg	And/or	90–99 mmHg
Level two (Moderate)	160–179 mmHg	And/or	100–109 mmHg
Level three (Severe)	≥180 mmHg	And/or	≥110 mmHg
Isolated systolic hypertension	≥140 mmHg	And	<90 mmHg

Table 5.6   Fuzzy data types determined and identified in the hypertension fuzzy description logic

Fuzzy data type	Definition	Vague data modelled
MidSystolic = LeftShoulderSystolic (0,200,140,159) MidDiastolic = LeftShoulderDiastolic (0,120,90,99)	Denoting that the numeric value of the Mid should comply with leftShoulder membership function leftShoulderSystolic (0,200,140,159) and leftShoulderDiastolic (0,120,90,99)	Hypertension with its Systolic value range 0–159 mmHg and Diastolic 0–99 mmHg could be regarded as small to some value. The value distribution complies with a leftShoulder membership function
ModerateStageSystolic = TrapezoidalSystolic (130,139,160,179) ModerateStageDiastolic = TrapezoidalDiastolic (90,99,100,109)	Denoting that the numeric value of the Moderate should comply with trapezoidal membership function trapezoidalSystolic (130,139,160,179) and trapezoidalDiastolic (90,99,100,109)	Hypertension with its Systolic value range 130–179 mmHg and Diastolic 90–109 mmHg could be regarded as small to some value. The value distribution complies with a trapezoidal membership function
SevereSystolic = RightShoulderSystolic (160,179,180,200) SevereDiastolic = RightShoulderDiastolic (100,109,110,120)	Denoting that the numeric value of the Severe should comply with RightShoulder membership function RightShoulderSystolic (160,179,180,200) and RightShoulderDiastolic (100,109,110,120)	Hypertension with its Systolic value range 160–200 mmHg and Diastolic 100–120 mmHg could be regarded as small to some value. The value distribution complies with a RightShoulder membership function

the fuzzy concept data and provide in corresponding order. As an example, in fuzzy data a numeric representation date has to be changed to linguistic representation like Stage_one hypertension diagnosis and also to generate a probabilistic linguistic specification of hypertension risk level like mid stage. It imprecise that the fuzzy

Table 5.7   Determination of appropriate fuzzy concepts in the hypertension-specific diagnosis

Fuzzy concept	Definition	Vague information modelled
HypertensionStage	Representing the superclass of a set of sub-concepts, including MidStage, ModerateStage and SevereStage	Hypertension stage could be described by linguistic variables, such as mid-stage, moderate stage and severe stage
MidStage	Containing a collection of diagnosis whose level is assigned with the MidStage Fuzzy data type. *MidStage =* ∋ *hasNumericValue.MidLevel*	Hypertension diagnosis Mid stage ranging Systolic 140–159 mmHg and Diastolic 90–99 mmHg is classified as mid complying with a leftshoulder membership function
ModerateStage	Containing a collection of diagnosis whose level is assigned with ModerateStage Fussy data type. *ModerateStage =*∋ *hasNumericValue.ModerateLevel*	Hypertension diagnosis Moderate stage ranging Systolic ≥180 mmHg and Diastolic 100–109 mmHg is classified as moderate complying with a trapezoidal membership function
SevereStage	Containing a collection of diagnosis whose level is assigned with SevereStage Fussy data type diagnosis *SevereStage =*∋ *hasNumericValue.SevereLevel*	Hypertension diagnosis Severe stage ranging Systolic 160–179 mmHg and Diastolic ≥110 mmHg is classified as severe complying with a rightshoulder membership function

data characteristic of the crisp set hasNumericValue must convert into the linguistic specification to specify the relationship between different concepts like Mid, Moderate and Severe fuzzy data prefixes like MidStage, ModerateStage and SevereStage. Tables 5.5 and 5.6 provide detailed information by healthcare providers on the vague and imprecise boundary level among mid, moderate and severe hypertension stages, applying three different fuzzy value sets, defined as membership functions. Figure 5.5 demonstrates how the fuzzy data type represents in Fuzzy-Ontology hypertension diagnosis in a certain specification.

5.11.9   Step 8: identify appropriate crisp ontology elements

This step is to define the model architecture of appropriate crisp ontology elements in the hypertension diagnosis domain. To avoid the data inconsistency, the ontology precise information should be considered to create new crisp ontology elements from the traditional subsisting ontology. The appropriate Fuzzy-Ontology elements are already identified in Step 7. Table 5.8 demonstrates the crisp ontology concept, data characteristics and proposes, supplied by the healthcare professional.

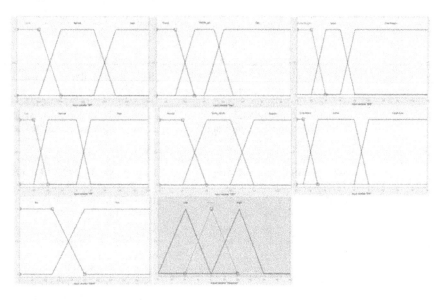

Figure 5.5   Fuzzy input and output data types for the hypertension diagnosis

Table 5.8   The appropriate crisp ontology elements in the hypertension diagnosis

Crisp Concept	Definition	Certain health data modelled
HypertensionStage	Defining a superclass of different stages of hypertension	A specific age and BMI could be identified as a specific type. The type of a specific stage of hypertension is a significant feature for hypertension diagnosis to be considered during the study
Normal	Representing Normal with generally the systolic blood pressure between ≤120 and 139 mmHg and the diastolic blood pressure between ≤80 and 89 mmHg	Health expert thinks that the recognition of normal stage as Normal and important to hypertension diagnosis
Hypertension	Representing hypertension with generally the systolic blood pressure between 140 and 179 mmHg and the diastolic blood pressure between 90 and 109 mmHg	Health expert thinks that the recognition of hypertension stage as Hypertension and important to hypertension diagnosis for the treatment
Hypertensive	Representing hypertensive which generally the systolic blood pressure ≤180 mmHg and the diastolic blood pressure ≤110 mmHg	The provider considers the fact of the hypertension stage as a Severe stage

Table 5.9 describes the description of the hypertension-related dataset, as follows:

Table 5.9   Description of hypertension-related dataset

No	Feature	Description	Data type	Domain	Number of entry
1	Age	Patient age in year	Numeric	[15–85]	
2	Sex	Gender	Binary	[0,1]	
3	BPS	Blood pressure systolic	Numeric	[0–200]	35
4	BPD	Blood pressure diastolic	Numeric	[0–122]	35
5	BMI	Body mass index	Numeric	[0–67]	11

Table 5.10 describes the hypertension Fuzzy dataset corresponding to feature with the numerical presentation, as follows:

Table 5.10   Hypertension fuzzy dataset corresponding to feature with numerical presentation

No	Feature	Fuzzy set	Data intervals			
1	Age	Young	15	15	25	30
		Middle_Age	25	35	45	55
		Old	45	55	85	85
2	BP (blood pressure systolic/diastolic)	Low	80/20	80/20	100/55	120/65
		Normal	100/55	120/65	150/85	170/90
		High	150/85	170/90	200/120	200/120
3	BMI (body mass index)	Under_weight	15	15	20	25
		Ideal	20	25	30	35
		Over_weight	30	35	40	40
4	HR (heart rate)	Low	30	30	40	50
		Normal	40	50	70	80
		High	70	80	100	100
5	DBT (diabetic)	Normal	70	70	80	90
		Early_Diabetic	80	90	100	110
		Diabetic	100	110	120	120
6	PA (physical activity)	Less_Active	0.5	0.5	1	3
		Active	1	3	8	10
		Very_Active	8	10	16	16
7	GEN (genetic)	No	0	0	0.25	0.5
		Yes	0.25	0.5	1	1

Table 5.8 is different from the traditional hypertension diagnosis. There are three extra patterns associated with hypertension Fuzzy-Ontology because traditional hypertension ontology is inappropriate to deal with all requirements for the healthcare domain. The argument behind the age, BMI and unknown, is that the healthcare professional has defined that three kinds of extra diagnoses are essential, namely normal, hypertension and hypertensive. They are knapping between each other in all kinds of hypertension diagnoses.

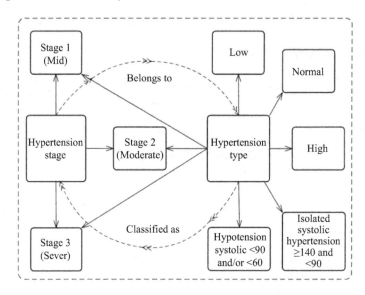

*Figure 5.6   The overall visualised structure of the fuzzy hypertension-specific
ontology*

5.11.10   Step 9: formalisation

OWL2 is chosen as use case approach. It is the formalism language to illustrate
the ontology design architecture. We have deployed the fuzzy OWL2 scope and
ontology performer portage to easily converting the theoretical concept into OWL2-
supported signification, in this section. The ontology performer portage is used for
visualised structures and realises comfortably for the modelled hypertension specific
Fuzzy-Ontology. Web Ontology Language (OWL) or Resource Description Framework (RDF) is sufficient enough for the ontology performer portage and automatic
code creation ontology. There are many OWL files approachable online constructed
hypertension-specific Fuzzy-Ontology diagnosis. Figure 5.6 demonstrates the overall
visualised structure of the hypertension-specific Fuzzy-Ontology diagnosis.

5.11.11   Step 10: Fuzzy-Ontology result affirmation

The affirmation is defined as the evidence of the approach appropriateness of the
constructed approach consequences, in our case consequences of the HIDAs. The
appropriateness of the data consistency and accuracy characterisation is appraised
by the fuzzy description logic reasoner. Other appropriateness of the HIDAs consequences is subjectively verified by all stockholders who have been directly engaged
in the approach evaluation procedure. The affirmation consequences are provided as
follows:

- *Data accuracy affirmation*: The approached HIDAs hypertension diagnosis has
  been accurately illustrated and architected from the EHRs domain. Data have been
  collected from healthcare professionals, and it has been followed all actual instruc-
  tions including recommendations accurately to keep the correct boundary line

between specific data and uncertain vague data. All subsisting uncertain elements have been identified accurately to present accurately appropriate Fuzzy-Ontology elements, amalgamated by appropriate fuzzy dataset. In addition, the correct relationship has been established between Fuzzy-Ontology and crisp ontology elements, defined by HIDAs expert and healthcare professionals.

- *Data inconsistency affirmation*: The fuzzy description logic reasoner has been introduced to define and verify the hypertension diagnosis for data consistency. And ontology has been introduced to observe the HIDAs data architecture and data elements. There are no debatable concept and data existing in the EHRs domain for the hypertension diagnosis development process, verified by the healthcare professional.
- *Data completeness affirmation*: The hypertension diagnosis model has satisfied the entire specification of the HIDAs contrivance and excellence, including the complete knowledge base concept that has been specified in Step 1. Especially, all imprecise and vague data have been integrated and converted in the hypertension diagnosis representation.
- *Data logicalness affirmation*: All controversial boundary lines between the specific and uncertain data are logically rational and it has been identified by a healthcare professional. Different imprecise and vague data types and categories that have been operated by the fuzzy approximation concept have made sense to other HIDM experts and healthcare professionals.
- *Data reliability affirmation*: The developed HIDAs hypertension diagnosis is easily understandable and reliable by all stakeholders. The EHRs domain terminologies that have been identified in the HIDAs are specified clear enough for the reliability.
- *Data validity affirmation*: According to all stakeholders numerous investigation and verification, the EHRs domain terminology is sufficient enough to declare the accurate and consistent hypertension diagnosis. Also no data redundancy has been noticed or identified in the HIDAs architecture or model.

5.11.12 Step 11: documentation and notes

We exclude this section to introduce fuzzy hypertension-specific ontology as our main contribution approach fails out on it.

5.12 Mathematical simulation of hypertension diagnosis based on Markov chain probability model

A Markov model is a stochastic process whose dynamic behaviour is such that its future development depends only on the present state space. In another way, the Markov process can be explained as it is a stochastic process by its present state. That is, the distinctions of events are independent of the history of the system. In other words, the description of the present state fully captures all the information that could influence the future evolution of the process. Being a stochastic process means that all state transitions are probabilistic. At each step, the system may change its state from the current state to another state (or remain in the same state) according to a probability distribution.

Here we have included the interval when each symptom reflects the visualisation of the condition. The set of Markov state equations describes the probabilistic transition from the initial states to the final states. The transition visualisation probabilities obey the following two rules:

1. *Transitive aspect*: Transitive aspect defines how a symptom passes from one condition to another condition. We will provide a mathematical simulation including conditional graph where the other describes the matrix probabilities passes. The probabilities of more than one transition in time are infinitesimals of higher order and can be neglected.
2. *Temporary aspect*: Temporary aspect is defined as the interval needed to the requirements on passes from one condition to the others. In another word, the probability of transition in time Δt from one condition to another is given by gain into Δt.

The interval is estimated with the point of views condition and refers to as transformation probabilities or simply perceived the probabilities. The transformation probability is represented by itself the average interval probabilities, passes from the condition of end diagnosing/monitoring of the condition and, before reception, by them next probability condition during the same interval. The Markov model can be illustrated by means of a state transition diagram, which shows all the states and transition probabilities.

The Markov chain describe as follows: We have a set of states, $S = \{S_0, S_1, S_2, \ldots, S_r\}$. The process starts in one of these states and moves successively from one state to another. Each move is called a step. If the chain is currently in state S_i, then it moves to state S_j at the next step with a probability denoted by S_{ij}, and this probability does not depend upon the state in which the chain was before the current state. The probabilities S_{ij} are called transition probabilities. The process can remain in the state it is in, and this occurs with probability S_{ij}. An initial probability distribution, defined on S, specifies the starting state. Usually this is done by specifying a particular state as the starting state. Using the transition matrix S, the hypertension probability could be represented as $S_{00}, \ldots, S_{06}$.

Figure 5.7 shows the Markov chain with respect to the different hypertension probabilities.

The other two events also have probabilities that can be written as products of entries of S. In general, if a Markov chain has r states, then

$$S_{06}^{(2)} = \Sigma_{k=0}^r S_{ik} S_{kj} \tag{5.11}$$

The following general theorem is easy to be proved by using the above observation and induction. There is an initial probability distribution to the set of states. We can define a Markov model as follows:

$$S_0(k+1) = 0 + 0 + 0 + 0 + 0 + 0 + 0 \tag{5.12}$$

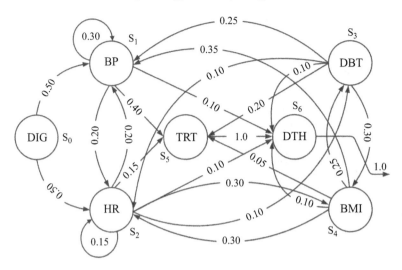

Figure 5.7 *The Markov chain probability link structure of hypertension progression risk model (DIG, start diagnosis/monitoring; BP, blood pressure, HR, heart rate; TRT, on treatment/under control; DBT, diabetic; BMI, body mass index; DTH,death/extremely critical; EXT, exit from diagnosis/monitoring)*

$$S_1(k+1) = 0.5 \times S_0(k) + 0.3 \times S_1(k) + 0.2 \times S_2(k) + 0.25 \\ \times S_3(k) + 0.35 \times S_4(k) + 0 + 0 \tag{5.13}$$

$$S_2(k+1) = 0.5 \times S_0(k) + 0.2 \times S_1(k) + 0.15 \times S_2(k) + 0.10 \\ \times S_3(k) + 0.3 \times S_4(k) + 0 + 0 \tag{5.14}$$

$$S_3(k+1) = 0 + 0 + 0.1 \times S_2(k) + 0 + 0.25 \times S_4(k) + 0 + 0 \tag{5.15}$$

$$S_4(k+1) = 0 + 0 + 0.3 \times S_2(k) + 0.3 \times S_3(k) + 0 + 0 + 0 \tag{5.16}$$

$$S_5(k+1) = 0 + 0.4 \times S_1(k) + 0.15 \times S_2(k) + 0.2 \times S_3(k) + 0.05 \\ \times S_4(k) + 0 + 0 \tag{5.17}$$

$$S_6(k+1) = 0 + 0.1 \times S_1(k) + 0.1 \times S_2(k) + 0.2 \times S_3(k) + 0.1 \\ \times S_4(k) + 1.0 \times S_5(k) + 0 \tag{5.18}$$

Therefore,

$$(S_0(k+1), S_1(k+1), S_2(k+1), S_3(k+1), S_4(k+1), S_5(k+1), S_6(k+1))$$

$$= [S_0(k), S_1(k), S_2(k), S_3(k), S_4(k), S_5(k), S_6(k)]$$

$$\times \begin{bmatrix} 0 & 0.5 & 0.5 & 0 & 0 & 0 & 0 \\ 0 & 0.3 & 0.2 & 0 & 0 & 0.4 & 0.1 \\ 0 & 0.2 & 0.15 & 0.1 & 0.3 & 0.15 & 0.1 \\ 0 & 0.25 & 0.1 & 0 & 0.3 & 0.2 & 0.1 \\ 0 & 0.35 & 0.3 & 0.25 & 0 & 0.05 & 0.1 \\ 0 & 0 & 0 & 0 & 0 & 0 & 1 \\ 0 & 0 & 0 & 0 & 0 & 0 & 0 \end{bmatrix}$$

When $k = 0$

$\quad S_0 = 1$

$\quad S_1 = S_2 = S_3 = S_4 = S_5 = S_6 = 0$

When $k = 1$,

$\quad S_0 = 0$

$\quad S_1 = 0.5 \times S_0(k_0) = 0.5$

$\quad S_2 = 0.5 \times S_0(k_0) = 0.5$

$\quad S_3 = S_4 = S_5 = S_6 = 0$

When $k = 2$,

$\quad S_0 = 0$

$\quad S_1 = 0.3 \times S_1(k_1) + 0.2 \times S_2(k_1) = 0.25$

$\quad S_2 = 0.2 \times S_1(k_1) + 0.15 \times S_2(k_1) = 0.18$

$\quad S_3 = S_4 = S_5 = 0$

$\quad S_6 = 0.1 \times S_1(k_1) + 0.1 \times S_2(k_1) = 0.1$

When $k = 3$,

$\quad S_0 = 0$

$\quad S_1 = 0.25 \times S_1(k_2) + 0.2 \times S_2(k_2) = 0.1$

$\quad S_2 = 0.2 \times S_1(k_2) + 0.1 \times S_2(k_2) = 0.07$

$\quad S_3 = 0.1 \times S_2(k_2) = 0.02$

$\quad S_4 = S_5 = 0$

$\quad S_6 = 0.1 \times S_1(k_2) + 0.1 \times S_2(k_2) + 0.1 \times S_6(k_2) = 0.05$

When $k = 4$,

$\quad S_0 = 0$

$\quad S_1 = 0.35 \times S_1(k_3) + 0.2 \times S_2(k_3) = 0.05$

$$S_2 = 0.2 \times S_1(k_3) + 0.3 \times S_2(k_3) = 0.04$$

$$S_3 = 0.1 \times S_2(k_3) + 0.25 \times S_4(k_3) = 0.01$$

$$S_4 = 0.3 \times S_2(k_3) + 0.3 \times S_3(k_3) = 0.02$$

$$S_5 = 0$$

$$S_6 = 0.1 \times S_1(k_3) + 0.1 \times S_2(k_3) + 0.1 \times S_3(k_3) + 0.1 \times S_6(k_3) = 0.02$$

When $k = 5$,

$$S_0 = 0$$

$$S_1 = 0.3 \times S_1(k_4) + 0.2 \times S_2(k_4) + 0.25 \times S_3(k_4) + 0.35 \times S_4(k_4) = 0.06$$

$$S_2 = 0.2 \times S_1(k_4) + 0.15 \times S_2(k_4) + 0.1 \times S_3(k_4) + 0.3 \times S_4(k_4) = 0.02$$

$$S_3 = 0.1 \times S_2(k_4) + 0.25 \times S_4(k_4) = 0.01$$

$$S_4 = 0.3 \times S_2(k_4) + 0.3 \times S_3(k_4) = 0.01$$

$$S_5 = 0.4 \times S_1(k_4) + 0.15 \times S_2(k_4) + 0.2 \times S_3(k_4) + 0.05 \times S_4(k_4) = 0.03$$

$$S_6 = 0.1 \times S_1(k_4) + 0.1 \times S_2(k_4) + 0.1 \times S_3(k_4) + 0.1 \times S_4(k_4) + 0.1$$
$$\times S_5(k_4) = 0.01$$

The result of graphical representation of the Markov chain probability when 'BMI to BP = 0.35' and 'BMI to HR = 0.30' is demonstrated in Figures 5.8. In addition, different matrix probability simulation according to 'BMI to BP' transmission in hypertension diagnosis has been demonstrated in Figure 5.9 and Table 5.11.

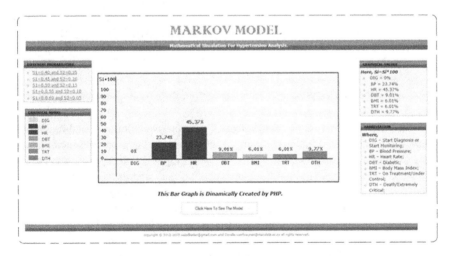

Figure 5.8   Graphical representation of the Markov chain probability link structure of hypertension progression risk when 'BMI to BP = 0.35' and 'BMI to HR = 0.30'

Different matrix probability of "BMI to BP"

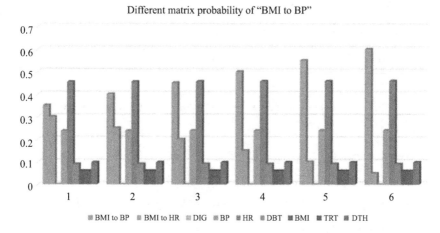

BMI to BP ▪ BMI to HR ▪ DIG ▪ BP ▪ HR ▪ DBT ▪ BMI ▪ TRT ▪ DTH

Figure 5.9   Different matrix probability simulation according to 'BMI to BP' transmission in hypertension diagnosis

Table 5.11   Different matrix probability simulation according to 'BMI to BP' transmission in hypertension diagnosis

Conditions		DIG (%)	BP (%)	HR (%)	DBT (%)	BMI (%)	TRT (%)	DTH (%)
BMI to BP	BMI to HR							
0.35	0.30	0	27.25	52.08	10.34	6.89	6.89	11.21
0.4	0.25	0	27.30	52.19	10.36	6.91	6.91	11.23
0.45	0.20	0	27.36	52.30	10.38	6.92	6.92	11.26
0.5	0.15	0	27.42	52.41	10.41	6.94	6.94	11.28
0.55	0.10	0	27.25	52.08	10.34	6.89	6.89	11.21
0.60	0.05	0	27.53	52.62	10.45	6.97	6.97	11.33

5.13   Analysis of result

Step 4 has demonstrated the HIDAs successful implementation and addressing the DQ issues for hypertension diagnosis in LSDB following the guideline accumulated by the proposed approaches. During the HIDAs implementation process, each and every step has been specified for diaphanous contrivance and the specific to-do lists. As the development process has been used in the formal ontology associated with fuzzy logic, it could assume the appropriateness and efficiency achievement from the HIDAs hypertension diagnosis. But our fundamental contrivance of the HIDAs performance is an incorporate statement which needs to be constructed in a logical order as Fuzzy-Ontology. The eventual contrivance of our proposed HIDAs is to provide a methodological instruction to efficiently handle the big data as an accomplishment confirmation of appropriate achievement. In spite of this, as emphasised between indication and philosophical introduction, it is not easy to implement a universal qualitative and quantitative corresponding analysis with another subsistence approach. Widely accepted circumstances confirm still quantitative limitation present in the entire subsisting ontology [40], together with the contrivance for constructing Fuzzy-Ontology, crisp or probabilistic ontologies. Vice-like, METHONTOLOGY is the renowned approach, which does not comprise any evaluation even if it allows the systematic approach for constructing crisp ontology from scratch. Another example, applicability of NeOn has proven in several exploration platforms but did not provide any meticulous appraisement.

The possibility of the diligent approach is evaluating many use case crisp ontologies except providing any range of appraisements. According to Carvalho *et al.* [44] determination, the latest probabilistic ontology development approach omits the appraisement segment too. Therefore, this chapter just accommodates a corresponding way of constructing a use case hypertension diagnosis in big data environment using the HIDAs methodology. Inasmuch as ontology is an existing approach which cannot be appraised rigorously, it makes clear that generally all stakeholders including the HIDAs professionals are selecting from existing approaches and simply combine appropriate approaches to achieve the best performance according to their needs.

According to the above-mentioned phenomenon, the ontology remained as unapprised evaluation approach like other existing consequential approaches along with Fuzzy-Ontology non-methodological elaboration approaches. Therefore, the following lineament of the proposed HIDAs evaluated methodology could be anticipated to introduce affix in the Fuzzy-Ontology evaluation excursion:

- *Analogies of HIDAs*: The proposed HIDAs follow all generic rules and procedure as a formal Fuzzy-Ontology approach, excluding a few significant rules such as using single or combined approaches where needed, and reuse the existing knowledge base Fuzzy-Ontology elements in appropriate occurrences. As HIDAs is the new way HA based on Fuzzy-Ontology evaluation process, so initially it may need additional time to understand the implementation process.
- *Methodological guideline of HIDAs*: The proposed HIDAs provide the first methodological guideline for elaborating HA based on Fuzzy-Ontology from scratch. Analogies to other existing approaches, HIDAs are more mature, complete and compressive. For the non-methodological evaluation process, it is absolutely significant when easily excludes an important step. The similar incident can be identified in existing hybrid evaluation approaches. For example, reusing the Fuzzy-Ontology elements is not a common consideration in present hybrid evaluation approaches.
- *Applicability and interoperability of HIDAs*: The proposed HIDAs are a generic HA based on Fuzzy-Ontology and have higher applicability and interoperability compared to other present approaches. The possibility of HIDAs is to build own Fuzzy-Ontology elements to reuse them, rather than fuzzified each and every existing crisp ontology which imposes extra resources for their uses. This reduces the applicability performance and provides a limitation on the domain-specific

dependency, where the approaches previously implemented. The main contribution of HIDAs is to grant a different generic solution approach from scratch for the big data domain that does not depend on existing domain-specific ontology.

There are two different types of knowledge base data in HIDAs: (1) appropriate data and (2) fuzzy-related data. This concept easily draws the borderline among them and accomplishes them with the specific strategical methodology. Here Fuzzy-Ontology deals with vague data and existing associative approach deals with appropriate data.

Although the main contribution of HIDAs is to illustrate a methodological guideline to develop an HA to deal with big data, this approach also has all possibility to deal with the crisp ontology development. The applicability and interoperability of HIDAs development have been demonstrated in the crisp ontology evaluation process. This feature declares that the HIDAs approach can be used as a methodological guideline for crisp ontology development. To accomplish, the HIDAs approach can be appropriate for both crisp ontology and Fuzzy-Ontology development as a guideline according to the extensive and generic features.

5.14 Conclusion

This chapter described the applicability of the HAs based on Fuzzy-Ontology by illustrating its use in a hypothetical hypertension diagnosis project, the HIDAs. A novel Fuzzy-Ontology development approach for big data presented HAs as HIDAs. The HIDAs demonstrate the approaching directive for constructing approach Fuzzy-Ontology for hypertension diagnosis in big data environment from the base. According to our implicit wisdom delegation, the HIDA has been considered to aiming at the data standardisation to deal with DQ issues including imprecise and vague data according to the lesson learned from existing different approaches. The entire HIDAs construction process is divided into 11 development steps and determined and implemented where the necessary in each step. The HIDA provides a structured approach for the selection of an appropriate HA based on Fuzzy-Ontology that can support the interoperability of big DI systems. This chapter demonstrated the usefulness of HAs for big data communication.

References

[1] John P., Julien M., Laurent L. and Jaakko L. (2012). Quality analysis of sensors data for personal health records on mobile devices. In *Pervasive Health Knowledge Management*, R. Bali, I. Troshani, S. Goldberg, and N. Wickramasinghe (eds.). Part of the series Healthcare Delivery in the Information Age. New York, NY: Springer, pp. 103–133, DOI: 10.1007/978-1-4614-4514-2_10.

[2] Malcolm P.A., Peter B. and Ronald M. (2012). *Data Types and Persistence.* Berlin, Heidelberg: Springer-Verlag.

[3] Creswell J.W. (2013). *Research Design: Qualitative, Quantitative, and Mixed Methods Approaches*. Thousand Oaks, CA: Sage Publications.

[4] Matthias J, Maurizio L, Yannis V. and Panos V. (2013). *Fundamentals of Data Warehouses*, 2nd ed. Berlin, Heidelberg: Springer-Verlag.

[5] Jiawei H., Micheline K. and Jian P. (2011). *Data Mining: Concepts and Techniques*, 3rd ed. Waltham, MA: Elsevier.

[6] Yusuf, M.K. and Azlan, A. (2012). Comparative study of techniques in reducing inconsistent data. *International Journal of Database Theory and Application*, vol. 5, no. 1, pp. 37–46.

[7] Ralph K. and Margy R. (2013). *The Data Warehouse Toolkit: The Definitive Guide to Dimensional Modeling*. Indianapolis, IN: John Wiley & Sons.

[8] Saiod A.K., Darelle V.G. and Veldsman A. (2017). Electronic health records: benefits and challenges for data quality. In U.K. Samee, A.Y. Zomaya, and A. Abbas (eds.), *Handbook of Large-Scale Distributed Computing in Smart Healthcare, Scalable Computing and Communications*. Switzerland AG: Springer International Publishing AG 2017. DOI: 10.1007/978-3-319-58280-1_6

[9] Hai B.T., Trong H.D. and Ngoc T.N. (2013). A hybrid method for fuzzy ontology integration. *Cybernetics and Systems, An International Journal*, vol. 44, pp. 133–154.

[10] Jarrar M. and Meersman R. (2009). Ontology engineering – the DOGMA approach. In *Adv. Web Semantics I*, vol. 4891, T.S. Dillon, E. Chang, R. Meersman, and K. Sycara (eds.). Berlin, Germany: Springer, pp. 7–34.

[11] Maio D.P., White L.M., Bleakney R., Menezes R.J. and Theodoropoulos J. (2014). Diagnostic Accuracy of an iPhone DICOM viewer for the interpretation of magnetic resonance imaging of the knee. *Clinical Journal of Sport Medicine*, vol. 24, no.4, pp. 308–314. DOI: 10.1097/JSM.0000000000000005.

[12] Abdullah G., Aisha S., Shahaboddin S. and Fariza H. (2015). A survey on indexing techniques for big data: taxonomy and performance evaluation. *Knowledge and Information Systems*, vol. 46, no. 2, pp. 241–284.

[13] Uthayan K.R. and Anandha Mala G.S. (2015). Hybrid ontology for semantic information retrieval model using keyword matching indexing system. *The Scientific World Journal*, vol. 2015, pp. 9. Article ID 414910, http://dx.doi.org/10.1155/2015/414910.

[14] Zadeh L.A. (1965). Fuzzy sets.' *Inf. Control*, vol. 8, no. 3, pp. 338–353.

[15] Fernando B. and Umberto S. (2013). Aggregation operators for fuzzy ontologies. *Applied Soft Computing*, vol. 13, no. 9, pp. 3816–3830, DOI:10.1016/j.asoc.2013.05.008.

[16] Pérez I.J., Wikström R., Mezei J., Carlsson C. and Herrera-Viedma E. (2013). A new consensus model for group decision making using fuzzy ontology. *Soft Computing - A Fusion of Foundations, Methodologies and Applications*, vol. 17, no. 9, pp. 1617–1627.

[17] Haibo C., Lingling X., Peng W., Peng Z. and Haibin Y. (2017). Discrete manufacturing ontology development. *2017 IEEE International Conference on Industrial Technology (ICIT)*, 22–25 March, 2017, Toronto, ON, Canada. IEEE. DOI: 10.1109/ICIT.2017.7915568

[18]   Lukasiewicz T. and Straccia U. (2008) Managing uncertainty and vagueness in description logics for the semantic web. In *Web Semant. Sci. Services Agents World Wide Web*. Cham: Springer.

[19]   Bobillo F. and Straccia U. (2011). Fuzzy ontology representation using OWL 2. *Int. J. Approx. Reasoning*, vol. 52, no. 7, pp. 1073–1094.

[20]   Cross V.V. (2014). Fuzzy ontologies: the state of the art. In *Proc. IEEE Conf. Norbert Wiener 21st Century (21CW)*, June 2014. Cham: Springer, pp. 1–8.

[21]   Chanchal Y., Shuliang W. and Manoj K. (2013). Algorithm and approaches to handle large data – a survey. *IJCSN International Journal of Computer Science and Network*, vol. 2, no. 3, pp. 1–5. ISSN (Online): 2277–5420

[22]   Pawlak Z. (1982). Rough sets. *International Journal of Parallel Programming*, vol. 11, no. 5, pp. 341–356. DOI:10.1007/BF01001956.

[23]   Pawlak Z. (1991). *Rough Sets: Theoretical Aspects of Reasoning About Data*. Dordrecht: Kluwer Academic Publishing. ISBN 0-7923-1472-7.

[24]   Silberschatz, A., Korth, H. and Sudarshan, S. (2006) *Database System Concepts*. Beijing: Higher Education Press.

[25]   Wenfei F., Floris G., Shuai M. and Heiko M. (2010). Detecting inconsistencies in distributed data. In *2010 IEEE 26th International Conference on Data Engineering (ICDE 2010)*. 1–6 March 2010, Long Beach, CA, USA. IEEE. DOI: 978-1-4244-5446-4/10.

[26]   Sha F. and Guo-bing F. (2016). A multiple attribute decision-making method based on exponential fuzzy numbers. *Mathematical and computational Applications*, vol. 21, no. 2. DOI: 10.3390/mca21020019.

[27]   Lakshmana G.N.V., Muralikrishnan S. and Sivaraman G. (2011). Multi-criteria decision-making method based on interval-valued intuitionistic fuzzy sets. *Expert Syst.*, vol. 38, pp. 1464–1467. DOI: https://doi.org/10.1016/j.eswa.2010.07.055.

[28]   Park J.H., Park I.Y., Kwun Y.C. and Tan X. (2011). Extension of the TOPSIS method for decision making problems under interval-valued intuitionistic fuzzy environment. *Appli. Math. Model.*, vol. 35, pp. 2544–2556. DOI: https://doi.org/10.1016/j.apm.2010.11.025.

[29]   Xu Z.S. (2007). Models for multiple attribute decision-making with intuitionistic fuzzy information. *Int. J. Uncertain. Fuzziness Knowl.-Based Syst.*, vol. 15, pp. 285–297. DOI: https://doi.org/10.1142/S0218488507004686.

[30]   Wang, C., Zhang, J. and Qin, L. (2016). Design & research of legal affairs information service platform based on UIMA and semantics. *International Journal of Future Generation Communication and Networking*, vol. 9, no. 3, pp. 1–14.

[31]   Wei G.W. (2008). A method of interval-valued intuitionistic fuzzy multiple attributes decision making with incomplete attribute weight information. *Chin. J. Manag.*, vol. 5, pp. 208–211, 217.

[32]   Mendel J.M. (2016). A comparison of three approaches for estimating (synthesizing) an interval type-2 fuzzy set model of a linguistic term for computing with words. *Granul. Comput.*, vol. 1, pp. 59–69. DOI: http://dx.doi.org/10.1007/s41066-015-0009-7.

[33]   Francky C.S., Wuytack G.E. (2013) *Custom Memory Management Methodology: Exploration of Memory Organisation for Embedded Multimedia System Design.* de Greef Florin Banica Lode Nachtergaele Arnout Vandecappelle. Boston, MA: Springer-Science + Business Media.

[34]   Fernández M., Gomez-Perez A. and Juristo N. (1997). METHONTOLOGY: from ontological art towards ontological engineering. Stanford Univ., Stanford, CA, USA, Tech. Rep. SS-97-06, 1997.

[35]   Suarez-Figueroa M.C. (2010) NeOn methodology for building ontology networks: specification, scheduling and reuse. Universidad Politécnica de madrid, Tech. Univ. of Madrid, Spain, 2010.

[36]   Vrandečič D., Pinto S., Tempich C. and Sure Y. (2005). The DILIGENT knowledge processes. *Journal of Knowledge Management*, vol. 9, no. 5, pp. 85–96.

[37]   Sure Y., Staab S. and Studer R. (2004). On-to-knowledge methodology (OTKM). In S. Staab and R. Studer (eds.). *Handbook Ontologies.* Berlin, Heidelberg: Springer, pp. 117–132.

[38]   Kotis K. and Vouros G.A. (2006). Human-centered ontology engineering: the HCOME methodology. *Knowl. Inf. Syst.*, vol. 10, no. 1, pp. 109–131.

[39]   Noy N.F. and McGuiness D.L. (2001). Ontology development 101: a guide to creating your first ontology. *Stanford Med. Informat.*, Stanford, CA, USA, Tech. Rep. SMI-2001-0880, 2001.

[40]   Alexopoulos P., Wallace M., Kafentzis K. and Askounis D. (2012) IKARUSOnto: a methodology to develop fuzzy ontologies from crisp ones. *Knowl. Inf. Syst.*, vol. 32, no. 3, pp. 667–695.

[41]   Ghorbel H., Bahri A. and Bouaziz R. (2010). Fuzzy ontologies building method: fuzzy ontomethodology. In *Proc. Annu. Meeting North Amer. Fuzzy Inf. Process. Soc. (NAFIPS)*, Toronto, ON, 12–14 July, 2010. IEEE, pp. 1–8.

[42]   Tho Q.T., Hui S.C., Fong A.C.M. and Cao T.H. (2006). Automatic fuzzy ontology generation for semantic Web. *IEEE Trans. Knowl. Data Eng.*, vol. 18, no. 6, pp. 842–856.

[43]   Mancia G., Fagard R., Narkiewicz K., *et al.* (2014). 2013 ESH/ESC Practice guidelines for the management of arterial hypertension: Task Force for the management of arterial hypertension of the European Society of Hypertension and the European Society of Cardiology. *Blood Pressure*, pp. 3–16.

[44]   Carvalho R.N., Laskey K.B. and Costa P.C.G.D. (2016). Uncertainty modeling process for semantic technology. *PeerJ Comput. Sci.*, vol. 2, p. e77.

Chapter 6
Deep generative models for recommender systems

Vineeth Rakesh[1], Suhang Wang[2], and Huan Liu[3]

6.1 Introduction

The complexity of modern recommender system has grown significantly with the evolution of web data. Therefore, conventional recommendation models such as collaborative and content-based filtering are quickly fading away due to their inability to capture complex heterogeneous relationships in data. For example, Figure 6.1 shows the layers of information that collectively impact the item-selection process of a user. Here, the movie Moana is chosen as the item; nonetheless, this example holds good for other products such as books, electronics, apps and games. One can observe that a user's interest to watch Moana is determined by five different layers, namely, social network layer, item layer, temporal layer, personal layer and geo-location layer. The social network layer is attributed by social media platforms such as Twitter, Facebook and Instagram where users are constantly exposed to product promotions and celebrity endorsements. These social signals play a decisive role in influencing the purchase behavior of users. The item layer signifies the content quality of the movie. This includes attributes such as story line, music and visual effects. The personal layer represents the choice of individual users, which is usually determined by analyzing their historical data. In this example, this is the preference over the genre and the cast members of the movie. Finally, the geo-location of users also has a strong influence over the selection of items. For example, the movie Moana was a huge box office success in the USA but had a mediocre reception in other parts of the world. Consequently, to build a robust recommendation model, it is important to incorporate such heterogeneous signals from various data sources. This chapter introduces some recent trends in generative and deep-learning (DL) models for hybrid recommendation systems that have proven to be extremely effective in integrating different modalities of data.

[1]Researcher (Machine Learning and AI) at Technicolor, Palo Alto, CA, USA
[2]College of Information Sciences and Technology, The Pennsylvania State University, USA
[3]Computer Science and Engineering, Ira A. Fulton Schools of Engineering, Arizona State University, USA

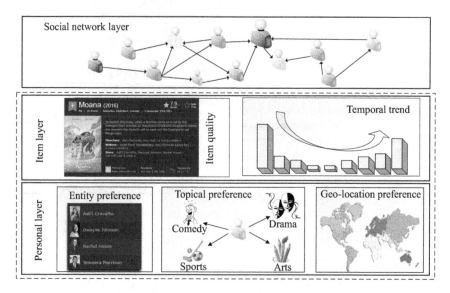

*Figure 6.1   The collective impact of social network, product quality, temporal trend
and personal choice over the item selection process of users*

Probabilistic generative models (PGMs) such as probabilistic matrix factorization (MF) (PMF) [1], probabilistic latent semantic analysis (PLSA) [2] and latent
Dirichlet allocation (LDA) [3] are powerful techniques that are capable of learning
implicit relationships in data in a condensed feature space. While PMF is predominantly used for collaborative filtering (CF)–based recommendation, PLSA and LDA
can be formulated as both topic and recommendation models. Additionally, the generative principle adopted by these models allows them to seamlessly integrate with
each other. For instance, the collaborative topic regression (CTR) model [4] combines LDA with PMF to efficiently handle the *cold-start* problem and improve the
recommendation performance. Nevertheless, the latent representations learned by
CTR are often not effective enough, especially when the auxiliary information is very
sparse. DL on the other hand has emerged as the state-of-the-art technique for natural
language processing, image analysis and speech recognition due to its ability to learn
effective representations and capture nonlinear relationships in data [5]. Recently,
it has also demonstrated impressive performance over applications such as YouTube
video recommendation [6], Yahoo news recommendation and [7] and app recommendation in Google Play store [8]. However, it is not without its flaws; DL techniques
are generally inferior to shallow models such as CF in capturing and learning the
similarity and implicit relationship between the items. This calls for the integration of
PGMs and DL models to create a unified framework that leverages the best of both
worlds.

This chapter is organized into three main sections. The first section introduces the
readers to some classic algorithms such as PMF and LDA and illustrates the generative
principle of a hybrid recommendation model called CTR that jointly models the

latent interests of users and items. The second section presents recommendation models that are exclusively based on DL techniques. This includes models such as Restricted Boltzmann-machine-based CF (RBM-CF) [9], autoencoder (AE)-based recommendation (AutoRec) [10], neural CF (NCF) [11] and recurrent recommender network (RRN) [12]. Finally, the third section explains models such as collaborative denoising AE (DAE) (CDAE) [13] and collaborative variational AE (VAE) (CVAE) [14] that integrates PGMs with DL to create a *generative DL* framework.

6.2 Generative models

PGMs are powerful techniques that are capable of capturing implicit relationship between the attributes of a dataset. This section begins by introducing the PMF, which will be followed by the discussion of two topic models, namely, (1) PLSA and (2) LDA. Specifically, we will show how to reframe the generative principle of topic models for recommender systems and how to integrate PMF with topic models to create hybrid recommendation systems. The topics discussed in this section will serve as fundamentals to understand advanced recommendation models such as deep generative models that will be discussed in the later part of this chapter.

6.2.1 Probabilistic matrix factorization

MF [15] and its probabilistic counterpart PMF [1] are classic model-based techniques for CF-based recommendation. Unlike MF, the PMF follows a generative approach which allows the model to seamlessly integrate with topics models such as LDA and generative DL models such as VAEs. From simple addition of attributes to a more complex change in the generative process, researchers have experimented with several variations of PMF. For example [16], incorporate travel distance, utility index and popularity of locations into PMF for point-of-interest (POI) recommendation and [17] introduce a new distribution into PMF to create social Poisson factorization. The graphical structure of PMF is shown in Figure 6.2, where v represents the latent vector of an item, u represents the latent vector of a user. The plate notations I and J denote the total number of users and items, respectively. PMF assumes that both the users and the items have their own respective latent attributes u and v and the observed rating r_{ij} is generated from these latent attributes. This generative process is shown in Algorithm 1 where the ratings r_{ij} could be categorical or binary valued and K is the number of latent attributes. It should be noted that when $r_{ij} = 0$, there

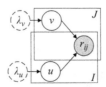

Figure 6.2   Graphical structure of the probabilistic matrix factorization

are two ways to interpret this scenario: (1) a user is not interested in item j or (2) a user is unaware of this item. To resolve this ambiguity, a confidence parameter c_{ij} is introduced where c_{ij} is large when r_{ij} is trusted more and low otherwise.

Algorithm 1: Generative process of the PMF

---

1 **for** *each user $i \in I$* **do**
2 $\quad|\quad$ draw a user latent factor $u_i \sim \mathcal{N}(0, \lambda_u^{-1} I_K)$
3 **end**
4 **for** *each item $j \in J$* **do**
5 $\quad|\quad$ draw item latent factor: $v_i \sim \mathcal{N}(0, \lambda_v^{-1} I_K)$
6 **end**
7 **for** *each user-item pair (i,j)* **do**
8 $\quad|\quad$ draw a rating $r_{ij} \sim \mathcal{N}(u_i^T v_j, c_{i,j}^{-1})$
9 **end**

Parameter inference: The objective of the PMF model is to estimate the following posterior distribution:

$$P(U, V|R) \propto P(R|U, V) \cdot P(U) \cdot P(V) \tag{6.1}$$

parameters U and V are learned using the *maximum a posteriori* (MAP) estimate. Expanding the above likelihood using the graphical structure and taking the negative log of the resultant expression produces the following equation:

$$-ln\, P(U, V|R) \propto \frac{c_{ij}}{\lambda^2} \sum_{(i,j) \in R} (r_{i,j} - u_i^T v_j)^2 + \frac{1}{\lambda_u^2} \sum_{i,K} u_{i,k}^2 + \frac{1}{\lambda_v^2} \sum_{j,k} v_{j,k}^2 \tag{6.2}$$

One can observe that the above equation is simply the squared error between the observed and the predicted rating along with some regularization terms λ_v and λ_u. Parameters U and V can be obtained by performing gradient descent.

Rating prediction: After learning the parameters, the predicted rating of an item j by a user i can be estimated by taking the dot product of the user and the item latent vector as follows:

$$\widetilde{r_{ij}} \approx u_i^T \cdot v_j \tag{6.3}$$

6.2.2   *Probabilistic latent semantic analysis*

PLSA was originally proposed as a topic model for document clustering [2] and later introduced as a model for CF-based recommendation by Hofmann *et al.* [18].

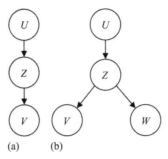

(a)   (b)

Figure 6.3   Graphical structure of PLSA models: (a) shows the graphical structure of simple CF-based PLSA and (b) shows the hybrid-PLSA that incorporates content information

Since then, it has been extended by several researchers to incorporate content information in the form of text [19], social network information [20] and geo-location information [21] to create hybrid recommender systems. The graphical structure of the CF-PLSA and the hybrid PLSA (H-PLSA) is shown in Figure 6.3(a) and (b), respectively. Here, $U = \{u_j\}_1^U$ denotes the set of users, $V = \{v_i\}_1^V$ denotes the set of items, $W = \{w_i\}_1^W$ are the set of words for an item v_i and $Z = \{z_i\}_1^Z$ is the set of latent attributes (or topics). The generative algorithm of PLSA assumes that users have some interests Z based on which they choose an item V. In reality, the interests of users are not observed; hence, the objective is to infer the latent attribute Z using the observed variables U and V (and W in case of H-PLSA).

Parameter inference: The central inferential problem of H-PLSA is to estimate the following posterior probability.

$$P(z|u, v, w) = \frac{P(u)P(z|u)P(i|z)P(w|z)}{\sum_z P(u)P(z|u)P(v|z)P(w|z)} \tag{6.4}$$

where $n(u, v, w)$ is the number of times a user chooses an item v that has the content (i.e., word) w. Since, the variable z is latent, explicitly finding the maximum likelihood estimates of the parameters is hard. Therefore, maximization is done over the expected value of the log-likelihood as follows:

$$\mathbb{E}(\mathscr{L}) = \sum_{U,V,W} n(u, v, w)Q(z) \sum_z \log P(u)P(z|u)P(v|z)P(w|z) \tag{6.5}$$

where the Q-function $Q(z)$ is generally set to the posterior $P(z|u, v, w)$. The expected likelihood function is solved by introducing Lagrange multipliers and taking the partial derivatives of (6.5) w.r.t. $P(u), P(u|z)$, $P(v|z)$ and $P(w|z)$ to yield the following expressions:

$$P(u) \propto \sum_{V,W,Z} n(u, v, w)P(z|u, v, w) \tag{6.6a}$$

$$P(v|z) \propto \sum_{U,W} n(u, v, w)P(z|u, v, w) \tag{6.6b}$$

$$P(w|z) \propto \sum_{U,V} n(u, v, w)P(z|u, v, w) \tag{6.6c}$$

$$P(z|u) \propto \sum_{V,W} n(u, v, w)P(z|u, v, w) \tag{6.6d}$$

Using (6.4) and (6.6)(a)–(d), the expectation maximization (EM) algorithm can be explained as follows:

1. **Initialization:** Begin by randomly initializing the parameters $P(u)$, $P(u|z)$, $P(v|z)$ and $P(w|z)$.
2. **E-step:** Estimate the posterior $P(z|u, v, w)$ using (6.4).
3. **M step:** Use the newly calculated posterior from **Step 2** to recalculate the parameters using expressions (6.6)(a)–(d).
4. Repeat **Steps 2 and 3** until convergence.

It should be noted that the parameter inference of CF-PLSA (Figure 6.3(a)) is exactly same as that of H-PLSA, except it does not include the term $P(w|z)$.

Item recommendation: The convergence of the EM algorithm results in learning the parameter z and consequently the probabilities in (6.6)(a)–(d). Given a user u, the predicted score of an item v can be obtained by marginalizing the contents W and the topics Z of the likelihood function as follows:

$$P(v|u) \propto \sum_{W} \sum_{Z} P(u, v, w, z) \tag{6.7}$$

6.2.3   *Latent Dirichlet allocation*

LDA is the most widely used topic model for document and word clustering [3]. The generative process of words and documents is very similar to that of PLSA; however, LDA introduces additional constraints in the form of Dirichlet priors that smoothens the document topic proportion and the word topic proportion which alleviates the problem of overfitting. The algorithm of LDA is usually explained from a perspective of document and word generation. Nonetheless, similar to PLSA, LDA can also be used for CF-based recommendation for implicit ratings. For example, in [22], the authors use LDA for location-based recommendation, [23] propose a generative group recommendation model for crowdfunding domains and [24] recommend sequence of POIs for travelers by incorporating temporal, historical and popularity-based features into a unified LDA model. Figure 6.4(a) shows a toy example of an LDA-based

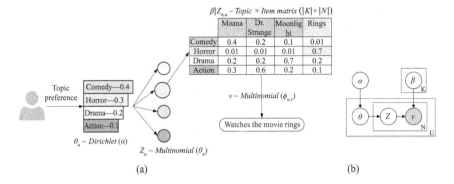

Figure 6.4 *Generative framework of recommendation using LDA topic model:*
(a) shows a toy example of the movie-selection process of a user and
(b) represents the formal graphical structure of the model

recommender system, which illustrates the decision-making process of a user u to watch a movie v. In this example, there are four topics (i.e., a distribution θ) that are color coded and four movies, which are depicted as columns of the ϕ matrix. The following steps delineate the generative process of LDA.

- A user has interests over *multiple topics* with different proportions which follows a Dirichlet distribution θ with hyperparameter α.
- From the topical interests θ, he then picks a single topic z (denoted by the color coded coins) using a multinomial distribution. In this example, the user picks the topic *horror* that is denoted by the orange coin.
- To watch a movie, he then consults a topic-movie matrix ϕ, which indicates probability of a movie v belonging to a topic z and picks a single movie that matches his topical interests using a multinomial distribution. In Figure 6.4, the user picks the movie *Rings* that corresponds to the genre *horror*.

However, in reality, we do not observe the topic selection z, which implies both the user-topic proportion θ and the movie-topic proportion ϕ are not observed. The only observed variables are the set of users $U = \{u_i\}_1^U$ and their corresponding item selections $N_u = \{v_{ju}\}_{j=1}^N$. Therefore, the central inferential problem of LDA is to estimate θ and ϕ from the observed variables v and u. The formal representation of LDA's graphical model is shown in Figure 6.4(b).

Parameter inference: The posterior of LDA is defined as follows:

$$P(\theta, z | v, \alpha, \beta) = \frac{P(\theta, z, v | \alpha, \beta)}{P(v | \alpha, \beta)} \tag{6.8}$$

By examining the graphical structure of the model, the likelihood for a single user u can be expanded as follows:

$$P(\theta, z, v | \alpha, \beta) = P(v | \beta, z) P(z | \theta) P(\theta | \alpha) \tag{6.9}$$

where $P(\theta|\alpha)$ is the Dirichlet distribution and $P(v|\beta, z)$ is the $K \times V$ probability matrix β. Substituting these values in the likelihood function results in the following expression:

$$P(\theta, z, w | \alpha, \beta) = \left(\frac{\Gamma(\sum_{k=1}^{K} \alpha_k)}{\prod_{k=1}^{K} \Gamma(\alpha_k)} \prod_{k=1}^{K} \theta_k^{\alpha_k - 1} \right) \prod_{i=1}^{U} \prod_{k=1}^{K} \prod_{j=1}^{V} (\theta_k \beta_{k,j})^{w_i^j z_i^k} \qquad (6.10)$$

the normalizing factor of (6.8) is defined as follows:

$$P(v | \alpha, \beta) = \frac{\Gamma(\sum_{k=1}^{K} \alpha_k)}{\prod_{k=1}^{K} \Gamma(\alpha_k)} \int \prod_{k=1}^{K} \theta_k^{\alpha_k - 1} \prod_{i=1}^{U} \sum_{k=1}^{K} \prod_{j=1}^{V} (\theta_k \beta_{k,j})^{w_i^j z_i^k} d\theta \qquad (6.11)$$

The above expression is similar to the likelihood except for the marginalization integral θ and the summation over the topic space $\{z_k\}_1^K$. However, this normalizing factor is intractable to compute. This is because, in the graphical model of LDA (Figure 6.4(b)) since v is observed, there is a coupling between θ and β. Therefore, when taking the log of (6.11) it is not possible to separate parameters θ and β. To overcome this problem, LDA tries to approximate the parameters using Gibbs sampling or variational inference (VI). The prior approximates the parameters by drawing MCMC samples from the posterior, while the latter achieves this objective by optimizing the evidence lower bound (ELBO) of the likelihood function. Here, we restrict our explanation to the VI technique. Readers interested in Gibbs sampling-based inference are suggested to refer to the tutorial on parameter estimation for text analysis [25].

The VI solves the problem of coupling by assuming that the distribution θ and β depends only on their respective variational parameters γ and ϕ [26,27]. Under this assumption, the ELBO can be stated as follows:

$$ln\,P(v | \alpha, \beta) = \mathscr{L}(\alpha, \beta) + KL(q(\theta, z | \lambda, \phi) || P(\theta, z | v, \alpha, \beta)) \qquad (6.12)$$

The objective of VI is to make $\mathscr{L}(\alpha, \beta)$ as close as possible to $ln\,P(v | \alpha, \beta)$. In other words, the goal is to learn the parameters γ and ϕ which minimizes the KL divergence between the variational distribution $q(\theta, z | \cdot)$ and the true posterior $P(\theta, z | \cdot)$. One way of achieving this objective is to use iterative fixed-point method, which yields the following update expressions:

$$\phi_{uk} \propto \beta_{kv_u} \exp\{\mathbb{E}[\log(\theta_k) | \gamma]\} \qquad (6.13)$$

$$\gamma_k = \alpha_k + \sum_{i=1}^{U} \phi_{ik} \qquad (6.14)$$

where the expectation is defined as follows:

$$\mathbb{E}_q[\log(\theta_k) | \gamma] = \psi(\gamma_k) - \psi\left(\sum_{k=1}^{K} \gamma_k \right) \qquad (6.15)$$

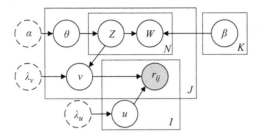

Figure 6.5   Graphical structure of the collaborative topic regression (CTR) model

where ψ is the digamma function. With the update expressions defined, the variational parameters can be estimated using EM algorithm as follows:

- **E-step**: Randomly assign some initial values for α and β. For every user $u \in U$, find the optimal values of the variational parameters γ and ϕ using (6.13) and (6.14), respectively.
- **M-step**: Using the updated ϕ and γ from the E-step maximizes the following lower bound with respect to α and β.

$$\mathcal{L}(\alpha, \beta) = \sum_{i=1}^{U} \log P(v_i | \alpha, \beta) \qquad (6.16)$$

Item recommendation: Once the EM algorithm converges, it returns the word-topic distribution β and the document-topic hyperparameter α. The user-topic distribution θ can be obtained by normalizing α over the set of topics K. The predicted score of a user i for an item j is defined as follows:

$$\tilde{r}_{ij} \approx \theta_i^T \cdot \beta_j \qquad (6.17)$$

6.2.4   Collaborative topic models

Although topic models such as PLSA and LDA can be formulated as standalone hybrid recommendation models, this technique has not been widely acknowledged as the best way to integrate content with CF. In fact, the most popular way of creating a hybrid recommendation model is to infuse the generative framework of topic model into PMF to create *collaborative topic models*. The very first model that leveraged this technique is known as CTR [4]. Figure 6.5 shows the graphical structure of CTR where the bottom part is the PMF and the top part is the LDA topic model. Similar to PMF, CTR assumes that the observed rating r_{ij} is generated from the latent attributes of users and items, but unlike PMF, CTR assumes that a user i selects (or rates) an item j mostly based on its contents θ_j and the user might diverge from this decision by an offset distribution ϵ_j, which is drawn from the PMF part (i.e., CF part) of the CTR model (see Algorithm 2). In this way, the model seamlessly integrates both the content information of items and the rating information of users to create a hybrid recommendation framework.

Algorithm 2: Generative process of CTR

---

1 **for** *each user $i \in I$* **do**
2 | draw user latent vector $u_i \sim \mathcal{N}(0, \lambda^u_{-1} I_K)$
3 **end**
4 **for** *each item $j \in J$* **do**
5 | Draw topic proportions $\theta_j \sim Dirichlet(\alpha)$
6 | Draw item latent offset $\epsilon_j \sim \mathcal{N}(0, \lambda_v I_K)$
7 | Set the item latent vector $v_j = \epsilon_j + \theta_j$
8 | **for** *each word $n \in N$* **do**
9 | | Draw topic assignment $z_{jn} \sim Mult(\theta)$
10 | | Draw word $v_{jn} \sim Mult(\beta_{z_{jn}})$
11 | **end**
12 **end**
13 **for** *each user-item pair (i,j)* **do**
14 | Draw the rating $r_{ij} \sim \mathcal{N}(u_i^T v_j, c_{ij}^{-1})$
15 **end**

Parameter inference: There are four latent parameters in this model, namely, θ, ϕ, U and V. The authors adopt a MAP estimate to infer these parameters by maximizing the following log likelihood.

$$\mathcal{L} = -\frac{\lambda_u}{2} \sum_{i=1}^{I} u_i^T u_i - \frac{\lambda_v}{2} \sum_{j=1}^{J} (v_j - \theta_j)^T (v_j - \theta_j)$$

$$+ \sum_{j=1}^{J} \sum_{n=1}^{N} \log \left(\sum_k \theta_{jk} \beta_{k,w_{jn}} \right) - \sum_{i,j} \frac{c_{i,j}}{2} (r_{ij} - u_i^T v_j)^2 \qquad (6.18)$$

Coordinate ascent is used to learn parameters by iteratively optimizing the CF variables U, V and the item-topic proportions θ. The procedure of learning U and V remains same as that of PMF (Section 6.2.1). Given U and V, the log likelihood function for the topic proportions is derived by applying Jensen's inequality as follows:

$$\mathcal{L} \geq \frac{\lambda_u}{2} (v_j - \theta_j)^T (v_j - \theta_j) + \sum_n^N \sum_k^K \phi_{jnk} (\log \theta_{jk} \beta_{k,w_{jn}} - \log \phi_{jnk})$$

$$= \mathcal{L}(\theta_j, \phi_j) \qquad (6.19)$$

where ϕ_{jnk} is the variational distribution $q(z_{jn} = k)$ [3]. $\mathcal{L}(\theta_j, \phi_j)$ gives the tight lower bound of $\mathcal{L}(\theta_j)$, and projection gradient [28] is used to obtain parameter θ. After estimating the user latent attribute U and item latent attribute V, parameters ϕ, β can be obtained using the M-step update of LDA that was explained in Section 6.2.3.

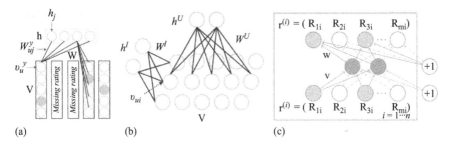

Figure 6.6   An illustration of RBM and autoencoder-based recommender systems:
(a) RBM-CF, (b) UI-RBM-CF and (c) AutoRec

Rating prediction: Once the parameters are learned, the ratings are estimated based on the availability of information, i.e., when user–item ratings are available, the ratings are estimated as follows:

$$\tilde{r}_{ij} \approx (u_i)^T (\theta_j + \epsilon_j) \tag{6.20}$$

when the ratings are sparse (i.e., cold start), the predicted ratings are obtained using the following equation:

$$\tilde{r} \approx (u_i)^T \theta_j \tag{6.21}$$

6.3   Deep learning for recommender systems

DL has demonstrated a great capability in learning useful representations of data in domains such as computer vision, natural language processing and speech recognition. The impressive feature-learning ability of DL has attracted the attention of researchers in recommender system community. Recently, DL models such as AutoRec [10], NCF [11] and visual-content recommendation [29] have shown significant improvement over traditional recommender systems. In this section, we will briefly introduce representative recommender systems based on DL algorithms, which includes restricted Boltzmann machine, AE, multilayer perceptron and long short-term memory (LSTM).

6.3.1   Restricted Boltzmann-machine-based collaborative filtering

RBM-CF [9] is probably the first recommendation model that built atop DL. An illustration of RBM-CF is shown in Figure 6.6(a). It is composed of two layers, i.e., input layer V and hidden layer h. The input/visible layer $V \in \{0, 1\}^{K \times m}$ encodes the ratings of a user to the items, where m is the total number of items and K is the rating range, i.e., the rating is from 1 to K. Each rating is converted to one-hot-coding. For example, the first column of V as shown in Figure 6.6(a) is $[0, 0, 0, 1, 0]$, denoting that the rating the user give to the first item is 4. The hidden layer $h \in \{0, 1\}^{F \times 1}$ is the corresponding latent features of a user we want to learn, where F is number of latent dimensions. The joint distribution of V and h is defined as

$$P(V,h) = \frac{\exp(-E(V,h))}{\sum_{V',h'} \exp(-E(V',h'))} \qquad (6.22)$$

with the energy term $E(V,h)$ given as

$$E(V,h) = -\sum_{i=1}^{m}\sum_{j=1}^{F}\sum_{k=1}^{K} W_{ij}^k h_j v_i^k + \sum_{i=1}^{m} \log Z_i - \sum_{i=1}^{m}\sum_{k=1}^{K} v_i^k b_i^k - \sum_{j=1}^{F} h_j b_j \qquad (6.23)$$

where W_{ij}^k is the weight between the rating k of item i and the hidden unit j, which models the interaction between the visible and hidden layers, and b_i^k is the corresponding bias. $Z_i = \sum_{k=1}^{K} \exp(b_i^k + \sum_j h_j W_{ij}^k)$ is the normalization term that ensures $\sum_{k=1}^{K} p(v_i^k = 1|h) = 1$. With the joint distribution, we can derive the conditional distributions as

$$p(v_i^r = 1|h) = \frac{\exp(b_i^r + \sum_{j=1}^{F} h_j W_{ij}^r)}{\sum_{k=1}^{K} \exp(b_i^l + \sum_{j=1}^{F} W_{ij}^k)}, \quad p(h_j = 1|V)$$

$$= \sigma\left(b_j + \sum_{i=1}^{m}\sum_{k=1}^{K} v_i^k W_{ij}^k\right) \qquad (6.24)$$

The goal of training RBM-CF is to learn the weights and bias by maximizing the likelihood $\sum_n P(V^{(n)})$, where $V^{(n)}$ means the ratings of user n. After the model is trained, $p(v_i^r = 1|h)$ can be used for rating prediction. RBM-CF clamps a given user's ratings on the visible layer. Similarly, we can easily design an item-based RBM-CF if we clamp a given item's ratings on the visible layer. Georgiev *et al.* [30] proposed UI-RBM-CF, which combines the user-based and item-based RBM-CF in a unified framework. In the case, the visible units are determined both by user and item hidden units. An illustration of UI-RBM-CF is shown in Figure 6.6(b), where h^U is the latent feature for users and h^I is the latent feature for items. W^U and W^I are the weights for modeling users and items, respectively.

6.3.2 Autoencoder for recommender systems

AE is another widely used DL model for recommendation. An AE is a neural network trained to learn latent representation that is good at reconstructing its input. AE is strongly related to principle component analysis. In fact, a one hidden layer AE without nonlinear activation function is similar to PCA, which is one of the reason AE can be used for recommendation. AutoRec [10] applies AE for rating prediction. AutoRec takes user partial vectors $r^{(u)}$ or item partial vectors $r^{(i)}$ as input and aims to reconstruct them at output layer. Based on the input type, it has two variants, i.e., Item-based AutoRec (I-AutoRec) and User-based AutoRec. Figure 6.6(c) gives an illustration of I-AutoRec. Given the input $r^{(i)}$, AutoRec encodes it to latent representation as

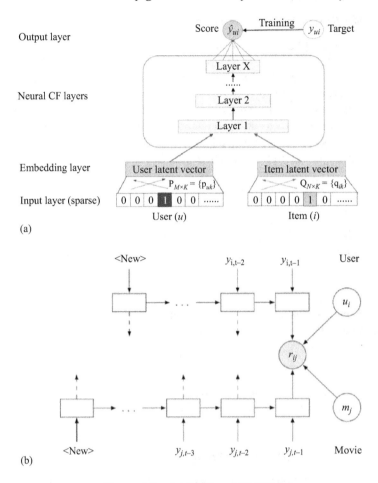

Figure 6.7 (a) NCF and (b) RRN

$g(V \cdot r + \mu) + b$, where g is some activation function such as sigmoid and V is the weight matrix and μ is the bias. The decoder then reconstructs the latent representation as $f(W \cdot g(V \cdot r + \mu) + b)$, where f is another activation function and W and b are weights and bias, respectively. The objective function of I-AutoRec is then to learn weights that can approximate the input as

$$\sum_{r \in R} \|r - h(r; \theta)\|_f^2, \qquad h(r; \theta) = f(W \cdot g(V \cdot r + \mu) + b) \qquad (6.25)$$

Collaborative filtering neural network [31] further extends AutoRec by using DAE. The structure of DAE is the same as shown in Figure 6.6(c), except that the input data is first corrupted with noises and the AE need to reconstruct the uncorrupted data. The advantage of using DAE is to alleviate overfitting.

6.3.3 Multilayer perceptron based recommender systems

Recently, NCF [11] based on multilayer perceptron is proposed, which also shows promising results. Unlike the reconstruction-based methods, such as RBM-CF and I-AutoRec, NCF fuses MF with MLP, which tries to capture the nonlinear two-way interaction between users and items. The architecture of the NCF is shown in Figure 6.7(a). It takes in a (user, item) pair as input to a multilayer perceptron. The user and item are represented using one-hot-coding, which are first projected to latent representation as shown in the embedding layer. The projection is simply the multiplication of sparse user/item representation with the embedding matrix, i.e., $U^T \cdot s_u^{user}$ and $V^T \cdot s_i^{item}$. The embedding matrix then goes to Layer 1 of NCF layers and the Output Layer gives the rating score as

$$\hat{r}_{ui} = f(U^T \cdot s_u^{user}, V^T \cdot s_i^{item} | U, V, \theta) \tag{6.26}$$

where $f(\cdot)$ is the multilayer perceptron and θ is the parameters of the network. For explicit ratings, the loss function is defined as the weighted square error

$$\mathcal{L} = \sum_{(u,i) \in \mathscr{O} \cup \mathscr{O}^-} w_{ui} \cdot (r_{ui} - \hat{r}_{ui})^2 \tag{6.27}$$

where $\mathscr{O}$ is the set of positive training data and $\mathscr{O}^-$ is a subset of missing ratings. For implicit ratings, the cross-entropy loss is used

$$\mathcal{L} = - \sum_{(u,i) \in \mathscr{O} \cup \mathscr{O}^-} r_{ui} \log \hat{r}_{ui} + (1 - r_{ui}) \log (1 - \hat{r}_{ui}) \tag{6.28}$$

One thing to note is that traditional MF is a special case of NCF by removing the NCF layers. In other words, without the NCF layers, (6.26) reduces to $\hat{r}_{ui} = (U^T \cdot s_u^{user}) \cdot (V^T \cdot s_i^{item})^T$.

6.3.4 RNN/LSTM for recommendation

As LSTM is good at modeling sequence data and user rating history is also sequential, LSTM is of great potential for temporal/dynamic recommender systems. One representative work of is RRN proposed in [12], which exploits LSTMs to model the seasonal evolution of items and changes of user preferences over time for rating prediction. As shown in Figure 6.7(b), RRN uses two LSTMs as the building block to model dynamic user state of user and item, respectively. The input to the LSTM for modeling user is a sequence of rating actions of the user. Specifically, the sequence $y_1, y_2, \ldots, y_t$ is defined as

$$y_t = W_{embed}[x_t, 1_{newbie}, \tau_t, \tau_{t-1}] \tag{6.29}$$

where W_{embed} is the transformation to be learned to project source information into embedding space. $x_t \in \mathbb{R}^m$ denotes the rating for a given user at time t. $x_{tj} = k$ if the user rated item j with the score k at time step t and $x_{tj} = 0$ otherwise. τ_t is the wall clock at time step t and $1_{newbie} = 1$ indicates that the user is new. With such inputs, the users latent representation at time t is

$$u_t = LSTM(u_{t-1}, y_t) \tag{6.30}$$

Note that at time $t - 1$, user's latent feature is u_{t-1}. And LSTM computes u_t based on u_{t-1} and $t - 1$ so as to capture the evolving of user preferences. Similarly, the input to the LSTM for modeling items is a set of ratings users give to this item and the latent representation of items v_t can be calculated using LSTM. In addition to the changing user and item latent features, RRN also assumes that users have static features, which are denoted as u_i and m_j in the figure. With user i's dynamic latent features u_{it} and static latent features u_i, and the item j's dynamic latent feature v_{jt} and static latent features v_j, the rating is predicted as

$$\hat{r}_{ij|t} = u_{it}^T v_{it} + u_i^T v_{it} \tag{6.31}$$

The objective function is then to learn the weights of LSTMs and the static latent features to make $r_{ij|t}$ close to the ground truth.

6.4 Deep generative models

The CTR (Section 6.2.4) is a robust model that integrates LDA and PMF into a unified framework for recommendation. That being said, the performance of CTR strongly depends on the representation capability of the LDA topic model. Unfortunately, the latent representation learned by LDA is not effective when the auxiliary information is very sparse. The previous section showed that DL models are extremely good in learning the representations of data. However, when it comes to recommendation, PMF and its variants still reign as the state-of-the-art techniques due to their ability to capture and learn implicit relationship between items (and users) [32]. This necessitates the integration of generative and DL models to create a unified framework that can provide the best of both worlds. To this end, we now introduce two most recent papers on *generative DL*, namely, CDAE [13] and CVAE [14].

6.4.1 *Collaborative denoising autoencoders*

The CDAE [13] is a hierarchical Bayesian model that bridges the gap between generative models and DL for recommendation. Figure 6.8 shows the graphical structure of CDAE, which is composed of two parts: (a) a stacked DAE (SDAE) [33] and (b) the PMF component. The DAE is a feedforward neural network for learning latent representations (or encoding) of the input data. Similar to AEs, the DAE has an input layer, a hidden layer, and an output layer. The difference between these two models lies in the input layer, where, in DAE, the input is corrupted before being passed on to the network. The AE is then trained to *reconstruct the original input from the corrupted version*. Figure 6.8(a) shows the graphical structure of CDAE and (b) explains the layers of SDAE. Here, W denotes the weights of the neural network, X_c is the *corrupted* data (i.e., the input layer) and X_0 is the *original* data of size $J \times S$, where J is the number items and S is the size of vocabulary. The input X is usually the textual contents of items such as product reviews and images. l indicates a specific layer of the neural network, L is the total number of layers and $\{g_1, \ldots, g_l\}$ are the

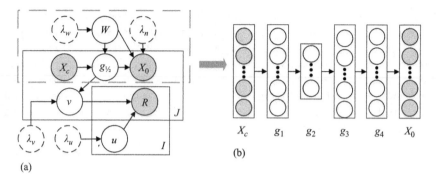

*Figure 6.8   Graphical structure of (a) the collaborative denoising autoencoder
(CDAE) and (b) the expanded portion of the stacked denoising
autoencoder with four hidden layers*

intermediate layers (the function approximators) of the SDAE. The item-latent vector
v, the user latent-vector u and the observed rating R are same as that of CTR.

Algorithm 3 delineates the generative process CDAE, where lines 1–9 illustrate
the DAE block (i.e., the orange box in Figure 6.8) and lines 10–19 illustrate the

---

Algorithm 3: Generative process of CDAE

---

1 **for** *each layer $l \in L$ of SDAE* **do**
2   **for** *each column n of the weight matrix $\mathbf{W}_l$* **do**
3   Draw $\mathbf{W}_{l,*n} \sim \mathcal{N}(0, \lambda_w^{-1}\mathbf{I}_{K_l})$
4   **end**
5   Draw bias vector $\mathbf{b}_l \sim \mathcal{N}(0, \lambda_w^{-1}\mathbf{I}_{K_l})$
6   **for** *each row j of $\mathbf{g}_l$* **do**
7   Draw $\mathbf{g}_{l,j*} \sim \mathcal{N}(\sigma(\mathbf{g}_{l-1,j*}\mathbf{W}_l + \mathbf{b}_l), \lambda_D^{-1}\mathbf{I}_{K_l})$
8   **end**
9 **end**
10 **for** *each item $j \in J$* **do**
11   Draw original input $\mathbf{X}_{0,j*} \sim \mathcal{N}(\mathbf{g}_{L,j*}, \lambda_n^{-1}\mathbf{I}_j)$
12   Draw the latent item offset vector $\epsilon_j \sim \mathcal{N}(0, \lambda_v^{-1}I_K)$
13   Set latent item vector as $v_j = \epsilon_j + \mathbf{g}_{L/2,j*}$
14 **end**
15 **for** *each user $u \in U$* **do**
16   Draw $u_i \sim \mathcal{N}(0, \lambda_u^{-1}I_K)$
17 **end**
18 **for** *each user-item pair (i,j)* **do**
19   Draw $R_{i,j} \sim \mathcal{N}(u_i^T v_j, C_{ij}^{-1})$
20 **end**

PMF block. Here, $X_{0,j*}$ indicates the bag of words vector of an item j, and $g_{l,j*}$ is the row of the layer g_l. Essentially, CDAE follows the same generative principle as that of the CTR that was discussed in Algorithm 2. One key difference is that, instead of using LDA, the CDAE uses a DAE to embed the content information of items in a latent space (i.e., lines 11–12). One can observe that the content of the latent item vector v_j is drawn from $g_{L/2}$, which is the middle layer of SDAE. The objective of CDAE is defined as follows:

$$\arg\min_{W_l,b_l} ||X_0 - X_L||_F^2 + \lambda \sum ||W_l||_F^2 \tag{6.32}$$

where λ is the regularization parameter and $|| \cdot ||_F$ is the Frobenius norm. Similar to CTR, the posterior $P(U, V, g_l|\cdot)$ is derived using a MAP estimate. The likelihood of CDAE is defined as follows:

$$\mathcal{L}(U, V, W_l, b_l) = -\frac{\lambda_u}{2} \sum_i ||u_i||_2^2 - \frac{\lambda_w}{2} \sum_l (||W_l||_F^2 + ||b_l||_2^2)$$

$$-\frac{\lambda_v}{2} \sum_j ||v_j - g_{L/2,j*}||_2^2 - \frac{\lambda_n}{2} \sum_j ||g_{L,j*} - X_{0,j*}||_2^2$$

$$-\frac{\lambda_s}{2} \sum_l \sum_j ||\sigma(g_{l-1,j*}W_l + b_l) - g_{l,j*}||_2^2$$

$$-\sum_{i,j} \frac{C_{i,j}}{2}(R_{ij} - u_i^T v_j)^2 \tag{6.33}$$

To obtain parameters u_i and v_j, coordinate ascent is used. Given U and V, the weights W_l and biases b_l can be learned using back propagation. This process is repeated iteratively until a local optimum for $\mathcal{L}$ is reached.

Rating prediction: After obtaining the user and item latent vectors and the weights of SDAE, the ratings of an item j by a user i can be estimated as follows:

$$E[R_{ij}|D] \approx E[u_i|D]^T(E[g_{L/2,j*}(W)|D] + E[\epsilon_j|D]) \tag{6.34}$$

where $E(\cdot)$ denotes the expected value, and D is the observed dataset.

6.4.2 Collaborative variational autoencoder

Although CDAE is a powerful DL model that delivers excellent recommendation performance, it is not without its flaws. First, the denoising component of the model works by corrupting the input data, which is extremely data specific and requires specialized corruption schemes that are designed for the type of data. In other words, a corruption scheme that is used for image data cannot be applied over text data and vice versa. This in turn degrades the quality of the learned representations. Second, the DAE used in CDAE does not have a probabilistic approach; instead, it has a frequentist approach, which makes it difficult to perform Bayesian inference when integrating with other generative models. To overcome these limitations, Li *et al.* [14] propose a model called CVAE that replaces the DAE part of CDAE with a VAE [34].

The graphical structure of CVAE is represented in Figure 6.9 where the top part (the red box) indicates the VAE component and the bottom part indicates the PMF component. The integration of VAE with PMF results in two major advantages. First, VAE induces stochasticity in the latent layer Z, which results in better representations of the latent feature space compared to the deterministic AEs [35]. Second, the probabilistic nature VAE allows the model to seamlessly integrate with other generative models such as PMF; this enables powerful Bayesian inference techniques such as MCMC and VI. The generative process of CVAE is shown in Algorithm 4. For the most part, the algorithm remains similar to CDAE with the major difference in steps 14–19. This block illustrates the sampling process of mean μ covariance Σ and the latent layer Z that are unique to VAE. For details on the working of VAE, readers are suggested to refer the paper by Kingma *et al.* [34].

Algorithm 4: Generative process of CVAE

---

1 **for** *each layer $l \in L$ of VAE* **do**
2   **for** *each column n of the weight matrix $\mathbf{W}_l$* **do**
3   │   Draw $\mathbf{W}_{l,*n} \sim \mathcal{N}(0, \lambda_w^{-1} \mathbf{I}_{K_l})$
4   **end**
5   Draw bias vector $\mathbf{b}_l \sim \mathcal{N}(0, \lambda_w^{-1} \mathbf{I}_{K_l})$
6   **for** *each row j of $\mathbf{g}_l$* **do**
7   │   Draw $\mathbf{g}_{l,j*} \sim \mathcal{N}(\sigma(\mathbf{g}_{l-1,j*}\mathbf{W}_l + \mathbf{b}_l), \lambda_D^{-1} \mathbf{I}_{K_l})$
8   **end**
9 **end**
10 **Decoder**
11 **for** *each item $j \in J$* **do**
12 │   Draw $\mathbf{X}_j \sim \mathcal{N}(\mathbf{g}_L, \lambda_n^{-1} \mathbf{I}_V)$
13 **end**
14 **Encoder**
15 **for** *each item $j \in J$* **do**
16 │   Draw $\mu_j, \sim \mathcal{N}(\mathbf{g}_L \mathbf{W}_\mu + \mathbf{b}_\mu, \lambda_n^{-1} \mathbf{I}_K)$
17 │   Draw $\Sigma_j, \sim \mathcal{N}(\mathbf{g}_L \mathbf{W}_\Sigma + \mathbf{b}_\Sigma, \lambda_n^{-1} \mathbf{I}_K)$
18 │   Draw $Z_j \sim \mathcal{N}(\mu, \Sigma)$
19 **end**

Parameter inference: Essentially, there are two ways to learn the parameters of CVAE: (1) a partial VI that is more like a MAP estimate and (2) a full VI. Here, we restrict our explanation to the prior. For details on the full variational estimate, readers are suggested to refer to [14]. The central inferential problem of CVAE is to learn the posterior distribution $P(Z, U, V | X, R)$. However, as is the case with LDA

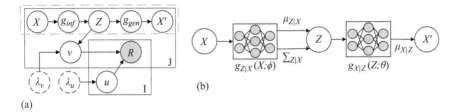

Figure 6.9   Collaborative variational autoencoder: (a) shows the integrated graphical structure of PMF and VAE and (b) shows the content generation part using VAE

(Section 6.2.3), this posterior is intractable to compute; consequently, we resort to VI. The ELBO for this model is given as follows:

$$\log P(X, R) \geq E_q \left[\log P(Z, U, V, R, X) - \log q(U, V, Z) \right] \tag{6.35}$$

Here, the variational distribution q is over three latent variables, namely, U, V and Z. The RHS of the above expression (i.e., the likelihood term) can be expanded as follows:

$$\mathcal{L}(U, V, \theta, \phi) = E_{q_\phi(Z|\cdot)} \left[\log P_\theta(X|Z) - \mathcal{D}(q_\phi(Z|X) \| P_\theta(Z)) \right]$$
$$+ E_{q_\phi((Z|\cdot))} \left[\log P_\theta(V|Z) + \log P(R|U, V) + \log Pr(U) \right] \tag{6.36}$$

where ϕ and θ is the set of weights for the encoder and decoder networks, respectively. The first term of the above equation is simply the ELBO of VAE, while the second term is likelihood of PMF. One can observe that the ELBO of VAE has two parts, the first is simply the sum squared error between the predicted and actual inputs, while the second and the term $\mathcal{D}$ is the KL divergence between two multivariate normal distributions which is given as follows:

$$\mathcal{D}(q_\phi(Z|x) \| Pr(Z)) = -\frac{1}{2} \left(tr\left(\Sigma_\phi(x)\right) + \left(\mu_\phi(x)\right)^T \left(\mu_\phi(x)\right) - \log det\left(\Sigma_\phi(x)\right) \right) \tag{6.37}$$

In the likelihood function $\mathcal{L}(U, V, \theta, \phi)$, it is quite straightforward to take the gradient w.r.t. to θ; however, the gradient w.r.t. ϕ cannot be estimated since the sampling operation is not a continuous deterministic function. This in turn makes back-propagation unfeasible. To overcome this problem, a reparameterization trick is adopted to obtain samples of z from an isotropic normal distribution where $z = \mu_\phi(x) + \epsilon \odot \Sigma_\phi(x)$, $\epsilon \sim \mathcal{N}(0, \mathbf{I})$ and x is the attribute vector of a single item [34]. Substituting the corresponding distributions in 6.36, the following MAP estimate is obtained:

$$\mathcal{L}^{MAP^*}(U, V, \theta, \phi) = \mathcal{L}(\text{VAE}) - \sum_{i,j} \frac{C_{i,j}}{2} (R_{i,j} - U_i^T V_j)^2$$

$$- \frac{\lambda_U}{2} \sum_i \|U_i\|_2^2 - \frac{\lambda_V}{2} \sum_j E_{q_\phi(Z|\cdot)} \|V_j - Z_j\|_2^2 \tag{6.38}$$

where $\mathscr{L}(VAE)$ indicates the ELBO of VAE. Readers should note that the above expressions is not strictly a MAP estimate since the parameters parameter Z is still inferred using a variational distribution. Hence, we denote the above expression as $\mathscr{L}^{MAP*}$.

Rating prediction: After learning the parameters U, V and Z, for an observed data D the predicted rating for an item j by a user i can be obtained as follows:

$$\mathbb{E}[R_{ij}|D] \approx \mathbb{E}[u_i|D]^T(\mathbb{E}[v_j|D] + \mathbb{E}[z_j|D]) \tag{6.39}$$

If there are no ratings for an item v_j, the term $\mathbb{E}[v_j|D]$ will not have any effect over the above expression, and the predicted rating will be purely based on the content information of the item.

6.5   Summary

This chapter presents some recent trends in generative and DL models for recommendation systems. It begins by introducing classic generative models such as PMF and LDA and explains the methodology of integrating PMF with LDA to create a hybrid model called CTR. The second section introduces recommendation frameworks that are purely based on DL, where we discuss models such as RBM-CF, AutoRec, NCF and RRN. The final section of this chapter illustrates the strengths and weaknesses of generative and DL models and explains the methodology of merging these two techniques to create deep generative models such as CDAE and CVAE.

References

[1]   Mnih A, Salakhutdinov RR. Probabilistic matrix factorization. In: Advances in Neural Information Processing Systems; 2008. p. 1257–1264.

[2]   Hofmann T. Probabilistic latent semantic indexing. In: Proceedings of the 22nd Annual International ACM SIGIR Conference on Research and Development in Information Retrieval. ACM; 1999. p. 50–57.

[3]   Blei DM, Ng AY, Jordan MI. Latent Dirichlet allocation. The Journal of Machine Learning Research. 2003;3:993–1022.

[4]   Wang C, Blei DM. Collaborative topic modeling for recommending scientific articles. In: Proceedings of the 17th ACM SIGKDD International Conference on Knowledge Discovery and Data Mining. ACM; 2011. p. 448–456.

[5]   Schmidhuber J. Deep learning in neural networks: An overview. Neural Networks. 2015;61:85–117.

[6]   Covington P, Adams J, Sargin E. Deep neural networks for YouTube recommendations. In: Proceedings of the 10th ACM Conference on Recommender Systems. ACM; 2016. p. 191–198.

[7]   Cheng HT, Koc L, Harmsen J, et al. Wide & deep learning for recommender systems. In: Proceedings of the 1st Workshop on Deep Learning for Recommender Systems. ACM; 2016. p. 7–10.

[8] Okura S, Tagami Y, Ono S, *et al.* Embedding-based news recommendation for millions of users. In: Proceedings of the 23rd ACM SIGKDD International Conference on Knowledge Discovery and Data Mining. ACM; 2017. p. 1933–1942.

[9] Salakhutdinov R, Mnih A, Hinton G. Restricted Boltzmann machines for collaborative filtering. In: Proceedings of the 24th International Conference on Machine Learning. ACM; 2007. p. 791–798.

[10] Sedhain S, Menon AK, Sanner S, *et al.* AutoRec: Autoencoders meet collaborative filtering. In: Proceedings of the 24th International Conference on World Wide Web. ACM; 2015. p. 111–112.

[11] He X, Liao L, Zhang H, *et al.* Neural collaborative filtering. In: Proceedings of the 26th International Conference on World Wide Web. International World Wide Web Conferences Steering Committee; 2017. p. 173–182.

[12] Wu CY, Ahmed A, Beutel A, *et al.* Recurrent recommender networks. In: Proceedings of the Tenth ACM International Conference on Web Search and Data Mining. ACM; 2017. p. 495–503.

[13] Wang H, Wang N, Yeung DY. Collaborative deep learning for recommender systems. In: Proceedings of the 21th ACM SIGKDD International Conference on Knowledge Discovery and Data Mining. ACM; 2015. p. 1235–1244.

[14] Li X, She J. Collaborative variational autoencoder for recommender systems. In: Proceedings of the 23rd ACM SIGKDD International Conference on Knowledge Discovery and Data Mining. ACM; 2017. p. 305–314.

[15] Koren Y, Bell R, Volinsky C. Matrix factorization techniques for recommender systems. Computer. 2009;42(8):30–37.

[16] Liu B, Fu Y, Yao Z, *et al.* Learning geographical preferences for point-of-interest recommendation. In: Proceedings of the 19th ACM SIGKDD International Conference on Knowledge Discovery and Data Mining. ACM; 2013. p. 1043–1051.

[17] Chaney AJ, Blei DM, Eliassi-Rad T. A probabilistic model for using social networks in personalized item recommendation. In: Proceedings of the 9th ACM Conference on Recommender Systems. ACM; 2015. p. 43–50.

[18] Hofmann T, Puzicha J. Latent class models for collaborative filtering. In: IJCAI. vol. 99; 1999. p. 688–693.

[19] Popescul A, Pennock DM, Lawrence S. Probabilistic models for unified collaborative and content-based recommendation in sparse-data environments. In: Proceedings of the Seventeenth conference on Uncertainty in Artificial Intelligence. Morgan Kaufmann Publishers Inc.; 2001. p. 437–444.

[20] Ye M, Liu X, Lee WC. Exploring social influence for recommendation: A generative model approach. In: Proceedings of the 35th International ACM SIGIR Conference on Research and Development in Information Retrieval. ACM; 2012. p. 671–680.

[21] Yuan Q, Cong G, Ma Z, *et al.* Who, where, when and what: Discover spatio-temporal topics for twitter users. In: Proceedings of the 19th ACM SIGKDD International Conference on Knowledge Discovery and Data Mining. ACM; 2013. p. 605–613.

[22] Kurashima T, Iwata T, Hoshide T, *et al.* Geo topic model: Joint modeling of user's activity area and interests for location recommendation. In: Proceedings of the Sixth ACM International Conference on Web Search and Data Mining. ACM; 2013. p. 375–384.

[23] Rakesh V, Lee WC, Reddy CK. Probabilistic group recommendation model for crowdfunding domains. In: Proceedings of the Ninth ACM International Conference on Web Search and Data Mining. ACM; 2016. p. 257–266.

[24] Rakesh V, Jadhav N, Kotov A, *et al.* Probabilistic social sequential model for tour recommendation. In: Proceedings of the Tenth ACM International Conference on Web Search and Data Mining. ACM; 2017. p. 631–640.

[25] Heinrich G. Parameter estimation for text analysis. University of Leipzig, Tech Rep.; 2008.

[26] Blei DM, Kucukelbir A, McAuliffe JD. Variational inference: A review for statisticians. Journal of the American Statistical Association. 2017;112(518): 859–877.

[27] Wainwright MJ, Jordan MI. Graphical models, exponential families, and variational inference. Foundations and Trends® in Machine Learning. 2008; 1(1–2):1–305.

[28] Bertsekas DP. Nonlinear programming. Athena Scientific, Belmont, MA; 1999.

[29] Wang S, Wang Y, Tang J, *et al.* What your images reveal: Exploiting visual contents for point-of-interest recommendation. In: Proceedings of the 26th International Conference on World Wide Web. International World Wide Web Conferences Steering Committee; 2017. p. 391–400.

[30] Georgiev K, Nakov P. A non-IID framework for collaborative filtering with restricted Boltzmann machines. In: International Conference on Machine Learning; 2013. p. 1148–1156.

[31] Strub F, Mary J. Collaborative filtering with stacked denoising autoencoders and sparse inputs. In: NIPS Workshop on Machine Learning for eCommerce; 2015.

[32] Koller D, Friedman N. *Probabilistic Graphical Models: Principles and Techniques.* Cambridge, MA: MIT Press; 2009.

[33] Vincent P, Larochelle H, Lajoie I, *et al.* Stacked denoising autoencoders: Learning useful representations in a deep network with a local denoising criterion. Journal of Machine Learning Research. 2010;11:3371–3408.

[34] Kingma DP, Welling M. Auto-encoding variational Bayes. arXiv preprint arXiv:13126114; 2013.

[35] Rumelhart DE, Hinton GE, Williams RJ. Learning internal representations by error propagation. No. ICS-8506. California University, San Diego, La Jolla Institute for Cognitive Science; 1985.

Chapter 7
Recommendation algorithms for unstructured big data such as text, audio, image and video

Madjid Khalilian[1], Mahshid Alsadat Ehsaei[1], and Saloomeh TaheriFard[1]

In recent times, the recommender system (RS) played a significant role in assisting users select the ideal product from a huge amount of data. The gradually increasing amount of customers, services and online information due to yielding the large data analysis turns into a problem for service RSs. Approaches which are greatly successful cover a wide variety of recommendation tasks such as video, music, image, books.

The recommendation algorithms require a variety of parameters to propose suggestions for new users, and this is where limitations and challenges of the RSs emerge. Recommendation algorithms for unstructured big data and their challenges will be discussed in this chapter.

RS is an innovative technique which has transformed the content-based applications to customer centric ones. This method figures out what the customers exactly want; it can either be data or an item. Feature of collecting and computing information in recommendation techniques provide a better understanding among users and clients [1]. Large amount of data is being generated from radio-frequency identification and other sensors. Therefore, big data technique is being used to handle such large amount of data in producing recommendations. There are various applications which use Item based collaborative filtering (CF). For instance applications in business sections, e-business, recommendation of items in online shopping, recommendation of exciting sites, web browsing, discovering music, books, movies, etc. Considerable efforts in Collective Intelligence are the root of the RSs. The emergence of RS goes back to the 1990s, during the time when recommendations were only provided based on the rating structure. Over recent years, innumerable ways turn out to recognize user's interest for special items, including tagging, voting, reviewing or even the number of likes users provide. Besides, it can be in a form of a review written in blogs, descriptions about the item or a reply to an online community. In spite of how preferences are communicated or being presented, they should be defined as numerical values as described in [2].

[1]Department of Computer Engineering, Karaj Branch, Islamic Azad University, Iran

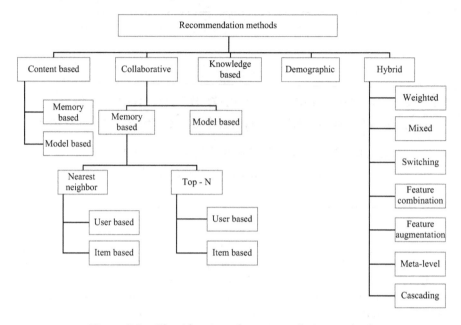

Figure 7.1   Classification of recommendation methods

7.1   Recommender methods

The various recommendation methods can be categorized into different types based on the information or knowledge source they develop to make the appropriate recommendations. The diagrammatic representation of the classification is shown in Figure 7.1. They are categorized as [1]

- content-based recommendations,
- collaborative recommendations,
- knowledge-based recommendations,
- demographic recommendations and
- hybrid recommendations.

7.1.1   Content-based recommendations

In content-based recommendation, the recommended items are based on the previously preferred items by the users [1]. In creating recommended applications, content is the foundation for recommender applications. These recommendations are totally based on item descriptions rather than the similarity of other users. Machine-learning algorithms are being used to induce a model of user preferences based on feature factors. There are various accessible contents, such as articles, photos, video, blogs, wikis, classification terms, polls and lists [3].

It can either be

- memory/heuristic based—term frequency, inverse document frequency (TF–IDF) text retrieval method or
- model based—uses decision trees, neural networks, Bayesian classifiers, clustering or vector-based representation.

Large number of approaches are available to study the model of content-based recommendations; however, if the content does not contain enough information, content-based recommendations would not be able to promise accurate predictions. Various limitations it encounters are being listed as follow: (1) limited content analysis: examining sufficient set of features that would represent the entire content sounds like a hard job to do. If the documents contain same terms and phrases, it is also difficult to examine whether the case is good or a bad one. Furthermore, it would not guarantee the quality of the document or item. For the case of multimedia data, audio streams, video streams and graphical images, extracting the feature factors turns up to be a complexity. (2) Overspecialization: you can label different titles for same events, e.g., different news article can have identical content with different headings. Billus and Pazzani in [4] recommended filtering out items that are too similar along with the items that are too different from each other. (3) Cold start: in cold start, lack of information about the user also makes it hard to recommend items to the users. There are two types of cold starts:

- New user: In the case of new user's entrance to the system, lack of previous information such as browsing history and interested items makes it hard to suggest items to the users.
- New item: New item entering the system has no rating and possibly they will not be entered.

7.1.2   Collaborative recommendations

In CF recommendation system, the services recommended to the user are those that users with comparable tastes desired in the past, i.e., recommendations are being given based on the people who have similar tastes and preferences. The simple assumption in CF is that user A and user B's personal tastes are in fact connected if each user rates *n* items similarly. CF systems produce recommendation, first by collecting the ratings from users and keep user's judgment in a database, then by diagnosing the correlations between the two of a kind user to determine a user's neighbor in taste space. It observes computation provided by these neighbors to make recommendations. CF filtering is additionally arranged into memory-based and model-based CF [3]:

- In memory-based CF, the input ought to be as a form of matrix. They make guesses by working on data (users, things and ratings) kept in memory. They can be classified as follows:
  - Nearest neighbor algorithms—Users who are similar to the present users regarding preferences are called as neighbors. This algorithm finds out those precedent users who previously had the similar taste as that of the new user.

Items which were preferred by neighbors are recommended to the new user, and s/he will probably like them as well.

- Top-N recommendation algorithms—It recommends a set of N top-ranked items that will be of notice to a specific user.

• Matrix factorization (MF) or association rule mining produces a model in model based. References [5,6] indicate dissimilar model-based methods. MF, fuzzy systems, Bayesian classifier and neural networks, etc., are the most well-known model-based methods. CF can be used depending upon the algorithmic technique or the application both user based and item based [3]. Item-based CF—the predicted rating depends totally on the ratings by the same user on other similar items.

• User-based CF—User-based classification, however, raises a number of problems for a content-based filtering system and CF such as follows:

- **Credibility:** Not all customers believe in the concept of honesty is the best policy, so they might not always tell the truth (especially online), and users with small rating history can twist the data. Additionally, various vendors might present positive ratings to their own products but intentionally provide negative ratings to their competitor's products, obviously not a fair play!

- **Scarcity:** Not all items will be rated or will have sufficient ratings to make helpful data.

- **Inconsistency:** Users do not apply similar keywords in order to tag an item, even if the meaning may possibly be the same. Furthermore, a number of attributes can be subjective.

Ibrahim *et al.* [3] try to merge location-aware recommender system (LARS) [7] and keyword-aware service recommendation (KASR) [8]. LARS is an item-based CF method which produces recommendation based on the spatial properties of the user and item. This reduces the number of items to be compared when compared to the traditional-item-based CF. KASR is user-based CF technique that produces the recommendations based on the preferences of the user. KASR analyzes the reviews of previous users and stores it. The keywords which are extracted from these reviews will serve as a factor to recommend a new user. Item-based CF is used to decrease the complexity of the user-based CF. It is true that recommendations are being produced more accurately compared to user based but the complexity remains high. LARS (item-based CF) decreases this complexity. It does this by reducing the number of users and items by taking into consideration their spatial properties. Dealing with the unstructured data (reviews) given by the user is upon the KASR which is a user-based CF. Integration of these two CF systems would definitely leave behind the conventional recommendation system in all measure of accuracy. In this section, keyword and spatial properties of user are integrated and categorized in collaborative recommendation. Location-based RS is item-based CF and keyword-based RS is user-based CF. Producing personalized recommendation with accuracy is a benefit provided by both the RS techniques. A comparison between the hybrid approaches and traditional approaches proved that hybrid approaches are more precise than the

Table 7.1   Collaborative filtering technique

CF technique	Memory-based collaborative filtering (neighborhood based)	Model-based collaborative filtering	Hybrid collaborative filtering
Representative algorithm	User-based CF Item-based CF	Slope-one CF Dimensionality reduction (matrix factorization) E.g., SVD	Combination of memory-based and model-based CF
Advantages	Easy implementation New data can be added easily and incrementally Need not consider the content of items being recommended Scales well with correlated items	Better addresses the sparsity and scalability problem Improve prediction performance	Overcome limitations of CF such as sparsity Improve prediction performance
Limitations	Are dependent on human ratings Cold-start problem for new user and item Sparsity problem of rating matrix Limited scalability for large datasets	Expensive model building Trade-off between the prediction performance and scalability Loss of information in dimensionality reduction technique (SVD)	Increased complexity and expense for implementation

original techniques [3]. Table 7.1 illustrates a detail description of CF together with their pros and cons.

7.1.3   Knowledge-based recommendations

Knowledge-based RSs recommend desired items to the users, according to item's characteristics and user's profiles. It makes the most of the knowledge about users and products and defines which products meet up the users requirements. This kind of RS requires a thorough modeling of items and users to work properly; accessibility of the necessary knowledge and its maintenance over time is the common obstacle to their progress. Here comes up an advantage, its recommendations do not rely on any database of user ratings, so it would not result in a ramp up problem. Also they do not require a large amount of data to offer or compute recommendations; in contrast to other systems, a minimal amount of users will suffice. A drawback emerges when it requires an engineer's knowledge database to provide users with helpful recommendations, a knowledge that should get updated regularly to keep up with ever-changing consumer ratings and preferences [9].

7.1.4 Demographic recommendations

Demographical data such as age, gender, social class, education, location can be used and achieved both explicitly and implicitly based on the demographical data which a user profile can be made of. A demographic profile can recommend definite identical items. As an example, teenagers obviously rather different products than the olds; rich class of society may rather different type and items quality and definitely are willing to pay more on mentioned features. So the demographic recommendation takes into account personal characteristic of users and makes recommendations accordingly. Demographic approach does not apply user–item ratings even before rating any item; new users are able to take advantage of receiving recommendations. The technique is domain independent due to an independency of item's knowledge and their features. To gather the demographic data, this approach faces the privacy issues which can be grouped in disadvantages of the technique. For highly personalized recommendations, demographic classification is a little too basic [10].

7.1.5 Hybrid recommendations

Very simple recommendation techniques are being used by current RSs, such as content-based, collaborative, demographic, utility-based and knowledge-based. Using these techniques alone will lead to both advantages and disadvantages. The fact is a total inspiration to more research in hybrid RS which has merged different techniques to enhance performances. Numerous hybrids have been investigated, i.e., the hybridization techniques that are being named as weighted, switching, feature combination, feature augmentation, meta-level, cascading and mixed. They are described as follows [11]:

- **Weighted:** Applying collaborative and content-based system individually and afterward unite their predictions.
- **Switching:** System applies a specific switching criterion to swap between two recommendation systems that are working on the similar object.
- **Feature combination:** Features related to dissimilar recommendation system's data sources are gather into a single recommendation algorithm.
- **Feature augmentation:** We can sometimes utilize output of a system as an input feature of another; for instance, we can use a produced model to form features used by another model.
- **Meta-level:** Here a feature can be used as input of another, like model learned by one recommendation.
- **Cascading:** In this category, one recommendation system improves the outcome presented by another.
- **Mixed:** Integrating two or more techniques simultaneously; for instance, content based and CF.

CF, content-based and knowledge-based methods are the most commonly used recommendation techniques [3].

7.2 Big data analytic

Big data for all types of machine-automated systems is nowadays admitted as a challenge by computer industry. Many concerns are in storage, management and retrieval data which is known as big data. However, the main issue is how to apply this data in order to enhance business and improve the living standard of people. Process of collecting, organizing and analyzing large amount of data to determine various outlines and other helpful information is referred to as big data analytics. The primary objective of the big data analytic is assisting organization to get better decisions in business, help them with future predictions and provide them with analysis of large numbers of transactions done in organizations and update those forms of data used by them [12]. Extracting information from current data in order to predict future outcomes and trends or determining pattern can be done by predictive analysis; this will not act as a prophecy but with an acceptable level of reliability will predict what may happen in future, including what-if-then scenarios and risk considerations. Predictive analytics has application areas, namely, customer relationship management, clinical decision support, collection analytics, cross sell, customer retention, direct marketing, Fraud detection risk management and underwriting [12].

7.2.1 Text analytics

Information in database is being provided in textual form. Effective extraction of important information or manual analytics of these contexts is somehow impossible, due to its relevance in supplying a quantity of automatic tools for analyzing large textual data. A procedure of obtaining major information from text data is called text analytics or text mining. This procedure is used to extract meaningful data from texts. It utilizes numerous ways like associations among entities, predictive rule, designs, patterns, concepts, events based on rules. Text analytics is widely used in government, research and business requirements. Letting you know what people did is what data do, but text analytic let you know why they have done it. All information in unstructured or semi structured text data is recoverable and will extract significant information which can be categorized, and finally, based on all these categorized information, they can take decisions for business.

7.2.1.1 Steps for text analytics system
1. **Text:** Data is unstructured in primary phase.
2. **Text processing:** All information will be transferred in semantic syntactic text.
3. **Text transformation:** Notable text will be extracted in this phase for future use.
4. **Feature selection:** Data is calculated and illustrated in statistics format.
5. **Data mining:** All data is classified and clustered.

7.2.1.2   Text recommendation using an angle-based interest model

An interest model consisting of two kinds of angle is suggested by Xu *et al.* [13]: persistence and pattern which are able to unite and form complex angles. The model makes use of a new method to signify the long-term interest and the short-term interest; it also discriminates the interest in object and interest in the link structure of objects [13]. Extracting the data structure that stands for the interest of the texts, in the history of reading, is what they aim to achieve. They will do so by a text-scanning mechanism that considers the following point:

- **Simulating the human reading features to emerge interest**
  Link is a way to emerge interest in reading. On one side, a link is undeniably able to raise the chance of creating a new interest from an existing one. The text scanning mechanism knows how to simulate the association process which exists in the human-reading process. On the other side, people undoubtedly will create impressions based on the objects in text, and afterward they link the impressions throughout association in order to comprehend the text [14]. What associations are able to do is they can develop the impression made of those linked objects.
- **The data structure for calculating the angles of interest**
  A weighted graph is used by data structures which is responsible to compute the angles of interest; it records and calculates interests where nodes are indicators of objects and undirected edges are indicators of associations. Nodes or edges consist of two weights: short-term weight that represents the degree related to a short-term interest node or edge, and the long-term weight represents the degree related to the long-term interest. Construction of the interest graph is totally based on the dynamic growth of reading history. Limitation in the amount of nouns or noun phrase is the reason of the small-sized graph.

  As shown in Figure 7.2, by scanning every text in reading history, the interest graph will be more enhanced. We add extracted edges and objects in every text and put them into the graph if they have not come into view earlier. Accretion assumption and proximity distribution assumption are considered by the computation of the short-term weight. The preceding weights will be updated immediately after scanning a text. Superior weight is the reflection of stronger short-term interest or long-term interest. The nodes with comparatively great short-term or long-term weights in the interest graph are the indicator of the short-term (or long-term) interested objects. The connection between the objects in the text and objects in the interest graph is established by the degree in which a text meets the short-term (or long-term) object interest. Each intersection has three different features: size of an intersection, the short-term (or long-term) weights related to the objects in the intersection and the times which the common objects appear in the text. In order to assess the degree of a text meeting the short-term (or long-term) object interest, a variable node match degree is used and its computations consists of three features. If we consider the short-term (or long-term) weight as a second attribute, it will assess the degree of the short-term or long-term object interest; accordingly a text contains two node match degrees, both having an interest graph. Node matches with a high degree are indications of stronger interest in objects.

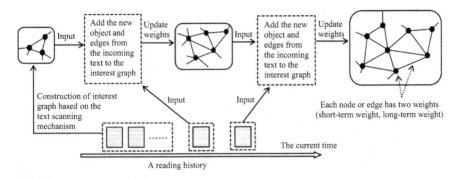

Figure 7.2   The construction of interest graph. A reading history is the sequence of the texts. The hollow arrow stands for the direction of the text scanning. The nodes and edges in interest graph are both enhanced with the scanning. The dotted arrows are indicators of notes. The solid arrows indicate the update of the interest graph and the construction as well. The dotted boxes are the indicators of the enriching processes

Nodes and the edges reflect the interest in link objects. What each link does is to join two nodes in order to form a basic unit. Compound basic units form a link structure. The overlap between the basic units in the interest graph and the text verifies the degree of the short-term (or long-term) link interest in a text. If even one sentence in a text includes the two nodes, a basic unite will appear. The mentioned overlap consists of three attributes. The quantity of basic units, edges short-term (long-term) weights of the basic units existing in the overlap because there may be more than one sentence which consists of a basic unit, and the times a common basic unit in the text appears. An edge match degree is being used by this method to assess the degree of a text meeting the short-term (or long-term) link interest.

- **Recommendation mechanism**
  The recommendation mechanism merges the four basic angles to order the candidate texts. Every basic angle is a correspondence of a rank of texts. For a compound joined by k basic angels points and the k basic angels compare to k rank, a content has a rank array (RA) that comprise k parts relating to the k areas of the content in the k positions, meant as $\vec{RA} = (r_1, r_2 \ldots, r_k)$ one RA can be changed into one value (*Integratedrank, Ir*) by multiplying a coefficient vector $\vec{CV} = (c_1, c_2, \ldots, c_k)$ where $c_1 + c_2 + \cdots + c_k = 1$ and $c_1, c_2, \ldots, c_k$ are within $[0, 1]$. It is calculated by

$$Ir = \vec{CV} \times \vec{RA} = \sum_{i=1}^{k} c_i * r_i \tag{7.1}$$

Then we are able to rank unread text based on the integrated ranks. Note that the integrated rank itself might not be there as an integer. The default value of $\vec{CV}$ is $(1/k, 1/k, \ldots, 1/k)$. In order to have a more specific service, the user is free to regulate coefficients in coefficient vector. The recommendation mechanism is capable to keep the coefficient vector's previous settings for future use. Two common complex angles that can be handled by the recommendation mechanism are mentioned below:

1. One of the angles is responsible for the new information on the short-term interested objects. Imagine a user who is interested in US economy history, reading various texts on Franklin Roosevelt on the topic of economy policies. The user is probably making interest in Roosevelt (object). Then the user has a tendency to get more information about Roosevelt, but in other areas except economy, may it be his dealings in WWII. The angels consist of two dimensions of meaning here: (1) new stands for the high-rank texts and it means that it should not concern economy, which is held by low-node match degree with long-term weight and (2) short-term interested objects means the high-rank texts should concern Roosevelt, which is held by high node match degree with short-term weight. Accordingly, the compound angle is a combination of the short-term object interest and the long-term object interest.

2. The other angle which is responsible for the new link structure holding the long-term interested objects. For instance, a user with a long-term interest in David Beckham desires to find extra information that s/he has not known yet. Meeting the compound angle here involves (1) meeting the long-term object interest, held by high node match degree with long-term weightž, (2) not meeting the short-term link interest, held by low edge match degree with short-term weight, also (3) not meeting the long-term link interest, held by low-edge match degree with long-term weightž.

Characteristics below are all within this method:

1. This method is able to differentiate the four basic angles of interest; it does so by a user's reading history.

2. Users must provide the interest in object and interest in link structure; two angles that are known as valuable elements in improving the effectiveness recommendation of texts. The interest in link structure emerges less frequently than the interest in object.

3. Recommending texts, according to the interest in object, make this method superior than the baseline methods. Somehow the advantage does not seem so great since the interest in object and the angle is similar to preceding methods.

4. Recommending texts according to the interest in link structure also makes this method superior than the baseline methods. Here, the advantage seems great while recommending a small number of texts. This is for the reason that the interest in link structure is not considered by preceding methods.

5. This method is able to handle the compound angles. The effectiveness of the two usual compound angles (when the coefficient vector changes effectiveness is advanced) vigorously supporting its effectiveness on the complex angles.

Recent experiments with news-scale text data confirm that the interest in object and the interest in link structure both have real requirements, and recommending texts according to the angles is definitely a useful approach.

7.2.2 Audio analytics

The process of compressing data and packaging it into single format called audio is what audio analytics does. Audio analytics extract information and meaning from audio signals, these extractions afterward can be used for investigation. To represent the audio analytic, two ways exist: (1) sound representation and (2) raw sound files. A special format for storing digital audio on systems is called audio file format. Audio formats are presented in three layouts: uncompressed audio format, lossless compressed audio format and lossy compressed audio format [15].

Audio is a file format being used to transfer data from one place to another. What audio analytics does is to make sure whether the provided audio data is accessible in proper format or in similar format that sender has already sent. The applications of audio analytics are many:

1. **Surveillance application:** That is derived from a technique for systematic choice of audio classes for detection of crimes done in society.
2. **Detection of threats:** By the audio mechanism we are able to recognize the thread occurring between sender and receiver.
3. **Tele-monitoring system:** Cameras with modern technologies are capable of recording the audio as well. Audio analytics may possibly offer useful detection of screams, breaking glass, gun sound, explosions, calling for help sound.
4. **Mobile networking system:** Information transferring from one side/place to another or having a talk is what we make out of this system.

7.2.2.1 Prediction of genre-based link in a two-way graph for music recommendation

Zhao *et al.* [16] have offered a music genre weight-based music recommendation (MGW) model which is able to suggest music rooted in the link prediction illustrated in Figure 7.3. The function of the proposed model is a bit similar to the majority off-line music recommendations; it provides a recommendation list which is construed of extract music feature [17]. The main feature it provides is constructing a recommendation model based on the complex representation-based link prediction

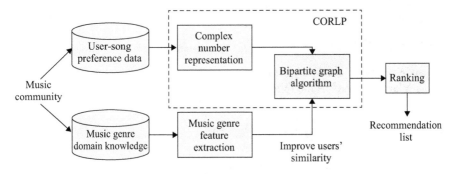

Figure 7.3 The framework of the MGW model

(CORLP) method. It also unites the similarity of users by taking out the genre weight feature of user's preference. The CORLP method is able to determine and represent both positive and negative preference of a user, this is in contrast with the old link prediction that is capable of representing only the one-sided music preference (positive or negative are not presented simultaneously). So as to build up the model, a process of extracting music-genre-preference feature from user was suggested. Afterward, they determine the connection between music-genre-preference feature and CORLP method. Once music preference and music-genre-preference weight are provided by the user, a recommendation list is generated by the model.

1. **CORLP method:** Rather than modeling a previously united relationship between users and items, the CORLP method models relational dualities through complex number. Comparing to the state-of-the-art methods, CORLP method has accomplished considerable performance. Directed graph $G = (V, E, w)$ is a representation of input data, where the set of nodes V contains all users U and items I, E is set of links that stand for diverse associations, and w comprise all of the links weight. Subsequently, set $w_{like} = i, w_{dislike} = -i, w_{similar} = 1, w_{dissimilar} = -1$, where i is an imaginary number with negative square. Therefore, they are able to change directed graph $G = (V, E, W)$ to $G' = (V', E', W')$ which is an unweighted and undirected network. The adjacency matrix A of the user–item graph (UIG) includes the following characteristics:

$$A(x, y) = \begin{cases} 1, & \text{if } x \text{ similar } y \\ -1, & \text{if } x \text{ dissimilar } y \\ i, & \text{if } x \text{ likes } y \text{ or } y \text{ dislikes } x \\ -i, & \text{if } x \text{ dislikes } y \text{ or } y \text{ likes } x \\ 0, & \text{if } (x, y) \notin E \end{cases} \tag{7.2}$$

where $A(x, y)$ is the value in row x and column y of matrix A. Matrix A can be signified as $\begin{bmatrix} A_{UU} & A_{UI} \\ A_{IU} & A_{II} \end{bmatrix}$ where A_{UU}, A_{II} are the similarity matrix of users and items; A_{UI}, A_{IU} are the preference matrices of users. Disregarding the primary relations between users and items, the G' is a bipartite graph and the adjacency matrix A can be simplified to $\begin{bmatrix} 0 & A_{UI} \\ -A_{UI}^T & 0 \end{bmatrix}$, and they can further convert A to $\begin{bmatrix} 0 & iB \\ -iB^T & 0 \end{bmatrix}$, where B is a real matrix. Based on path counting in the unweighted and undirected networks, the path counting for paths of length k can be derived similarly using A^k as the following equation:

$$A^k = \begin{cases} \begin{bmatrix} (BB^T)^n & 0 \\ 0 & (B^T B)^n \end{bmatrix}, & k = 2n \\ i \cdot \begin{bmatrix} 0 & (BB^T)^n B \\ -(B^T B)^n B^T & 0 \end{bmatrix}, & k = 2n + 1 \end{cases} \tag{7.3}$$

Hence, any sum of the powers of the adjacency matrix can be split into even and odd parts. Furthermore, they can, using the sum of odd parts for recommendation, be combined with the matrix exponential.

2. **Feature extraction:** Melody, rhythm, tempo, mode, key, harmony, dynamics and tone color are features provided by extraction music [18,19]. Music genre is able to recognize the user's preferred area of music according to the user's preference. The music-genre-preference weight is capable to mirror the similarity of users; this ability makes assessing the differences between the users. Customized similarities among users will definitely help improving the accuracy of music recommendation. In real music society, every user has its own favorite list of music or artist, and at least each artist has one or two music in the genre of pop or rock.

3. **Recommendation:** In a real situation, the improved CORLP method is capable of taking into consideration the influence of music preference weight of users to the similarity of users. They adjust the second power of the adjacency matrix A combined with music genre domain knowledge, and by doing so, they can suggest songs that they have never heard before by a user. Equation (7.4) based on CORLP method is able to represent the second power of the adjacency matrix A:

$$Precision = \frac{\sum_{u \in U} |R(u) \cap T(u)|}{\sum_{u \in U} |T(u)|} \tag{7.4}$$

where B is real matrix. After computation of similarity among users, again combined with music genre, it is possible to convert the top left matrix BB to matrix C. It is also possible to change A^2 to $(A^2)'$, as following:

$$A^2 = \begin{bmatrix} BB^T & 0 \\ 0 & B^T B \end{bmatrix} \tag{7.5}$$

$$(A^2)' = \begin{bmatrix} C & 0 \\ 0 & B^T B \end{bmatrix} \tag{7.6}$$

where C is a modified matrix, responsible of considering the music-genre-preference weight of the users. It is also possible to infer the modified $(A^3)'$ as

$$(A^3)' = \begin{bmatrix} C & 0 \\ 0 & B^T B.A \end{bmatrix} = \begin{bmatrix} 0 & -iC.B \\ -iB^T BB^T & 0 \end{bmatrix} \tag{7.7}$$

where the $-iC, B$ part of the $(A^3)'$ is music preference matrix of users. That part considers the relations between users which are represented as path counting for paths of length 3. Hence, it is probable to compare $(A^3)'$ with A and provide a music recommendation list which is resulted as well, to the users. Having experiments with the Xiami.com, music dataset provides evidence that MGW performance is superior to the CORLP method.

7.2.2.2 Personalized tag-based social media music recommendation

Quick rise of music data caused a huge increase in need of clarifying the customer's preferences; this is why knowing how to help customers gain what they desire from a great amount of music data has become a great challenge. To deal with such issues, a number of RSs have been proposed: Large amount of traditional RSs has failed to do so due to the inconsistency in rating relevant items by users which is called rating-diversity problem. To handle that, an innovative system called recommendation by tag-driven item similarity is introduced. It benefits from a feature named tag information to capture user's preference on music.

- **Framework of music recommendation**

  Initially as a support item-tag-driven and artist-tag-driven similarities are being used to have a precise prediction. Next, as a replacement for top N recommendation, it converts play counts into ratings to clarify the user's preferences [20]. The primary contributions can be summed up as follows:

  – The rating-diversity problem is abating considerably due to usage of tag information instead of rating. In fact, the item similarities are computed by tag frequency vectors.

  – Even though tag information is being used, instead of a ranking list, the user's preferences are signified as ratings, i.e., the final results are ratings derived by incorporating tag information into CF algorithms.

  – Even if data comes from social music websites with no ratings, play counts is used to figure it out statistically. That is, a formulator is needed to transform play counts into ratings by statistical theory. As shown in Figure 7.4, the framework of tag-based RS consists of two stages, namely, off-line preprocessing and online prediction stages.

  Off-line preprocessing makes use of formulator projects in the rating space to fill the requirement of representing the user preferences by playing counts of ratings. Figure 7.5 shows the scenario of transforming play counts into ratings. User's preferences can be embodied by play counts. That is, your preferred one in a music database consists of music you frequently listen to. Another work off-line stage offers is calculating similarities among items, and consequently item similarity matrix will be made. By constructing item similarities, we aim to decrease online prediction cost. With reference to Figure 7.4, the item similarity is derived by combining two similarities, i.e., item-tag-driven similarity and artist-tag-driven similarity [20].

  Afterward, a rating matrix and three similarity matrices are regenerate in online preprocessing. According to the generated matrices, the goal of online prediction stage is to infer the unknown ratings for the active user. It starts with an active user's visit and then the unknown ratings for the active user are predicted one by one [20].

- **Tag-based music recommendation challenges**

  In the future, various issues will be taken into consideration. Initially, to improve the recommendation result, context information will be used, as well as tags and ratings. Next, we will consider the optimal transformation between play counts and ratings. Afterward, we apply this idea on other multimedia recommendations in order to mine the social media tags.

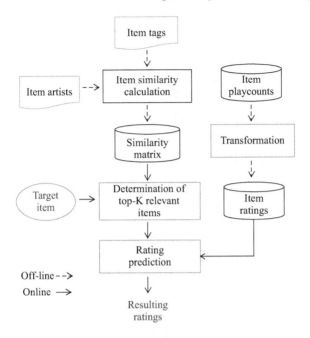

Figure 7.4   Framework of the tag-based music recommender system

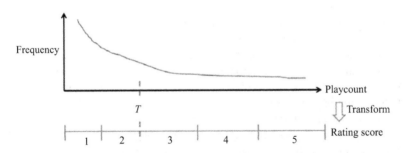

Figure 7.5   Scenario of transforming play counts into ratings

7.2.2.3   Graph-based quality model for music recommendation

We allocate this section to the detailed description of a music recommendation framework which is based on graph-based quality model. By this framework, generating a fine-grained music recommendation is possible. We will introduce the mentioned framework that has been divided into two stages: preference relation and graph-based quality model. Figure 7.6 is a display of the system framework. This algorithm is named as preference graph (PG)–based method.

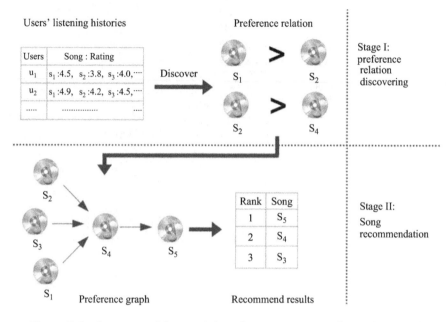

Users' listening histories   Preference relation

Figure 7.6   Overview of the graph-based music recommendation framework

- **Preference relation**

  $tr_i \rightarrow tr_j$ signify that track tr_j is more fair-sounding than track tr_i. Suppose a group of users in the music society listens to two tracks tr_j and tr_i. And these tracks have been rated by users according to their preferences. If user rates tr_j are higher than tr_i, then we know that his/her judgment for two tracks is $tr_i \rightarrow tr_j$.

  In order to find out the preference relation from the online music community, in the beginning it tries to infer user's judgment of various tracks. Suppose a user who has listened to two tracks tr_i and tr_j. In this case, users will definitely rate these two tracks according to their preferences. Their preferences could be deduced as follows: to start with, user u listens to track tr_i and tr_i and then rates the two tracks with the scores r_i and tr_j, respectively. If $r_i < r_j$ means u likes tr_j better than tr_i and vice versa. This is a sign that "u"s judgment for the two tracks is $tr_i \rightarrow tr_j$. Then afterward song preference relations are discovered by the RS from the user's listening history. Initially, track pairs rated by ten users will be discovered by the system, and then the user's judgment will be deduced as follows: for each track pair tr_i and tr_j, it counts the judgment for $tr_i \rightarrow tr_j$ and $tr_j \rightarrow tr_i$, respectively. It regards the one in $tr_i \rightarrow tr_j$ and $tr_j \rightarrow tr_i$ with more user's supports as the preference relation between track tr_i and tr_j [21].

- **Graph-based quality model**

  The graph-based quality model integrates each and every one of the preference relations in order to make use of them for music recommendation. The main idea is to measure probability of each track to be preferred by users. It also uses the preference probability to rank the tracks for recommendation. For example, if we know tr_i have a larger preference probability than tr_j, we should prefer tr_i as the recommendation for the user. The preference probability of track tr_j for user u_k is the probability that u_k likes to listen track tr_j

$$pr_j^k = Pr\{u_k \quad likes \quad tr_j\} \tag{7.8}$$

So as to estimate each track's preference probability, in the beginning, we must model the quality model as a PG. PG is a direct graph, and each track as the vertex signifies the edge weight from track tr_i to track tr_j as w_{ij}. The edge weight w_{ij} is set as the reliability of the preference relations. Assume that u_k likes to listen tr_j as $L(tr_j^k)$. Based on the graph theory, it uses the sum and product rule of probability and gets

$$Pr(L(tr_j^k)) = \sum_{tr_i^k \in TR_{in}^j} [Pr(L(tr_j^k)|L(tr_i^k)) * Pr(L(tr_i^k))] \tag{7.9}$$

By knowing the preference probability of tr_j's in-degree tracks, we only need to estimate $Pr(L(tr_j^k)|L(tr_i^k))$, this is the probability that user u_k likes to listen tr_j, knowing the fact that u_k likes to listen tr_i which is the reliability of the preference ordering. The cold-start problem in recommendation has been solved by the framework [21].

- **Graph-based music recommendation challenges**
  Comparing with two traditional algorithms (user-based CF and UIG-based method) the suggested framework is apparently greater, particularly in solving the cold-start problem in recommendation. We can also model other factors such as friend relation, group information, and tag information and so on into the PG in order to figure out whether they are able to improve the performance.

7.2.2.4 Music recommendation using acoustic features and user access patterns

CF and content-based recommending systems have their advantages and limitations. In this section, we suggest an approach which is a combination of CF and acoustic contents of music. Figure 7.7 shows the framework of the music recommendation system [22]. First we gather music data and user access patterns and process them beforehand.

- **Dynamic music similarity measurement**
  Dynamic music similarity measurement system is used by the music recommendation. Dynamic music-similarity measurements combine the acoustic content features and user-access patterns [22]. This scheme is based on the assumption that two pieces of music are similar in human perception when they share similar access patterns across multiple users. Table 7.2 shows a toy example of user access patterns on four pieces of music by four different users. To calculate the new similarity measure, a metric-learning method is being used by the music recommendation. This metric-learning approach learns the appropriate similarity metrics which are based on the correlation between acoustic feature and

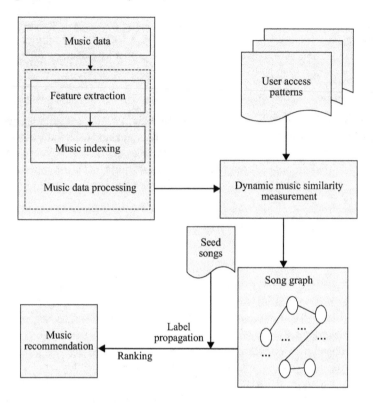

Figure 7.7   Framework of the user access patterns music recommendation

Table 7.2   Example of user access patterns

	M_1	M_2	M_3	M_4
U_1	1	1	0	0
U_2	1	1	0	0
U_3	0	0	1	1
U_4	0	0	1	1

user-access pattern of music. This will determine the weights for audio features, automatically as well [22]. A comprehensive study of extracting audio features for music similarity search has been done in literature [23–25]. Acoustic feature has proved that similar music pieces make use of similar instruments and possess similar sound textures [26].

- **Music feature extraction and indexing**
  The music recommendation develop mel-frequency cepstral coefficients and short-term Fourier transform features [27] for feature extraction. Efficient data

structures can be made for similarity search the moment features/signatures for each song are acquired. In this RS, for indexing music, min-wise hashing [28] is applied to speed up similarity computation for large datasets, particularly in online calculation. Being able to make a small signature for each song here is the core idea as well as figuring out the resemblance of any pair of songs which can be accurately estimated based on their min-wise hashing signatures.

- **Music recommendation and label propagation on song graph**
  Music recommendation will construct the song graph immediately after obtaining the music similarity [29], then it will be possible to treat it as a label propagation from labeled data (i.e., items with ratings) to unlabeled data.

  Definition 7.1. *(Song graph): A song graph is an undirected weighted graph* $G = (V, E)$, *where*
  - $V = L$ *is the node set (L is the song set, which means that each song is represented as a node on the graph G);*
  - *E is the edge set. Associated with each edge* $e_{pq} \in E$ *is the similarity* w_{pq}, *which is nonnegative and satisfies* $w_{pq} = w_{qp}$.

  The label propagation [22] is like a diffusive process of the labeled information [30,31]. The Green's function of the Laplace operator is being used by music recommendation to recommend music [32].

- **Music ranking**
  After label propagation, the ratings for unrated songs are obtained and many of them may have the same rating [22]. In fact, we require having a ranked list of the items to recommend. The music ranking over a song graph is somehow enclosing a problem, finding the shortest path from the seed song node to the rest of the nodes in the song graph is a complexity to deal with. Low similarity edges have already been eliminated consequently to build the shortest paths no more than the remaining edges can be used. To recommend songs, the system basically selects the M songs that are the closest to a seed songs S.

- **User access patterns music recommendation challenges**
  Several venues are present for further research. It is possible to develop current framework to personalized music recommendation. Additionally, for similarity measurements, investigation on further comprehensive music content features is also possible.

7.2.2.5 Learning content similarity for music recommendation

In this section, a method is introduced for improving content-based audio similarity by learning from a sample of collaborative filter data sample.

- **Learning similarity: collaborative filters and metric learning to rank**
  We have applied the metric learning to rank (MLR) [33] algorithm. At a high level, distance metric is optimized by MLR, and an optimal ranking of songs is created when each song is used as a query. We must supply a set of similar songs for each training query in order to apply the algorithm. We can do so by leveraging the side information accessible for items.

Particularly, a notion of similarity from collaborative filter data is used by the music recommendation. Therefore, content-based audio similarity is optimized by this approach. It will be done by learning a sample of collaborative filter data. Collaborative filters [34] form the basis of state-of-the-art recommendation systems but are neither able to form recommendations directly nor answer the queries for items which have not been consumed or rated yet. Due to optimizing content-based similarity from a collaborative filter, music recommendation makes use of definitely a simple mechanism to alleviate the cold-start problem. It also extends the recommendation of new or less known songs.

By taking advantage of implicit feedback in the user's listening history, we are able efficiently to gather high-quality training data even without active user's participation. Accordingly, we can train on greater collections of music than what explicit feedback or survey data would have offered. The concept of similarity is originated from user activity in a bottom-up fashion; it also fades the need for common simplification such as genre or artist agreement [35].

The MLR algorithm combines these two approaches of metric learning and structural support vector machine (SVM) [36], and this is planned specifically for the query-by-example setting [33].

- **Audio representation**

The metric learning framework is strong as a consequence of the code-book size choice and vector quantization (VQ) threshold and defers stable performance over a broad range of VQ configuration.

The top-VQ audio illustration facilitates efficient and compact description of the acoustic content of music data. Integrating audio representation with an optimized distance metric defers similarity calculations that are both efficient to compute and significantly more accurate than other competing content-based methods [35].

7.2.3   Video analytics

In considering the big data, video is a major issue. Eighty percentages of unstructured data is contributed from videos and images. Today, CCTV cameras go into the category of digital information and surveillance. Each and every single one of this information is kept and processed for further use. As you know, videos contain countless amount of information, so they are normally large in size. Applications of video analytics are useful in schools, in accident cases, security, business, traffic police, video analytics for business intelligence, video analytics for investigation (video search), target and scene analytics, direction analytics and removing the human equation through the automation [12].

7.2.3.1   Real-time video-recommendation system

Recommendation system aims to provide personalized recommendations so as to help users discover high-quality videos consistent with their interest. To enhance user's satisfaction, recommendations should be provided in real-time and be reflect of user's recent activities on the site. In this section, we will discuss a real-time top-N video-recommendation system.

- **Real-time matrix factorization model update based on stochastic gradient descent (SGD)**

  First, a real-time MF [37] based on CF algorithm, which is an online updating strategy will be developed. MF presume user preferences which are modeled merely by a small number of latent factors and then attempts to explain the observed user–item ratings by these factors which have been inferred from the rating patterns. MF aims to uncover the latent factors which are able to explain observed ratings. Specifically, particularly, each user u is associated with a vector $x_u \in R^f$, and each item i is associated with a vector $y_i \in R^f$. For a given item i, the elements of y_i measure the extent to which the item belongs to those factors. Similarly, for a given user u, the elements of x_u measure the extent of interest the user has in items that are high on the corresponding factors. The user "u"s rating of item i is r_{ui}, which indicates the preference by user u of item i. Higher r_{ui} values mean stronger preference, and the goal of MF is to predict the unknown ratings. The prediction is done by taking an inner product, i.e., $\hat{r}_{ui} = x_U^T * y_i$. The major challenge MF is dealing with "i"s to compute the mapping of each user and item to factor vectors $x_u, y_i \in R^f$. To learn the factor vectors (x_u and y_i), the training is performed by minimizing the regularized squared error on the set of known ratings:

  $$\min_{x_*, y_*} \sum_{(u,i) \in D} (r_{ui} - x_u^T y_i)^2 + \lambda(\|x_u\|^2 + \|y_i\|^2) \tag{7.10}$$

  where D is the set of user–item pairs for which r_{ui} is known, i.e., the training set, and λ is a parameter used to control the extent of regularization. The regularization term $\lambda(\|x_u\|^2 + \|y_i\|^2)$ is used to avoid overfitting, and the value of λ is data-dependent and usually determined by experiments. By taking the biases effect into account, the prediction of rating r_{ui} could be extended as follows:

  $$\hat{r}_{ui} = \mu + b_u + b_i + x_u^T y_i \tag{7.11}$$

  where μ stands for the overall average rating, and the parameters b_u and b_i indicate the observed deviations of user u and item i, respectively, from the average.

  $$\min_{x_*, y_*, b_*} \sum_{(u,i) \in D} (r_{ui} - \mu - b_u - b_i - x_u^T y_i)^2 + \lambda(\|x_u\|^2 + \|y_i\|2 + b_u^2 + b_i^2) \tag{7.12}$$

  The most successful method to solve MF optimization problem is SGD [38], specifying a training dataset which contains tuples in the form $\langle user, item, rating \rangle$, SGD performs various passes through the dataset until the moment of stopping criteria is met, which is generally a union bound or a maximum number of iterations. At each iteration, SGD hits every known rating in the training set. For each rating, SGD updates the parameters by correcting them in the inverse direction of the gradient of error. $\eta \leq 1$ is the factor which the extent of correcting is determined with and it is known as step size of the learning rate. Based on (7.11), the associated prediction error of rating r_{ui} can be computed as below:

$$e_{ui} = r_{ui} - \mu - b_u - b_i - x_u^T y_i \tag{7.13}$$

The updating operations are done as follows:

$$b_u \rightarrow b_u + \eta(e_{ui} - \lambda b_u) \tag{7.14}$$

$$b_i \rightarrow b_i + \eta(e_{ui} - \lambda b_i) \tag{7.15}$$

$$x_u \rightarrow x_u + \eta(e_{ui}x_u - \lambda x_u) \tag{7.16}$$

$$y_i \rightarrow y_i + \eta(e_{ui}y_i - \lambda y_i) \tag{7.17}$$

The confidence levels of various implicit feedback data instances are considered by the online updating strategy. The learning rate of the training process is adjustable to each data instance.

- **Real-time video recommendation generation**
  The procedure of real-time video recommendation generation is discussed in this section. In order to make accurate video recommendations in real-time, a similar video table should be built to pick high-quality candidate videos for recommendation; for each video, it will record the most related videos. The factors are leveraged from three aspects to compute the similarity of videos. These three aspects are the MF similarity, the type similarity and the time factor [39]. The definition of CF similarity goes as

$$S1_{ij} = y_i^T y_j \tag{7.18}$$

For video i and j, the type similarity is defined as follows:

$$S2_{ij} = \begin{cases} 1 & \text{type}(i) \text{ equals type}(j) \\ 0 & \text{type}(i) \text{ not equals type}(j) \end{cases} \tag{7.19}$$

Specifically, the similarity of video pairs will decrease when their update time go up from the current time. The update time refers to the time of the latest user action that touches off the similarity computation (similarity of video i and j will be updated only when new user action relating to i or j happens). Officially, a damping factor which is used to measure this time factor is as follows:

$$d_{ij} = 2^{-\Delta t/\xi} \tag{7.20}$$

where Δt is the time difference between sim_{ij}'s update time and current time, and ξ is a parameter which controls the rate of decay. By giving two videos, i and j, the overall relevance between them [39] is defined as

$$sim_{ij} = d_{ij}((1 - \beta) * S1_{ij} + \beta * S2_{ij}) \tag{7.21}$$

where β is a parameter adjusting the weight of different similarity factors in the final relevance function. The exact values of ξ and β are determined by the experiments. The model is scalably implemented on Storm, a distributed real-time computation system for processing streams of data. The video recommendation system was in production at Tencent Video. Every day it dealt with billions of user action tuples with data size of more than 1 TB. In online testing experiments, its performance is undoubtedly superior in production [39].

- **Real-time video recommendation challenges**
  For real-time video recommendations, there exists loads of further works to be done. Only the video-type information was used to measure the content features of videos here. And yet, there exists so many other useful information which can be employed, like the videos directors and actors. Furthermore, combining results from different algorithms to leverage benefit of different methods is a better methodology for improving the diversity and novelty of video recommendations.

7.2.3.2   Recommendation system for micro-video on big data

One innovative form of information media called micro-video is what we are going to discuss at this point. With the development of the Internet, 3G (the 3rd Generation mobile communication technology), and 4G (the 4th Generation mobile communication technology) network, the bandwidth expands and the speed of network increasingly rises. The mentioned technologies make the distribution of information media swift and simple. Micro-video is a type of short video [40] [41], which only lasts for 30 up to 300 s [42]. We can formulate the recommendation issue as follows: assume that C is the set of all users and S is the set of all probable items which might be recommended and assume that u is an utility function which measures usefulness of item s to user c, i.e., $u : C \times S \longrightarrow R$, where R is a totally ordered set. Then for each user $\in C$, we want to choose such item $s \in S$ that maximize the user's utility.

$$\forall c \in C, S_c = \arg\max_{s \in S} u(c, S) \tag{7.22}$$

The utility of an item usually is represented by ratings in recommendation system, which specifies how a particular item is liked by a particular user.

1. **Content-based recommendation:** To represent a text document, Shang *et al.* always make use of features. The importance of the feature word is measured by feature weighting. The best well-known feature weighting algorithm is TF–IDF algorithm [43]. Consider N as the total number of documents that can be recommended to users, and feature w_i appears n_i of them. Supposed that $f_{i,j}$ is the frequency feature w_i appears in document d_j. Hence, $TF_{i,j}$, the term frequency of feature w_i in document d_j can be defined as

$$TF_{i,j} = \frac{f_{i,j}}{\max_z f_{z,j}} \tag{7.23}$$

where the maximum can be calculated over the frequencies $f_{z,j}$ of all features w_z that appear in the document d_j. Yet the features are neither important nor useful, if they appear in various documents. Afterward we can identify the inverse document frequency (IDFi) of feature w_i as log

$$IDF_i = \log \frac{N}{n_i} \tag{7.24}$$

Therefore, the TF–IDF weight for feature w_i in document d_j is defined as

$$\omega_{i,j} = TF_{i,j} \times IDF_i \tag{7.25}$$

So, the recommended document d_j can be represented as a vector, $d_j = \{\langle t_{1,j}, \omega_{i,j} \rangle, \langle t_{2,j}, \omega_{2,j} \rangle\}, \ldots, \langle t_{i,j}, \omega_{i,j} \rangle$, where $t_{i,j}$ is the ith feature in document d_j, and $\omega_{i,j}$ is the $t_{i,j}$'s weight.

Several candidate documents are weighed against the input document; this will be done in recommendation system. And then the best matching documents will be recommended accordingly. The utility function $u(c,s)$, in 7.21, is generally an indication of the similarity between the candidate document and the input document, for instance cosine similarity measure.

$$u(c,s) = \cos(\omega_c, \omega_s) = \frac{\omega_c.\omega_s}{\|\omega_c\| \times \|\omega_s\|} = \frac{\sum_{i=1}^{k} \omega_{i,c}\omega_{i,s}}{\sqrt{\sum_{i=1}^{k} \omega_{i,c}^2}\sqrt{\sum_{i=1}^{k} \omega_{i,s}^2}} \tag{7.26}$$

where ω_c is the candidate document vector and k is the total number features in the recommendation system.

As an example, in order to suggest videos to user c in the micro video application, the collaboration system attempts to discover other users with similar tastes in videos liked by user c. Initially, the similarity among users should be calculated by particular items. The adjust cosine [44], as following formula, is used in some CF methods for similarity among users where the difference in each user's use of the rating scale is taken into account.

$$sim(i,j) = \frac{\sum_{s \in I_{ij}} (R_{is} - A_s)(R_{js} - A_s)}{\sqrt{\sum_{s \in I_{ij}} (R_{is} - A_s)^2 \sum_{c \in I_{ij}} (R_{is} - A_s)^2}} \tag{7.27}$$

where $R_{i,s}$ stands for the rating of item s by user i, A_s indicates the average rating of user i for all the co-rated items and $I_{i,j}$ signifies the items set both rating by user i and user j.

2. **Slope one recommendation:** An open-source machine learning library called Apache Mahout comprises a framework of tools that permits researchers to create powerful and scalable recommendation and classification applications. Slope one algorithm [45,46] is a CF algorithm in Mahout. Slope one, Mahout and Hadoop platform are all based on big data. They are able to deal with the computation of large volume data space, like large amount data similarity computing. The main idea of Slope one algorithm is to find the similarities between two items along with the users. If we calculate the average rating of the two items and then compare the difference of them, the results would lend us a hand in predicting another user's rating of those items.

3. **Slope one algorithm based on MapReduce:** MapReduce [47] A parallel computing model which is based on Hadoop framework is called MapReduce [44] and consists of two stages, the Mapper stage and Reducer stage. It divides the input data into n parts and start n Mappers. Each Mapper handles one data part at a time. The inputs and outputs of Mapper are ⟨*key, value*⟩ pairs. If there are *n* ⟨*key, value*⟩ pairs of Mapper output, then in order to get the final result, *n* Reducers should be established. Two MapReduce stages and one Mapper stage are required to apply the Slope one algorithm.

   Calculating difference matrix D_{ij} for each user is the first MapReduce stage of the Slope one algorithm. The Mapper does not modify anything in the first MapReduce stage; merely the Reducer requires calculating the difference matrix D_{ij}.

   The second MapReduce stage of Slope one algorithm is to compute the average difference matrix, counts. Besides, the Mapper stage does not modify anything, and the average difference matrix D_{ij} is calculated by Reducer stage as well as computing the total number of the same pair ⟨*itemsi, itemj*⟩. Calculating the prediction rating of the user happens in the final stage. One Map stage is used to complete the task. The Mappers input refers to the users rating list and the Mappers output refers to the prediction rating list. Therefore, Shang *et al.* [42] make use of Map Reduce programming model in order to implement the Slope one algorithm. The challenges what they need at present is how to find the favorite video. Somehow micro-video producer's issue is discovering how many viewers liked a video and what kind of videos has been liked by users. This system is capable of suggesting the favorite videos to the viewer according to the viewers' browsing or watching history. Then again, this system is able to gather feedbacks and accordingly provide suggestions for micro-video producers with how many viewers like the micro-video.

7.2.4 Image analytics

A method of extracting information from an image using automatic or semiautomatic techniques: scene analysis, pattern recognition, image understanding, image description, computer/machine vision, etc. Two methods of image analysis for designing-recommendation systems will be discussed.

7.2.4.1 An images-textual hybrid recommendation system

Nowadays, the best replacement for the hotel rooms are vacation rental SNS, thanks to their affordable rental and scalable O2O interaction platform. The most important factors influencing user's decisions while they are setting up for their vacation are accommodation reviews, descriptions and images available on the website. For improving the search efficiency, three methods have been proposed by Cheung *et al.* [48]: images-based cosine similarity calculation, textual-description-based Jaccard similarity calculation and the fusion of both prior-mentioned methods [48]. This methodology include three phases: (1) similarity between accommodations based on bag of features (BoF), (2) similarity between accommodations based on textual descriptions and (3) hybrid RS. In first phase, each image is signified with a BoF [49], which illustrates an image with a vector. Later on, the vector can be used to determine similarities between images. In creating a BoF, the following steps are required:

1. **Feature extraction:** The images are overlaid with a regular grid, and for each grid point, the histogram of oriented gradients descriptor are calculated.
2. **Codebook generation:** The extracted feature descriptors are clustered with k-means in order to create the codebook and afterward that the set of cluster centers is used.
3. **Representing an image with BoF:** Each entry in the codebook allocates to features of every one of the images; later the number of assigned features will be counted.

Then, computation of the cosine similarities, between a single image (respectively, BoF) of the visited and the potentially recommended accommodations will be done. This process will be repeated for all images of the visited accommodation, and according to these similarities, the potentially recommended accommodation will be ranked, which later on the top N accommodations will be recommended consequently. In addition to stating the vacation destination, in the second phase, most of the vacation rentals SNS offer various filters that will assist users to narrow down their search. Filter setting which were manually inputted by users will later on reflect their travel preference. So Jaccard similarity is used to determine the text-based similarity. For the last phase, we should take into consideration that obtained information from both methods may be different but both reflect the traveling preferences in different angles. One should understand that not all preferences can be captured by textual data alone, and most of the time, the images have the power to tell the hidden information which cannot be captured by text simply. Seeing that both methods have their own strength as an images-textual hybrid RS is proposed. This is a multimodal recommendation approach combining the similarity results acquired from both images and textual description. It was proved that recommendation based solely on image similarities or textual description-based similarities are possible. Yet, it looks as if the traveling preferences of users could not be obtained completely via either one. Somehow the images-textual hybrid RS accomplished better results, and that is apparently due to the feature that can capture information missed out by image or textual data. However, this method is only applicable for users who have histories; hence the cold-start problem for first time users who do not have any travel history is challenge.

7.2.4.2   Recommendation system for styles and substitutes based on image

McAuley *et al.* [50] seek out a method to signify the preferences of users for the visual appearance of one object given that of another. Many appropriate models may well be developed for this purpose; however, hardly any of them will be able to scale to the volume of data available. They determine an F-dimensional feature vector $x \in R^F$ for every object in the dataset; they accomplish this by using a convolution neural network. A set R of relationships exists in the dataset, where $r_{ij} \in R$ relates objects i and j and each relationship is of one of the classes mentioned above. What they aim is

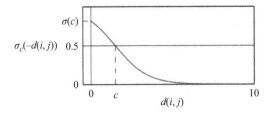

Figure 7.8   Shifted (and inverted) sigmoid with parameter $c = 2$

learning a parameterized distance transform $d(X_i, X_j)$ such that feature vectors $X_i; X_j$ for objects that are related $r_{ij} \in R$ are assigned a lower distance than those that are not $r_{ij} \notin R$. Particularly, they seek $d(0,0)$ such that $P(r_{ij} \in R)$ raise monotonically with $d(X_i, X_j)$. Distances and probabilities: they use a shifted sigmoid function to relate distance to probability thus

$$P(r_{ij} \in R) = \sigma_c(-d(X_i, X_j)) = \frac{1}{1 + e^{d(X_i, X_j) - c}}. \tag{7.28}$$

This is depicted in Figure 7.8

This decision permits us to cast the problem as logistic regression, which is carried out for scalability reasons. In fact if items i and j have distance $d(X_i, X_j) = c$, then they have probability 0.5 of being related; the probability increases above 0.5 for $d(X_i, X_j) < c$ and decreases as $d(X_i, X_j) > c$. Bear in mind that they do not state c in advance but rather choose c to maximize prediction accuracy.

Now a set of potential distance functions will be described.

Weighted nearest neighbor: Taking that into consideration, those different feature dimensions are almost certainly more important than the different relationships; our concern is how to acquire a method by which we can discover feature dimensions relevant to distinct relationships. They aim to learn which feature dimensions are relevant for a particular relationship. So they fit a distance function of the form.

$$d_{\mathbf{W}}(\mathbf{X_i, X_j}) = \| \mathbf{W} \circ (\mathbf{X_i} - \mathbf{X_j}) \|_2^2, \tag{7.29}$$

where $\circ$ is the Hadamard product.

Mahalanobis transform: Equation (7.29) is restricted in modeling the visual similarity between objects, although with varying emphasis per feature dimension. Modeling subtler notions is a bit trivial, like which pairs of pants and shoes regardless of having different appearances, fit in to the same style. To do so, they are supposed to learn how different feature dimensions relate to each other; to be precise they have to find out how the features of a pair of pants possibly will be transformed in order to help spot a well-matched pair of shoes. To identify such transformations, they relate image features via a Mahalanobis distance, which basically generalizes (7.29), so at the level of pairs of features, weights will be described. In particular they fit

$$d_{\mathbf{M}}(\mathbf{X_i, X_j}) = (\mathbf{X_i} - \mathbf{X_j})\mathbf{M}(\mathbf{X_i} - \mathbf{X_j})^{\mathbf{T}} \tag{7.30}$$

A complete ranked matrix $\mathbf{M}$ contains excessive parameters and it makes it hard to fit amenably into the given size of the dataset. For instance, if we want to use features with dimension $F = 2^1 2$, to learn a transform as in (7.30), around 8 million parameters are required to be fitted in; not only this is nearly overfitting, it is also not practical for any current solver. To deal with these issues, by considering the fact that M parameters a Mahalanobis distance, we can estimate M like $M \approx YY^T$ where Y is a matrix of *dimension* $\times K$. Consequently, they define

$$d_Y(X_i, X_j) = (X_i - X_j)\mathbf{Y}\mathbf{Y}^T(X_i - X_j)^T \parallel (X_i - X_j)\mathbf{Y} \parallel_2^2 \tag{7.31}$$

Remember that almost every one of distances (as well as their derivatives) can be calculated in $O(FK)$, which is noteworthy for the scalability of the method. Similar ideas emerge in [51] [17], which take the problem of metric learning into account by learning low-rank implanting, even if it uses a different objective than the one they have considered here.

1. **Style space:** In addition to being computationally useful, the low-rank transform in (7.31) has a convenient interpretation. Specifically, if they consider the K-dimensional vector $s_i = x_i Y$, then (7.31) can be rewritten as

    $$d_Y(X_i, X_j) = \parallel (S_i - S_j) \parallel_2^2 . \tag{7.32}$$

    In other words, (7.31) defers a low-dimensional embedding of the features x_i and x_j. This low-dimensional representation is referred to as style-space embedded products. Despite being visually dissimilar, they hope to identify Y in a way that related objects fall close to each other. The notion of style is automatically learned by training the model on pairs of objects Amazon regard as being related. Personalizing styles to individual users:

    A model has been developed to learn a universal notion; according to that, we learn which products go together or match. Rooted in the notion of style-related products should have similar style. This notion is adaptable and could be personalized for each user in order to discover which dimension of style they regard classy or important. To do so, they require to learn personalized distance functions $d_{Y,u}(X_i, X_j)$ which appraise the distance between item i and j according to the user u. They pick the distance function

    $$d_{Y,u}(X_i, X_j) = (X_i - X_j)\mathbf{Y}\mathbf{D}^{(u)}\mathbf{Y}^T(X_i - X_j)^T \tag{7.33}$$

    where $\mathbf{D}^{(u)}$ is a K_K diagonal (positive semidefinite) matrix. In this way, the entry $\mathbf{D}^{(u)}kk$ indicates the extent to which the user u "cares about" the kth style. In practice, they $_t a U_K$ matrix X such that $\mathbf{D}^{(u)}kk = Xuk$. Much like the simplification in (7.32), the distance $d_{Y,u}(X_i, X_j)$ can be conveniently written as

    $$d_{Y,u}(X_i, X_j) = \parallel (S_i - S_j) \circ X_u \parallel_2^2 \tag{7.34}$$

    Putting it differently, X_u is a personalized weighting of the projected style-space dimensions. The construction in (7.33) and (7.34) only seems right if users associated with each edge exists in their dataset, which is not right for the four graph types they have offered up until now. In order to study the issue of user personalization, they take advantage of ratings and review data. They sample a dataset of triples $(i; j; u)$ of products i and j which both are purchased by user u (i.e., u has reviewed them both).

2. **Features:** By occupying Caffe deep-learning framework, features can be calculated from the original image [17]. A Caffe reference model 3 with 5 convolutional layers is particularly utilized followed by three fully connected layers; a model relevant to 1.2 million Image Net (ILSVRC2010) images. An output of FC7, the second fully connected layer, is utilized and the outcome was a feature vector of length $F = 4,096$.

3. **Generating recommendation:** Here they have illustrated that the offered model is able to provide users with recommendations that possibly will be of use to them. Take a query item (e.g., a product a user is currently browsing or has just paid for) into account, you will understand that their objective is recommending a collection of other items that may well complement it. For instance, considering a user who has recently browsed pants, they may feel like recommending a jacket, shoes or accessories which belong to the similar style or are in harmony with the browsed item. At this point, Amazon's rich and comprehensive grouping hierarchy may well lend us a hand. For category like women's or men's clothing, they may perhaps categorize an outfit as a mixture of pants, a top, shoes and an accessory (they do this for the display, while far more compound combinations are likely their category tree for clothing alone consists of hundreds of nodes). When a query item occurs, they aim to choose the best matching items with it from each category. To be precise, assuming a query item, xq, for each category C (symbolizes a set of item index), they will make recommendations for it according to

$$arg \max_{j \in C} P_Y(r_{qj} \in \mathscr{R}), \qquad (7.35)$$

i.e., the minimum distance according to their measure (7.31) amongst objects belonging to the desired category. Generally speaking, the model produces apparently reasonable recommendations, with clothes in each category usually being of a consistent style.

McAuley *et al.* [50] have proved that it is probable to model the human notion of what is visually related. This will be done by considering a properly huge dataset, even if that information is somewhat imaginatively enclosed there. Moreover they have proved that the suggested method is able to model a range of visual relationships, which are even ahead of plain visual similarity. What makes this method to be prominent is the ability to model what makes items complementary. They assert that this is the foremost effort of modeling human preference for the appearance of one object which is suggested based on another by means of something more than the visual similarity between the two. It is true and it is definitely the first time that this has been done at this level. Visual and relational RSs are also offered as a latent concern of interest to their information retrieval community. They have provided a huge dataset for their training and evaluation. In the procedure, they deal with discovering what not to put on and how to judge a book by its cover.

7.2.5 Other recommender system

7.2.5.1 Personalized trip advisor service

Purpose of the system is to present a personalized list of suggestion services as well as offering the most appropriate services to the user. Keywords here particularly signify the preferences of related users and user-based CF algorithm will be the chief support. A list of keywords and domain thesaurus is there to elicit the preferences.

This recommendation system takes active users and passive user into account. Passive users are those who have already logged in to the trip advisor site, and active users are those in the need of recommendation. Active users possibly will require recommendation of preceding user who is previously in the dataset. By choosing keywords from a list of keywords, an active user can specify his or her preferences from the services indicated to her/him. According to the list of keywords and domain thesaurus, the preferences of a previous user can be extracted from his/her reviews for the services. [52].

1. **Preprocess:** The removal of HTML tags from hotel link and stop words in the reviews snippet collection should be done. The Porter stemmer algorithm for removing the morphological and in flexional endings from words in English is being used.
2. **Keyword extraction:** According to the list of keywords and domain thesaurus, reviews will be transformed into a corresponding keyword set.

Approximate and exact similarity computations are two similarity computation methods in use. For approximate similarity method, the weights of the keywords in the preference keyword set are not considered, whereas the exact similarity computation method will consider the weight of the keyword [52]. Jaccard coefficient is the best method for comparing the similarity and diversity of sample sets [8,53]. In order to extract the precise computation, we can make use of the Cosine-based similarity computation [8,54]. After checking the consistency of the matrix, calculation of the weights will be done. When the set of most similar users has been found, the personalized rating of each candidate service for the active user can be calculated. As a final point, a personalized service recommendation list will be offered to the user and the service with the highest rating will be recommended to him/her.

The trip advisor dataset was downloaded from UCI repository. The attributes of this dataset are hotel name, address, date of the review and users review. Then the active user gives their preferred item by keywords. That item was compared to the previous user preference. Then the recommendation to the active user was generated. Then similarity checking, ranking and rating, recommendation generation are the major steps. The system has keyword candidate list. Here it has been created manually. The problem was implemented by using the concept of MapReduce [55]. The accuracy was checked with original trip advisor and feedback from Facebook and Twitter had been collected. They all proved that while processing or analyzing such large-scale data, it considerably enhances the accuracy and scalability of service RSs.

7.2.5.2 Recommendation system with Hadoop Framework on big data

Verma *et al.* [56] offer a recommendation system for the huge amount data accessible on the web in the type of rankings, complain, opinions, remarks, reviews, feedback and comments regarding any item (product, event, individual and services) by using Hadoop Framework. A hybrid filtering technique is offered to filter different types of complains, opinions, remarks, reviews, feedback, comments, etc. Since recommendations are all based on ratings, ranks, content, reviewers behavior and timing of review created by various reviewers, they have devised a recommendation system for Movielans dataset on the Hadoop framework and made analyzing possible within different range of size files. It has been proved that when the size of a file increases, the execution time do not increase simultaneously, while data size in the type of ratings, ranks, review, feedback is notably increasing. Recommendation based on applying the weight age of summarized reviews and opinions on the rating of an item are proposed as a further investigation [56].

7.3 Recommender systems: challenges and limitations

Accuracy, novelty, sparsity, scalability and cold start are problems which RSs deal with while processing or analyzing large-scale data. These terms will be defined as follows:

- **High recommendation accuracy:** A good recommendation system should output a relatively short list of songs in which many pieces are favored by the user and few pieces are not.
- **High recommendation novelty:** RSs should be diverse and well-balanced, i.e., the system's content is wide ranged and informative while not diverging much from the user's preferences. Even though most traditional RSs use the similar ratings and rankings system, not all of them take diversity of user's preferences into account, and this is the reason why they fall short of meeting user's personalized requirements.
- **Data sparsity:** In fact, loads of commercial RSs stand on large datasets, and a large amount of items are left unrated by the majority of users. Therefore, the user–item matrix in CF will be extraordinarily large and sparse, and these are the challenges in the performances of the recommendation. Cold start is one of the common complexities caused by data sparsity. Recommendation of items in CF is based on user's previous preferences, and new users will need to rate sufficient number of items to enable the system to capture their preferences accurately and thus provide reliable recommendations. New items face the similar problem. Items newly added to system, require to be rated by considerable number of users. Then they possibly will be suggested to users with similar tastes with the ones who have rated them. The content-based recommendation will not face any limitation by the new item problem, since the recommendation of an item is totally based on its distinct set of descriptive qualities rather than its ratings.

- **Scalability:** At the same time as the numbers of users and items increase, traditional CF systems experience severe scalability difficulties. For instance, consider tens of millions of customers and millions of items; a CF system requires taking action instantaneously in online requirements, and irrespective of the user's purchases and ratings history provides recommendations for them all. Apparently, it requires a higher scalability of a CF system. To weigh up recommendations, great web companies such as Twitter employs clusters of machines for their millions of users. Nearly all calculations take place in extremely large memory machines.
- **Cold-start problem:** The cold start is a common problem in recommendation systems. When recommendations systems lack enough information about a user or an item, providing a reliable recommendation seem to be almost impossible; this is what a cold-start problem is all about. When a new user or item just comes into the system, almost no information about the user or item is available; as a result system fails to acquire assumption to suggest items to users. The cold-start problem refers to the situation when a new user or item just enters the system. Cold-start problem is in three forms: new user problem, new item problem and new system problem. In all these three cases, providing recommendation is almost a problem. Lack of information about new users and nonavailability of item ratings for newly added items make CF recommending nearly impossible.

Thus, what we realize is that the current systems apparently require serious enhancement and upgrading in order to provide high-quality recommendations.

7.4 Summary

Recently, RSs have gained much popularity; they are also used in various fields like music, movies, news, music, books, search queries, research papers, social tags and products in general. Recommendation systems are all about users and items. CF is used by a second class of recommendation system, these determine similarity of users by their item setting and/or determine similarity of items via the users who has preferred them. Recommendation methods are categorized as follows:

1. **Content-based recommendations:** These measure similarity by looking for common features of the items.
2. **Collaborative recommendations:** These determine similarity of users through their item setting and/or determine similarity of items by the users who has liked them.
3. **Knowledge-based recommendations:** Items are recommended to the users according to their preferences perceived from both item's attributes and user's profile.
4. **Demographic recommendations:** With the help of a demographic profile, specific harmonizing items can be recommended. Age, gender, etc., are demographic data which are obtainable both explicitly and implicitly.
5. **Hybrid recommendations:** Prior methods have many corresponding advantages and disadvantages when applied alone. So the combination of different techniques which are collaborative, content based, demographic and utility based and knowledge-based is the key to enhanced performance.

In real time, the volume of data is large and is in different forms like statistical, audio, video, text, sensor and biometric data that emerged from the term big data. The term big data describes innovative techniques and technologies to capture, store, distribute, manage and analyze petabyte or larger sized datasets with high-velocity in different forms such as audio, video, image and text. This unstructured data are tough challenges for the big data. Despite these challenges, recommendation systems have been introduced for big data, yet they are facing challenges—specifically, cold-start problem, high-recommendation novelty, high-recommendation accuracy, scalability and data sparsity can be mentioned. Therefore, the current recommended systems in the field of big data require improving the quality for enhanced recommendation.

References

[1] Venkatesh P. A survey on algorithm used in recommenders system. Int J Innovative Res Comput Commun Eng. 2016;4(6):27–38.

[2] Alag S. Collective intelligence in action. Shelter Island, NY: Manning Publications; 2008.

[3] Suganeshwari G, Syed Ibrahim SP. A survey on collaborative filtering based recommendation system. In: Proceedings of the 3rd International Symposium on Big Data and Cloud Computing Challenges, Feb 2016. Cham: Springer; vol. 49, pp. 503–518.

[4] Pazzani M. A framework for collaborative, content-based, and demographic filtering. Artif Intell Rev Spec Issue Data Min. 1999;13(5–6):393–408.

[5] Adomavicius G, Tuzhilin A. Toward the next generation of recommender systems: A survey of the state-of-the-art and possible extensions. IEEE Trans Knowl Data Eng. 2005;17(6):734–749.

[6] Su X, Khoshgoftaar TM. A survey of collaborative filtering techniques. Adv Artif Intell. 2009:19; Article ID 421425.

[7] Sarwat M, Levandoski JJ, Eldawy A, Mokbel MF. LARS*: An efficient and scalable location-aware recommender system. IEEE Trans Knowl Data Eng. 2014;26(6):1384–1399.

[8] Meng S, Guo W, Zhang X, *et al.* KASR: A keyword-aware service recommendation method on MapReduce for big data applications. IEEE Trans Parallel Distrib Syst. 2014;25(12):3221–3231.

[9] D Dell'Aglio, Celino I, Cerizza D, editors. Anatomy of a semantic web-enabled knowledge-based recommender system. In: Semantic Web Conf. Italy; 2010.

[10] Hiralall M. Recommender Systems for e-Shops. Amsterdam: Vrije Universiteit; 2011.

[11] Burke R. Hybrid Recommender Systems: Survey and Experiments. User Model User-Adapted Interact. 2002;12(4):331–370.

[12] Verma J P Agrawal S, Patel B, Patel A. Big data analytics: Challenges and applications for text, audio, video, and social media data. Int J Soft Comput Art Int App. 2016;5(1):41–51.

[13] Xu B, Zhuge H. An angle-based interest model for text recommendation. Future Gener Comput Syst. 2016;64:211–226.

[14]   Xu B, HZ. A text scanning mechanism simulating human reading process. In: 23th International Joint Conference on Artificial Intelligence, IJCAI 2013. ACM; August 3–9, 2013; pp. 2190–2196.

[15]   Liu H, TW, He J, Song W, Du X. Combining user preferences and user opinions for accurate recommendation. Electr Commerce Res Appl. 2013;12(1):14–23.

[16]   Zhao D, LZ, Zhao W. Genre-based link prediction in bipartite graph for music recommendation. Procedia Comp Sci. 2016;91:959–965.

[17]   Jia Y, JD, Shelhamer E, Girshick R, editors. Caffe: Convolutional architecture for fast feature embedding. Florida: ACM; 2014.

[18]   Sotiropoulos D N, GAT, Lampropoulos A S, MUSIPER: A system for modeling music similarity perception based on objective feature subset selection. User Model User Adapted Interac. 2008;18(4):315–348.

[19]   Shan M K MFC, Kuo F-F, Lee SY. Emotion-based music recommendation by affinity discovery from film music. Expert Syst Appl. 2009;36(4):666–7674.

[20]   Su J H, Chang W Y, Tseng V S. Personalized music recommendation by mining social media tags. Procedia Comput Sci. 2013;(22):303–312.

[21]   Mao K, Chen G, Hu Y, *et al.* Music recommendation using graph based quality model. Signal Process. 2016;120:806–813.

[22]   Shao B, Wang D, Li T, *et al.*. Music recommendation based on acoustic features and user access patterns. IEEE Trans Audio Speech Lang Process. 2009;17(8):1602–1611.

[23]   Foote J, Uchihashi S. The beat spectrum: A new approach to rhythm analysis. In: Proc. IEEE Int. Conf. Multimedia Expo. IEEE; 2001. p. 881–884.

[24]   Li T, Ogihara M, Li Q. A comparative study on content-based music genre classification. In: Proc. SIGIR. IEEE; 2003. p. 282–289.

[25]   Logan B, Salomon A. A content-based music similarity function. Technical Report, Cambridge Research Laboratory, CRL 2001/02, 2001.

[26]   Foote J, Cooper M, Nam U. Audio retrieval by rhythmic similarity. In: Proc. ISMIR'02; 2002. p. 265–266.

[27]   Tzanetakis G, Cook P. Music genre classification of audio signals. IEEE Trans Speech Audio Process. 2002;10:293–302.

[28]   Broder AZ, Charikar M, Frieze AM, *et al.* Minwise independent permutations. J Comput Syst Sci. 2000;60(3):630–659.

[29]   Szummer M, Jaakkola T. Partially labeled classification with Markov random walks. In: Advances in Neural Information Process. Syst. vol. 14; 2001.

[30]   Zhou D, Bousquet O, Lal T, *et al.* Learning with local and global consistency. In: Proc. 18th Annu. Conf. Neural Inf. Process. Syst.; 2003.

[31]   Zhu X, Ghahramani Z, Lafferty J. Semi-supervised learning using Gaussian fields and harmonic functions. In: Proc. ICML.; 2003.

[32]   Ding C, Jin R, Li T, *et al.* A learning framework using Green's function and kernel regularization with application to recommender system. In: Proc. KDD '07: 13th ACM SIGKDD Int. Conf. Knowledge Discovery Data Mining. New York; 2007. p. 260–269.

[33]   McFee B, Lanckriet G, Fürnkranz J, *et al.* Metric learning to rank. In: Proc. 27th Int. Conf. Mach. Learn., Ser. ICML, Haifa, Israel; 2010. p. 775–782.

[34] Sarwar B, Karypis G, Konstan J, *et al.* Item-based collaborative filtering recommendation algorithms. In: Proc. 10th Int. Conf. World Wide Web, ser. WWW '01., New York; 2001. p. 285–295.

[35] McFee B, Barrington L, Lanckriet G. Learning content similarity for music recommendation. IEEE Trans Audio Speech Lang Process. 2012;20(8):2207–2218.

[36] Tsochantaridis I, Joachims T, Hofmann T, *et al.* Large margin methods for structured and interdependent output variables. J Mach Learn Res. 2005;6:1453–1484.

[37] Koren Y, Bell R, Volinsky C. Matrix factorization techniques for recommender systems. Computer. 2009;(8):30–37.

[38] Bell RM, Koren Y. Scalable collaborative filtering with jointly derived neighborhood interpolation weights. In: Proc of the 2007 7th IEEE ICDM Conference. IEEE; 2007. p. 43–52.

[39] Huang Y, Cui B, Jiangx J, *et al.* Real-time video recommendation exploration. In: Proceedings of the 2016 International Conference on Management of Data San Francisco, CA, USA, June 26–July 1, 2016. pp. 35–46.

[40] Li Y Z, TG, Li X Y. Design of video recommender system based on cloud computing. J Commun. 2013;34(Z2):138–140, 147.

[41] Balachandra K. The video recommendation based on machine learning. Int J Inn Res Comp Comm Eng. 2018;6(6):6434–6439.

[42] Shang S, WS, Shi M, Hong Z. A Micro-video recommendation system based on big data. *IEEE/ACIS 15th International Conference on Computer and Information Science (ICIS)*, 2016. pp. 34–45.

[43] Lan M, JS, Tan C L, Lu Y. Supervised and traditional term weighting methods for automatic text categorization. IEEE Trans Pattern Anal Mach Intell. 2008;31(4).

[44] Gong S J, HWY, Tan HS. Combining memory-based and model-based collaborative filtering in recommender system. Pacific-Asia Conference on Circuits, Communications and Systems, May 2009, Chengdu, China. pp. 22–35.

[45] Bamnote GR, Agrawal SS. Evaluating and implementing collaborative filtering systems using apache Mahout. In: International Conference on Computing Communication Control and Automation, Feb 2015, Pune, India. pp. 11–24.

[46] Song SY, Wu KJ. A creative personalized recommendation algorithm— User-based slope one algorithm. In: International Conference on Systems and Informatics, May 2012, Yantai, China. pp. 56–65.

[47] Li L N, HC, Du X Y. MapReduce-Based SimRank computation and its application in social recommender system. In: 2013 IEEE International Congress on Big Data, Santa Clara, CA, USA. pp. 18–25.

[48] Ng P C, MC, She J, Cebulla A. An images-textual hybrid recommender system for vacation rental. In: 2016 IEEE Second International Conference on Multimedia Big Data, Taipei, Taiwan, Apr 2016. pp. 34–41.

[49] Nowak E, FJ, Triggs B. Sampling strategies for bag-of-features image classification. In: European Conference on Computer Vision; 2006. pp. 490–503.

[50] McAuley J, CT, Shi Q, Hengel A. Image-based Recommendations on Styles and Substitutes. In: Proceedings of the 38th International ACM SIGIR Conference on Research and Development in Information Retrieval, Santiago, Chile, August 9–13, 2015. pp. 43–52.

[51] Der M, Saul L. Latent coincidence analysis: A hidden variable model for distance metric learning. NIPS.

[52] Reshma M, Remesh Babu KR. Recommendation system: A big data application. In: INC-BEAT'16; 2016. p. 76–83.

[53] Yang X, Guo Y, Liu Y. Bayesian-inference based recommendation in online social networks. IEEE Trans Parallel Distrib Syst. 2013;24(4):642–651.

[54] Gang Q, Shamik S, Yuelong G, *et al.*, editors. Similarity between Euclidean and cosine angle distance for nearest neighbor queries. In: Proceedings of the 2004 ACM Symposium on Applied Computing. ACM; 2004.

[55] Jin Y, Hu M, Singh H, *et al.*, editors. MyS-pace video recommendation with MapReduce on Qizmt. In: Proceedings of the 4th Semantic Computing International Conference. IEEE; 2010.

[56] Verma J P, BP, Patel A. Big data analysis-recommendation system with Hadoop Framework. In: International Conference on Computational Intelligence & Communication Technology. IEEE; 2015.

Chapter 8

Deep segregation of plastic (DSP): segregation of plastic and nonplastic using deep learning

K. Sreelakshmi[1], R. Vinayakumar[1], and K.P. Soman[1]

Due to industrialization and urbanization, the rapid rise in the volume and amount of hazardous waste and the disposal of it is becoming a burgeoning problem that the world is facing today. One of the best ways out for this problem is to collect, sort and reuse or recycle these waste. This work proposes christened deep segregation of plastic (DSP) architecture which sorts waste materials into plastic and nonplastic using deep learning technique, convolutional neural network (CNN). CNN is one among the efficient modern machine learning techniques, which is able to provide maximum learning efficiency by taking raw input samples. CNN has become a state-of-the-art method for many of the tasks existing in computer vision (CV). In most of the tasks, it has performed well in comparison to the human. This has performed well in various tasks of CV compared to standard neural network. The developed framework is highly scalable on commodity hardware server. The framework collects data from different sensors, preprocess, and analyze using distributed algorithms. Now this framework is specifically developed for plastic segregation. Moreover, the framework can be easily extended to handle large volumes of other waste categories by adding additional resources. These characteristics have made the proposed framework stand out from any other system of similar kind. The proposed design also consists of a prototype which acts as a real-time classifier. The hardware setup consists of a conveyor belt over which the waste materials are placed, and these are captured by a camera fitted on the system. The captured image is sent to the DSP which classifies it into plastic and nonplastic, and accordingly it is moved to two different bins. This system can reduce the human efforts in separating plastics from nonplastics and also in keeping the environment neat and clean. The performance of the system is analyzed on various data sets. These data sets are collected from public and private sources. Various experiments are run for identifying the optimal parameters for CNN networks and structures. All these experiments are run till 1,000 epoch with varied learning rate 0.01–0.5.

[1]Center for Computational Engineering and Networking (CEN), Amrita School of Engineering, Amrita Vishwa Vidyapeetham, India

8.1   Introduction

Due to advancement of technology, the world today is producing uncountable products for the use of men. When it becomes unusable, we keep them with us and look for ways to dispose them off. The choices we have are to dispose them either in land or in water bodies. Either of these affects the environment and its living beings adversely. To a great extent, we can reduce harm caused by the disposal of waste in land or water by recycling them through some process [1–3]. To recycle, the waste material has to be collected and then segregated as per its nature and then recycled. Many of the disposed wastes can be recycled and new products made out of it. Metal items can be easily recycled and given shape to new products. Similarly, paper waste can be recycled and reused for printing purposes. As said earlier, in order to recycle the disposed wastes, we have to collect and segregate the materials. Commonly, this is done manually by people engaged for it. This manual method is causing harm to the life of the people. It is, therefore, highly important that we implement automation for the collection and segregation of waste.

There are so many techniques that are used for automatic waste segregation. Some methods use image-processing techniques to classify the waste. Size, color, texture, etc., of waste material is used to segregate them, and such systems are implemented using microcontrollers [1]. There are also waste segregators which work based on sensors. Different types of sensors such as capacitive sensors to detect plastic, glass, wood; inductive proximity sensors to detect metals, gas detection and optical sensors for detecting food items, etc., are used to segregate waste [3,4]. Segregation of waste is also done using radio frequency identification (RFID). In this type of segregation, the RFID is attached on each type of material during manufacturing, so that classification becomes easier [5].

Currently, different supervised learning techniques in machine learning are used for classification [6]. In supervised learning, the data set is labeled and the algorithm predicts the output from input data. The supervised learning algorithm learns to inherit structure from input data. Traditional supervised learning techniques rely on feature engineering, feature representation and feature-selection techniques. This requires extensive domain knowledge. Recently, deep learning algorithms have performed well in comparison to the traditional machine learning in various long standing intelligence tasks which are related to CV, natural language processing, speech processing, etc. They have the capability to learn optimal features by taking raw input samples. They pass the input data across many input hidden layers and try to learn the abstract feature representation. CNN is a type of deep learning algorithms. It has proved as a best classifier in several CV tasks [7]. This has also performed well on text [8–13] and time series data [14–16]. In this work, we employ CNN for waste segregation. The main objectives of this system are as follows:

- To develop scalable framework that can handle huge data set.
- Framework employs distributed and parallel algorithms with various optimization techniques that are capable of analyzing the plastic and nonplastic data.
- To implement a hardware setup to demonstrate the segregation of plastic and nonplastic trash.

The rest of the sections are organized as follows: Section 8.2 discusses the related work. Section 8.3 provided information of deep learning. Section 8.4 discusses the scalable architecture. Section 8.5 discusses software framework. Section 8.6 provides information about the used software packages. Section 8.7 discusses about the hardware components used. Section 8.8 discusses the hardware setup. Section 8.9 explains the detailed experiment and observation. Conclusion and future work is placed at Section 8.10.

8.2   Related work

This section discusses the related works of waste segregation. Initially, different machines were used to separate the waste into different categories. Few of them are as follows [17]:

- Trommel separators/drum screens: Trommel separator consists of a rotating drum perforated with holes in it. This separates wastes based on their sizes. When wastes are passed though the drum, the particles with small size pass out through the holes and large particles stay in the drum.
- Eddy current separator: It is used to separate metallic materials in waste. It makes use of electromagnetics for dividing the wastes into ferrous and nonferrous metal categories.
- Induction sorting: Here the system makes use of different type of sensors connected over a conveyor belt to segregate the waste.
- Near infrared sensors: This system uses the reflectance property as its parameter for distinguishing various waste materials, since different materials exhibit different reflective properties.
- X-ray technology: This system makes use of the density property of various material for distinguishing them.
- Lastly, the manual method is the most widely used method for separating waste. Here the wastes are segregated manually by hand.

George E Sakr automated the recognition of different type of wastes from their images using machine learning techniques. He used two learning algorithms, namely, CNN and support vector machines (SVM). The classifier was built to separate the waste into three main categories: plastic, paper and metal, and the accuracies obtained for the model by using both the models were noted and the best one was implemented using Raspberry Pi 3. A mechanical system controlled by Pi guides the waste from its initial position into the corresponding trash cans to which it was classified. The final implemented model produced in this research had very low average execution time (0.1s) on the Raspberry Pi 3 [18].

Mittal developed a smart phone-based application which detects a pile of garbage and identifies the location where the garbage is present by using the location access of the smart phones called as "spot garbage." It is built based on CNN and the model obtained an accuracy of 87%. The model was trained by using the patches which were extracted from the Bing Image Searches. This research showcases an architecture which reduces the memory consumed and also the time taken for prediction with zero accuracy loss, thus minimizing and optimizing the space consumed in the device used [19].

A research was done by Mindy Yang on garbage classifying. He classified them in to six different classes, namely, metal, paper, cardboard. He carried out the experiment on the hand collected data set which numbered approximately 400 plus images of each category. The models that he applied to classify the images into different categories were SVM with scale-invariant feature transform features and CNN. To construct the CNN classifier, Torch7 framework for Lua was used. A total of eleven layer CNN architecture was implemented, which is quite identical to AlexNet. The experiment proved that the SVM performs much efficiently compared to the CNN. The quantum of data used to train the model was 70%, and the data used to test is 30%. As optimal hyper parameters could not be obtained, certain categories were to be ignored to find the optimal accuracy, denoting the fact that CNN use was not trained to its entire potential [20].

8.3   Deep learning

Some of the most commonly used programs today are deep learning, artificial neural networks, deep neural networks and artificial intelligence. Application of these programs brings excellent result especially in the fields of CV (recognition of object and face [21]). Machine learning is an application of artificial intelligence which primarily aims at making the computer without human assistance. Of late, deep learning has been very much depended by researchers and industry people to derive solutions to their problems of varied domains. Figure 8.1 represents classification of deep learning architecture. The terms such as machine learning, neural networks and deep learning are part and parcel of any discussion on artificial intelligence. There exists a confusion among people as to whether deep learning, which is a sub field of machine learning, evolved from neural networks. It acts like human brain like processing of data and creating patterns for decision making. While traditional machine learning develops algorithms with data in a linear way, deep learning bears several neurons

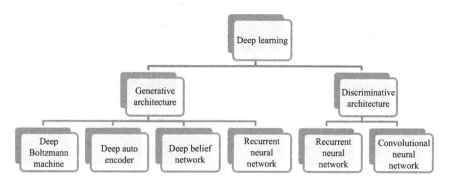

Figure 8.1   Taxonomy of deep learning models

connected like web, and it handles the data through a nonlinear method. With the tremendous advancement made in the computing technology and storage capacity, machine learning algorithms become capable to train on massive data sets. It learns hierarchical feature representation by transforming features from one layer to another. Deep learning has been extensively applied so solve problems existing in natural language processing, CV, robotic planning, etc. It has performed exceedingly well in artificial intelligence tasks existing in different domains compared to the statistical methods such as machine learning. With the advent and extensive application of deep learning, the areas like CV, speech processing, natural language processing have gained importance [7]. It is one of the features of deep learning algorithm that it has the ability to extract optimal feature representation by itself automatically by drawing raw input samples in security domain as well. Following are the two most commonly used deep learning algorithms:

- Recurrent structures
- CNN.

In machine learning, we do three things for classification:

- Collect data
- Train a model using the collected data
- Test the trained model to make new predictions.

To make machine learning easier, we need to do two things:

- Feature engineering
- Feature learning.

Feature engineering: Feature engineering is extraction of useful patterns of images or the features of images which will make the machine learning models to distinguish between different classes. Feature engineering will increase the accuracy of the result but it is a very different task because for, different data set, we require different feature engineering techniques. So we prefer to use algorithms that extract feature automatically.

Feature learning: Feature learning is nothing but feature engineering done automatically by algorithms. Feature learning algorithm extracts patterns automatically that are important and make the distinction between classes easier.

Although neural networks were developed in 1960s, it did not get much popularity due to nonavailability of proper training methods. This made it an unworthy program. Then in 1980, with the inclusion of some mathematical applications, position improved and it gained popularity. While it slowly picked up again in 1990s and 2000, it has been affected by the application of SVM. Though neural networks are far superior to other programs, it was not feasible due to both algorithmic and computational limitations. However, of late, neural network has again appeared in the form of deep learning due to improvements made in the algorithmic and its implementation on graphical processing units (GPUs). Deep learning is successfully applied in almost all fields [21].

CNN: It is a form of neural network commonly used for image classification. Unlike the other traditional network which has densely connected layers, CNN shares weights between receptive fields. This reduces the number of parameters and CNN employs convolution mechanism with filters. CNN is a network that learns the filters to use, i.e., the features to extract, in order to classify. The network takes input data, transforms it by calculating a weighed sum over the input and applies a nonlinear filter for this transformed input to find an intermediate state. These three steps constitute a layer. The commonly used nonlinear activation function is rectified linear unit (*ReLU*).

CNN constitute combination of the following layers:

Convolution layer: This layer contains many filters, and each filter produced an image containing a particular feature. So the output of a convolution layer will be a stack of images called Tensor.

Maxpool layer: This layer is used to reduce the size of the input by merging the neighboring elements by taking the maximum value. Hence, a two-dimensional window is chosen, and it is convolved over each image in steps. After each step, we get values which fall within the window; from these values, the maximum value is chosen and after all convolution steps, a matrix of all these chosen values is formed which is of low dimension. This will help to reduce the number of parameters and hence the amount of computation.

Fully connected layer: In this layer, we have many units. In this layer, each unit is connected to every other unit of the succeeding layer. Fully connected layer map the data to higher dimension. As the dimension increases, the accuracy of output also increases. In this work, the *sigmoid* activation function with binary cross entropy as loss function is used. The binary cross entropy is defined mathematically as follows:

$$loss(pd, ed) = -\frac{1}{N}\sum_{i=1}^{N}[ed_i \log pd_i + (1 - ed_i)\log(1 - pd_i)] \tag{8.1}$$

where *pd* is a vector of predicted probability for all samples in testing data set and *ed* is a vector of expected class label, values are either 0 or 1.

8.4 Scalable architecture

With the aim to train deep learning models at scale, two types of Apache Spark cluster setup are implemented by following [22]:

- Distributed deep learning on GPUs (NVidia GK110BGL Tesla k40)
- Distributed deep learning on CPUs.

As the research work is of confidential nature, we cannot disclose the scalable framework details. A prototype of distributed computing architecture is shown in Figure 8.2. The configuration of each system goes as in Table 8.1.

Figure 8.2   Distributed computing platform

Table 8.1   System configuration

RAM	32 GB
Hard disk	2 TB
CPU	Intel® Xeon® CPU E3-1220 v3 @ 3.10 GHz
Ethernet network	1 Gbps

Above the Apache Hadoop[1] one more resource negotiator (YARN), Apache Spark[2] cluster arrangement is provided. This setup permits the end users to quickly distribute, carry out and complete the jobs. Each machine, whether it is physical or virtual device in Apache Spark cluster, is considered as a node. The framework setup consists of the following three types of nodes:

- Master node
- Slave node
- Data storage node

Master node: What it does is, it oversees all other nodes and makes it possible for the end user to communicate to the other nodes in the cluster by providing an interface. Apart from this, it helps distribute the workload to the slave nodes and consolidate the output from all other slave nodes. In off-line evaluation, it gets data from the data storage node and does preprocessing and then segmentation.

Slave nodes: It is in slave nodes the actual computation takes place. In off-line system, it gathers the preprocessed data from the master node and then carries out the actual computation.

Data storage node: Its role is to serve as a data base to help store the data in off-line evaluations. As per the command of the master node, the data storage node

---

[1] http://hadoop.apache.org/
[2] https://spark.apache.org/

acts as a slave node. It maintains the data on day-to-day basis, consolidate and store in NoSQL data base. The advantage of it is that the data can be retrieved in whatever basis we require, that is, daily, weekly or monthly format.

The distributed deep learning framework has been developed keeping in view the advantages listed below:

- It supports to increase the speed of training deep learning models, thereby the task of hyper parameter selection becomes easier.
- We can deploy this type of system in large scale in real time to analyze huge quantity of data. This will detect and issue an alert in proper time.

8.5 Software framework

With the addition of software frameworks, it has become easy to implement deep learning program. A comparative study of deep learning software has been conducted on CPU and GPU devices and discussed on its speed, hardware utilization and extensibility [23]. It was also tested in Google's data flow search engine TensorFlow [1]. It permits the programmers to build numerical systems as unified data flow graphs. The data flow graphs have nodes and edges representing mathematical operations and the tensors, respectively. It also permits the programmers to use more than one device, i.e., CPU, GPU or mobile to experiment. To accelerate the gradient descent computations, all experiments are run on GPU-enabled TensorFlow in single NVidia GK110BGL Tesla k40. CNNs are parameterized functions such as learning rate, epochs, filters and to find out the optimal values for them, various configurations for network parameters and structure are used for all the experiments.

8.6 Software and packages

8.6.1 TensorFlow

It is an open-source software library which is used computing complex mathematical operations especially numerical methods. Hence, this is also used as a machine-learning tool especially for CNN and deep learning. TensorFlow uses dataflow graphs for computing. Dataflow graphs are made of edges and nodes. All the data are stored in the edges which are multidimensional arrays. The nodes are used to build computational graphs. Three types of nodes, namely, constant, variable and placeholder can be used to build a dataflow graph:

Constant: Constants are nodes which hold a value which cannot be changed throughout and operation.

Placeholder: In order to place a value with another value once an operation is done with former value, a placeholder is needed.

Variable: To make a model trainable, the value of the weights should be changed every cycle. Hence, a variable node is needed to do a training operation.

Designing a dataflow graph involves two processes. Building a dataflow graph and running a dataflow graph. As a first process, nodes are designed and interconnected. Running the dataflow graph involves getting the input from edges and starting the computation process. Codes interact with TensorFlow system using sessions [1].

Computational graph for a deep learning network includes bias node (b) and weight node (W) as variables and input node (X) as placeholder. Values at input node and weight node are multiplies, and the product is added to a bias node. The reason is explained at the beginning of the report. The value is given to an activation function which is connected to the output.

$$h = \text{ReLU}(WX + b) \tag{8.2}$$

The h variable holds the output value for given input. The values of the bias and weight nodes are changed at every cycle using back propagation method; the input nodes are given input at every cycle.

The activation functions available in TensorFlow are **sigmoid function** and **ReLU** function. Sigmoid function quashes the given input into a bounded interval. ReLU function reduces the processing time by 50% especially during the input cycle.

When images are used for training, the RGB features of the images are extracted and stored in an array. When image is given as input, instead of taking the whole image, the images are resized for computer interpretation.

8.6.2 Keras

Keras is a tool in python to work on neural network as application program interface. Keras is built for the convenience of the users in designing a neural network. It reduces the efforts of users by using many in-built functions. Compared with TensorFlow it provides a clear idea in designing and showing outcomes of a neural network.

8.6.3 OpenCV

CV is a programming tool for a computer to interpret and process images and video, or in simple terms, it can be said as an eye of a computer. As the cornea in our eyes receive images and processes the images and sends to our brain, OpenCV receives an image as input by capturing and processing it for a purpose needed by the user. It is now used in many fields such as engineering, technology and entertainment and thus, being a free open-source tool, has led to many uses for commercial purposes. Bringing a small change in OpenCV can create a lot of change when it is used for commercial purposes. OpenCV which offers us with many packages and in-built functions for free has also assured with optimized, portable and easy-coding environment, thus enabling the users to code easily. To advance the vision research, to improve the vision knowledge, it is necessary to have programming functions.

OpenCV library has several modules, where each and every module is dedicated to single group of CV tasks. "Namespace cv" is used to call any functions or classes. To access the cv2 into a coding environment, "import cv2" is used, and in order to call any class or function within the libraries of open cv, it is required to give cv2.function name, for example, in order to read an image, which is captured by a camera and which

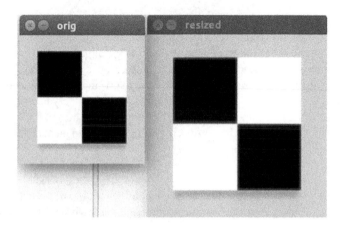

Figure 8.3   Resized enlarged image

is to be given as input, the command "cv2.imread()" is given. Image is given as digital input to the computer in the form of pixels where each pixel has a value depending on its intensity. Each pixel should be processed in an effective manner so that each image being a collection of more than 10,000 pixel are effectively processed. Image is considered to be a matrix of pixels, and each pixel represents one entry of a matrix.

If Grey level images are used for processing, then each pixel is of 8-bit length, whereas for a colored image, where each pixel is made of RGB colors, each color is considered to have 8-bit length. Hence, as a whole for three colors, 24 bit are used, thereby making each pixel 24 bit-length. It is necessary to combine images for doing mathematical operations. Combining images has numerous functions, namely, add, multiply, and divide.

OpenCV for CNN: Before an image is given as an input for neural network either for training or testing, the image is to be preprocessed. The image has to be resized, dimensions to be changed and at last normalized. Each function is an in-built library in OpenCV software. Hence, the images are processed in an easier manner without any complex coding.

In order to read the captured image, cv2.imread("img file") is given. Then the pixel values of the images are extracted. These images, instead of being given directly, are resized, and then further preprocessing is done. All the collected images are converted to images of same size Figure 8.3.

As a next process, images are to be converted from BRG to RGB format. This is done as images are processed in TensorFlow as RGB format, but the input image is always in BRG format.

At last the images are to be normalized for convenience of training the neural network. As each pixel value can have a maximum of 255 pixel, each pixels are divided by 255 and the normalized image is given as input for neural network. For testing, the captured image is resized and normalized and then given to neural network for testing Figure 8.4.

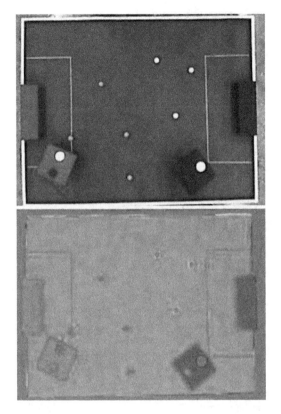

Figure 8.4　Original image (top) and normalized image (bottom)

8.7　Hardware components used

8.7.1　Arduino UNO

The Arduino UNO microcontroller board shown in Figure 8.5 works based on ATmega 328 datasheet. The board has 14 digital input/output pins; out of this, 6 are PWM output pins and 6 analog pins. It can be powered by using a 9 V battery or by connecting it to a computer via a USB cable. It uses STK500 protocol for communication and ATmega 16U2 as a USB to serial converter [24]. Arduino can be coded by using C or C++. The specifications of the board is given in Table 8.2.

Specifications: There are two types of pin functions, namely, general pin function and special pin function.

- General pin function
  - LED: There is a built-in LED which is driven by the digital pin 13. When the pin is given a high value, the LED is on and when it is given a low value, the LED is off.
  - VIN Pin: Voltage required for the board is supplied through this pin.

Figure 8.5   Arduino UNO

Table 8.2   Specifications

Operating voltage	5 V
DC current per input/output pin	20 mA
Dc current for 3.3 V pin	50 mA
Flash memory	32 KB
SRAM	2 KB
EEPROM	1 KB
Clock speed	16 MHz

- 5 V Pin: This pin provides an output voltage of 5 V.
- 3.3 V Pin: An output voltage of 3.3 V can be drawn from this pin.
- GND Pin: There are two ground pins; one for 5 V and one for 3.3 V pin.
- IOREF Pin: This pin provides a reference voltage with which the board operates.
- Reset Pin: It is used to add a reset button.
- 2. Special pin function
  - Serial: Pin 0 and Pin 1 are the serial pins. Pin 0 is used to receive serial data and Pin 1 is used to transmit serial data.
  - External interrupts: Pins 2 and 3 are the interrupt pins. These pins can be used to trigger an interrupt.
  - PWM: PWM is the pulse width modulation pin. Pins 3, 5, 6, 9, 10 and 11 provide 8 bit PWM output.
  - TWI: TWI stands for two wire interface. Analog pins A4 and A5 are the TWI pins that used for TWI communication.

8.7.2 Windshield wiper motor

Windshield wiper motor with an in-built permanent magnet is a most commonly used one in automotive vehicle. It is used to drive the wiper of the vehicle to provide clear view to the driver. The rotation of a wiper motor makes the wiper to move back and forth. The motor works on an input voltage of 12 V. The motor can work in two different speeds; they are single speed and two speed. When the motor works in a normal speed, it makes 40 wipes per minute, and when it works in high speed, it makes 60 wipes per minute.

Operation: A windshield wiper motor consists of an armature shaft and three brushes which are brush 1, brush 2 and brush g. When we connect the motor to a power supply, maximum of 12 V, the brushes 1 and g get current. This current received by the brushes generates a magnetic field. We know by Fleming's left hand thumb rule that the current, magnetic field and force are mutually perpendicular to each other. So the magnetic field generated by the current is perpendicular to armature shaft. This perpendicular magnetic field creates a force on the shaft which makes the shaft to rotate. In this case, the magnetic fields generated by the two brushes 1 and g are opposite to each other, so the motor runs at high speed. Like before, the current generates a magnetic field on brush 2 and g. The magnetic fields on brushes 2 and g are perpendicular to the force on copper winding. This force on copper winding generated by brushes 1 and g is less compared to the force generated by brushes 2 and g, so the armature shafts rotates at low speed in this case [25].

8.7.3 Stepper motor

The stepper motor is a brushless DC motor. It has a small piece of iron in the center around which electromagnets are arranged. Permanent magnet stepper, Hybrid synchronous stepper and variable reluctance stepper are the three different types of stepper motors. Stepper motor finds wide range of applications in the field of lasers and optics. It is also used in commonly used devices such as printers, scanners.

To make the shaft of the motor run, power is given to one electromagnet which will magnetically attract the gear teeth. The gear teeth slightly align to the next electromagnet which will make the first electromagnet turn off and turns on the second electromagnet. This process continues for all the electromagnets which will make the shaft rotate. The motor has a main advantage that it can be positioned anywhere.

Two-phase stepper motor: There are two types of stepper motors. Based on the electromagnetic coil arrangement, they are divided as unipolar and bipolar stepper motor. The difference between them is that the bipolar motor has only a single winding for a phase, whereas a unipolar motor also has a single winding for one phase but with a center tap. The specification of 4SGH-050A 51S stepper motor is shown in Table 8.3.

8.7.4 Switching power supply

Switching power supply/switching mode power supply (SMPS) transfers power from a DC or AC source to DC load. It is commonly installed in computers. The main

*Table 8.3   Specification of 4SGH-050A 51S
stepper motor*

Operating voltage	5 V
Resistance	5 W
Current	1 mA
Phase	4
No. of leads	6
Step angle	1.8 degree per step

advantage of SMPS is that it can supply three different voltage values, i.e., 3.3, 5 and 12 V. As it receives power supply from AC/DC source, it can constantly supply the required voltage and will not get drained up like a battery. A fan is provided inside the SMPS to avoid the equipment getting heated up even when used continuously for long time.

The functioning of an SMPS is as follows:

- Input rectifier stage: The input to the rectifier can either be from AC or DC source. If it is from DC source, no conversion takes place, whereas if it is from AC source, it has to be converted to DC. This process of conversion from AC-to-DC value is called rectification.
- Inverter chopper stage: The function of this stage is to convert the DC output received from the previous stage or the direct DC input received from the main supply to convert to AC. This conversion is happening by passing the DC through an oscillator with an output transformer
- Output rectifier and filtering stage: If the required output is DC, the AC output received from the transformer is rectified. The rectification could be done by using silicon diodes or Schottky diodes or MOSFETs. For higher voltage, silicon diodes are preferred and for lower voltage Schottky diodes are preferred. For very low voltage, MOSFETs are used. The rectified output is further smoothened by inductive and capacitive filters.

8.7.5   ULN 2003

ULN 2003 is most commonly used IC to drive a stepper motor. It has an array of Darlington transistors. These Darlington pair has two bipolar transistors which can amplify current. Since there are two bipolar transistors, the current amplified by one is further amplified by the other resulting in double amplification.

The IC has a total of 16 pins which includes 7 input pins, 7 output pins, 1 Vcc and 1 Ground Pin. The IC can withstand current of 500–600 mA.

8.7.6   Webcam

Webcam is used to capture a stream of real-time images or videos. It can be connected to the computer through a USB. These cameras find a wide range of applications in

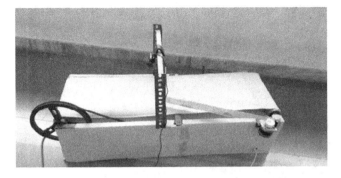

Figure 8.6 Hardware setup for segregation

the areas of security, health monitoring, traffic control and in houses for making video calls, etc.

The hardware setup includes the following minor components apart from the major ones mentioned above:

- Wheel: for the movement of the conveyor belt.
- Belt: for the movement of the conveyor belt.
- Canvas conveyor bearing: for the smooth movement of the conveyor.

8.8 Hardware setup for segregation

As shown in Figure 8.6, the hardware setup consists of a conveyor belt which is run by a wind shield wiper motor, a camera, a gate which is moved by a stepper motor. The motor is controlled using a motor driver ULN 2003 and an Arduino board. The power supply required for the entire system is given by an SMPS. The waste material to be segregated is placed on the conveyor belt such that it is captured by the camera. The demo of the working of the hardware prototype is shown in footnote 4,[3] and the video showing each components whose pictures are not shown in the chapter is shown in footnote 5.[4]

The image captured by the camera is sent to the CNN code for preprocessing and classifying as plastic or nonplastic. The grouping of picture is done in framework utilizing CNN. CNN comprises two hidden layers, and one completely associated layer which give the outcome whether the picture is plastic or nonplastic. The output is given as probability value. If the probability value is more than 0.5, then the waste material is plastic, and if the probability value is more than 0.5, then the waste material is nonplastic.

Figure 8.7 shows the plastic image on the conveyor belt. If the system identifies the material as plastic, that is, if the probability value obtained is greater than 0.5, a

---

[3]http://nlp.amrita.edu/DSP/index.html
[4]http://nlp.amrita.edu/DSP/index.html

Figure 8.7   Plastic object in the conveyor belt

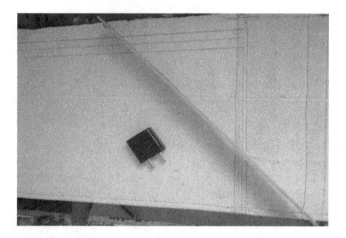

Figure 8.8   Use of motor to dispose plastic wastes to the bin

Figure 8.9   Nonplastic disposal

character (e.g., "o") is sent (serial communication) to the Arduino board. The board immediately switches on the stepper motor which moves the gate to an angle of 45 degrees (i.e., 25 stages) with a speed of 60 rpm. And after few seconds, the motor returns back to its default state Figure 8.8.

Now if the system identifies the material as nonplastic as shown in Figure 8.9, that is, if the probability value obtained is less than 0.5, then the gate will be in the open state and the material over the belt moves straight to the end and falls to the bin.

8.9   Experiments and observation

Generally, any machine learning model contains two modules, training and testing. The images used for training is required to train the neural network, whereas the images for testing is used to predict the accuracy of the system. Data set of waste materials required for our setup is collected; they are trained and tested using CNN. The images of plastic waste and nonplastic waste are collected real time using mobile camera as well as from internet for training. The detailed statistics of various data sets is reported in Table 8.4. Data sets 1 and 2 is collected from Internet sources. Data set 3 is collected from real-time camera. Data set 4 is a combination of data sets 1, 2 and 3. The experiment is done in four different ways:

- The network is trained with images from the internet and tested using the images from the internet (data set 1).
- The network is trained with images from the internet and tested using the images from the internet (data set 2).
- The network is trained with images from the captured real time and tested using the images captured real time (data set 3).
- The network is trained with images captured real time and tested using the images captured real time.
- The network is trained with images captured in real time and tested using the images from internet and captured real time.

8.9.1   Training process

The function block diagram shown in Figure 8.10. It consists of three different sections, namely, input layer, hidden layer and output layer. In input layer, collection of

Table 8.4   Detailed statistics of data set

Data	Training	Testing
Data set 1	2,021	506
Data set 2	3,974	994
Data set 3	1,980	1,230
Data set 4 (data set 1 + data set 2 + data set 3)	7,975	2,730

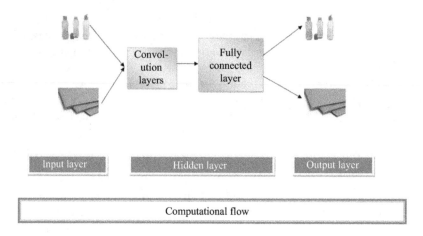

Figure 8.10   Function block diagram

samples and preprocessing is done, and then it is passed to a hidden layer where we have CNN layer and full connected layer. CNN layer extracts features implicitly on its own and pass it to fully connected layer for classification. In the output layer, the sigmoid activation function outputs values as 0s and 1s where 0 represents plastic and 1 represents nonplastic.

Preprocessing: The images are converted to HDF5 file format as the images cannot be given directly to the neural networks. The images are labeled as 1 if it is plastic and 0 if nonplastic. All the images together are put into a folder, and these images are shuffled irrespective of classes. 80% of the images are used for training and 20% for testing. First an empty hdf5 file is created. These images are preprocessed and properly fed to this empty hdf5 file. This hdf5 file is later used for training. The images are resized to dimensions of (56, 56), and each image has three channels. The data order is given as (56, 56, 3) if theano is used as backend, else the data order goes as (3, 56, 56) if TensorFlow [26]. CV2 loads image as BRG, hence it has to be changed to RGB, and this is further preprocessed by resizing and normalizing. The images and labels of training and testing data are extracted using SciKit package.

Building neural network: Neural network consists of convolutional layer, maxpooling layer, activation layer. By following hyper parameter tuning method, best CNN network is selected. CNN has a parameterized function; thus, the performance depends on the optimal parameters. Initially, two trials of experiments are run for filters in the range [4–32] and filter length 3 with the moderately sized CNN composed of CNN, maxpooling followed by fully connected layer. The CNN network with filter 32 performed well in comparison to the other filters. Thus, number of filters value is set to 32 for the rest of the experiments. To select optimal learning rate, three trials of experiments were run with learning rate in the range [0.01–0.5]. CNN network with learning rate 0.1 performed well in comparison to the other experiments. The detailed results are reported in Table 8.5 and the configuration details of CNN network are reported in Table 8.6.

Table 8.5 Detailed statistics of data set

Data set	Accuracy	Recall	Precision	*F*-score
1	0.978	0.913	0.979	0.945
2	0.969	0.967	0.979	0.973
3	0.480	0.480	1.000	0.648
4	0.953	0.937	0.980	0.958

Table 8.6 Detailed statistics of model

Layer (type)	Output shape	Param
conv2d_1(Conv2D)	(None,32,56,56)	896
activation_1(Activation)	(None,32,56,56)	0
conv2d_2(Conv2D)	(None,32,56,56)	9,248
activation_2(Activation)	(None,32,56,56)	0
max_pooling2d_1(MaxPooling2)	(None,32,27,27)	0
dropout_1(Dropout)	(None,32,27,27)	0
conv2d_3(Conv2D)	(None,64,27,27)	18,496
activation_3(Activation)	(None,64,27,27)	0
conv2d_4(Conv2D)	(None,64,25,25)	36,928
activation_4(Activation)	(None,64,25,25)	0
max_pooling2d_2(MaxPooling2)	(None,64,12,12)	0
dropout_2(Dropout)	(None,64,12,12)	0
flatten_1(Dense)	(None,9216)	0
dense_1(Dense)	(None,128)	1,179,776
activation_5(Activation)	(None,128)	0
dropout_3(Dropout)	(None,128)	0
dense_2(Dense)	(None,1)	129
activation_6(Activation)	(None,1)	0

To identify CNN network architecture to train a model that can classify the waste into plastic or nonplastic, two trials of experiments are run for the following network topologies:

- CNN 1 layer
- CNN 2 layer
- CNN 3 layer

The performance of CNN 2 layer is good in comparison to CNN 1 layer and CNN 3 layer. Due to over fitting, the CNN 3 layer performance trails the CNN 2 layer. The optimal CNN model configuration details are given in Table 8.6.

Testing:

Preprocessing: The image captured by the camera is preprocessed for prediction. Hence, the image is resized and BRG to RGB conversion is also done. Then the image is normalized by dividing the pixels by 255. The image is resized for dimension (56, 56).

8.10   Conclusion and future work

In the current research work, waste-segregation-management system is thoroughly studied and developed an automated proof of concept model by leveraging the application of deep learning techniques. Specifically, segregation of plastic and nonplastic problem is considered. Deep learning techniques provide facility to pass raw image samples as such to the model and obtain an optimal feature representation. This feature representation helps to segregate the plastic and nonplastic images. The hardware setup model demonstrates the segregation of plastic and nonplastic waste implemented using CNN. The performance of the CNN model is evaluated on various data sets. It performed well in almost all the data sets. The prototype designed has given a better idea of how a waste-segregating machine can be designed. This system can be used for commercial purpose by any manufacturing company. This model, when used for commercial purpose, can be more advantageous, as it can reduce humans getting infected due to wastes and reducing the efforts of them.

Due to computational time and other requirements, we were unable to try out experiments with the more complex architecture. Thus, even more images can be used to train and even more epochs can be done to increase the accuracy, thus reducing the error of prediction. The machine can be designed in even more user friendly manner so that this product can be commercialized in future. Additionally, CNN methodology can be integrated with other machine learning techniques such as SVM so that it can prove to achieve a greater efficiency [17]. Additionally, the recent trend in artificial intelligence is switching towards CapsNet because it has the capability to use 3D imaging and can achieve good performance with less data set. Thus, this CapsNet outperforms CNN in image-classification tasks [27].

Appendix A

Pin configuration for ULN 2003: The pin configuration for ULN 2003 is shown in Figure A.1.

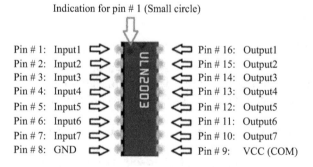

Figure A.1   Pin configuration for ULN 2003

Appendix B

Pin diagram of Arduino UNO: The pin diagram of Arduino UNO is shown in Figure B.1.

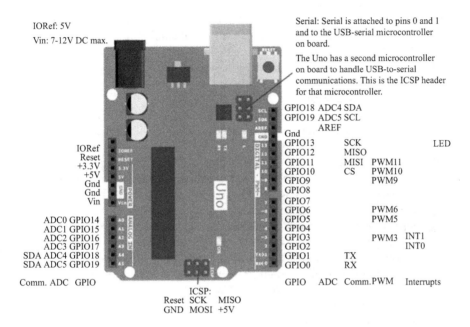

Figure B.1   Pin diagram of Arduino UNO

Acknowledgments

We are grateful to NVIDIA India, for the GPU hardware support to research grant. We are also grateful to Computational Engineering and Networking (CEN) department for encouraging the research.

References

[1]   Abadi M, Barham P, Chen J, *et al.* TensorFlow: A system for large-scale machine learning. In: OSDI. vol. 16; 2016. p. 265–283.

[2]   Ante L. Cem surgere: Surgite postquam sederitis, qui manducatis panem doloris. Omnes. 1916;13:114–119.

[3]   Chandramohan A, Mendonca J, Shankar NR, *et al.* Automated waste segregator. In: India Educators' Conference (TIIEC), 2014 Texas Instruments. IEEE; 2014. p. 1–6.

[4] Sharanya A, Harika U, Sriya N, *et al.* Automatic waste segregator. In: Advances in Computing, Communications and Informatics (ICACCI), 2017 International Conference on. IEEE; 2017. p. 1313–1319.

[5] Tim Dettmers, NVIDIA. Available at https://devblogs.nvidia.com/deep-learning-nutshell- core-concepts/, accessed on 4.5.18. 2015.

[6] Kittali RM, Sutagundar A. Automation of waste segregation system using PLC. International Journal on Engineering Technologies (ICRIET). 2016;7(2): 265–268.

[7] Kotsiantis SB, Zaharakis I, Pintelas P. Supervised machine learning: A review of classification techniques. Emerging Artificial Intelligence Applications in Computer Engineering. 2007;160:3–24.

[8] Vinayakumar R, Soman K, Poornachandran P. Detecting malicious domain names using deep learning approaches at scale. Journal of Intelligent & Fuzzy Systems. 2018;34(3):1355–1367.

[9] Vinayakumar R, Soman K, Poornachandran P. Evaluating deep learning approaches to characterize and classify malicious URLs. Journal of Intelligent & Fuzzy Systems. 2018;34(3):1333–1343.

[10] Vinayakumar R, Soman K, Poornachandran P, *et al.* Evaluating deep learning approaches to characterize and classify the DGAs at scale. Journal of Intelligent & Fuzzy Systems. 2018;34(3):1265–1276.

[11] Mohan VS, Vinayakumar R, Soman K, *et al.* Spoof net: Syntactic patterns for identification of ominous online factors. In: 2018 IEEE Security and Privacy Workshops (SPW). IEEE; 2018. p. 258–263.

[12] Hiransha M, Unnithan NA, Vinayakumar R, *et al.* Deep Learning Based Phishing E-mail Detection.

[13] Vinayakumar R, Barathi Ganesh HB, Anand Kumar M, Soman KP. DeepAnti-PhishNet: Applying Deep Neural Networks for Phishing Email Detection.

[14] Vinayakumar R, Soman K, Poornachandran P. Applying convolutional neural network for network intrusion detection. In: Advances in Computing, Communications and Informatics (ICACCI), 2017 International Conference on. IEEE; 2017. p. 1222–1228.

[15] Selvin S, Vinayakumar R, Gopalakrishnan E, *et al.* Stock price prediction using LSTM, RNN and CNN-sliding window model. In: Advances in Computing, Communications and Informatics (ICACCI), 2017 International Conference on. IEEE; 2017. p. 1643–1647.

[16] Vinayakumar R, Soman K, Poornachandran P. Secure shell (ssh) traffic analysis with flow based features using shallow and deep networks. In: Advances in Computing, Communications and Informatics (ICACCI), 2017 International Conference on. IEEE; 2017. p. 2026–2032.

[17] Sabour S, Frosst N, Hinton GE. Dynamic routing between capsules. In: Advances in Neural Information Processing Systems; 2017. p. 3856–3866.

[18] Sakr GE, Mokbel M, Darwich A, *et al.* Comparing deep learning and support vector machines for autonomous waste sorting. In: Multidisciplinary Conference on Engineering Technology (IMCET), IEEE International. IEEE; 2016. p. 207–212.

[19]   Mittal G, Yagnik KB, Garg M, *et al.* SpotGarbage: Smartphone app to detect garbage using deep learning. In: Proceedings of the 2016 ACM International Joint Conference on Pervasive and Ubiquitous Computing. ACM; 2016. p. 940–945.

[20]   Yang GTM, Thung G. Classification of Trash for Recyclability Status. CS229 Project Report. 2016;2016.

[21]   Culjak I, Abram D, Pribanic T, *et al.* A brief introduction to OpenCV. In: MIPRO, 2012 Proceedings of the 35th International Convention. IEEE; 2012. p. 1725–1730.

[22]   Vinayakumar R, Poornachandran P, Soman K. Scalable Framework for Cyber Threat Situational Awareness Based on Domain Name Systems Data Analysis. In: Big Data in Engineering Applications. Singapore, Springer; 2018. p. 113–142.

[23]   Bahrampour S, Ramakrishnan N, Schott L, Shah M. Comparative study of deep learning software frameworks. arXiv preprint arXiv:151106435. 2015.

[24]   Louis L. Working principle of Arduino and using it as a tool for study and research. Journal of Control Automation Communication and Systems. 2016;1:21–29.

[25]   Ashik K, Basavaraju A. Automatic wipers with mist control. American Journal of Engineering Research (AJER). 2014;3:24–34.

[26]   Bergstra J, Breuleux O, Bastien F, *et al.* Theano: A CPU and GPU math compiler in Python. In: Proc. 9th Python in Science Conf. vol. 1; 2010.

[27]   Capel C. Waste sorting—A look at the separation and sorting techniques in today's European market. Waste Management World. 2008:1–8. http://waste-management-world com/a/waste-sorting-a-look-at-the-separation-and-sorting-techniques-in-todayrsquos-european-market [Accessed 1 July 2008].

Chapter 9

Spatiotemporal recommendation with big geo-social networking data

Weiqing Wang[1] and Hongzhi Yin[2]

Recommendation has become an important mobile application on *location-based social networks (LBSNs)*, especially when users travel to a new place far away from their home. Compared to traditional recommender systems, this type of recommendation is very challenging. A user on geo-social network usually visits only a very limited number of spatial items (points of interest), resulting in sparse user–item matrix. As most users tend to visit the spatial items nearby their homes, the user–item matrix will become even sparser when users travel to a distant place. Another major challenge is that, users' interests and behavior patterns tend to vary dramatically across different time period and different geographical regions. In this chapter, we focus on effective spatial item recommendation by exploiting both spatial and temporal information on geo-social networks. To solve the sighted challenges, we propose ST-SAGE, a spatial–temporal sparse additive generative (SAGE) model for spatial item recommendation. ST-SAGE considers both personal interests of the users and the preferences of the crowd in the target region at the given time by exploiting both the co-occurrence patterns of spatial items and the content of spatial items. To further alleviate the data sparsity issue, ST-SAGE exploits the geographical correlation by smoothing the crowd's preferences over a well-designed spatial index structure called *spatial pyramid*. To speed up the training process of ST-SAGE, we implement a parallel version of the model inference algorithm on the GraphLab framework. We conduct extensive experiments, and the experimental results clearly demonstrate that ST-SAGE outperforms the state-of-the-art recommender systems in terms of recommendation effectiveness, model training efficiency and online recommendation efficiency.

9.1 Introduction

The rapid development of Web 2.0, location acquisition and wireless communication technologies have fostered a number of *LBSNs*, such as Foursquare, Gowalla, Facebook Places and Loopt, where users can check in at different venues and share life

[1]Faculty of Information Technology, Monash University, Australia
[2]School of Information Technology and Electrical Engineering, The University of Queensland, Australia

experiences in the physical world via mobile devices [1–3]. Developing recommendation systems for LBSNs to provide a user with spatial items that maybe interesting for him/her (e.g., a venue or an event associated with a geographic location) has recently attracted increasing research attention [4–6]. This application becomes even more useful and important when a user travels to an area far away from his/her hometown, where he/she has little knowledge about the neighborhood. In this scenario, the spatial item recommendation has been proposed as *recommendation for out-of-town users in LBSNs* [7,8]. In this chapter, we focus on the effective and efficient spatial item recommendation, aiming to offer accurate spatial item recommendations for users on LBSNs in both hometown and out-of-town scenarios by mining their historical behavior data in LBSNs. As suggested in many existing work about LBSNs [9–12], human geographical movement demonstrates significant temporal patterns on LBSNs and is also highly relevant to the location property. Therefore, the recommendation should be both time aware and location oriented.

Spatial item recommendation is highly challenging because of the following three main reasons: (1) *travel locality*: with the rapid expansion of LBSNs, the number of spatial items visited by each individual user is rather small compared to the total number of spatial items in an LBSN, leading to a very sparse user–item matrix. Travel locality refers to the scenario that most users tend to check in nearby their living regions [13]. According to the survey in [13], the check-in activities generated by users in their nonhome cities only take up 0.47% of the ones generated in their home cities. The *travel locality* aggravates the data sparsity problem in spatial item recommendation in out-of-town scenarios (e.g., recommending spatial items in Beijing to people from New York). (2) *Spatial dynamics of user behavior*: when users travel in different geographical regions, their behavior patterns tend to change [14]. We have conducted a survey on Foursquare dataset. Specifically, with the application programming interfaces (APIs)[1] published by Foursquare, we extract the top three categories of check-in spatial items in three different cities including Boston, Las Vegas and Gold Coast for a specific group of users. The number of users in the group is 3,000 and each user in this group has checked-in in all these three cities. The percentage of check-ins of each spatial item category is shown in Table 9.1. We observe that for the same group of users, they are more interested in visiting casino (80.32%), nightlife (10.61%) and outlet (5.82%) when they are in Las Vegas, while prefer beach (71.36%), surf spot (14.82%) and theme park (9.60%) when they are in Gold Coast. (3) *Temporal dynamics of user behavior*: temporal influence also plays an important role in impacting users' daily activities in LBSNs [9–12,15]. For example, a user is more likely to go to a restaurant rather than a bar at noon. Therefore, the spatial item recommendation on LBSNs should also be time-aware. An intuitive solution of temporal influence modeling is splitting time into slices at the predefined granularity (e.g., hourly or seasonal) and then modeling the temporal preference to spatial items of a user in each time slice by mining the activities of the user in the time slice. However, splitting the users' activities into multiple slices according to the time will

---

[1] https://developer.foursquare.com/

Table 9.1   Illustration of spatial dynamics of user interests

City	Top item types	Percentage of check-ins (%)
Gold Coast (AU)	Beach	71.36
	Surf spot	14.82
	Theme park	9.60
Las Vegas (US)	Casino	80.32
	Nightlife	10.61
	Outlet	5.82
Boston (US)	College	78.32
	Museum	9.45
	Park	7.65

make the activity data even sparser. Thus, modeling the temporal dynamics of user behavior is also very challenging.

Recently, several methods [1,7] have been developed to make spatial item recommendations in both hometown and out-of-town scenarios. These existing approaches either do not address all three aforementioned challenges or address the challenges with ineffective strategies. For example, [7] proposed a CF-based method which makes recommendation for a target user based on the activities of both users who have visited many common spatial items and the friends mined from the target user's social connections in LBSNs. Including social friends is supposed to handle the travel locality when users travel to a distant places where the target user has limited check-in activities, by making recommendation according to activities of social friends in the target region. However, according to the survey in [11], when a user travels to a target region more than 100 km away from his/her hometown, the check-in probability at the target region visited by any of his/her social friends is merely 10%. This means that, in a place far away from a user's hometown, his/her friends also have few history activities in LBSNs. Bao *et al.* model individual users' interests based on the category information of spatial items and consider both user personal interests and the opinions of local experts in [1]. The opinions of local experts are expected to solve the *travel locality* problem. Nevertheless, the local experts are chosen from the users who demonstrate same or similar interests with the target user by mining the history activities. In this way, the chosen local experts still have similar history activities with the target user, and thus this approach is unable to address *spatial dynamics of user behaviors*.

In this chapter, we focus on effective and efficient spatial item recommendation by dealing with the aforementioned challenges and propose ST-SAGE, an ST-SAGE model. Traditional mixture models (e.g., [16]) usually combine multiple facets (e.g., time and location) which influence a user's choice of spatial items by introducing additional latent variables acting as "switches" to control which factor is currently active. It is not only computationally expensive to learn personalized "switching" variables for individual users to enable personalized recommendation but also difficult to learn these variables accurately when data is sparse, which is usually the case in most recommender systems. Inspired by the SAGE model [17], we have designed our model in a way by adding the effect of all the facets in the log space to avoid the inference of the massive latent "switching" variables, with the aim of achieving improved robustness and predictive accuracy.

While modeling user-visiting behaviors, ST-SAGE takes into account both users' personal interests and dynamics of user behaviors caused by spatial–temporal drift. ST-SAGE learns a user's preference as a topic-based vector, by mining both the co-occurrence patterns of spatial items and their associated content information (e.g., comments and categories). One advantage of exploiting the content information of spatial items is to address the travel locality problem in out-of-town scenarios, where the content information associated with spatial items serves as the medium for transferring preference of a user mined from his/her hometown to the unfamiliar regions.

To adapt to *spatial–temporal dynamics of user behaviors*, ST-SAGE recognizes two roles of each individual user in a specific spatial region: local or tourist. Given a specific location and a specific time, ST-SAGE mines the visiting records from local users to learn *temporal native preferences* as a topic-based vector. In the similar way, ST-SAGE mines visiting records from tourists to learn *temporal tourist preferences*. Users with the same role at a location are more likely to share similar preferences and behavior patterns at a specific time. Thus, to recommend spatial items to a target user u at location l and time t, we consider not only u's personal interests but also the temporal preferences of the crowd who have the same role as u. In this way, we leverage the crowd's temporal preferences to overcome the sparsity of individuals' activity data at out-of-town regions at a specific time. Specifically, given a user u, a specific time t and his/her current location l, we first find a group of users sharing the same role with u when they visited l and then produce the time-aware recommendation based on their temporal preferences and the user's personal interests.

When using the visiting history to learn the temporal native preferences and tourist preferences of a specific region, however, we still face the data sparsity issue, especially when the target region is small. Given a specific region r and time t (e.g., at night), when there are insufficient visiting records generated at the given spatiotemporal context, its native preferences and tourist preferences cannot be inferred accurately. To overcome the data sparsity problem, ST-SAGE integrates a spatial index called *spatial pyramid*, which is a tree structure proposed in [13]. It is first constructed by partitioning locations of spatial items into spatial grids of varying sizes at different hierarchies. Then, ST-SAGE applies the *additive* framework [18,19] to learn the temporal native preferences and tourist preferences of each region. Briefly, when learning the temporal native preferences and tourist preferences in a region, the two variables learned for all of the region's ancestor grids in the spatial pyramid will be added. Given a specific region r and time t, if there are few or no activities, we can still infer its native preferences and tourist preferences guided by its ancestor grids, which have larger scales of geo-regions and thus have more check-in records. Another advantage of the integration of the spatial pyramid is allowing users to switch between different scales of geo-regions (e.g., zoom in/out on a Google Map) without relearning the parameters. In this way, this model can be seamlessly connected with Google Map.

9.2 Preliminaries about SAGE

Our proposed model is inspired by the SAGE model [17]. SAGE is an effective
generative mixture model in the situation where a variable is affected by several
factors as it does not need to infer explicit switching variables and has been widely
used in many existing work [20–23]. The key technical difference from traditional
mixture models is that the mixture occurs in terms of the natural parameters of the
exponential family instead of distributions. Such a model is robust given limited
training data as it does not have to infer a complex indicator variable to distinguish
the set of causes.

To provide a clearer explanation of SAGE, we compare it with a traditional
probabilistic mixture generative model, LCA–LDA [16], as an illustrative example.
LCA–LDA is a location-content-aware model which aims to mimic the process of
human decision-making on visiting spatial items. There are two factors considered
in affecting users' decision-making in checking in spatial items: the user's personal
interest θ_u^{user} and the influence of local preference θ_l^{crowd} (note that, it does not distinguish between native preference and tourist preference). LCA–LDA combines the
two factors in a unified manner. Specifically, in this traditional probabilistic mixture
generative model, given a querying user u at a target location l, the likelihood that
u will prefer spatial item v is computed by combining the considered two factors
through a linear combination as follows:

$$P(v|\theta_u^{user}, \theta_l^{crowd}) = \lambda_u P(v|\theta_u^{user}) + (1 - \lambda_u)P(v|\theta_l^{crowd}) \tag{9.1}$$

where λ_u is the "switching" variable and obviously it needs to be trained for each
user. For each record, other than the latent topic, we also need to sample the switching variable. Thus, the complexity is doubled. Other than the increased complexity,
when the data is sparse, it cannot be inferred accurately as the training data for each
individual user is even sparser. In contrast, SAGE combines the two generative facets
through simple addition in log space, as shown in (9.2). Clearly, SAGE avoids the
computation for latent switching variables.

$$P(v|\theta_u^{user}, \theta_l^{crowd}) = P(v|\theta_u^{user} + \theta_l^{crowd}) = \frac{exp(\theta_{u,v}^{user} + \theta_{l,v}^{crowd})}{\sum_{v'} exp(\theta_{u,v'}^{user} + \theta_{l,v'}^{crowd})} \tag{9.2}$$

9.3 Spatial–temporal SAGE model

In this section, we first present the formulated problem definition and then propose
our ST-SAGE model.

9.3.1 Problem definitions

We first define the key data structures used in this chapter and then introduce
the research problem. For ease of reference, the involved notations in this part is
summarized in Table 9.2.

Table 9.2   Notations of the input data

Variable	Interpretation
U, V, R, T	The set of users, spatial items, locations and time slices
W	The vocabulary set
D_u	User u's profile
$v_{u,i}$	The spatial item of ith record in D_u
$l_{u,i}$	The location of spatial item $v_{u,i}$
l_u	The home location of user u
$W_{u,i}$	The set of words describing spatial item $v_{u,i}$
$w_{u,i,n}$	The nth word describing spatial item $v_{u,i}$
$s_{u,i}$	A Boolean value indicating whether the user u is a local or tourist on location $l_{u,i}$
$t_{u,i}$	The occurring time of ith record in D_u

Definition 9.1. *(Spatial item) A spatial item is an item associated with a geographical location (e.g., a hotel or a scenic spot).*

A spatial item in our model has three attributes: identifier, location and content, represented by v, l_v and W_v, respectively. The content associated with the spatial items refers to the set of words describing the item, such as tags and categories. The location information available for each spatial item v in the collected raw datasets is in the form of the (latitude, longitude) pair. A spatial pyramid structure [13,24,25] is first adopted to partition and index the entire geographic area, and then for a location, the index of the area containing this location is used as the identifier l_v of this location. The granularities can range from cities to streets, depending on the nature of the applications. The details of the spatial pyramid are described in Section 9.3.4.

Definition 9.2. *(User home location) Given a user u, following the recent work of [26], we define the user's home location as the place where he/she lives, denoted as l_u.*

Due to the privacy problem, user home locations are not always available. For a user whose home location is not given explicitly, the method proposed in [27] is adopted to infer the user's home location as the cell in the spatial pyramid containing the most of his/her check-ins.

Definition 9.3. *(Time) t is an ordinal variable and we use t to index the tth time slice which corresponds to a specific time period.*

The time information available for each record in the collected raw datasets is usually in the form of timestamps (e.g., "2010-07-24, 13:45:06"). We divide the timestamps into time slices using predefined granularity when preprocessing the datasets. The model in this chapter focuses on the daily patterns of users' behaviors as the experimental results show that the performance of exploring this pattern is best. Thus, we divide the timestamps into 24 slices based on the hours. However, the recommendation ability of ST-SAGE is not limited to one specific temporal pattern.

Definition 9.4. *(User activity) A user activity consists of a six tuple* $(u,\ v,\ l_v,\ W_v,\ t,\ s)$.

A user activity indicates that the user u visits the spatial item v, located at l_v and described as W_v, at time t, in the role of s. If $s = 0$, the user is recognized as a local and the activity occurs in u's hometown. If $s = 1$, the user u plays the role of tourist when visiting v.

Definition 9.5. *(User profile) For each user u, we create a user profile D_u, which is a set of user activities associated with u.*

Given a dataset D as the union of a collection of user profiles, we aim to provide spatial item recommendation for both hometown and out-of-town users. We formulate our problem as follows, following our previous work [28,29].

Problem 9.1. (Spatial item recommendation) Given a user activity dataset D, a target user u with his/her current location l and the querying time t (i.e., the query is $q = (u, l, t)$), our goal is to recommend top-k spatial items that the target user u would be most interested in. Given a distance threshold d, the problem becomes an **out-of-town recommendation** if the distance between u's current location and his/her home location (i.e., $|l - l_u|$) is greater than d. Otherwise, the problem is a **hometown recommendation**.

We set $d = 100$ km in our work following related studies [7,30–32]. A distance around 100 km is the typical radius of human "reach" as it usually takes 1–2 h to drive such a distance.

9.3.2 Model description

In this chapter, we propose an ST-SAGE model to model users' visiting activities in LBSNs. The graphical representation of ST-SAGE is demonstrated in Figure 9.1. The notations of our model are summarized in Table 9.3. The shaded circles in Figure 9.1 model the observed random variables. More specifically, the shaded circles model the input data, that is, users' activity profiles. Following existing models [16,20], the topic index of each user activity is modeled with a latent random variable, denoted as z.

User interest modeling. Intuitively, a user chooses a spatial item at a given location and a specific time by matching his/her personal interests with the content of that item. Inspired by the early work on user interest modeling [16,20,33], ST-SAGE also adopts latent topics to characterize users' interests. Specifically, we infer an individual user's interest vector over a set of topics according to his/her visited spatial items and their associated contents, denoted as θ_u^{user}. As the content of spatial items can play the role of medium through which user preferences inferred from their hometown can be transferred to out-of-town regions, our proposed model is able to alleviate the travel locality problem for out-of-town recommendation. Moreover, beyond θ_u^{user}, we also introduce a background vector over topics θ^0. This background vector is able to capture common topics among all users. The purpose of using a background model is to make the user interests encoded in θ_u^{user} more discriminative.

Spatial dynamic modeling. To adapt to spatial dynamics of user behavior, we exploit the preferences of the crowds who share the same role as the target user u. For example, the preferences of the tourists will be leveraged if the target user is currently

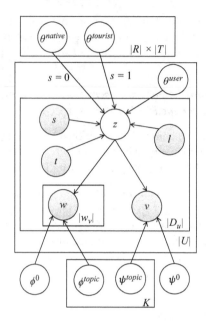

Figure 9.1   The graphical representation of our model

Table 9.3   Notations of model parameters

Variable	Interpretation
K	The number of latent topics
$z_{u,i}$	The topic assigned to spatial item $v_{u,i}$
θ^0	The background topic vector
θ_u^{user}	The topic vector representing the intrinsic interests of user u
$\theta_{l,t}^{native}$	The topic vector of l on time t, representing the native preferences at l on time t
$\theta_{l,t}^{tourist}$	The topic vector of l on time t, representing the tourist preferences at l on time t
ϕ^0	The word vector of the background
ψ^0	The spatial item vector of the background
ϕ_z^{topic}	Content word vector of topic z
ψ_z^{topic}	Spatial item vector of topic z

out-of-town. Technically, we introduce two parameters: *native preferences* θ^{native} and *tourist preferences* $\theta^{tourist}$. Given a location l, the native preferences θ_l^{native} represent the preferences of people living at location l. In contrast, the tourist preferences $\theta_l^{tourist}$ represent the preferences of tourists traveling in location l. Note that, distinguishing native preferences from tourist preferences is one of the fundamental differences between our models ST-SAGE and the LCA–LDA [16] which also exploits local activity records at the target location.

Temporal dynamic modeling. As presented before, users tend to visit different spatial items at different time, we expect that the proposed ST-SAGE model is able to capture this temporal dynamic of user behaviors. An intuitive approach in modeling the temporal influence is to split time into multiple slices at a predefined granularity (e.g., hourly or seasonal) and then model the temporal preferences of a user based on his/her visited spatial items inside each single time slice. However, as we know, the data in many real recommender systems are very sparse and dividing a user's activity data into multiple slices will make the data much sparser in a specific time slice, which inevitably makes the inference of personal temporal preferences over-fitting. In light of this, we propose to exploit and integrate the collective temporal preferences of the crowd with the same role as the target user, as shown in Figure 9.1. The collective preferences of the public with the same roles, θ_l^{native} and $\theta_l^{tourist}$, are extended to be temporal vectors $\theta_{l,t}^{native}$ and $\theta_{l,t}^{tourist}$.

Topics modeling. To take full advantage of the strengths of both content-based and collaborative filtering-based recommendation methods, a topic z in our ST-SAGE model is not only associated with a word vector ϕ_z^{topic}, but also with a vector over spatial items ψ_z^{topic}. This design enables ϕ_z^{topic} and ψ_z^{topic} to be mutually influenced and enhanced during the topic-discovery process by associating each other. Thus, the discovered topic z, on one hand, can cluster the content-similar items together. On the other hand, it can also capture the item co-occurrence patterns to link relevant items together, similar to item-based collaborative filtering methods. We also introduce two background models for words and items, respectively: ϕ^0 and ψ^0. The purpose of using background models is to make the topics learned from the dataset more discriminative, since ϕ^0 and ψ^0 assign high probabilities to non-discriminative and non-informative words and items.

For an individual user activity in the user profile D_u, the generative process of the ST-SAGE model is as follows:

- Draw a topic index $z_{u,i} \sim P(z_{u,i}|s_{u,i}, l_{u,i}, t_{u,i}, \theta^0, \theta^{user}, \theta^{native}, \theta^{tourist})$
- For each content word $w_{u,i,n}$ in $W_{u,i}$, draw $w_{u,i,n} \sim P(w_{u,i,n}|\phi^0, z_{u,i}, \phi^{topic})$
- Draw a spatial item $v_{u,i} \sim P(v_{u,i}|\psi^0, z_{u,i}, \psi^{topic})$

For each user activity, ST-SAGE first chooses the topic this activity is about. To generate the topic index z, we utilize a multinomial model as follows.

$$P(z_{u,i}|s_{u,i}, l_{u,i}, t_{u,i}, \theta^0, \theta^{user}, \theta^{native}, \theta^{tourist})$$
$$= P(z_{u,i}|\theta_u^{user} + (1 - s_{u,i}) \times \theta_{l_{u,i},t_{u,i}}^{native} + s_{u,i} \times \theta_{l_{u,i},t_{u,i}}^{tourist}) \quad (9.3)$$

where $P(z|\theta_u^{user} + (1 - s) \times \theta_{l,t}^{native} + s \times \theta_{l,t}^{tourist})$, denoted as $\alpha_{u,s,l,t,z}$, is computed as (9.6). Once the topic z is generated, the spatial item v and the associated content words are generated as expressed in (9.4) and (9.5), respectively.

$$P(v_{u,i}|\psi^0, z_{u,i}, \psi^{topic}) = P(v_{u,i}|\psi^0 + \psi_{z_{u,i}}^{topic}) \quad (9.4)$$

$$P(w_{u,i,n}|\phi^0, z_{u,i}, \phi^{topic}) = P(w_{u,i,n}|\phi^0 + \phi_{z_{u,i}}^{topic}) \quad (9.5)$$

where $P(v|\psi^0 + \psi_z^{topic}) = \gamma_{z,v}$ and $P(w|\phi^0 + \phi_z^{topic}) = \beta_{z,w}$ are computed as in (9.6). Note that, in order to model topics based on the background word/item vectors, for each topic, ST-SAGE models the difference from the background word/item vector in log-frequencies, instead of the frequencies themselves.

9.3.3 Model inference

The goal of model inference is to learn parameters which maximize the marginal log-likelihood of the observed random variables **w**, **v**, **t** and **s**, and the marginalization is performed with respect to the latent random variable **z**. However, the latent variable is difficult to be maximized directly. Therefore, the Gibbs EM algorithm [34], a mixture of EM and a Monte Carlo sampler, is adopted to maximize the complete data likelihood in (9.7), where $\ominus$ represents the set of all the parameters. There are two steps in each iteration of the Gibbs EM algorithm: E-step and M-step. In the E-step, we sample latent topic assignments for the activity records using the Gibbs sampling and fixing all other parameters. In the M-step, we optimize the model parameters $\ominus$ and fixing all topic assignments by using the gradient descent learning algorithm. The two steps are iterated until convergence.

$$\alpha_{u,s,l,t,z} = \frac{exp(\theta_z^0 + \theta_{u,z}^{user} + (1-s) \times \theta_{l,t,z}^{native} + s \times \theta_{l,t,z}^{tourist})}{\sum_{zz} exp(\theta_{zz}^0 + \theta_{u,zz}^{user} + (1-s) \times \theta_{l,t,zz}^{native} + s \times \theta_{l,t,zz}^{tourist})},$$

$$\beta_{z,w} = \frac{exp(\phi_w^0 + \phi_{z,w}^{topic})}{\sum_{ww} exp(\phi_{ww}^0 + \phi_{z,ww}^{topic})}, \quad \gamma_{z,v} = \frac{exp(\psi_z^0 + \psi_{z,v}^{topic})}{\sum_{vv} exp(\psi_z^0 + \psi_{z,vv}^{topic})}$$

$$(9.6)$$

$$P(\mathbf{z}, \mathbf{w}, \mathbf{v}|\ominus, \mathbf{s}, \mathbf{u}, \mathbf{l}, \mathbf{t}) = P(\mathbf{z}|\mathbf{s}, \mathbf{u}, \mathbf{l}, \mathbf{t}, \theta^0, \theta^{user}, \theta^{native}, \theta^{tourist})$$

$$\times P(\mathbf{w}|\mathbf{z}, \phi^0, \phi^{topic}) \times P(\mathbf{v}|\mathbf{z}, \psi^0, \psi^{topic})$$

$$= \prod_{u=1}^{|U|} \prod_{i=1}^{|D_u|} \alpha_{u,s_{u,i},l_{u,i},t_{u,i},z_{u,i}} \prod_{u=1}^{|U|} \prod_{i=1}^{|D_u|} \prod_{n=1}^{|W_{v_{u,i}}|} \beta_{z_{u,i},w_{u,i,n}} \prod_{u=1}^{|U|} \prod_{i=1}^{|D_u|} \gamma_{z_{u,i},v_{u,i}}$$

$$(9.7)$$

More specifically, we iteratively draw latent topic **z** for all activity records in the E-step. When sampling $z_{u,i}$ as expressed in (9.8), we assume all other variables are fixed. $z_{\neg u,i}$ represents the topic assignments for all user activities except the ith activity for user u.

$$P(z_{u,i}|z_{\neg u,i}, \mathbf{w}, \mathbf{v}, \mathbf{s}, \mathbf{u}, \mathbf{l}, \mathbf{t}, \ominus) \propto \alpha_{u,s_{u,i},l_{u,i},t_{u,i},z_{u,i}} \times \prod_{n=1}^{|W_{v_{u,i}}|} \beta_{z_{u,i},w_{u,i,n}} \times \gamma_{z_{u,i},v_{u,i}} \quad (9.8)$$

In the M-step, we optimize the parameters $\ominus$ to maximize the log likelihood of the objective function with all topic assignments fixed. To update the parameters, we use PSSG (projected scaled sub-gradient) [35], which is a gradient descent learning algorithm and designed to solve optimization problems with L1 regularization on parameters. What's worth noting is that, PSSG is scalable because it uses the quasi-Newton strategy with line search that is robust to common functions. Let L be the log-likelihood of the model. According to the limited-memory BFGS [36] updates for the quasi-Newton method, the gradients of model parameters θ^0, θ^{user}, θ^{native} and $\theta^{tourist}$ are provided as follows.

$$\frac{\partial L}{\partial \theta_z^0} = d(z) - \sum_{u=1}^{|U|} \sum_{i=1}^{|D_u|} \alpha_{u,s_{u,i},l_{u,i},t_{u,i},z}, \qquad \frac{\partial L}{\partial \theta_{u,z}^{user}} = d(u,z) - \sum_{i=1}^{|D_u|} \alpha_{u,s_{u,i},l_{u,i},t_{u,i},z} \qquad (9.9)$$

$$\frac{\partial L}{\partial \theta_{l,t,z}^{native}} = (1-s) \times (d(l,t,z) - \sum_{j=1}^{|D(l,t)|} \alpha_{u_j,s_j,l,t,z}), \qquad (9.10)$$

$$\frac{\partial L}{\partial \theta_{l,t,z}^{tourist}} = s \times (d(l,t,z) - \sum_{j=1}^{|D(l,t)|} \alpha_{u_j,s_j,l,t,z}) \qquad (9.11)$$

where $d(z)$ represents the number of user activities assigned to the topic z, $d(u,z)$ denotes how many activities are assigned to topic z in u's activity profile D_u, $d(l,t,z)$ is the number of visiting activities assigned to topic z at location l and time t, $D(l,t)$ represents the set of activities occurring at location l and time t, and u_j denotes the user who generates the jth activity record. Similarly, the gradients of model parameters ϕ^0, ϕ^{topic}, ψ^0 and ψ^{topic} are computed as follows:

$$\frac{\partial L}{\partial \phi_w^0} = d(w) - \sum_{z=1}^{K} d(z) \times \beta_{z,w}, \qquad \frac{\partial L}{\partial \phi_{z,w}^{topic}} = d(z,w) - d(z) \times \beta_{z,w} \qquad (9.12)$$

$$\frac{\partial L}{\partial \psi_v^0} = d(v) - \sum_{z=1}^{K} d(z) \times \gamma_{z,v}, \qquad \frac{\partial L}{\partial \psi_{z,v}^{topic}} = d(z,v) - d(z) \times \gamma_{z,v} \qquad (9.13)$$

where $d(w)$ is the total number of activities where word w appears, and $d(z,w)$ is the number of user activities where the word w is assigned to the topic z. $d(v)$ is the number of user activities associated with item v, and $d(z,v)$ represents the number of activities in which topic z is assigned to item v.

Time complexity. There are two steps in each iteration in the Gibbs EM algorithm: Gibbs sampling and gradient descent learning. We assume that the algorithm needs I iterations to reach convergence. For each iteration, its time complexity is analyzed as follows. In the E-step, it needs to go through all user check-in records, and for each check-in activity, it requires $O(K)$ operations to compute the posterior probability distribution for sampling topic z. Thus, the time complexity in this step is $O(K \times D)$ where $D = \sum_u |D_u|$ is the total number of check-ins in the dataset. In the M-step, we use the gradient descent learning algorithm to update the model parameters $\ominus = \{\theta^0, \theta^{user}, \theta^{native}, \theta^{tourist}, \phi^0, \phi^{topic}, \varphi^0, \varphi^{topic}\}$ based on the topic assignments sampled in the E-step. We assume that the gradient descent algorithm needs J iterations to converge, and in each iteration, the time complexity to compute the gradients for the model parameters $\ominus$ is $O(K \times D)$.

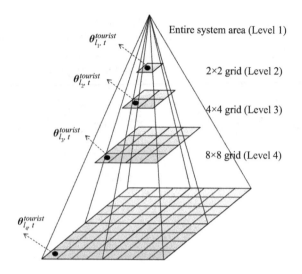

$\theta_{l_1, t}^{tourist}$

Entire system area (Level 1)

$\theta_{l_2, t}^{tourist}$

2×2 grid (Level 2)

4×4 grid (Level 3)

$\theta_{l_3, t}^{tourist}$

8×8 grid (Level 4)

$\theta_{l_4, t}^{tourist}$

Figure 9.2　The spatial pyramid

9.3.4　Spatial smoothing

To combat the data-sparsity problem when modeling the *temporal native preferences* and *temporal tourist preferences*, we adopt a quad tree structure called spatial pyramid, proposed in [13], to partition and index the entire geographic area. The spatial pyramid is constructed by partitioning item locations into spatial regions of varying sizes at different hierarchies. More specifically, the spatial pyramid decomposes the space into H levels. Level 0 has only one grid cell. For a given level h, the space is partitioned into fourth grid cells of equal area. Thus, the space can be divided recursively into numerous cells at different levels with different granularity. The graphical representation of the spatial pyramid is shown in Figure 9.2.

The proposed spatial pyramid structure can encode one important assumption in spatial data mining effectively. The assumption is that everything is related to everything else, but nearby things are more related than distant things and has been proposed in [37] as the first law of geography [38]. This law is also known as the "spatial autocorrelation." The spatial pyramid structure can encode this law in an effective manner. Specifically, each location l in the spatial pyramid can be represented by a path from the root node to its corresponding leaf node. A vector can be used to describe the path, $(l_1, l_2, ..., l_h, ..., l_H)$, where l_h is a grid at level h that contains the location l. Then, the proximity between two locations can be computed with the vector representation of locations. The basic idea is that, if two locations in the spatial pyramid share more ancestors, then these two locations are more proximate.

If user activity data at location l and time t are very sparse, both the associated temporal native preference $\theta_{l,t}^{native}$ and the temporal tourist preference $\theta_{l,t}^{tourist}$ may not be estimated accurately. To address this issue, we exploit geographical correlation to enhance the prior knowledge about the model parameters $\theta_{l,t}^{native}$ and $\theta_{l,t}^{tourist}$. Intuitively, if two locations l and l' have a proximate geographical distance, their associated $\theta_{l,t}^{native}$ and $\theta_{l',t}^{native}$ should be similar to each other. Similarly, this intuition can also be applied to the temporal tourist preferences $\theta_{l,t}^{tourist}$ and $\theta_{l',t}^{tourist}$. As a result, given a location l and time t, we propose an *additive* framework [18,19] to compute temporal native preference $\theta_{l,t}^{native}$ and tourist preference $\theta_{l,t}^{tourist}$ based on the path vector representation. Specifically, given a location l, its temporal native preference and temporal tourist preference at time t are represented as follows.

$$\theta_{l,t}^{native} = \sum_{h=1}^{H} \theta_{l_h,t}^{native}, \quad \theta_{l,t}^{tourist} = \sum_{h=1}^{H} \theta_{l_h,t}^{tourist} \tag{9.14}$$

According to the above equations, both the temporal native preferences and the temporal tourist preferences of a location depend on all of its ancestors up to the root. The advantage of this representation method is three-fold. First, this representation method is able to integrate the information of geographical correlation into our ST-SAGE model by enabling neighboring locations to share similar preferences as desired (i.e., the preferences are smoothed over the spatial pyramid). Second, this method is able to solve the data-sparsity problem, as if there are few or no activities at a location, we can still infer its preference guided by its ancestors. Last, once *temporal native preferences* and *temporal tourist preferences* for each level are learned, this modeling makes the switch between various granularity fast and convenient by changing the lowest level in the model without retraining the parameters.

Figure 9.3 demonstrates a detailed application scenario of ST-SAGE where the input consists of four elements: the current location, the current time, the number of the recommendations and the size of the target region (e.g., zoom in/out on Google Map [1]). Most smart mobile phones are able to capture both the location and time automatically.

As we mentioned before, by indexing the geographical space using a spatial tree structure, our model supports users to change the scale of the target region efficiently by switching between different levels in the tree structure. Although the previous work in [16] also supports the change of space granularity, it has to retrain all parameters for the new granularity while our model does not. Take the application in Figure 9.3 as an example. Assume that the current scale corresponds to "Level 3" of the spatial pyramid. If the querying user zooms out on the map, the map becomes smaller and the granularity of the regions becomes coarser. ST-SAGE will automatically change the scale from "Level 3" to "Level 2" or above based on the new granularity. As the model parameters for all levels have been pretrained and the parameters for the new "level" can be retrieved directly, the model does not need to retrain the parameters for this "zooming out." Similarly, if the user zooms in on the map, ST-SAGE simply switches the scale from the upper level into one lower level without any parameter retraining.

9.3.5 Parallel implementation

We proposed a two-step inference algorithm to train ST-SAGE: Gibbs EM algorithm containing Gibbs sampling and gradient descent learning. This two-step inference

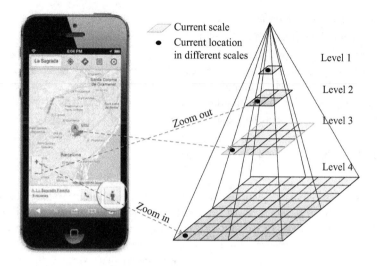

Figure 9.3   The application scenario

algorithm is quite expensive in many large-scale applications. In this section, we focus on proposing a scalable parallel inference algorithm to enable the large-scale applications. We implement a parallel ST-SAGE inference algorithm on the distributed GraphLab framework [39] and parallel gradient descent learning framework PSSG [35]. PSSG is scalable because it not only uses the quasi-Newton strategy with line search that is robust to common functions but also adopts the multicore parallel-processing strategy. Specifically, in the E step, we implement the Gibbs sampling algorithm in the GraphLab framework [39]; in the M step, PSSG [35] is adopted as the parallel gradient descent-learning framework in ST-SAGE.

GraphLab framework is proposed to support asynchronous, dynamic, graph-parallel computation while ensuring data consistency, which is required by Gibbs Sampling to ensure statistical correctness, and achieving a high degree of parallel performance in the shared-memory setting. GraphLab framework has demonstrated superior performance over popular parallel systems, e.g., MapReduce and Spark, for many machine-learning algorithms [40].

This framework implements the *gather* − *apply* − *scatter* (*GAS*) model which abstracts the program into three phases. In the *gather* phase, each vertex aggregates data from the *scope* of the vertex. The *scope* of a vertex *ve* includes the data stored in *ve* as well as the data stored in all adjacent vertices and adjacent edges. The gather result is used to update the data stored in this vertex in the *apply* phase. Lastly, each vertex triggers its neighboring vertices or modifies adjacent edge data. GraphLab framework stores the algorithm state as an undirected graph called the **data graph**. In this graph, users can associate arbitrary data with each vertex and edge. In ST-SAGE, we store the state as a graph in Figure 9.4. Specifically, we construct an undirected graph that connects each user with each spatial item. An edge between a user *u* and a spatial item *v* contains the location of the item l_v, the role of *u* at *l* (a tourist or a local)

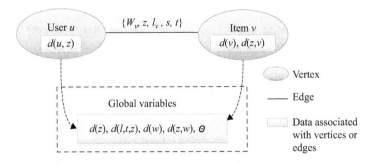

Figure 9.4   Data graph

denoted as s, the time t, content words of item v and the topic indicator z. For each user u, the number of his/her check-ins assigned to each topic z, denoted as $d(u, z)$, is stored in her associated vertex. Similarly, for each spatial item v, the number of its associated check-ins (i.e., $d(v)$) and the number of its associated check-ins assigned to each topic z (i.e., $d(z, v)$) are stored in its corresponding vertex.

We accelerate the Gibbs EM algorithm by simultaneously sampling new topics according to (9.8). The variables in (9.8) are either maintained globally or in vertices. To improve efficiency further, the global variables are periodically aggregated from the vertices, while the variables in vertices are updated during the *gather* and *apply* phases. New topics are sampled in the *scatter* phase. As the variables in the Gibbs EM algorithm are updated with the BFGS algorithm, we run the BFGS algorithm during the *apply* phase when *gather_result* is applied to update the related variables. Algorithm 9.1 shows the GAS procedure of the ST-SAGE Gibbs Sampler.

Algorithm 9.1: *GAS* program of ST-SAGE Gibbs Sampler

Gather (v, e);
if $v.type = user$ **then**
| return α related parameters and $d(z), d(u, z), d(l, t, z)$;
end
if $v.type = item$ **then**
| return β, γ related parameters and $d(w), d(z, w), d(v), d(z, v), d(z)$;
end

Apply $(v, gather\_result)$;
if $v.type = user$ **then**
| call BFGS to update α related parameters with (9.9) according to *gather_result*;
end
if $v.type = location$ **then**
| call BFGS to update β, γ related parameters with (9.12) according to
| *gather_result*;
end

Scatter (v, e);
sample z according to (9.8);

With this two-step parallel processing using the GraphLab framework and the PSSG framework, respectively, our inference implementation achieves satisfying efficiency and scalability on large data, as shown in the empirical study.

9.4 Spatial item recommendation using ST-SAGE

Once we have estimated the model parameter set $\ominus$, given a querying user u_q with the querying time t_q and location l_q, we first infer the role of target user s_q according to the distance between his/her home location l_{u_q} and the querying location l_q. Then, we compute the probability of user u_q choosing each unvisited spatial item v based on the new query $q = (u_q, t_q, l_q, s_q)$ as follows:

$$
\begin{aligned}
P(v, W_v | u_q, l_q, s_q, t_q, \ominus) &= \sum_{z=1}^{K} P(v, W_v, z | u_q, l_q, s_q, t_q, \ominus) \\
&= \sum_{z=1}^{K} P(z | u_q, s_q, t_q, l_q, \theta^0, \theta^{user}, \theta^{native}, \theta^{tourist}) \\
&\quad \times P(W_v | z, \phi^0, \phi^{topic}) P(v | z, \psi^0, \psi^{topic}) \qquad (9.15) \\
&= \sum_{z=1}^{K} \alpha_{u_q, s_q, t_q, l_q, z} \left(\prod_{n=1}^{|W_v|} \beta_{z, w_{v,n}} \right)^{(1/|W_v|)} \gamma_{z,v}
\end{aligned}
$$

where W_v are the content words describing item v. We should note that the reason why we use the geometric mean ($\prod_{n=1}^{|W_v|} \beta_{z,w_{v,n}})^{(1/|W_v|)}$ instead of the product $\prod_{n=1}^{|W_v|} \beta_{z,w_{v,n}}$ for the probability of topic z generating the word set W_v is that the number of content words associated with each spatial item is different. As we know, β_z is a distribution over all the content words, thus $\beta_{z,w}$ is a value in $(0, 1]$. As a result, without $1/|W_v|$, the spatial items with more content words tend to have lower scores as the product of $\beta_{z,w}$ is always less than 1.

As we know, the efficiency of online recommendation is quite critical as users would not be willing to wait for a long time for the recommendation results. To accelerate the online recommendation process, we first propose a ranking framework in (9.16) which separates the offline modeling from the online computation to the maximum extent.

$$
S(q, v) = \sum_{z=1}^{K} F(z, v) W(q, z)
$$

$$
F(z, v) = \left(\prod_{n=1}^{|W_v|} \beta_{z, w_{v,n}} \right)^{(1/|W_v|)} \times \gamma_{z,v}, \quad W(q, z) = \alpha_{u_q, l_q, s_q, l_q, z} \qquad (9.16)
$$

where $F(z, v)$ denotes the score of spatial items v with respect to topic z, which is computed offline. This part is computed offline since it is independent from the query $q = (u_q, t_q, l_q, s_q)$. On the other hand, $W(q, z)$ denotes the part which need to compute online, representing the preference of query q on topic z. Note that the principal time-consuming components of $W(q,z)$ are also computed offline (e.g., $\theta^0, \theta^{user}, \theta^{native}$ and $\theta^{tourist}$). This design enables the maximum separation of the online computation from the offline calculation, which in turn reduces the query time.

Note that, even after the maximum separation of online computation from the offline calculation, a straightforward method of generating the top-k recommendations is still quite expensive especially in the situation where the item corpus is large, as it still needs to compute the ranking scores for all items according to (9.16) and select top-k ones with highest ranking scores. To further improve the online recommendation efficiency, we adopt the TA-based query processing technique for top-k recommendation developed in [41], inspired by the observation that a query usually has a sparse preference over the latent topics. More specifically, a query q usually has obvious preferences over a small number of attributes (say 5–10 latent dimensions) and the query weights on most attributes are extremely small. Since $W(q,z)$ is nonnegative, the proposed ranking function in (9.16) is monotonically increasing given a query q, which meets the requirement of the TA-based query-processing technique. This technology has the nice property of finding top-k results correctly by examining the minimum number of items without scanning all ones, which enables the ST-SAGE model scalable to large-scale datasets with large item corpus.

9.5 Experiments

In this section, we first describe the experimental settings including the datasets, comparative approaches and the evaluation method. We then demonstrate the experimental results.

9.5.1 Experimental settings

9.5.1.1 Datasets

Our experiments are conducted on two real large-scale LBSN datasets: Foursquare and Twitter. The detailed information about the two datasets is described as follows.

Foursquare. This dataset contains the check-in history of 4,163 users living in California, USA, on 111,813 spatial items from Dec 2009 to Jul 2013. For each user, it contains his/her social ties, visiting POI IDs, locations of each check-in POI in terms of latitude and longitude, check-in time and the contents associated with each visited POI. Each check-in is stored as *user-ID, POI-ID, POI-location, check-in time, POI-content*. Each record in social networks is stored as *user-ID, friend-ID* and the total number of social relationship is 32,512.

Twitter. This dataset is based on the publicly available Twitter dataset [42]. Twitter supports the third-party location sharing services like Foursquare and Gowalla, where users of these services opt in to share their check-ins on Twitter. But the original data on Twitter does not contain the content information about spatial items. So, we crawled the category and tag information associated with each spatial item from Foursquare with the help of the publicly available API[2] supplied by Foursquare. The final dataset used in our experiments contains 114,058 users, 62,547 spatial items and 1,434,668 check-in activities from Sep 2010 to Jan 2011. Each check-in record has the same format as the aforementioned Foursquare dataset except that this dataset does not contain user social tie information.

To make the experiments repeatable, we will make the datasets and our codes publicly available.[3]

9.5.1.2 Comparative approaches

We compare our ST-SAGE model with the following five methods representing the state-of-the-art spatial item recommendation techniques.

JIM. JIM [29] is a joint probabilistic generative model which integrates the content effect, geographical-social influence, temporal effect and word-of-mouth effect. The word-of-mouth effect refers to the scenario that, given a target region, the popularity of a spatial item has a large effect on the probability of a user visiting that item.

LCA–LDA. LCA–LDA is a location-content-aware recommender model which has been recently developed to support spatial item recommendation for out-of-town users [16]. This model takes into account both personal interests and local preferences of each location by exploiting both item co-visiting patterns and content of spatial items. Compared with ST-SAGE, LCA–LDA is a traditional mixture model which introduces "switching" variables to consider multiple factors. Besides, LCA–LDA ignores the roles of users and does not distinguish between *tourist preference* and *native preference*. Moreover, LCA–LDA has not integrated the temporal information.

UTE+SE. UTE+SE [9] is a collaborative recommendation model which incorporates both the temporal and spatial information. Given a user and his/her querying time, this model first finds the users sharing similar temporal preference with him/her and then produces the time-aware recommendations based on these similar users' historical visiting records made around the querying time.

CKNN. CKNN, proposed in [1], projects a user's activity history into the category space and models user preference using a weighted category hierarchy. When receiving a query, CKNN retrieves all users and items located in the querying location, formulates a user–item matrix online and then applies a user-based CF method to predict the rating of a querying user on an unvisited item. Note that the similarity between two users in CKNN is computed according to their weights in the category hierarchy, making CKNN a hybrid recommendation method.

UPS-CF. UPS-CF [7] is a collaborative recommendation framework which is especially designed for out-of-town users. This framework integrates user-based collaborative filtering and social-based collaborative filtering. That is, it recommends spatial items to a target user according to the activity records of both his/her friends and similar users.

---

[2]https://developer.foursquare.com/
[3]https://sites.google.com/site/dbhongzhi/

To further validate the benefits brought by exploiting temporal information and spatial smoothing based on the spatial pyramid, we compare our model with three simplified versions of ST-SAGE.

ST-SAGE-S1 is the first simplified version of the ST-SAGE model, and it does not consider the temporal influence. This means that θ^{native} and $\theta^{tourist}$ in this version are $|R|$ instead of $|R| \times |T|$ vectors. For each user activity, the topic index z is sampled according to the following equation instead of the (9.3). This simplified version is equal to the Geo-SAGE model proposed in [28].

$$P(z_{u,i}|s_{u,i}, l_{u,i}, \theta^0, \theta^{user}, \theta^{native}, \theta^{tourist})$$
$$= P(z_{u,i}|\theta^{user}_u + (1 - s_{u,i}) \times \theta^{native}_{l_{u,i}} + s_{u,i} \times \theta^{tourist}_{l_{u,i}}) \tag{9.17}$$

ST-SAGE-S2 is the second simplified version, and it models the temporal information without smoothing over the proposed spatial pyramid. More specifically, the topic index z is sampled according to the following equation:

$$P(z_{u,i}|s_{u,i}, l_{u,i}, t_{u,i}, \theta^0, \theta^{user}, \theta^{native}, \theta^{tourist})$$
$$= P(z_{u,i}|\theta^{user}_{u,t_{u,i}} + (1 - s_{u,i}) \times \theta^{native}_{l_{u,i}} + s_{u,i} \times \theta^{tourist}_{l_{u,i}}) \tag{9.18}$$

ST-SAGE-S3 is the third simplified version of ST-SAGE which does not exploit the geographical correlation in the spatial pyramid. Thus, this model cannot deal with the problem that the inferred temporal native preference and temporal tourist preference for location l at time t are not reliable when there are few or even no user activity records in the corresponding region.

9.5.1.3 Evaluation methods

We aim to evaluate both the effectiveness and efficiency of the proposed ST-SAGE. For the efficiency part, both the model training and the online recommendation efficiency are to be evaluated.

Recommendation effectiveness. Since our ST-SAGE model is designed for both hometown recommendation and out-of-town recommendation, we evaluate the recommendation effectiveness of our model under each of the scenarios. Given a user profile containing a collection of user activities, we divide these activities into a training set and a test set. For the hometown recommendation scenario, we randomly select 30% of the activity records occurring at the user's hometown as the test set, and use the remaining activity records as the training set. Similarly, for the scenario of out-of-town recommendation, we randomly select 30% of the activity records generated by the user when he/she travels out of town as the test set and use the remaining activity records as the training set. To decide whether an activity record occurs in his/her hometown or elsewhere, we measure the location distance between the user's hometown and the spatial item (e.g., $|l_u - l_v|$). If the distance is greater than 100 km, we assume the activity occurs when the user is out-of-town. The threshold $d = 100$ km is selected because a distance of around 100 km is the typical radius of "human reach," which takes 1–2 h to drive.

According to the above dividing strategies, we split the user activity dataset D into the training set D_{train} and the test set D_{test}. To evaluate the recommendation methods, we adopt the evaluation methodology and measurement Accuracy@k, which is applied in [16,20,43–45]. Specifically, for each user activity record (u, v, l_v, W_v, s, t) in D_{test}: (1) we compute the ranking score for spatial item v and all other spatial items which are within the circle of radius d centered at l_v and unvisited by u previously; (2) we form a ranked list by ordering all of these spatial items according to their ranking scores. Let r denote the position of the spatial item v within this list. The best result corresponds to the case where v precedes all the unvisited spatial items (that is, $r = 1$) and (3) we form a top-k recommendation list by picking the k top ranked spatial items from the list. If $r \leq k$, we have a hit (i.e., the ground truth item v is recommended to the user). Otherwise, we have a miss.

The computation of Accuracy@k proceeds as follows. We define hit@k for a single test case as either the value 1, if the test item v appears in the top-k results, or the value 0, if otherwise. The overall Accuracy@k is defined by averaging the overall test cases:

$$Accuracy@k = \frac{\#hit@k}{|D_{test}|} \tag{9.19}$$

where $\#hit@k$ denotes the number of hits in the test set and $|D_{test}|$ is the number of all test cases.

Recommendation efficiency. The time cost of training ST-SAGE is mainly affected by the number of activity records in the dataset and the number of nodes in the GraphLab framework. Therefore, we evaluate the model training efficiency of ST-SAGE with various numbers of nodes. For the online recommendation, the efficiency mainly depends on (1) the number of all spatial items in the target region and (2) the number of spatial items recommended. Thus, we test the recommendation efficiency of ST-SAGE by varying these two factors.

9.5.2 Recommendation effectiveness

In this part, we first present the experimental results by comparing our model with the state-of-the-art recommendation methods on two real-life datasets for both out-of-town recommendation and hometown recommendation. Second, we validate the benefits brought by different strategies adopted by ST-SAGE, such as exploiting temporal effect and spatial smoothing based on the spatial pyramid.

9.5.2.1 Results and analysis

First, we present the experimental results of the comparison between recommendation methods with well-tuned parameters. Figures 9.5 and 9.6 report the effectiveness of recommendation on the Foursquare and Twitter datasets, respectively. From the figures, we observe that the accuracy values gradually rise with respect to the increase of k. This is because, by returning more spatial items, it is more likely that items that users would like to visit will be discovered. We show the performance when k is set to 5 and 10.

It is apparent that the recommendation methods have significant performance disparity in terms of the top-k accuracy. Figure 9.5(a) presents the recommendation accuracy in the scenario of out-of-town recommendation where the accuracy of

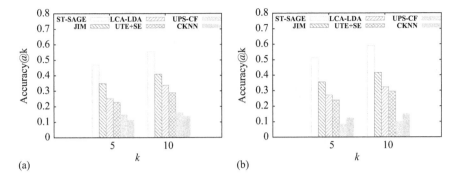

Figure 9.5   Performance on Foursquare dataset: (a) out-of-town and (b) hometown

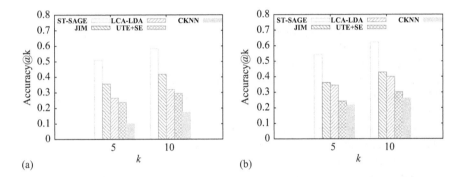

Figure 9.6   Performance on Twitter dataset: (a) out-of-town and (b) hometown

ST-SAGE is about 0.457 when $k = 5$ and 0.535 when $k = 10$. This means that there is a probability of 45.7% that ST-SAGE will place an appealing point of interest in the top-5 recommendations and a 53.5% probability that it will be placed in the top-10 recommendations. Clearly, our proposed ST-SAGE model outperforms other competitor models significantly, demonstrating the advantages of ST-SAGE over other competitor methods. Several observations are made from the results: (1) ST-SAGE outperforms two other models which also integrate the temporal information: UTE+SE [9] and JIM [29], demonstrating the advantages of ST-SAGE over other competitor methods which also integrate the temporal information. (2) CKNN performs worst as it does not explore the spatial–temporal dynamics since the local experts discovered by CKNN have the same or similar interests as target users. (3) UPS-CF falls behind ST-SAGE and LCA–LDA, showing the advantages of using the latent topic models to capture users' interests by exploiting the content of their visited spatial items. Through the medium of content, ST-SAGE and LCA–LDA transfer users' interests inferred in the hometown to out-of-town regions. In contrast, UPS-CF is a mixture of collaborative filtering and social filtering, which ignores the effect of content. Besides, according to the recent survey in [11], for movement farther than

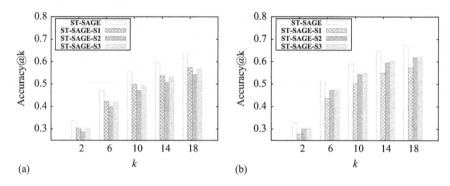

Figure 9.7   Impact of different factors on Foursquare dataset: (a) out-of-town and (b) hometown

100 km from home location, the probability of visiting the exact same locations as a friend has visited in the past is low.

Figure 9.6 shows the recommendation effectiveness on the Twitter dataset. As the social relationship is unavailable on this dataset, UPS-CF has not been evaluated in this experiment. The trend of the comparison result is similar to that presented in Figure 9.5.

There are two parameters in ST-SAGE: the height of the spatial pyramid (H) and the number of topics (K). The experimental results presented above are obtained with the optimal parameter settings: (1) the optimal height of the spatial pyramid is 5 for both Foursquare and Twitter datasets and (2) the optimal values of K are 60 for the Foursquare dataset, and 100 for the Twitter dataset.

9.5.2.2   Impact of different factors

To validate the respective benefits acquired by exploiting the temporal information and the spatial smoothing based on the spatial pyramid, we compare ST-SAGE with the three variant versions: ST-SAGE-S1, ST-SAGE-S2 and ST-SAGE-S3. The results of this comparison are shown in Figures 9.7 and 9.8. From the results, we observe that ST-SAGE consistently outperforms the three variant versions for both out-of-town recommendation and hometown recommendation, which demonstrates the benefits of exploiting the temporal information and the spatial smoothing. By comparing ST-SAGE-S1 and ST-SAGE-S2, we also observe that ST-SAGE-S1 performs better in out-of-town recommendation while ST-SAGE-S2 performs better in hometown recommendation. This is because the personal activity data is extremely sparse in out-of-town recommendation, and this sparsity leads to inaccuracy in inferring the personal temporal preferences in ST-SAGE-S2.

To study the impact of two parameters in ST-SAGE, i.e., H and K, we tried different setups for these two parameters. Due to space constraints, we only show the Accuracy@10 for the out-of-town recommendation on the Foursquare dataset. We tested the performance of the ST-SAGE model by varying the height of the spatial pyramid H from 2 to 7 and the number of topics K from 30 to 80. The results are

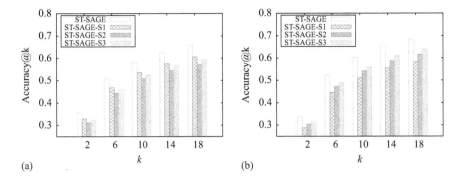

*Figure 9.8   Impact of different factors on Twitter dataset: (a) out-of-town and (b)
hometown*

Table 9.4   Impact of parameters

Height	Number of topics					
	30	40	50	**60**	70	80
2	0.46	0.498	0.518	0.53	0.534	0.535
3	0.464	0.502	0.525	0.539	0.54	0.543
4	0.471	0.502	0.529	0.546	0.551	0.554
5	0.478	0.513	0.534	**0.554**	0.556	0.555
6	0.456	0.492	0.513	0.522	0.522	0.527
7	0.421	0.451	0.476	0.485	0.489	0.492

presented in Table 9.4. From the results, we observe that as H increases, the *Accuracy* values of ST-SAGE first increase, and then decrease. One possible reason for the early increase of the *Accuracy* values is that increasing the height exploits the spatial effect at finer levels and makes the inference of native and tourist preferences more precise. Later, *Accuracy* decreases as H gets larger, because increasing the height makes users' activity data in a region cell sparser. ST-SAGE achieves its best performance when the height of the spatial pyramid is set to 5 on the Foursquare dataset. On the other hand, we also observed that the performance first improves with the increase of the number of topics K and then the increment becomes small. The reason is that K represents the model complexity. Thus, when K is too small, the model has limited ability to describe the data. However, when K exceeds a threshold (e.g., $K = 60$ in this dataset), the model is complex enough to handle the data. At this point, it is less helpful to improve the model performance by increasing K. Thus, we choose $H = 5, K = 60$ as the best trade-off between the accuracy and efficiency on the Foursquare dataset.

9.5.3   Recommendation efficiency

In this part, we first present the evaluation of the offline model training efficiency. Then, we present the online recommendation efficiency.

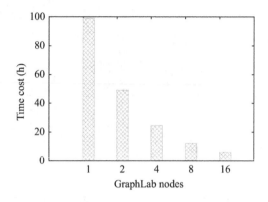

Figure 9.9   Training time of ST-SAGE on GraphLab

9.5.3.1   Model training efficiency

To make our ST-SAGE model scalable to large-scale datasets, we implement it based on the GraphLab framework. The training time of ST-SAGE on the Twitter dataset is reported under different numbers of nodes in Figure 9.9. From the result, we observe that the training time of ST-SAGE decreases significantly with growing size of distributed GraphLab nodes. We reduce the training time for ST-SAGE from approximately 100 h to less than 10 h. Though the basic implementation of ST-SAGE is costly, the parallel implementation guarantees the scalability of our ST-SAGE model. This model is thus feasible in practical deployment.

9.5.3.2   Online recommendation efficiency

In this section, we evaluate the recommendation efficiency using the Foursquare dataset. In the efficiency study, we tested top-k recommendations for the target region with 50 km × 50 km and 100 km × 100 km, respectively. Obviously, there are more spatial items in the target region with 100 km × 100 km than in the region with 50 km × 50 km. All recommendation algorithms are implemented in Java 1.7 and run on a Windows Server with "Intel E5-2690" CPU and 256G RAM.

For the online recommendation efficiency test, we compare ST-SAGE with UPS-CF, CKNN and UTE+SE. We did not compare our model with LCA–LDA and JIM due to the fact that the TA algorithm can also be employed to speed up the online recommendation in the two recommender models, as their ranking functions are also monotonous. For the online recommendation of ST-SAGE, we adopt two methods to utilize the knowledge learned offline to produce recommendations. The first method extends the TA algorithm to produce top-k recommendations and is denoted as "ST-SAGE-TA." The second method linearly scans all the spatial items in the target region, computes their ranking scores and then recommends the top-k items with the highest scores. This method is called "ST-SAGE-LS."

Figure 9.10 presents the average online efficiency of the four different methods. On average, our proposed "ST-SAGE-TA" produces top-10 recommendations

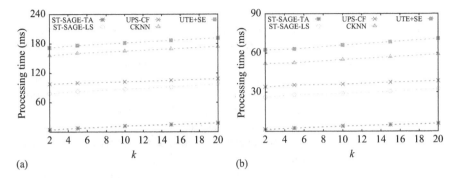

Figure 9.10   Efficiency of online recommendations: (a) target region with 100 km × 100 km and (b) target region with 50 km × 50 km

in 12.1 and 3.9 ms for the target region with 100 km × 100 km and 50 km × 50 km, respectively. From the figures, we observe that (1) "ST-SAGE-TA" outperforms "ST-SAGE-LS" significantly in all querying regions, which demonstrates that the TA-based query processing technique is efficient; (2) "ST-SAGE-TA" and "ST-SAGE-LS" consistently outperform "CKNN," "UPS-CF" and "UTE+SE" significantly in both querying regions, showing that the model-based methods produce faster responses to querying users than memory-based methods once the model parameters have been learned offline; (3) the time costs of all algorithms in the target region with 100 km × 100 km are higher than that in the target region with 50 km × 50 km due to the increase of the number of the candidate spatial items; and (4) the time costs of all algorithms increase slowly with the increase of the number of recommendations (*k*).

9.6   Related work

With the availability of large-scale user activity records in the physical world, many recent works have tried to improve spatial items recommendation by exploiting the GPS data, geographical and social influence, temporal effect and content information of spatial items.

GPS data. The task of spatial item recommendation is highly related to human mobility. It is traditionally studied on mobile data, i.e., cellphone-based GPS data. Various works have explored these information to study human mobility and have promoted a set of location-based applications including spatial item recommendation [46–50]. The raw GPS data is a sequence of time-stamped latitude/longitude pairs and there is no mapping information between geo-coordinates and specific real-world spatial items. Thus, a spatial item is usually extracted from users' GPS trajectory logs as the stay points on which a user spends sufficient time [51,52]. The data availability of GPS data is limited due to the user privacy problem since GPS data is obtained from users' cell phones through telecommunication services. Generally speaking, existing systems fall into two categories: systems without content or social information and system with limited content information. For the recommender systems without content information, spatial and temporal patterns are commonly adopted with collaborative filtering methods to perform spatial item recommendation [53–56]. The content information could be available in certain types of GPS data. Zheng et al. [51,57] have proposed a user-centered collaborative location and activity filtering approach to find like-minded users and similar activities at different locations with tensor decomposition. In tour recommendation [58,59] and tourist spatial item recommendation [60], contents related to travel packages or tourist spatial items, such as package description and spatial item attributes, are used to analyze user interested topics for spatial item recommendation.

Geo-social influence. Geo-social influence indicates that people tend to explore spatial items near a spatial item that they or their friends have visited before [61]. Many recent studies [5,11,61,62] show that there is a strong correlation between user check-in activities and geographical distance as well as social connections. Most of the current spatial item recommendation work mainly focuses on leveraging the geographical and social influences to improve recommendation accuracy. For example, Ye et al. [61] have delved into spatial item recommendation by investigating geographical influence between locations and proposed a system that combines user preferences, social influence and geographical influence. Cheng et al. [62] have investigated the geographical influence through combining a multicenter Gaussian model, matrix factorization and social influence together for location recommendation. Lian et al. [5] have incorporated the spatial clustering phenomenon resulted from geographical influence into a weighted matrix factorization framework to deal with the matrix sparsity. Ference et al. [7] have designed a collaborative recommendation framework which considers the activity records generated by both friends and similar users in a mixture way.

Temporal effect. The temporal effect of user check-in activities in LBSNs has also attracted much attention from researchers. Spatial item recommendation with temporal effect mainly leverages temporal cyclic patterns and temporal sequential patterns on LBSNs. Gao et al. [63] have investigated the temporal cyclic patterns of user check-ins in terms of temporal nonuniformness and temporal consecutiveness. [64,65] focus on the task of successive personalized spatial item recommendation in LBSNs by embedding the temporal sequential patterns. Yin et al. have proposed a temporal recommender system [66] and modeled user behaviors based on intrinsic interest as well as the temporal context in [16,41]. In recent years, deep neural networks have been successfully applied to many recommender systems [24,67] such as word embeddings to incorporate auxiliary information and recurrent neural networks (RNN) to capture sequential properties of observed user–item interactions. Manotumruksa et al. have proposed a deep recurrent collaborative filtering framework with a pairwise ranking function that aims to capture user–venue interactions in a CF manner from sequences of observed feedback by leveraging multilayer perception and RNN architectures in [67].

Content information. Most recently, researchers have explored the content information of spatial items to alleviate the problem of data sparsity. Hu et al. have proposed a spatial topic model for spatial item recommendation considering both spatial and textual aspects of user posts from Twitter in [20]. Yin *et al.* [16] have exploited both personal interests and local preferences based on the contents associated with spatial items. Wang *et al.* [28] leverage the content information as the medium to transfer the users' personal interest in the hometown to a new place. Liu *et al.* [33] have studied the effect of spatial item-associated tags for spatial item recommendation with an aggregated LDA and matrix factorization method. Gao *et al.* [68] have studied both spatial item-associated contents and user sentiment information (e.g., user comments) in spatial item recommendation and reported good performance. There are also researchers who focus on supplementing the content information based on temporal and spatial patterns of topics [69].

9.7 Conclusion

In this chapter, we proposed an ST-SAGE model for spatial item recommendation, which effectively overcomes the challenges arising from travel locality and spatial–temporal dynamics of user behaviors. Specifically, to combat travel locality, ST-SAGE exploited both the co-occurrence patterns of spatial items and their content to infer and transfer user interests. To address spatial dynamics of user behavior, ST-SAGE incorporated the native or tourist preference at the target location. To combat the data sparsity in modeling the temporal dynamics of user behaviors, we enhanced the model with smoothing by taking advantage of the temporal preferences of the crowd of similar users. To alleviate the data sparsity confronted by the inference of temporal native preferences and tourist preferences for each region, ST-SAGE employed an additive framework to smooth the preferences over a well-designed spatial pyramid. Besides, we developed a scalable and parallel learning algorithm for ST-SAGE based on the GraphLab framework to improve the efficiency of the model training, and efficient top-*k* query processing techniques (i.e., TA) are employed to speed up the process of online recommendation. We conducted extensive experiments to evaluate the performance of our ST-SAGE model on two real datasets. The experimental results reveal the advantages of ST-SAGE over other spatial item recommendation methods, for both out-of-town and hometown recommendations in terms of both recommendation effectiveness and efficiency, which demonstrate the effectiveness of ST-SAGE in facilitating travel for users in their hometowns as well as in regions they are not familiar with.

References

[1]   Bao J, Zheng Y, Mokbel MF. Location-based and Preference-Aware Recommendation Using Sparse Geo-Social Networking Data. In: Proceedings of the 20th International Conference on Advances in Geographic Information Systems. SIGSPATIAL; 2012. p. 199–208.

[2]   Yin H, Cui B. Spatio-Temporal Recommendation in Social Media. Singapore: Springer; 2016.

[3]   Cui B, Mei H, Ooi BC. Big Data: The Driver for Innovation in Databases. National Science Review. 2014;1(1):27–30.

[4]   Bao J, Zheng Y, Wilkie D, *et al.* Recommendations in Location-based Social Networks: A Survey. Geoinformatica. 2015;19(3):525–565.

[5]   Lian D, Zhao C, Xie X, *et al.* GeoMF: Joint Geographical Modeling and Matrix Factorization for Point-of-Interest Recommendation. In: Proceedings of the 20th ACM SIGKDD International Conference on Knowledge Discovery and Data Mining. SIGKDD; 2014. p. 831–840.

[6]   Xie M, Yin H, Xu F, *et al.* Learning Graph-based POI Embedding for Location-based Recommendation. In: the 25th ACM International Conference on Information and Knowledge Management. CIKM; 2016.

[7]   Ference G, Ye M, Lee WC. Location Recommendation for Out-of-Town Users in Location-based Social Networks. In: Proceedings of the 22nd ACM International Conference on Information Knowledge Management. CIKM; 2013. p. 721–726.

[8]   Wang H, Fu Y, Wang Q, *et al.* A Location-Sentiment-Aware Recommender System for Both Home-Town and Out-of-Town Mobile Users. In: SIGKDD; 2017.

[9]   Yuan Q, Cong G, Ma Z, *et al.* Time-Aware Point-of-Interest Recommendation. In: Proceedings of the 36th International ACM SIGIR Conference on Research and Development in Information Retrieval. SIGIR; 2013. p. 363–372.

[10]   Noulas A, Scellato S, Mascolo C, *et al.* An Empirical Study of Geographic User Activity Patterns in Foursquare. In: Proceedings of the Fifth International AAAI Conference on Weblogs and Social Media. ICWSM; 2011.

[11]   Cho E, Myers SA, Leskovec J. Friendship and Mobility: User Movement in Location-based Social Networks. In: Proceedings of the 17th ACM SIGKDD International Conference on Knowledge Discovery and Data Mining. SIGKDD; 2011. p. 1082–1090.

[12]   Lee K, Hong S, Kim SJ, *et al.* SLAW: A Mobility Model for Human Walks. INFOCOM; 2009. p. 855–863.

[13]   Levandoski JJ, Sarwat M, Eldawy A, *et al.* LARS: A Location-Aware Recommender System. In: IEEE 28th International Conference on Data Engineering. ICDE; 2012. p. 450–461.

[14]   Yin H, Zhou X, Cui B, *et al.* Adapting to User Interest Drift for POI Recommendation. IEEE Transactions on Knowledge and Data Engineering. 2016;28(10):2566–2581.

[15]   Hosseini S, Yin H, Zhang M, *et al.* Jointly Modeling Heterogeneous Temporal Properties in Location Recommendation. In: DASFAA; 2017. p. 490–506.

[16]   Yin H, Cui B, Sun Y, *et al.* LCARS: A Spatial Item Recommender System. ACM Transactions on Information Systems. 2014;32(3):11:1–11:37.

[17]   Eisenstein J, Ahmed A, Xing EP. Sparse Additive Generative Models of Text. In: International Conference on Machine Learning. ICML; 2011. p. 1041–1048.

[18]   Ahmed A, Kanagal B, Pandey S, *et al.* Latent Factor Models with Additive and Hierarchically-Smoothed User Preferences. In: Proceedings of the Sixth ACM International Conference on Web Search and Data Mining. WSDM; 2013. p. 385–394.

[19] Kanagal B, Ahmed A, Pandey S, *et al.* Supercharging Recommender Systems Using Taxonomies for Learning User Purchase Behavior. Proceedings of the VLDB Endowment. 2012;5(10):956–967.

[20] Hu B, Ester M. Spatial Topic Modeling in Online Social Media for Location Recommendation. In: Proceedings of the 7th ACM Conference on Recommender Systems. RecSys; 2013. p. 25–32.

[21] Wang W, Yin H, Sadiq S, *et al.* SPORE: A Sequential Personalized Spatial Item Recommender System. In: 2016 IEEE 32nd International Conference on Data Engineering. ICDE; 2016. p. 954–965.

[22] Yin H, Chen L, Wang W, *et al.* Mobi-SAGE: A Sparse Additive Generative Model for Mobile App Recommendation. In: ICDE; 2017. p. 75–78.

[23] Wang W, Yin H, Chen L, *et al.* ST-SAGE: A Spatial-Temporal Sparse Additive Generative Model for Spatial Item Recommendation. ACM Transactions on Intelligent Systems and Technology. 2017;8(3):48:1–48:25.

[24] Yin H, Wang W, Wang H, *et al.* Spatial-Aware Hierarchical Collaborative Deep Learning for POI Recommendation. IEEE Transactions on Knowledge and Data Engineering. 2017;29(11):2537–2551.

[25] Chen W, Yin H, Wang W, *et al.* Exploiting Spatio-Temporal User Behaviors for User Linkage. In: CIKM; 2017.

[26] Li R, Wang S, Deng H, *et al.* Towards Social User Profiling: Unified and Discriminative Influence Model for Inferring Home Locations. In: Proceedings of the 18th ACM SIGKDD International Conference on Knowledge Discovery and Data Mining. SIGKDD; 2012. p. 1023–1031.

[27] Scellato S, Noulas A, Lambiotte R, *et al.* Socio-Spatial Properties of Online Location-Based Social Networks. In: ICWSM; 2011.

[28] Wang W, Yin H, Chen L, *et al.* Geo-SAGE: A Geographical Sparse Additive Generative Model for Spatial Item Recommendation. In: Proceedings of the 21th ACM SIGKDD International Conference on Knowledge Discovery and Data Mining. SIGKDD; Sydney, NSW, Australia; 2015. New York, NY: ACM; 2015. pp. 1255–1264.

[29] Yin H, Zhou X, Shao Y, *et al.* Joint Modeling of User Check-in Behaviors for Point-of-Interest Recommendation. In: the 24th ACM International Conference on Information and Knowledge Management. CIKM; 2015. p. 1631–1640.

[30] Mok D, Wellman B, Carrasco J. Does Distance Matter in the Age of the Internet?. Urban Studies. 2010;47(13):2747–2783.

[31] Yin H, Cui B, Huang Z, *et al.* Joint Modeling of Users' Interests and Mobility Patterns for Point-of-Interest Recommendation. In: Proceedings of the 23rd ACM International Conference on Multimedia. MM; 2015. p. 819–822.

[32] Yin H, Cui B, Zhou X, *et al.* Joint Modeling of User Check-in Behaviors for Real-time Point-of-Interest Recommendation. ACM Transactions on Information Systems. 2016;35(2):11:1–11:44.

[33] Liu B, Xiong H. Point-of-Interest Recommendation in Location Based Social Networks with Topic and Location Awareness. In: Proceedings of

the 2013 SIAM International Conference on Data Mining. SDM; 2013. p. 396–404.

[34]   Wallach HM. Topic Modeling: Beyond Bag-of-words. In: International Conference on Machine Learning. ICML; 2006. p. 977–984.

[35]   Schmidt M, Niculescu-Mizil A, Murphy K. Learning Graphical Model Structure Using L1-regularization Paths. In: AAAI Conference on Artificial Intelligence. AAAI; 2007. p. 1278–1283.

[36]   Liu DC, Nocedal J. On the Limited Memory BFGS Method for Large Scale Optimization. Mathematical Programming. 1989;45(3):503–528.

[37]   Gale S, Olsson G. Philosophy in Geography. Dordrecht: D. Reidel; 1979.

[38]   Shekhar S, Zhang P, Huang Y, *et al.* Data Mining: Next Generation Challenges and Future Directions. AAAI/MIT Press; 2004.

[39]   Low Y, Bickson D, Gonzalez J, *et al.* Distributed GraphLab: A Framework for Machine Learning and Data Mining in the Cloud. Proceedings of the VLDB Endowment. 2012;5(8):716–727.

[40]   Hu Z, Yao J, Cui B, *et al.* Community Level Diffusion Extraction. In: Proceedings of the 2015 ACM SIGMOD International Conference on Management of Data. SIGMOD; 2015. p. 1555–1569.

[41]   Yin H, Cui B, Chen L, *et al.* A Temporal Context-aware Model for User Behavior Modeling in Social Media Systems. In: Proceedings of the 2014 ACM SIGMOD International Conference on Management of Data. SIGMOD; 2014. p. 1543–1554.

[42]   Cheng Z, Caverlee J, Lee K, *et al.* Exploring Millions of Footprints in Location Sharing Services. In: Proceedings of the Fifth International AAAI Conference on Weblogs and Social Media. ICWSM; 2011.

[43]   Chen WY, Chu JC, Luan J, *et al.* Collaborative Filtering for Orkut Communities: Discovery of User Latent Behavior. In: Proceedings of the 18th International Conference on World Wide Web. WWW; 2009. p. 681–690.

[44]   Cremonesi P, Koren Y, Turrin R. Performance of Recommender Algorithms on Top-n Recommendation Tasks. In: Proceedings of the Fourth ACM Conference on Recommender Systems. RecSys; 2010. p. 39–46.

[45]   Koren Y. Factorization Meets the Neighborhood: A Multifaceted Collaborative Filtering Model. In: Proceedings of the 14th ACM SIGKDD International Conference on Knowledge Discovery and Data Mining. SIGKDD; 2008. p. 426–434.

[46]   Beeharee A, Steed A. Exploiting Real World Knowledge in Ubiquitous Applications. Personal Ubiquitous Computing. 2007;11(6):429–437.

[47]   Horozov T, Narasimhan N, Vasudevan V. Using Location for Personalized POI Recommendations in Mobile Environments. In: SAINT; 2006. p. 124–129.

[48]   Park MH, Hong JH, Cho SB. Location-based Recommendation System Using Bayesian User's Preference Model in Mobile Devices. In: Proceedings of the 4th International Conference on Ubiquitous Intelligence and Computing. UIC; 2007. p. 1130–1139.

[49]   Simon R, Fröhlich P. A Mobile Application Framework for the Geospatial Web. In: Proceedings of the 16th International Conference on World Wide Web. WWW; 2007. p. 381–390.

[50] Takeuchi Y, Sugimoto M. CityVoyager: An Outdoor Recommendation System Based on User Location History. In: Proceedings of the 3th International Conference on Ubiquitous Intelligence and Computing. UIC; 2006. p. 625–636.

[51] Zheng VW, Zheng Y, Xie X, *et al.* Collaborative Location and Activity Recommendations with GPS History Data. In: Proceedings of the 19th International Conference on World Wide Web. WWW; 2010. p. 1029–1038.

[52] Zheng Y, Zhang L, Xie X, *et al.* Mining Interesting Locations and Travel Sequences from GPS Trajectories. In: Proceedings of the 18th International Conference on World Wide Web. WWW; 2009. p. 791–800.

[53] Zheng Y, Zhang L, Ma Z, *et al.* Recommending Friends and Locations Based on Individual Location History. ACM Transactions on the Web. 2011;5(1):5:1–5:44.

[54] Ge Y, Xiong H, Tuzhilin A, *et al.* An Energy-efficient Mobile Recommender System. In: Proceedings of the 16th ACM SIGKDD International Conference on Knowledge Discovery and Data Mining. SIGKDD; 2010. p. 899–908.

[55] Zheng Y, Xie X. Learning Travel Recommendations from User-generated GPS Traces. ACM Transactions on Intelligent Systems and Technology. 2011;2(1):2:1–2:29.

[56] Leung KWT, Lee DL, Lee WC. CLR: A Collaborative Location Recommendation Framework Based on Co-clustering. In: Proceedings of the 34th International ACM SIGIR Conference on Research and Development in Information Retrieval. SIGIR; 2011. p. 305–314.

[57] Zheng VW, Zheng Y, Xie X, *et al.* Towards Mobile Intelligence: Learning from GPS History Data for Collaborative Recommendation. Artificial Intelligence. 2012;184–185:17–37.

[58] Ge Y, Liu Q, Xiong H, *et al.* Cost-aware Travel Tour Recommendation. In: Proceedings of the 17th ACM SIGKDD International Conference on Knowledge Discovery and Data Mining. SIGKDD; 2011. p. 983–991.

[59] Liu Q, Ge Y, Li Z, *et al.* Personalized Travel Package Recommendation. In: Proceedings of the 2011 IEEE 11th International Conference on Data Mining. ICDM; 2011. p. 407–416.

[60] Kang E-y, Kim H, Cho J. Personalization Method for Tourist Point of Interest (POI) Recommendation. Proceedings of the 10th International Conference on Knowledge-Based Intelligent Information and Engineering Systems. 2006;4251:392–400.

[61] Ye M, Yin P, Lee WC, *et al.* Exploiting Geographical Influence for Collaborative Point-of-Interest Recommendation. In: Proceedings of the 34th International ACM SIGIR Conference on Research and Development in Information Retrieval. SIGIR; 2011. p. 325–334.

[62] Cheng C, Yang H, King I, *et al.* Fused Matrix Factorization with Geographical and Social Influence in Location-based Social Networks. In: Proceedings of the Twenty-Sixth AAAI Conference on Artificial Intelligence. AAAI; 2012. p. 17–23.

[63] Gao H, Tang J, Hu X, *et al.* Exploring Temporal Effects for Location Recommendation on Location-based Social Networks. In: Proceedings of the 7th ACM Conference on Recommender Systems. RecSys '13; 2013. p. 93–100.

[64]   Cheng C, Yang H, Lyu MR, *et al.* Where You Like to Go Next: Successive Point-of-interest Recommendation. In: Proceedings of the Twenty-Third International Joint Conference on Artificial Intelligence. IJCAI; 2013. p. 2605–2611.

[65]   Zhang W, Wang J. Location and Time Aware Social Collaborative Retrieval for New Successive Point-of-Interest Recommendation. In: CIKM; 2015. p. 1221–1230.

[66]   Chen C, Yin H, Yao J, *et al.* TeRec: A Temporal Recommender System over Tweet Stream. Proceedings of the VLDB Endowment. 2013;6(12):1254–1257.

[67]   Manotumruksa J, Macdonald C, Ounis I. A Deep Recurrent Collaborative Filtering Framework for Venue Recommendation. In: CIKM; 2017. p. 1429–1438.

[68]   Gao H, Tang J, Hu X, *et al.* Content-Aware Point of Interest Recommendation on Location-Based Social Networks. In: AAAI Conference on Artificial Intelligence. AAAI; 2015. p. 1721–1727.

[69]   He T, Yin H, Chen Z, *et al.* A Spatial-Temporal Topic Model for the Semantic Annotation of POIs in LBSNs. ACM Transactions on Intelligent Systems and Technology. 2016;8(1):12:1–12:24.

Chapter 10

Recommender system for predicting malicious Android applications

Tanya Gera[1], Jaiteg Singh[1], Deepak Thakur[1], and Rajinder Sandhu[1]

Hackers spread malware for various reasons, yet regularly the thought processes are money related. Malignant Android battles intended to take charge card and keeping money-related data from tainted gadgets were most common, regularly notwithstanding utilizing the official Google Play Store to trap casualties into entering their Master card data. Guiltless client does not know about the way that the application which he will download is sheltered or pernicious. The key thought is to manufacture a central server that will accumulate the clients' applications information and play out the static and dynamic investigation of an Android application to locate the risky examples and will group it as malicious or benign. This assignment will require huge processing power. Here, the importance of big data comes into picture.

Already existed and suggested frameworks have been tremendously helpful, and huge information is the main impetus behind proposal frameworks. Our planned mechanism additionally plans to gather a lot of client information; for example, it adds up to a number of downloads, clients' audits, consents required by an application, and designers data to give relevant and powerful proposals. There is a need of a dynamic malware investigation system which uses the innovations of graphical user interface (GUI)-based testing, big data examination, and machine figuring out how to identify malignant Android applications. The system can be utilized as a part of conjunction with other existing attempts to enhance the discovery rate of malware.

10.1 Background

Albeit many existing works have been proposed to distinguish malware on PCs, Android frameworks are distinctive in a few ways: application framework, touchscreen-based graphical user interface (GUI), and administration of individual information. Numerous re-penny papers can be found for the Android malware

[1]Department of Computer Science and Engineering, Chitkara University Institute of Engineering and Technology, Chitkara University, India

discovery. We can arrange them into two sorts of the identification system: static examination and dynamic analysis. Both static and dynamic investigations have their qualities and shortcomings. Static examination uses the show of the Android applications and recovers data, e.g. authorizations and application programming interface (programming interface) calls to distinguish malware. Some methodologies, e.g. RiskRanker [1], DroidMat [2], and DREBIN [3], figure out the Android Bundle (APK) records to acquire data from the dismantled smali code arrangement and the decompiled Java code. Some methodologies simply use the consent blends of the Android applications or signature, e.g. Kirin [4]. The benefits of static examination are little overhead, effective, and versatile, and expectation may base on physically created detection examples or learning-based identification. Dynamic examination concentrates on the runtime practices and the framework measurements of the applications. The greater part of the dynamic investigation approaches includes executing applications in the emulator to get the runtime data. Andromaly [5] utilizes the data of the framework measurements to do the malware location, TaintDroid [6] utilizes the data of framework calls, and other systems get to document read/compose practices. DroidScope [7] revamps the semantic data of the working framework and Java to break down the key practices of the malware families. Crowdroid [8] uses crowdsourcing to accumulate data from whatever number PDAs as could be expected under the circumstances, and exchange them to a cloud server for malware order with bunching calculations. A technique called STREAM [9] has a comparable way to deal with Andromaly, and this empowers quick substantial scale approval of portable malware machine learning classifiers. Contrasting with static investigation strategies, the previously mentioned dynamic examination techniques assemble dynamic data by means of the utilization of emulators, which requires the copying procedure to mimic GUI-based PDA applications by demonstrating human conduct. Dynamic investigation might have the capacity to assemble more data than static examination does; consequently, consolidating dynamic/static examination techniques would give better outcomes. Because of the unending advancement of the malware, it ends up noticeably increasingly hard for static strategies to recognize malware from APKs. Some malwares are capable of performing frequent behavioral changes [10]. Another basic issue is the Java reflection strategy, which is prevalently utilized as a part of JSON and XML deserialization, that may contain covered up or private programming interface calls summon and manage programming interface classes whose names change between variants. It is a capable strategy; however, it likewise turns into a solid weapon for a malware to conceal its vindictive conduct. All the over the confinements make static examination hard to completely identify all the malwares. Today, none of the previously mentioned static/dynamic investigation techniques can be viewed as the champ, since none of them can get all malwares. It is conceivable to manufacture a half breed location plot by joining a few techniques.

The greater part of the current malware depends on the establishment by the client who represents the last line of barrier in malware recognition. Another malware discovery technique is required that would concentrate on the data that the client can see preceding the establishment of an application metadata, e.g. maker ID, contact e-mail, contact site, limited time video, number of screenshots, promo writings, late changes, ID, bundle name, establishment measure, adaptation, application sort, appraisals tally, and application title inside the stages programming market. Contingent upon the stage, this will incorporate the applications depiction, its consents, the appraisals, or data about the designer, the last time changed, classification, value, portrayal, authorizations, rating, and number of downloads. To investigate these pieces of information, it's needed to make utilization of refined learning revelation forms and measurable techniques. An extensive variety of illustrations in light of genuine application metadata separated from the Android Market demonstrate the potential outcomes of the new strategy. It ought to be a basic piece of a complete malware investigation/discovery chain that incorporates other understood strategies, e.g. arrange activity examination, or static or dynamic code assessment. Accordingly, there is a need of a static and dynamic malware examination structures which use the advances of GUI-based testing, enormous information investigation, and machine figuring out how to distinguish vindictive Android applications. The system can be utilized as a part of conjunction with other existing attempts to enhance the location rate of malware.

10.1.1 Android operating system architecture

In this segment, we portray the engineering of the Android OS and its applications. Android is being created and kept up by Google and advanced by the Open Handset Partnership (OHA). Android OS is put over the Linux portion and it incorporates the middleware, libraries and APIs written in c dialect, and application programming running on an application system which incorporates Java-perfect libraries. Androids source code is discharged by Google under open source licenses. Android working framework is a heap of programming parts, which is generally divided into five segments and four fundamental layers as appeared in Figure 10.1. Android OS layers and segments are clarified as follows.

10.1.1.1 Applications

Application layer is situated at the highest point of the Android programming stack. Which further involves both the preinstalled applications that gave a specific Android usage and outsider applications created by people (informal) application engineers. Cases of such applications are Browser, Contacts Manager, and E-mail applications. More cases of such applications can be found from numerous official and informal application markets.

10.1.1.2 Application framework

The application system is an arrangement of administrations that on the whole shape the environment in which Android applications run and are overseen. Administrations are given to applications as Java classes. Application engineers are permitted to make utilization of these administrations in their applications. Application structure incorporates the accompanying real administrations: Movement Supervisor, Content Suppliers, Asset Director, Notices Administrator, and View Framework.

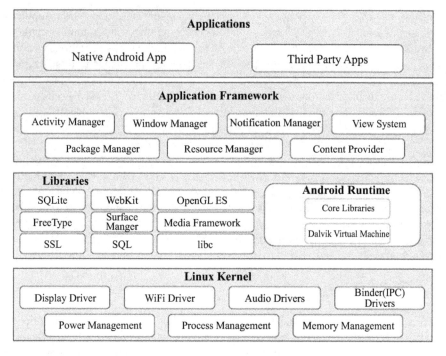

Figure 10.1   Android operating system architecture [11]

Activity manager
Action administrator oversees and controls all parts of the application lifecycle and action stack. This administration connects with the general exercises running in the framework.

Content providers
Content suppliers oversee access to an organized arrangement of information. They epitomize the information, and give components to characterizing information security. Content suppliers are the standard interface that associates information in one process with code running in another procedure. At the end of the day, this administration enables applications to distribute and share information with different applications.

Resource manager
This administration gives access to non-code installed assets, e.g. strings, shading settings, and UI designs from applications. This administration makes it conceivable to maintain applications assets freely.

Notifications manager
Warnings administrator enables applications to show alarms and notices to the client. With this administration, applications can tell the client of occasions that occur in the background

View system

This administration is an extensible arrangement of perspectives used to make application UIs.

10.1.1.3 Android runtime

This area portrays a key part called Dalvik Virtual Machine (DVM), which is a Java Virtua Machine (JVM) extraordinarily outlined and advanced for Android. Dalvik VM exploits Linux center highlights, e.g. multi-threading, multitasking execution condition, and memory administration, which are inborn in the Java dialect. Dalvik VM offers energy to applications to keep running as a procedure specifically on the Linux bit and inside its own VM (sandboxed). Since Dalvik is utilizing JVM, it provides the clients with an arrangement of libraries and APIs to create Android applications overwhelmingly utilizing Java programming dialect. The standard Java advancement condition includes a huge range of classes that are contained in the Java runtime libraries.

10.1.1.4 Libraries

The Android local libraries were created over the Linux bit. This layer empowers the gadget to deal with various sorts of information. It gives distinctive libraries utilize full to the well-working of Android working framework. These libraries are composed in C or C++ dialect and were created for specific equipment. Cases of some critical local libraries incorporate the open source Web program motor WebKit used to show HTML content, the notable library libc, SQLite database motor utilized for information stockpiling purposes, OpenGL used to render 2D or 3D illustrations substance to the screen, Media structure used to give distinctive media codecs, and SSL libraries for Web security.

10.1.1.5 Kernel

The Linux kernel is the fundamental layer of the entire system. This layer is customized specially for the embedded environment consisting of limited resources.

The entire Android OS is based over the Linux portion with some further architectural changes made by Google. This area likewise goes about as a deliberation layer between the equipment and other programming layers. Linux bit gives the essential framework usefulness, e.g. process administration, memory administration, and gadget administration. Linux bit likewise gives a variety of gadget drivers which make the assignment less demanding while at the same time interfacing the Android with fringe gadgets.

10.1.2 Android application structure

Android application is bundled into an .apk, a compress file comprising a few records and envelopes. Specifically, the AndroidManifest.xml stores the meta-information, e.g. bundle name, authorizations required, meanings of at least one parts like Exercises, Administrations, Communicate Collectors, or Substance Suppliers, least and maximum adaptation bolster, libraries to be connected, and so on. Envelope res stores

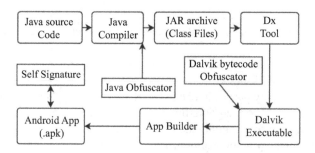

Figure 10.2   Application building process [11]

symbols, pictures, string/numeric/shading constants, UI formats, menus, and movements incorporated into the paired. Organizer resources contain noncompiled assets. Executable record classes.dex stores the Dalvik bytecode to be executed on the DVM. METAINF stores the mark of the application designer authentication to check the outsider developer character. As specified beforehand, the Android applications are created in Java. The improvement procedure is outlined in Figure 10.2. Assembled Java code produces various .class records, moderate Java bytecode of the classes characterized in the source. Utilizing the dx device, .class documents converged into a solitary Dalvik Executable (.dex). The .dex record stores the Dalvik bytecode to be executed on the DVM to speed up the execution.

10.1.3   Application threats

- Benefit acceleration assaults were utilized by misusing freely accessible Android part vulnerabilities to pick up root access of the gadget. Android sent out parts can be misused to access the risky consents.
- Security spillage or individual data burglary happens when clients give threats for authorization to malignant applications and unconsciously enable access to touchy information and exfiltration them without client learning as well as assent.
- Vindictive applications can likewise keep an eye on the clients by checking the voice calls, SMS/MMS, bank portable exchanges, recording sound/video, etc., without client information or consent.
- Malignant applications can acquire cash by influencing calls or subscribe to premium rate to number SMSes without the client learning or assent.
- Bargain the gadget to go about as a Bot and remotely control it through a server by sending different orders to perform malignant exercises.
- Forceful advertisement battles may allure clients to download possibly undesirable applications (PUAs) or malware applications.
- Conniving assault happens when an arrangement of applications, marked with same testament, gets introduced on a gadget. These applications would impart UID to each other, likewise any hazardous permission(s) asked for by one application will be shared by the plotting malware. For instance, an application with

READ SMS authorization can read SMSes and ask the intriguing accomplice with Web consent to exfiltrate the sensitive data to a remote server.

• Denial of Service (DoS) assault can happen when app(s) abuses officially restricted CPU, memory, battery, and data transfer capacity assets and controls the clients executing typical capacities.

10.2 The proposed recommender system for mobile application risk reduction

We built up a recommender framework for versatile application hazard lessening utilizing dynamic investigation strategy in light of the fact that numerous malwares of today can hide their conduct in the code to keep them from being identified by static examination methods. By gathering the runtime logs of an Android application, the recommendation framework can choose whether it is a malware or not, by method for machine learning strategies. The accomplishment of such a dynamic investigation approach relies upon two issues: (1) regardless of whether we have gathered adequate, helpful runtime logs and (2) how well the machine learning systems are connected. The proposed suggestion system will contain four stages: (1) preprocessing, (2) emulation and testing, (3) feature extraction, and (4) machine learning. Given an Android application bundle, the recommendation structure will naturally instrument and repackage the APK in Stage 1, introduces, executes, and uninstalls the APK in Stage 2, separates the highlights from the logged information in Stage 3, and foresees whether the application is vindictive in Stage 4.

10.2.1 Preprocessing

For the main stage, the recommender framework for versatile application hazard decrease will utilize API Monitor, to screen particular programming interface calls that might be called by malware. API Monitor first figures out an APK document and after that repackage it with observed codes. API Monitor will essentially wrap the first programming interface call with the droidbox adaptation that creates an investigate message before influencing the first programming interface to call. With the instrumented/repackaged APK, we would have the capacity to follow the calls to these APIs in this application amid the runtime, through logcat, the Android logging framework which gives a component to gathering and survey framework troubleshoot yield.

Preprocessing step likewise concentrates on the data that the client can see preceding the establishment of an application metadata, e.g. designer ID, contact e-mail, contact site, limited time video, number of screenshots, promo writings, late changes, ID, bundle name, establishment estimate, adaptation, application sort, appraisals tally, and application title inside the stages programming market. Contingent upon the platform, this will investigate the applications portrayal, its authorizations, the appraisals, or data about the engineer, the last time changed, class, value, depiction, consents, rating, and number of downloads. The recommender framework will monitor APIs, the recorded logs, and the gathered metadata and will be additionally broken down in the element extraction (Stage 3).

10.2.2   Emulation and testing

After the preprocessing, the repackaged APK in the Android Virtual Gadget will be introduced for gathering logs. We will apply the DroidBox, an Android Applications Sandbox, which empowers us to gather the runtime exercises including incoming/active system information, document read and compose operations, began benefits and stacked classes through DexClassLoader, data spills by means of the system, records, SMS, etc. There are absolutely a few sorts of exercises which can be recorded. The recommender framework will make utilization of Chimp testing device, which is a programmed Android malware testing system which is created to reproduce GUI-based occasions and navigate applications code ways.

Code scope is basic in powerful investigation. Contrasted with Monkey runner, Gorilla is more effective in activating GUI occasions by recognizing the catches and filling frames on the touch screen, which is the reason it can cover more code ways in a brief span and enhance the opportunity to get vindictive conduct. The recommender framework will gather thousands of lines of logged messages and will be sent to pool of servers for copying and testing. Every server runs a few emulators all the while to gather the logs from the approaching APKs. In the event that the application uncovers any vindictive conduct, at that point it is sorted as malware. Something else, the logged messages are put something aside for examination in the following stage.

10.2.3   Features extraction

Utilizing the logged information given by the past two stages, the highlights for every application will be extricated in this stage, and the yields are pre-handled into a document of highlight vectors speaking to the highlights separated from every application. Inside the vector, each element will be spoken to by 0 or 1, indicating nearness or nonattendance of the element.

The documents will be changed over to ARFF organization and encouraged into WEKA machine for additionally handling. A few highlights will be removed. These highlights at that point can be positioned utilizing the InfoGain (data pick up) include positioning calculation in WEKA. The main 100 positioned highlights can be then utilized for the analyses to look at the identification execution utilizing a few machine learning calculations.

10.2.4   Machine learning

In the last stage, the accompanying calculations will be utilized as a part of the tests: Support Vector Machine (SVM-linear), Naive Bayes (NB), Simple Logistic (SL), Multilayer Perceptron (MLP), Partial Decision Trees (PART), Random Forest (RF), and J48 Decision Tree to build a malware prediction model.

10.2.5 Dataset

Absolutely, there will be more than 1,20,000 amiable applications and 5,000 vindictive specimens in our dataset. The safe applications will be gathered from Google Play utilizing a crawler. The nature of the expectation increments with the amount of the applications in the dataset. As the quantity of the aggregate number of utilizations in the dataset developed from many applications to lakhs of utilizations, both precision and F-score get higher of course. This is empowering as our structure might be reached out to gather an ever-increasing number of information. This is the reason this work identifies with huge information.

10.3 Conclusion

Recommender system is a solution to the information overload problem on Play stores that allow users to choose the applications for downloading and express their interests about abundant of applications. Collaborative filtering is one of the most important methods in recommender systems which helps in predicting that whether an application is malicious or benign based on collected data from similar users group. Here, a novel method is proposed to determine malicious applications. For this purpose, the concept of preprocessing, emulation and testing, and feature extraction has been used to identify malicious patterns. As malware turns into a greater and greater risk to cell phone clients, machine learning based malware identification need to wind up plainly more dynamic and powerful. We trust the proposed recommender framework an entire, robotized outline work to complete dynamic investigation by incorporating different systems: application instrumentation, imitating, testing, include extraction, and machine learning. Collecting huge preparing datasets and separating helpful highlights is the way to enhance the after effects of machine learning. As observed in numerous applications of big data, preparing additional information in form of training data improves the outcomes without the need to grow new machine learning and malware detection algorithms over time. It is expected that the experimental results on huge dataset along with high computing server will help in improving accuracy of prediction when compared with several well-known state-of-the-art methods.

References

[1] Grace M., Zhou Y., Zhang Q., *et al.* RiskRanker: Scalable and accurate zero-day Android malware detection categories and subject descriptors. *Proceedings of the 10th International Conference on Mobile Systems, Applications, and Services*; Low Wood Bay, Lake District, UK, Jun 2012 New York, NY: ACM; 2012. pp. 281–294.

[2] Wu D.J., Mao C.H., Wei T.E., *et al.* DroidMat: Android malware detection through manifest and API calls tracing. *Seventh Asia Joint Conference on Information Security (Asia JCIS)*, 2012. IEEE. 2012; pp. 62–69.

234 Big data recommender systems, volume 1

[3]   Arp D., Spreitzenbarth M., Hübner M., *et al*. DREBIN: effective and explainable detection of Android malware in your pocket. *Proceedings 2014 Network and Distributed System Security Symposium*; Feb 2014; Vol. 14, pp. 23–36.

[4]   Enck W., Ongtang M., Mcdaniel P. On lightweight mobile phone application certification categories and subject descriptors. In *Proceedings of the 16th ACM Conference on Computer and Communications Security, CCS '09*, Nov 2009. New York, NY: ACM; pp. 235–245.

[5]   Shabtai A., Kanonov U., Elovici Y., *et al*. Andromaly: a behavioral malware detection framework for Android devices. *Journal of Intelligent Information System* 2012;38(1):161–190.

[6]   Enck W., Gilbert P., Han S., *et al*. TaintDroid: An information-flow tracking system for real-time privacy monitoring on smartphones. *ACM Trans Comput Syst*. 2014;32(2):5:1–5:29.

[7]   Yan L.K., Yin H. DroidScope: seamlessly reconstructing the OS and Dalvik semantic views for dynamic Android malware analysis. *Presented as part of the 21st {USENIX} Security Symposium ({USENIX} Security* 2012; pp. 569–584.

[8]   Burguera I., Zurutuza U., Nadjm-Tehrani S. Crowdroid: behavior-based malware detection system for Android. In *Proceedings of the 1st ACM Workshop on Security and Privacy in Smartphones and Mobile Devices - SPSM '11*. ACM. 2011;p. 15.

[9]   Amos B., Turner H., White J. Applying machine learning classifiers to dynamic Android malware detection at scale. In *2013 9th International Wireless Communications and Mobile Computing Conference, IWCMC 2013*. 2013; pp. 1666–1671.

[10] Rastogi V., Chen Y., Jiang X. DroidChameleon: evaluating Android anti-malware against transformation attacks. In *Proceedings of the 8th ACM SIGSAC Symposium on Information, Computer and Communications Security*, May 2013, Hangzhou, China. New York, NY: ACM; 2013; pp. 329–334.

[11] Faruki P., Bharmal A., Laxmi V., *et al*. Android security: a survey of issues, malware penetration, and defenses. *IEEE Communications Surveys and Tutorials* 2015;17(2):998–1022.

Chapter 11

Security threats and their mitigation in big data recommender systems

Madjid Khalilian[1], Maryam Fathi Ahmadsaraei[1], and Lida Farajpour[1]

11.1 Introduction

In intelligent applications, big data recommender systems help users to select an item among a vast set of products. Big data recommender systems analyze users' profiles and compare them with reference features. These features extract from users' social environment. Big data recommender systems are different from traditional recommender systems and need new security models and design methods. Big data recommender systems are very vulnerable to attacks, especially to profile injection attacks. So, we should use security mechanisms to protect big data recommender systems from different kinds of attacks. These vulnerabilities and attacks may decrease users' trust in accuracy of recommender systems. In addition, issues related to big data recommender systems and their security problems are based on security challenges in Hadoop architecture which is called Hadoop Distributed File System (HDFS). Recently using the term big data is increasing to refer to a number of information units that are stored, processed and analyzed. Big data features, its security, users' issues and the relation between them are studied from some points of view like collecting, storing and accessibility of data.

Recently researchers discuss the detection programs that are detect-and-defeat known attack models. In this chapter, we investigate a number of known attack models, examine their influence and suggest some solutions to combat with them. Furthermore, we represent some different methods that are used by attackers to modify an attack, not recognized as an attack. We recommend some important issues in creating secure big data recommender systems, focusing on attack models and their effect on different big data recommender approaches. We know the general effect on systems' ability to predict accurately, and we also know the amount of knowledge that attackers need to know about the system to deploy a realistic attack. In this chapter, we show that the two approaches, i.e. user-based and item-based algorithms, are particularly vulnerable to attack patterns, but the hybrid algorithms that are the combination of both

[1]Department of Computer Engineering, Karaj Branch, Islamic Azad University, Iran

user-based and item-based algorithms may present higher stability. Also, we study the basics of relevant research and advanced schemas, and discuss future thoughts.

11.2   Security issues and approaches in HDFS architecture

A big data recommender system gathers and analyzes a large amount of raw data. Hadoop is used to store and manage a large amount of data and distribute data analysis between a number of servers. HDFS is the file system for Hadoop architecture and has security problems. In this section, we present security problems in HDFS. The HDFS will become more secure by using some algorithms such as Kerberos.

HDFS is the Hadoop file system which is scalable and reliable and as its name shows, it is distributed. A cluster of Hadoop consists of a name node and a number of data nodes. By using special hardware, you can store a large amount of data in lower latency and do some operations such as Write Once and Read several times. In these special hardware devices, we can store in blocks of 64 MB, which is the default size. Different nodes communicate with each other by using remote procedure calls (RPCs). Name nodes reserve special data such as file name, copies of file, file properties and block addresses. These data can be stored in random access memory (RAM), for retrieving so fast. Also, this leads to decrease in loss of data and helps stop file system corruption. Moreover, name nodes enumerate blocks and if they find out that any block is absent or is not copied successfully, they create a right copy of that failed or lost block. A timestamp is attached to any block to recognize its current situation. It is not necessary to repair a failed node immediately, but failed nodes can be repaired in scheduled times. An operator supports more than 1,000 nodes in HDFS [1]. Blocks are copied, and sent and received between nodes. In Hadoop, original node that copies a block is called rack 1 and the other node is known as rack 2. This framework does not support caching data [2–4] because of large amount of data. Figure 11.1 shows HDFS architecture.

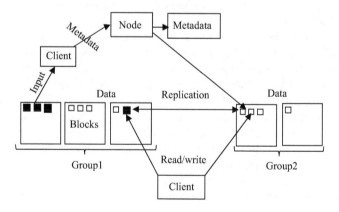

Figure 11.1   HDFS architecture [5]

11.2.1   Security issues in HDFS

Hadoop base layer is HDFS. HDFS has various data categories and has many security challenges. It cannot control security issues appropriately. In Hadoop, there is a risk of illegal accessing to data, stealing data and undesirable disclosure of data. Data that are copied are not secure too. These copies require more security plans to protect them from vulnerabilities. Most of government organizations do not use Hadoop to store their sensitive data, because of security problems in Hadoop. These organizations can use firewalls or intrusion detection systems and protect their sensitive data outside of Hadoop. Recent research shows that HDFS can be secure and data can be prevented from stealing and other vulnerabilities just by using encryption in blocks of file system in Hadoop. Although in some researches block encryption was used, there is not any completed algorithm that can secure the Hadoop. In the following, we present some approaches to enhance security in HDFS [5].

11.2.2   HDFS security methods

The following methods secure data in Hadoop file system. In Section 11.2.2.1, we are going to study a method that uses Kerberos to secure HDFS.

11.2.2.1   Kerberos construction

Kerberos [6] is an authentication protocol that is used for authentication over the network. Using this protocol for authentication lets nodes to use nonsecure and cheaper channel for transmitting data. Kerberos protocol secures data by tickets. Kerberos can be used to increase HDFS security. To connect client and name node, HDFS uses RPC [7] and for connecting client and data nodes, HDFS uses block transfer. In this section, we use Kerberos to authenticate an RPC connection. When a client gets a token, it means that the client uses Kerberos authenticated. A node which is using Kerberos protocol to authenticate uses Ticket Granting Ticket (TGT). TGT can be refreshed even if jobs are running for a long time. When Kerberos is refreshed, new TGT is distributed to jobs. When key distribution center (KDC) receives a request from a task it uses TGT. By using tokens, network traffic is forbidden KDC and just time can be extended, but tickets are fixed. The main benefit is that if an attacker stole the ticket, the attacker cannot refresh the ticket.

Also, there is another method for securing HDFS and preventing illegal access to file in HDFS. When clients from the data node want to achieve a block, first they should communicate to name node to know which data node keeps block files. Name node just gives permissions to access files and gives block token, and data node checks tokens. Also, data node gives name token which enforces name node to give correct permissions for accessing data blocks. Data node recognizes whether clients have permissions to access data blocks or not, by verifying block token. Both block token and name token are sent backward to clients who have permission to access the location.

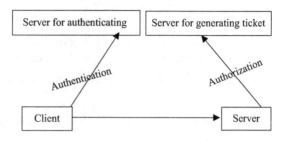

Figure 11.2   Kerberos KDC [5]

For increasing security, we have studied these two methods. These are used to prevent unauthorized clients from reading or writing in data blocks. Kerberos KDC is shown in Figure 11.2 [5].

11.2.2.2   Bull Eye algorithm

Sensitive data such as credit card numbers, passwords and other personal details are stored by Hadoop technology in big data recommender systems. Another approach to enhance Hadoop security for sensitive data is *Bull Eye approach*. Bull Eye is deployed on Hadoop to detect whether sensitive data stored are secure and without any risk or not. This approach allows authorized clients to protect their personal information. Also Bull Eye approach is used to enhance security in HDFS from node to node. Data node of rack 1 runs this algorithm and it investigates whether data are stored in block with no risk or not and whether authorized clients are allowed to store in particular blocks or not. This approach puts a gap for extracted data between original data node and copied data node. Bull Eye maintains clients who need to extract data from coping data nodes and also investigate whether there is a suitable communication between two racks or not. In this algorithm, authorized clients are just allowed to read or write, so data nodes are more secure. Clients read or write data in blocks, so this algorithm can be deployed in data node. To increase the security of blocks, Bull Eye algorithm is deployed in racks 1and 2. This algorithm investigates for any attacks, gaps or data stealing that are occurred in the data node blocks and encrypts data to protect it from illegal access. Using encryption in Bull Eye lets this algorithm to be the main security. This algorithm supports structured, unstructured and semi-structured data with size from less terabyte to multi-petabytes which are stored in HDFS. Data encryption in Bull Eye is deployed at the block level and not in file level. Data are scanned in two phases by this algorithm: first before entering the blocks and second after entering both racks 1 and 2. Generally, Bull Eye algorithm just focuses on the sensitive data that are stored in the data nodes [5].

11.2.2.3   Name node algorithm

In HDFS, if name node fails and cannot be reached, the data that are stored in HDFS become unavailable too. In this condition, accessing data in a protected way is not easy to achieve. Using two name nodes leads to data availability. Running two name node servers concurrently allows all tasks in the same cluster to execute successfully.

Name Node Security Enhance (NNSE) uses Bull Eye algorithm and provides redundant name nodes. This redundancy lets administrator to select different options for each node. One of these nodes works as master and the other one works as a slave. Master and slave work together to decrease the data loss of server crash and prevent from natural disasters. If master node fails, the administrator asks NNSE about the permission to retrieve data from a slave node and accessing to unavailable data in secure way. Without NNSE permission, administrator does not retrieve data from slave. There is a risk if two nodes play master role. Two master nodes lead to decrease security, data accessibility and local area network (LAN) or wide area network (WAN) performance. It's recommended to use a vital configuration to enhance the security that guarantees data available in a secure way for clients. This achieves when NNSE copies HDFS blocks between many nodes in many clusters [5].

11.3 Big data recommender system attacks

In big data recommender systems, an attacker injects fake ratings to force recommender system recommending the data that the attacker wants. These attacks are called "shilling" attacks [8–10]. This type of attack (profile injection attacks) is the only one way to recommend a special product. The main goal of profile injection attacks is to change output of the recommender system. In a profile injection attack, an attacker creates a number of fake profiles to interact with big data recommender system. These fake profiles communicate with dummy identities to hide their original identities.

11.3.1 Attack tactics

In this chapter, we divide attacks in two types: namely *push* attacks and *nuke* attacks. The goals of these two types of attacks are increasing or decreasing the rating for target items. All attacks are implemented as follows. A profile injection attacker attacks to identities and builds a fake profile for each identity. It is in this manner that attack data are inserted into a system—no other accessing to database of the system is accepted. There are two issues that attackers need to consider when building attack profiles. The first concerns the selection of items from which the profiles are constructed; the second relates to the ratings that are applied to the selected items [11].

11.3.2 Probe attack strategy

Attack profiles constructed using popular subdomain items have the potential drawback of being easy to detect, particularly if large numbers of such profiles are created. While an attacker could attempt to vary the items that are used, nevertheless a distinctive attack signature may exist. Thus, a less conspicuous strategy is desirable. One such approach involves probing the big data recommender system and using the system's recommendations as a means to select items. First an attacker rates to a small number of items and then increasingly creates fake profiles to make it close to the distribution of original users' ratings. Thus, there will be high similarities between original and fake profiles. Further, any attack profiles that are created are unlikely to be readily distinguishable from genuine profiles, thereby reducing the detectability of the attack. In this type of attack, an attacker needs less knowledge about the system. An attacker just needs to select a small number of items, and then big data recommender system is used for identifying other items [11].

11.3.3   Ratings strategy

The ratings strategy that we adopt is tailored to the particular automated collaborative filtering (ACF) algorithm that is used. We use a user-based algorithm which is described in [12]. This algorithm is used to calculate predictions by taking into account the differences between rating patterns for different users and using a deviation from mean. $p_{a,j}$ is the prediction and is calculated for a user "a" on an item "j" which is the neighbors' ratings average as follows:

$$p_{a,j} = \bar{r}_a + \frac{\sum_{i=1}^{n} w(a,i)(r_{i,j} - \bar{r}_i)}{\sum_{i=1}^{n} |w(a,i)|} \qquad (11.1)$$

where the average rating for user a is shown as $\bar{r}_a$ and $r_{i,j}$ is the rating which is attached by neighbor i to item j. The similarity $w(a,i)$ between the user a and neighbor i is typically computed using Pearson correlation [12].

Therefore, for successful product push and nuke attacks, it is essential to be sure that the magnitude of the deviation is maximized or minimized. The portion of any neighbor is a function of

1.   item rating for a desirable prediction,
2.   neighbor's rating tool and
3.   neighbor and user similarity.

Therefore, selecting ratings carefully is required. First, attack profiles need to have a high degree of similarity with genuine users if they are to influence predictions. Second, since Pearson correlation results in values between -1 and 1, it is important that all attack profiles correlate either positively or negatively with genuine users. Otherwise, the contributions of multiple attack profiles may be canceled out or attacked items may be inadvertently pushed instead of being nuked, or vice versa [11].

11.3.4   Dimensions of attacks

An attacker requires some knowledge to category profile injection attacks by considering the attack size and attack intention. From an attacker point of view, the best attack is an attack that has the biggest influence with the least attempt on the system. We use a relatively informal distinction between two types of attack based on knowledge:

1.   *High knowledge attacks:* These attacks need the detailed knowledge in the database of recommender systems. For an instance, the attacker needs to know about rating tools or the standard deviation for each item.

2. *Low knowledge attacks:* These attacks need some public information about sources. The goal of an attack is one of the dimensions of attacks. Two general goals of attacks are push and nuke. The effect of profile injection attack may make a fake product more likely, which is called push, or make an original product less likely, which is called nuke to be recommended. The attacker may have another goal to degrade system functionality. We focus more on economic motivation for an attacker, which wants to promote or demote a product rating.

In several ways, we can measure the size of an attack. We enumerate the number of fake profiles and the number of ratings that are generated in each profile. We assume that an attacker can automate the profile injection process. As online registration needs human intervention, so the number of profiles is very important and site owner may impose a cost due to create new profiles. When profiles consist of ratings, another risk will be added. Real users' ratings are just a small part of large recommendation space. Because a person with a profile cannot rate to every item, so, recognizing fake profiles with many ratings are very easy [13].

11.3.5 Models of attacks

In the following sections, we want to present a general framework for attack models and will begin with profile attacks.

11.3.5.1 Profile injection attacks

In this section, we introduce the basic concepts of profile injection attacks and dimensions. Profile injection attacks have two main aspects: profile injection attack models and profile injection attack dimensions. See [8,13–15] for additional details.

Profile injection attack models create profile attacks and are based on the information about recommender systems, its database and its clients. In Figure 11.3, you can see the general structure of these profiles. This structure consists of four items: a target item i_t, similar items with special features that are chosen by the attacker I_S, filler items that are selected randomly I_F and items that have no ratings $I_\emptyset$. These items define attack models, e.g. target item, selected items, filler items and how ratings are assigned to items defined the model of an attack. γ function determines the target item. σ function defines how ratings should assign to items and δ function defines filter items. The reason why these items are selected depends on target item. This

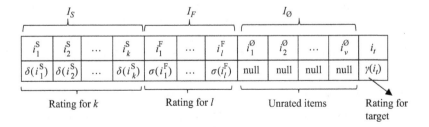

Figure 11.3 Push and nuke attack structure [16]

set of items might be empty for an attack. Profile attack may contain m-dimensional rating vector. The m variable is the number of items. When an item is attacked, the target item is shown by r_{target}. For push attack, we have $r_{target} = r_{max}$, but for a nuke attack, we have $r_{target} = r_{min}$. Here r_{max} and r_{min} are the number of ratings that are acceptable [16]. Figure 11.3 shows the push and nuke attack structure.

11.3.5.2 Push attacks

Push attack has two main models [9]: random and average. These attacks assign fake ratings to filler items. The random models assign fake ratings with respect to the users' ratings distribution. Average model assigns fake ratings to filler items with respect to the average of all users' ratings.

Random and average attack models

These attacks are discussed in [9]. As mentioned, random attack models assign fake ratings to filler items. For this in formal form, we consider I_S is empty, the set of I_F is chosen randomly and we need some information about the distribution of ratings in the system. The σ function calculates the overall average of ratings. The average attack model works like random attack model, but I_F is calculated for each filler item. So, for this model more information about the distribution of ratings in the system is needed. Average attack is more effective than random attack, but it infeasible to know the rating distribution details of the system. In this section, we discuss the Bandwagon and Segment attacks that are similar to random attack model. You can study the additional details in [8,14,15].

Bandwagon attack

Bandwagon attack model is like random attack model. Bandwagon model needs a little knowledge about the system—a little information that determines the most favorite item in specific domains such as blockbuster movies and top-selling recordings. Obtaining this information does not need detailed information about the system. A set that is named I_S consists of these favorite items. In profile attacks, high ratings are given to these items. The effect of Bandwagon attack is like average or other attacks that require detailed knowledge about the system [16].

Segment attack

Item-based algorithms are vulnerable to Segment attack. Item-based algorithms create clusters of similar items. The main aim of Segment attack is to increase the target item and the segment items in I_S similarity. To enhance the similarity between the target item and these items, which are members of I_S set, high ratings are given to filler items. To reduce the similarity between the target item and these items, low ratings are given to filler items. As we noted, Segment attack has high effect on item-based algorithms. Also, user-based collaborative recommendation is very vulnerable to Segment attack as well [16].

11.3.5.3 Nuke attacks

Attacks that we discussed above can nuke a target item too. For instance, as noted earlier, in random and average attacks, instead of r_{max} we can use r_{min} with i_t as the target item.

There are two attack models that are specially designed for nuking: Love and Hate attack and Reverse Bandwagon attack. Love and Hate attack has high effect on user-based algorithm and Reverse Bandwagon attack has high effect on item-based algorithm. These algorithms have decreased the cost of required knowledge, because these attacks do not need detailed data about the system. However, Reverse Bandwagon does require some general knowledge of product domain to be able to effectively select low-rated items that will have a significant number of ratings. These attack models are described in more detail as follows [13].

Love and Hate attack
Deploying Love and Hate attack is simple and there is no need for additional knowledge. Love and Hate attack contains profile attacks. In this attack r_{min} (the minimum rating) is given to i_t (the target item) and r_{max} (the maximum rating) is set for other ratings in the filler item set. By changing r_{min} to r_{max} and vice versa in push attack, we can define the variables of Love and Hate attack. In the following, we present the formal form of Love and Hate attack.

$$\mu_{bw} = <\chi_{lh}, \delta_{lh}, \sigma_{lh}, \gamma_{lh}> \tag{11.2}$$

Properties: $I_S = \emptyset$; I_F is a filler items set that is selected randomly; $\forall i \in I_F$, $\sigma(i) = r_{max}$, here r_{max} is the maximum value of ratings; and $\gamma(i_t) = r_{min}$, here r_{min} is the minimum value of ratings.

Love and Hate attack on a profile is shown in Figure 11.4. This attack needs a little detailed knowledge about the system. When Love and Hate attack is used as a push attack, it is not effective; but if this attack is used as a nuke attack, it is the most effective attack on user-based algorithms.

Reverse Bandwagon attack
One of the Bandwagon attack types is Reverse Bandwagon attack. In this attack, selected items are chosen with rating poorly by users. Low ratings are given to these items with the target item. So, the target item is affiliated to dislike items. The system may produce low ratings for these items. The Bandwagon attack takes advantage of the fact that high-rated items also tend to be very popular. Low-rated items, on the other hand, tend to have sparser ratings, making it more challenging to select items to be included in the attack that also have enough ratings to make a significant impact. Only a few number of users may rate items with the lowest average rating. To build

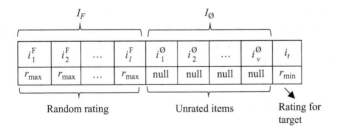

Figure 11.4   Love and Hate attack on a profile [13]

Table 11.1   The summary of attacks [13]

Attack type	Attack model	I_S	I_F	$I\emptyset$	i_t
Random	Push/ nuke	Not used	Ratings assigned with normal distribution around item mean	Filler size determines the value	r_{max}/r_{min}
Average	Push/ nuke	Not used	Ratings assigned with normal distribution around item mean	Filler size determines the value	r_{max}/r_{min}
Bandwagon	Push	Popular items assigned r_{max}	Ratings assigned with normal distribution around system mean	Filler size determines the value	r_{max}
Segment	Push	Chosen items define the segment assigned r_{max}	Ratings assigned with r_{min}	Filler size determines the value	r_{max}
Love/Hate	Nuke	Not used	Ratings assigned with r_{max}	Filler size determines the value	r_{min}
Reverse Bandwagon	Nuke	Disliked items assigned r_{max}	Ratings assigned with normal distribution around system mean	Filler size determines the value	r_{min}

an attack model that has a significant impact a large number of items would need to be known to have poor ratings, thus increasing the knowledge required for the attack. Reverse Bandwagon attack needs just a little detailed knowledge about the system, and only a few unpopular items are required. An attacker who uses Reverse Bandwagon attack model may select items that have poor ratings [13].

We will introduce a set of features to detect some attacks that use supervised learning algorithms. We use features that are introduced in [17–19] to know the effect of these features in detecting attacks. In this approach, we will produce training data by combining original profiles with attacked profiles (profiles that are under the attack discussed above). All profiles are tagged as an attacked user profile or as an original user profile. By using this training data set and the features, a binary classifier can be generated and there is no need to use any classified profiles to detect an attack. These features are divided into two types: generic and model-specific. Generic features use statistics to understand the attributes that make attackers' profile different from original user profiles. Model-specific features try to understand the attributes of each attack model [20]. You can see the summary of attack models in Table 11.1.

11.4   Recommender algorithms

First, we want to introduce the collaborative recommender algorithms that use association rule mining and then we will study the user-based recommender approaches that are base algorithms for recommender systems. In this section, we discuss two model-based algorithms that are used to cluster user profiles and standard memory-based k-nearest neighbor (kNN).

11.4.1 Association rule mining

Generally, association rule mining is used to analyze the market basket. The goal is to know customers' manner and find products that may buy together. The relations between items are discovered by association rules using patterns of transactions. In [21], association rules are used to personalize web pages. We use association rule mining for collaborative filtering. We can use the Apriori algorithm by assuming each user profile as a transaction. Also, in [22] association rules are used to create groups that contain similar items.

If an item is not repeated sufficiently, there will not be in any item set that contains frequent items. It means that this item will never be recommended. Decreasing the threshold leads to recommend more items, but these recommended items may not have adequate evidence of the pattern.

We must consider ratings of each profile before using association rule mining on the datasets. To calculate the zero-mean profile of each user profile, first we should subtract the average rating of each user profile from user's ratings. Then we divide rated items into two sets: Like and Dislike. If the calculated value of the item is >0, this item will be put in Like set and if the calculated value of the item is ≤ 0, this item will be put in Dislike set.

Effective deceiving can be gained by doubling the total number of features. To do this, an attacker must be able to infer the items that can be recommended items [23].

11.4.2 Base algorithms

To find users' profiles that are like a target user, we can use user-based collaborative filtering algorithms. By using the ratings that are assigned to the items of neighbor group, we can predict the rating values for missing items. In these approaches, a ranked list is generated and then the recommender system recommends the 20 or 50 top predictions [23].

11.4.3 k-Nearest neighbor

The kNN algorithm is very precise, so it is used extensively [24]. To calculate the similarity between items, Pearson's correlation coefficient is used in this algorithm. The k most similar users are chosen as neighbors who have rated the target item. It means that the target user can have different neighbors for each target item. It is usual to filter neighbors whose similarity is under the threshold. By using this approach, very distant correlations or negative correlations are prevented to predict. Then after recognizing neighbors, Resnick's algorithm can be used to predict the target item i and the target user u:

$$p_{u,i} = \bar{r}_u + \frac{\sum_{v \in V} sim_{u,v}(r_{v,i} - \bar{r}_v)}{\sum_{v \in V} |sim_{u,v}|} \tag{11.3}$$

Here, the variable V is used to express the k similar neighbors that have rated to item i; $r_{v,i}$ expresses the ratings of the item i for neighbor v; $\bar{r}_u$ is the overall average ratings for u and $\bar{r}_v$ is the overall average ratings for v; and $sim_{u,v}$ expresses the Pearson correlation between u and v variables [23].

11.4.4 k-Means clustering

To classify similar users, we can use a standard model-based collaborative filtering algorithm that uses k-means. We can partition users into k groups. In each group, users are similar to each other. The similarity measure is defined before.

To recommend for a target user u and a target item i, we choose user's neighbors who have at least a rate for i and their profile v_k is the most similar profile to u. This selected neighbor is the most similar user to the target user and it depends on the measures of similarity. We use Pearson's correlation coefficient for this approach. Now we can predict for item i, where neighbor V is the most similar profiles to the target user [23].

11.4.5 Probabilistic latent semantic analysis

Probabilistic latent semantic analysis (PLSA) models [26] are probabilistic methods for hidden semantic associations. In [27–29], PLSA is used to personalize user web pages. We combine this method to collaborative filtering [25].

For n users, $U = \{u_1, u_2, ..., u_n\}$, and m items, $I = \{i_1, i_2, ..., i_m\}$ and PLSA affiliates the unobserved variable Z with the observed rating data, where $Z = \{z_1, z_2, ..., z_i\}$. We can define the relation (11.4) for a target user u and a target item i:

$$P(u,i) = \sum_{k=1}^{I} \Pr(z_k) \cdot \Pr(u|z_k) \cdot \Pr(i|z_k) \tag{11.4}$$

11.4.6 Recommender algorithms and evaluation metrics

In this section, we discuss popular collaborative filtering algorithms that are divided into two classes: user-based and item-based. Hybrid recommender systems may provide higher robustness against profile injection attacks. Also, we introduce hybrid algorithms that increase the robustness of item-based systems [13].

11.4.6.1 User-based collaborative filtering

The standard collaborative filtering algorithm uses the similarity between users [24]. User-based collaborative filtering algorithm chooses the k most similar users to the target user. Extensively kNN is used and it is very accurate. By using the Pearson's correlation coefficient, we can calculate the similarity between the target user u and a neighbor v, shown in relation (11.5):

$$sim_{u,v} = \frac{\sum_{i \in I} (r_{u,i} - \bar{r}_u) * (r_{v,i} - \bar{r}_v)}{\sqrt{\sum_{i \in I} (r_{u,i} - \bar{r}_u)^2} * \sqrt{\sum_{i \in I} (r_{v,i} - \bar{r}_v)^2}} \tag{11.5}$$

Here I is items that users can rate for them, $r_{u,i}$ is the ratings of item i for the target user u and $r_{v,i}$ is the ratings of item i for a neighbor v. $\bar{r}_u$ is the average of the ratings of u and $\bar{r}_v$ is the average of the ratings of v over the items that are members of I set. Then the most similar users can be chosen by calculating the similarities using relation (11.5).

11.4.6.2 Item-based collaborative filtering

Item-based collaborative filtering compares items using users' ratings patterns. We can combine this approach with the nearest-neighbor approach. kNN algorithm discovers the k most similar items which different users rated them similarly. We measure the similarity by using relation (11.6), which is introduced in [29].

$$Sim_{i,j} = \frac{\sum_{u \in U} (r_{u,i} - \bar{r}_u) * (r_{u,j} - \bar{r}_u)}{\sqrt{\sum_{u \in U} (r_{u,i} - \bar{r}_u)^2} * \sqrt{\sum_{u \in U}^{n} (r_{u,j} - \bar{r}_u)^2}} \qquad (11.6)$$

Here $r_{u,i}$ is ratings which user u give for item i. As mentioned before, $\bar{r}_u$ is ratings average of user u. By calculating the similarity between items finished (by using relation (11.6)), we can choose the k most similar items to the target item and put them in a set. Then we can also predict by using the formula in relation (11.7):

$$p_{u,i} = \frac{\sum_{j \in J} r_{u,j} * sim_{i,j}}{\sum_{j \in J} sim_{i,j}} \qquad (11.7)$$

The set of k similar items is named J. $r_{u,j}$ is a prediction value for a user u on item j, and i and j items similarity is calculated by $sim_{i,j}$, which is defined in relation (11.6).

11.4.6.3 Enhanced collaborative filtering

As noted before, hybrid recommendation defenses more effectively against profile injection attacks. A recommendation system with multiple components does not only rely on profile data, so it prevents from manipulating data. Or, it may be that an attacker will have to attack all of the components in order to be successful [13].

11.4.7 Profile classification

Collaborative recommender systems' main ability is to suggest abnormal tasted users significantly by knowing users who have similar anomalies. This ability makes recommender systems challenging in securing field. The opinion diversity makes it difficult to detect whether a profile is an attack profile or it belongs to an abnormal user. It is not possible to classify all profiles correctly. We try to detect and response attacks for several goals such as

- To decrease the attack impact
- To reduce the successful attacks that have similar manner [30].

As we can classify successful attacks (because we know types of attacks traditionally), we can classify profiles into its matching known attacks by identifying the profile and attack patterns. Classifying original users' profiles as attackers may occur and has some consequences that will be discussed later. We identify suspicious profiles by investigating their overall properties. This is an extended approach of original approaches that were introduced in [17]. We use two types of analysis to classify features: the first type looks at the profile generally and not in detail for a specific attack and the second type is based on the attack patterns and extracts attack features [32].

11.5   Attack response and system robustness

After detecting attack profiles, the system should respond to the attack to remove or decrease the attack effects. The ideal situation is that all attack profiles are refused and the system does not suffer any profile injection attacks, but likely there may be a number of suspicious profiles which belong to attackers; however, we are not sure about it. We should measure the suspicious, so the probability whether a profile is under an attack or not can be used as a weight for profiles. We can use a simpler algorithm to deny attack labeled profiles. Although we have mainly discussed the effects of the push and nuke attacks, it is important to see the overall system as one of the aspects of robustness. To consider a robust system, it should be able to tolerate against attacks on different items and also be able to predict other items accurately [30].

11.5.1   Classification of attributes

Two types of attributes are used: generic attributes and model-derived attributes. For each profile, generic attributes are basic descriptive statistics. The model-derived attributes are used to detect attack features. Generic and model-derived attributes are based on the ratings, and classifiers use detection attributes [30].

11.5.1.1   Generic attributes

The attack profiles are not very similar to original user profiles. Attackers have always a main rating r_{target} goal to change the system in some aspects [30].

11.5.1.2   Model-derived attributes

Model-derived attributes try to recognize the differences between attack signatures. The Average and Random attacks consist of a partitioning form. As noted before, in these attacks one selected item is the target item, additional selected items are filler items and other items are ignored. Detection algorithms try to detect the similarity between each profile and the attack model [30].

Average attack detection

Average attack partitions the profile into three sections: a target item, filler items g and items that are not rated. In this model, just one target item is selected and other rated items are known as filler items. In Average attack, the filler rating is matched to the average rating for each filler item. We expect that the Average profile rating attack would be very similar to average rating for each item excludes the target item [30].

Random attack detection

Random attack is similar to Partitioning attack, but in Random attack filler items ratings are selected randomly as the average is gained from the overall system for all items. In average attack, different partitions can be examined by choosing different targets and calculating a measurement for each selection partition. The correlation between the average rating for each item and the profile is used in this model. We expect low correlation between filler items and individual ratings because of random ratings [30].

11.5.2 Enhanced hybrid collaborative recommender systems

We want to discuss a knowledge-based collaborative hybrid recommendation algorithm which, we believe, represents a potential solution to the profile injection attack problem. The reason this algorithm is more robust against such attacks is that it relies not only on user profiles, but also on semantic knowledge of the domain and items to be able to predict. So, profile injection attack may have less affect into the system [13].

11.5.2.1 Hybrid recommendation algorithm

Our semantically enhanced collaborative recommendation algorithm is a hybrid algorithm that uses semantic information and item-based collaborative recommender algorithm together [17,33]. Item-based recommendation relies on the similarity of ratings between items. This approach combines the item-based similarity with content-based similarity. This algorithm calculates the similarities by using semantic knowledge of items. To simplify these calculations, we need to convert class instances into a vector representation.

11.5.2.2 Push attacks against enhanced hybrid algorithm

We call item-based collaborative recommendation extension as the hybrid algorithm. We want to test and compare the robustness of the hybrid algorithm with the robustness of item-based algorithm. For example, an agent extracts samples of movies from Internet Movie Database. For each movie semantic attributes are extracted, some of these attributes are like: title of the movie, release year of the movie, movie director(s), movie cast, movie genre and plot. We use these attributes to create a binary attribute vector. Then we use the singular value decomposition to decrease the attribute vectors dimensions. Experiments were done in same situation by using the same target items and same users that are under Segment attack and average attack with 100% of filler sizes.

We examined the hybrid algorithm effective. Figure 11.5 shows that enhanced hybrid algorithm decreases the effect of Segment and average attacks. Also, the results show that Segment attack effect reduces by using semantic information. Segment attack can be effective against item-based algorithms by increasing the similarity between a pushed item and a group of items that are liked by some users. Figure 11.5 shows that enhanced hybrid algorithm effectively reduces an attacker ability to change the similarity between target movies and segment movies [13].

To protect completely from ratings attacks, we can use semantic similarity. For improving accuracy using ratings data and selecting $\alpha > 0$ is recommended. By

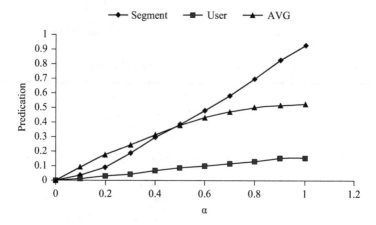

Figure 11.5 The comparison of semantically enhanced algorithm against Segment and average attacks [13]

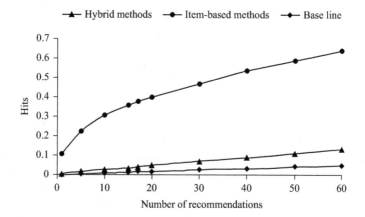

Figure 11.6 Hit ratio comparison of in-segment users

choosing semantic and rating data together, we would be able to provide the highest accuracy. We use mean absolute error (MAE) to analyze the semantically enhanced algorithm whether it provides the highest accuracy or not. In Figure 11.6, 40% of item rating similarity ($\alpha = 0.4$) and 60% semantic similarity lead to the highest prediction accuracy (or the lowest MAE) [13].

11.5.3 Defense against profile injection attacks

The vulnerabilities due to profile injection attacks are not just a theoretical concern. A collaborative recommender that applies usual algorithms would be vulnerable even without having detailed knowledge about the system. Hybrid recommendation noted before is a powerful protection against profile injection attacks. Also, weighted hybrid algorithm decreases the effect of attacks from the irritation to system's integrity. In addition to make the algorithm powerful, we should use effective approaches for detecting attacks.

One of the usual defenses is to make it difficult for an attacker to assemble a profile. These measures have a lot of costs for the owner of the system. Also, these measures may not be effective for recommender systems, e.g. data usage on web logs [13].

11.5.3.1 Detection methods

There are some methods that try to first detect and then prevent profile injection attacks. We want to discuss the multi-strategy method for attack detection and prevention that contains supervised and unsupervised methods, time analysis, abnormally detection and vulnerability analysis. Classifying profiles leads to detect suspicious profiles. Some attacks that do not follow these patterns of probability have lower impact than attacks that follow them. If we have a knowledge base of attack models and are able to detect attack models, then attackers may use other attack models that have lower effect. To have greater impact, larger attack models should occur and larger attack models are more detectable. Finally, we hope to minimize the effect of profile injection attacks [13].

11.5.3.2 Detection attributes for profile classification

Storing ratings data need a sparse and high-dimensional data structure. So, using supervised learning methods is not possible. Large number of combining needs to generate an appropriate training set that supports all attacks models. This idea is not possible and it is unrealistic. For creating a training set with lower dimensions, we use statistical computing on profiles and use attribute reduction techniques. As we noted before, each profile is assigned a label that expresses an attack profile or an original profile [13].

Generic attributes for detection
Using generic attribute technique believes that the general statistical signature of attack profiles is different from original profiles. The reasons of this difference are first for target item ratings and second for the distribution filler item ratings. In [9], [10], [19] and [34], authors prove that an attacker may not have the entire knowledge of system ratings in fact. Attack profiles have rating patterns deviation in comparison with original profiles.

Generic attributes discussed are used to classify the dataset and analyze its distribution deviation. In [34], some extended attributes are proposed as follows:

- *Rating average deviation (RAD):* RAD computes the average deviation of a profile for an item to recognize attackers by inversing the ratings number of that item. RAD is calculated by the relation (11.8):

$$RAD_u = \frac{\sum_{i=0}^{n_u} \frac{|r_{u,i} - \bar{r}_i|}{l_i}}{n_u} \qquad (11.8)$$

Here n_u is the rated item number of user u; $r_{u,i}$ is the item i rating that is rated by user u; l_i is the item i rating number; and $\bar{r}_i$ is rating average.

- *Weighted degree of agreement* (WDA) computes the sum of the differences between the profile's ratings and then divides into item's rating frequency. It is weighted by the number of RAD equations.
- *Weighted average deviation* (WAD) recognizes anomalies and registers high deviations for sparse items. This extended attribute gains the highest information. The difference between WAD and RAD is just using the squared number of ratings in sigma summation in WAD which is shown in relation (11.9), so outcome of this division decreases when many users rate the items. The WAD attribute is given by

$$WAD_u = \frac{\sum_{i=0}^{n_u} \frac{|r_{u,i} - \bar{r}_i|}{l_i^2}}{n_u} \qquad (11.9)$$

- *The similarity degree* (DegSim) [34] calculates the average of profile's similarity for kNNs. Recent researches show that profile attacks try to be similar to almost 25 closest neighbors [12,34]. If a neighbor gives ratings fewer than d, *DegSim* will reduce the average similarity. This attribute obtains more information using lower filler sizes.
- *Length variance* (LengthVar) investigates the diversity of a profile length from the average of all profiles' length in database. Usually, large profiles do not belong to original users. Probability, a profile injection attack may occur manually. Thus, attacks that have large filler sizes can be recognized by this attribute. Relation (11.10) calculates this feature:

$$Length\,Var_u = \frac{|n_u - \bar{n}|}{\sum_{k \in U} (n_k - \bar{n})^2} \qquad (11.10)$$

Here $\bar{n}$ shows the average number of users' ratings.

Model-specific attributes

Researches [12], [29] and [35] show that generic attributes are not enough to detect attack profiles, particularly when profiles are small with small number of filler items. We know attacks with their properties such as target item i_t, selected items I_S and filler items I_F. Model-specific attributes are able to detect particular attack model properties.

A proposed method detects the profile partitions that are the most similar part to an attack. This method splits each user profile u into three sets. Items that can be target are in $P_{u,T}$ set, items that can be filler items are in $P_{u,F}$ set and unrated items are in $P_{u,\emptyset}$ set. In this method, first the profile should be separated into the three parts: a target item, filler items and unrated items. This method necessarily requires only to choose two item sets: a target and other rated items as fillers. An Average attack changes each filler item ratings to make them close to the rating average. So, an Average attack generates a very similar profile to the average ratings for each item but not for the target item. The algorithm works as follows: the iteration continues up to when all rated items are processed. In each iteration, an item is chosen as the target item. Then the average of differences between filler items and the overall average is calculated. When this variance is minimized, it is likely that an average attack selects it as the target item. To calculate *MeanVar* for each profile p_t of a user u, P_u (p_t is rated r_t), we use relation (11.11) [13].

$$MeanVar - (p_t, u) = \frac{\sum_{i\in(pP_u - p_t)} P(r_{i,u} - \bar{r}_i)^2}{|pP_u|} \tag{11.11}$$

Here P_u is a user profile, p_{target} is the target item, $r_{i,u}$ is the rating that a user u rates for item i, $\bar{r}_i$ is the average of all users rating for item i and $|P_u|$ is the number of profile ratings. Then we choose the minimum *MeanVar(t, u)* as target t which is a member of $P_{u,target}$ set. For classification, *MeanVar(t, u)* is used as the *Filler Mean Variance* feature. To create a detection model, the item t converts to $P_{u,F}$ and other items converts to $P_{u,F}$. These two parts are used to detect push and nuke attacks:

- *Filler mean variance* which is a partition metric.
- *Filler mean difference* is the average variance between user's rating and average rating.
- *Profile variance* calculates the profile variance in comparison with low authenticated users.

The other attributes, set is used to detect Bandwagon and Segment attacks. In this method, $P_{u,T}$ is the set of P_u which has the maximum rating of a user profile u for push attacks (or minimum rating for nuke attacks) and other items which are members of P_u and $P_{u,F}$. The partitioning feature that compares the differences between ratings items in $i_{target} \cup I_S$ and items in I_F can maximize the impact of attacks. Filter mean target difference (FMTD) attribute is computed by relation (11.12):

$$FMTD_u = \left| \left(\frac{\sum_{i\in p_{u,T}} r_{u,I}}{|p_{u,T}|} \right) - \left(\frac{\sum_{k\in p_{u,F}} r_{u,K}}{|p_{u,F}|} \right) \right| \tag{11.12}$$

Here user u rates to item i is called $r_{u,i}$. To normalize this factor, we should subtract *FMTD* from $FMTD_u$ [13].

Intra-profile attributes
Intra-profile attributes use profiles' statistics unlike a single profile attribute. If an attack is occurred in a system, there would be many attack profiles that attack to the same item. To understand this better, we use *Target Model Focus* (TMF) attribute. This attribute determines partitions to detect target items weight. TMF attribute computes the partition weight that is assigned to a profile on items that are shared to other attack partitions. So, TMF attribute tries to find suspicion profiles which are probability the fake target items. To show TMF in formal form, we use $q_{i,m}$ to show the overall times that item i contains target set $P_{u,T}$ which is used to partition m. TMF is calculated by relation (11.13):

$$TargetFocus(u, i, m) = \frac{q_{j,m}}{\sum_{j\in I} q_{j,m}} \tag{11.13}$$

Here I is the items set. TMF_u is the maximum $TargetF ocus(u, t, m)$ in all m partitions [13].

11.6   Conclusion

In this chapter, we discuss the security issues of big data recommender systems. To enhance security in big data recommender systems, we can secure HDFS in Hadoop with so many blocks. We introduced approaches that aim to combat attacks on the name node or data node. In Future, other layers of Hadoop should become more secure. Also, in this chapter we introduce different methods to discover attacks on recommender systems. We noted that successful attacks can occur on collaborative recommender systems without any detailed knowledge about the system or users of the system. Item-based algorithms that had a robust imagine in past are much vulnerable against Segment attacks that require a little knowledge about the system. Researches show that nuke attacks are more difficult to detect than push attacks. We studied about two nuke attacks: Love and Hate attack and Reverse Bandwagon attack. These attacks do not need detailed knowledge about the system that suffers attacks. Love and Hate attack needs the least amount of knowledge about the system and has the most impact on the system. The hybrid recommender systems that merge collaborative recommender approach with other recommender system methods equip recommender systems with stronger defense component. The advantages of hybrid recommender systems are shown by using a knowledge-based component. The semantically enhanced item-based algorithm is an extension of standard item-based algorithms, which enhances the accuracy and robustness. An attacker can discover a solution to bias the inputs for many recommender systems simultaneously, but it is very difficult and contains more cost for the attacker. We introduced a supervised classification method to detect attacks. By using a merge method of statistical approach and model-derived features, we can enhance the recommender system stability against attacks. Attacks such as Segment attack and Love and Hate attack have malicious impacts on recommender systems. We want to research more on statistical methods to detect these attacks. Many items may effect on users' belief in big data recommender systems such as the system's trustiness and the system's ability to gain trust. Users' trust depends on their perception of a big data recommender system whether it does its duty or not. To enhance understanding big data recommender systems' attacks and their impact on big data recommender system algorithms and to develop attack detection algorithms, we should trust and use big data recommender systems.

References

[1]   A. Cloudera, "Hadoop and HDFS: storage for next generation data management," In 2014 International Conference on Developments in E-systems Engineering (DeSE), IEEE, 2014.

[2]   R. Baskaran, P. Victer Paul and P. Dhavachelvan, "Ant colony optimization for data cache technique in MANET," In International Conference on Advances in Computing (ICADC 2012), Advances in Intelligent and Soft Computing series, Vol. 174, New Delhi: Springer, June 2012, pp. 873–878.

[3]   P. Victer Paul, D. Rajaguru, N. Saravanan, R. Baskaran and P. Dhavachel-
      van, "Efficient service cache management in mobile P2P networks," Future
      Generation Computer Systems, vol. 29, no. 6, 2013, pp. 1505–1521.

[4]   N. Saravanan, R. Baskaran, M. Shanmugam, M.S. SaleemBasha and P. Victer
      Paul, "An effective model for QoS assessment in data caching in MANET
      environments," International Journal of Wireless and Mobile Computing,
      Inderscience, vol. 6, no. 5, 2013, pp. 515–527.

[5]   B. Saraladevi, N. Pazhaniraja, P. Victer Paul, *et al.* "Big data and Hadoop—a
      study in security perspective," In 2nd International Symposium on Big Data
      and Cloud Computing (ISBCC'15), Procedia Computer Science, vol. 5, 2015,
      pp. 596–601.

[6]   A. Janabi and M.A. Rasheed, "Public-key cryptography enabled Kerberos
      authentication," In 2011 International Conference on Developments in E-
      systems Engineering (DeSE), IEEE, pp. 209–214, 2011.

[7]   L.E. Heindel, "Highly reliable synchronous and asynchronous remote pro-
      cedure calls," In Proceedings of the IEEE Fifteenth Annual International
      Phoenix Conference on Computers and Communications, Scottsdale, AZ,
      March 27–29, IEEE, 1996.

[8]   R. Burke, B. Mobasher and R. Bhaumik, "Limited knowledge shilling attacks
      in collaborative filtering systems," In Proceedings of the 3rd IJCAI Workshop
      in Intelligent Techniques for Personalization, Edinburgh, Scotland, 2005.

[9]   S. Lam and J. Riedl, "Shilling recommender systems for fun and profit,"
      In Proceedings of the 13th International Conference on World Wide Web,
      New York, May 17–20, ACM, 2004.

[10] M. O'Mahony, N. Hurley, N. Kushmerick and G. Silvestre, "Collabora-
      tive recommendation: a robustness analysis," ACM Transactions on Internet
      Technology, vol. 4, no. 4, 2004, pp. 344–377.

[11] P. Michael, O'Mahony, J.N. Hurley, *et al.* "Recommender systems: attack types
      and strategies," In Proceedings of the 20th National Conference on Artificial
      intelligence – Volume 1, Pittsburgh, PA, July 09–13, AAAI Press, pp. 334–339,
      2005.

[12] P. Resnick, N. Iacovou, M. Suchak, P. Bergstrom and J. Riedl, "An open archi-
      tecture for collaborative filtering of netnews," In Proc. of the ACM Conference
      on Computer Supported Cooperative Work, Chapel Hill, NC, October 22–26,
      ACM, pp. 175–186, 1994.

[13] B. Mobasher, R. Burke, R. Bhaumik, C. Williams. "Towards trustworthy rec-
      ommender systems: an analysis of attack models and algorithm robustness,"
      ACM Transactions on Internet Technology, vol. 7, no. 4, 2007, pp. 1–47.

[14] R. Burke, B. Mobasher, C. Williams and R. Bhaumik, "Segment-based
      injection attacks against collaborative filtering recommender systems," In
      Proceedings of the Fifth International Conference on Data Mining (ICDM),
      Houston, TX, November 27–30, IEEE, 2005.

[15] R. Burke, B. Mobasher, R. Zabicki and R. Bhaumik, "Identifying attack models
      for secure recommendation," In Beyond Personalization: A Workshop on the
      Next Generation of Recommender Systems, San Diego, CA, January 9, 2005.

[16]   C.A. Williams, B. Mobasher and R. Burke, "Defending recommender systems: detection of profile injection attacks," Journal of Service Oriented Computing and Applications, vol. 1, no. 3, 2007, pp. 157–170.

[17]   P.A. Chirita, W. Nejdl and C. Zamfir, "Preventing shilling attacks in online recommender systems," In WIDM '05: Proceedings of the 7th Annual ACM International Workshop on Web Information and Data Management, New York, NY, November 04, ACM, 2005, pp. 67–74.

[18]   R. Burke, B. Mobasher, C. Williams and R. Bhaumik, "Detecting profile injection attacks in collaborative recommender systems," In 8th IEEE International Conference on E-Commerce Technology and The 3rd IEEE International Conference on Enterprise Computing, E-Commerce, and E-Services, San Francisco, CA, June 26–29, IEEE, 2006.

[19]   B. Mobasher, R. Burke, C. Williams and R. Bhaumik, "Analysis and detection of segment-focused attacks against collaborative recommendation," In 8th International Workshop on Knowledge Discovery on the Web, WebKDD 2006 Philadelphia, PA, August 20, 2006, pp. 96–118.

[20]   C. Williams, B. Mobasher, R. Burke, *et al.*, "Detection of Obfuscated Attacks in Collaborative Recommender Systems," In 17th European Conference on Artificial Intelligence, Riva del Garda, Italy, August 29–September 1, IOS Press, 2006, pp. 19–23.

[21]   M. Nakagawa and B. Mobasher, "A hybrid web personalization model based on site connectivity," In WebKDD Workshop at the ACM SIGKKDD International Conference on Knowledge Discovery and Data Mining, Washington, DC, August 24–27, ACM, 2003.

[22]   R. Agrawal and R. Srikant, "Fast algorithms for mining association rules," In Proceedings of the 20th International Conference on Very Large Data Bases, San Francisco, CA, September 12–15, Morgan Kaufmann Publishers Inc., 1994.

[23]   J.J. Sandvig, B. Mobasher and R. Burke, "Robustness of collaborative recommendation based on association rule mining," RecSys '07 Proceedings of the 2007 ACM Conference on Recommender Systems, Minneapolis, MN, October 19–20, ACM, 2007, pp. 19–20.

[24]   J. Herlocker, J. Konstan, A. Borchers and J. Riedl, "An algorithmic framework for performing collaborative filtering," In 22nd ACM Conference on Research and Development in Information Retrieval, Berkeley, August 1999.

[25]   T. Hofmann, "Probabilistic latent semantic analysis," In Fifteenth Conference on Uncertainty in Artificial Intelligence, Stockholm, Sweden, July 1999.

[26]   X. Jin, Y. Zhou and B. Mobasher, "Web usage mining based on probabilistic latent semantic analysis," In ACM SIGKDD Conference on Knowledge Discovery and Data Mining, Washington, August 2004.

[27]   X. Jin, Y. Zhou and B. Mobasher, "A unified approach to personalization based on probabilistic latent semantic models of web usage and content," In AAAI 2004 Workshop on Semantic Web Personalization, California, July 2004.

[28]   B. Mobasher, R. Burke and J. Sandvig, "Model-based collaborative filtering as a defense against profile injection attacks," In Proceedings of the 21st national

conference on Artificial intelligence – American Association for Artificial Intelligence, Boston, MA, July 16–20, AAAI Press, 2006, pp. 1388–1393.

[29]   B. Sarwar, G. Karypis, J. Konstan and J. Riedl, "Item-based collaborative filtering recommendation algorithms," In 10th International World Wide Web Conference, Hong Kong, 2001.

[30]   R. Burke and B. Mobasher, "Detecting profile injection attacks in collaborative recommender systems," In Proceedings of the 8th IEEE International Conference on E-Commerce Technology and 3rd IEEE International Conference on Enterprise Computing, E-Commerce, and E-Services, Washington, DC, June 26–29, IEEE Computer Society, 2006.

[31]   J.R. Quinlan, *C4.5: Programs for Machine Learning*. Boston, MA: Morgan Kaufmann Publishers, Inc., 1993.

[32]   X. Jin and B. Mobasher, "Using semantic similarity to enhance item-based collaborative filtering," In 2nd IASTED International Conference on Information and Knowledge Sharing, Scottsdale, 2003.

[33]   B. Mobasher, X. Jin and Y. Zhou, "Semantically enhanced collaborative filtering on the web," In Berendt B., Hotho A., Mladenič D., van Someren M., Spiliopoulou M., Stumme G. (eds) Web Mining: From Web to Semantic Web. EWMF 2003. Lecture Notes in Computer Science, vol. 3209. Springer, Berlin, Heidelberg.

[34]   R. Burke, B. Mobasher, C. Williams and R. Bhaumik, "Classification features for attack detection in collaborative recommender systems," In Proceedings of the 12th ACM SIGKDD International Conference on Knowledge Discovery and Data Mining, Philadelphia, PA, August 20–23, ACM, 2006, pp. 542–547.

[35]   R. Burke, B. Mobasher, C. Williams and R. Bhaumik, "Detecting profile injection attacks in collaborative recommender systems," In 8th IEEE International Conference on E-Commerce Technology and 3rd IEEE International Conference on Enterprise Computing, E-Commerce, and E-Services (CEC/EEE'06), San Francisco, CA, June 26–29, IEEE, 2006.

Chapter 12

User's privacy in recommendation systems applying online social network data: a survey and taxonomy

Erfan Aghasian[1], Saurabh Garg[1], and James Montgomery[1]

Recommender systems have become an integral part of many social networks and extract knowledge from a user's personal and sensitive data both explicitly, with the user's knowledge, and implicitly. This trend has created major privacy concerns as users are mostly unaware of what data and how much data is being used and how securely it is used. In this context, several works have been done to address privacy concerns for usage in online social network data and by recommender systems. This paper surveys the main privacy concerns, measurements and privacy-preserving techniques used in large-scale online social networks and recommender systems. It is based on historical works on security, privacy-preserving, statistical modeling and datasets to provide an overview of the technical difficulties and problems associated with privacy preserving in online social networks.

12.1 Introduction

Online social network services have become one of the most well-liked and accepted services on the Internet. These networks deliver an infrastructure so that individuals can connect with one another, share information, explicit their emotions and attitudes and shape and keep a connection with different individuals on the Internet [1,2]. These networks such as Facebook, LinkedIn, Google+, Twitter and other social networking sites all have advantages, both practical (such as sharing employment history in a LinkedIn profile) and social (like connecting with distant friends via Facebook).

In order to increase the data utility in such social networks, recommender systems can deliver personalization of a collection of items to online social network users based on their nature. Meanwhile, the personalized suggestions and recommendations in these systems are heavily dependent on users' information. This can increase the probability of information leakage of users in such networks [3]. Further, information

---

[1]Discipline of ICT, School of Technology, Environments and Design, University of Tasmania, Australia

sharing creates real threats to a user's privacy. In this case, there is a need for data protection. Fundamentally, data protection means clear sets of rules and regulations, policies and diverse measures that is provided for information security and lessening the invasion into a user's privacy. This invasion can be initiated by gathering, storing and distributing private data [4]. Hence, there is a need to understand the various types of recommender systems, privacy concerns in such systems and the ways which users' privacy can be protected.

In this survey, we first introduce recommender systems and their techniques. Then, in Section 12.3, we discuss the risks and concerns for users in online social networking sites and explain the different methods for scoring users' privacy in such networks. In Section 12.4, we describe the privacy preserving approaches. Finally, we describe privacy-preserving models in online social networks and recommender systems.

12.2   Recommender systems and techniques: privacy of online social network data

A recommender system delivers a set of items that is pertinent to a specific user of a system [3]. This set can vary based on the nature of each online social networking sites. Moreover, prediction in these systems is provided based on the characteristics of the users, and the item itself which would be recommended to users [5]. These systems do collaborate with users and just suggest specific items which the users may be interested in [6].

Several classifications have been mentioned and considered for recommender systems [6]. The most well-known one is collaborative [7] which is applicable in different fields of research and industry. The second method is content based. In this method, there is a need for long-term observation of users' preferences in social network [8]. The third technique is demographic. This technique is useful for the times that there is not much information about a user's preferences. Therefore, demographic information such as age or education level is used in such systems [9]. The last type is knowledge based. Providing feedback by users is the key point for designing these type of systems. By providing more feedback to the system, the knowledge of the system will improve, and better recommendations will be provided for users [10].

While these systems bring many advantages for the users in online social networking sites, the privacy risks inherent to data gathering and processing are often underrated or disregarded. In order to protect the privacy of a user's sensitive information and avoid any security concern, there is a need to apply encryption and anonymization techniques (the common method for privacy preservation in recommender systems is encryption-based while anonymization of dataset is common for privacy-preservation of online social networks users). In this section, first, the definition of privacy is discussed to understand what is considered as sensitive or private information. Then, classification and different types of online social network are discussed to clarify the goal of each online social network sites and what can lead to privacy concern or risk for users in such sites.

Table 12.1   Definitions for privacy and information privacy

Definition	Authors	Year
"Protecting personal information from being misused by malicious entities and allowing certain authorized entities to access that personal information by making it visible to them"	Bünnig and Cap [13]	2009
"An individual's claim to control the terms under which personal information identifiable to the individual is acquired, disclosed or used"	Kang [14]	1998
"Set of privacy policies that force the system to protect private information"	Ni *et al.* [15]	2010
"Is in disarray [and n]obody can articulate what it means"	Solove [16]	2006
"The ability of the individual to personally control information about one's self"	Stone *et al.* [17]	1983
"Applications that seek to protect users' location information and hide some details from others"	Taheri *et al.* [18]	2010
"Multidimensional, elastic, depending upon context, and dynamic in the sense that it varies with life experience"	Xu *et al.* [19]	2011

12.2.1   Privacy: definition

Increased utilization of information technology and communication has had a major effect on the connections between individuals. This is predominantly related to individuals who make use of transportable machines to interconnect with one another or to connect the World Wide Web [11]. The word privacy has numerous subtly various definitions. These can be vary from "personal privacy" to "information privacy" from one place to another, which privacy alone is being used for multipurpose on the Internet [12]. Table 12.1 shows some definitions for privacy and information privacy.

Meanwhile, the notion and idea of privacy is varied, one particular description of privacy cannot cover all characteristics of the phrase. Accordingly, based on the meaning of privacy, this study is concerned principally with information privacy of users. Regarding Kang's (1998) definition of privacy, user's information privacy concept is intensely connected to the notation of confidentiality, which is one of the main attributes (qualities) of information security (InfoSec), but not to be used in an interchangeable manner. It should be noted that confidentiality[1] is concerned with

---

[1]Confidentiality, integrity and availability are the main qualities of information security which are known as CIA-triad [20]. Confidentiality is related to unauthorized information publishing, integrity describes as modifying information in an unauthorized manner, and integrity is described as unauthorized denial of use of individual information [21].

disclosure of pieces of information of an individual or its secrecy, while information privacy deals with information ownership and the consequences that information disclosure has on the individual and his/her data-access permissions and controls.

12.2.2   Online social networks, classification, and privacy

Popularity and interest in social networks have increased considerably over the last era. Kaplan and Haenlein [22] described social networks as applications that permit individuals to form profiles, send requests to join friends and see other users' profiles. Many forms of information can be included in these profiles, including pictures, audio files, videos and even posts and blogs, each of which may be public or semipublic, visible to a subset of other users who use that social network site [23]. LinkedIn, Friendster, MySpace and Facebook are among the most well-known social networks that attract many users share their information. In these sites, recommender systems can undoubtedly support to expand user participation by providing new friend recommendations or content that a user may be interested in [24].

By raising the number of users in social networks and sharing more information in these sites and also with recommender systems, concerns about users' privacy will increase. The quantity of data that social network sites collect from users is constantly growing while users' data are extremely valuable for many purposes such as research, marketing and numerous additional goals [25]. Simultaneously, an important amount of sensitive information can be obtained from users' data, which should be preserved against unapproved access and revelation [26].

As mentioned, each social network follows a different goal compared with other ones. Basically, social network sites can be categorized based on different purposes. Some social networks were founded for dating purposes, while other social networks were established for purposes such as chatting, socializing, enforcing real-life relationships and also business. Beye *et al.* [12] considered two main social network types and provided the purpose of use of these social networks as well.

Moreover, the functionality of each online social network site differs from the others. Based on their functionality, the social network provider may ask users different information to provide and share. Hence, information can be shared and disclosed within the different sources of social networks. Moreover, privacy concerns for users may increase as they share more and more information within different online social networks. Therefore, the privacy of users should be taken into account. Privacy includes protecting a portion of information in its scope. Three factors define this scope [12]. The first dimension is breadth, which reflects the number of groups of people. The second factor is depth, which shows the degree of allowed usage. The last factor is lifetime, which indicates the duration.

In any of these three dimensions, when a portion of data or information is moved outside the planned scope, whether maliciously or accidentally, a breach of privacy happens. Apart from the scope, users in online social networks are contending with privacy boundaries. Three boundaries have been recognized for privacy. The first boundary for individuals is disclosure. Here, users try to handle the anxiety of disclosing their information in a public or private manner. The second boundary is identity.

The identity boundary is described as the ability to manage one's information with particular groups. For example, it shows users' behaviors in different situations: one at work and the other at a party. The last one is a temporal boundary. It shows how the conduct of individuals may differ over time [27].

12.3 Taxonomy of privacy

Privacy can be studied from different aspects: privacy concerns, scoring models and privacy-preserving models and approaches (Figure 12.1). The first two divisions illustrate the privacy concerns in online social networks and user-related concerns, while the third part illustrates the measurement techniques of privacy of users' data. The last two sections show the preserving approaches of privacy for users in online social networks and recommender systems.

12.3.1 Privacy concerns in social networks

Privacy in social network sites can be seen from two different perspectives. The first perspective is local privacy or user-centric, which is known as social privacy. The second perspective is global or network-centric which is known as institutional privacy [26]. From the user-centric perspective, users decide what to share with others while they can create various levels and circles of friends, posts and information to whom they intend to share. From the global view, social network sites take advantage of users' information for different goals as stated and detailed in data usage rule and policy. Moreover, the network-centric privacy can also be seen from two distinctive approaches. Considering the first approach, the data collector is the data owner of the users' information. While these social network sites have infinite access to a user's data, the concerns for privacy are less if the data collector is trustworthy for the user.

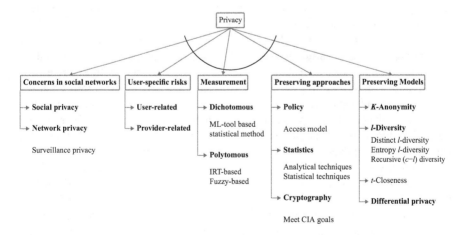

Figure 12.1   Taxonomy of privacy in online social networks

Table 12.2   Overview of privacy concerns in social networks

Privacy perspective	Related concerns
Social privacy	• User awareness • Complexity of privacy controls • Changes in privacy controls • Conflicts in privacy control
Network privacy	• Use and revenue from collected data • Lack of appropriate anonymization • Expand disclosing of collected data
Surveillance privacy	• Unauthorized data collection • Untrusted provider • Non oblivion—data may be published or stored forever

The second approach is known as surveillance privacy, where a user is suspicious about data collector. This happens when information is released to third parties by a reliable data collector [26]. Table 12.2 shows an overview of privacy concerns in social networks.

12.3.2   User-specific privacy risks and invasion

Privacy concerns and risks for users in an online social network can be differentiated in two groups: user related and provider related. Users may face several issues if their information being revealed and breaches happen. This type of breach can occur by a deliberate act of hacking or the individual can disclose the data accidentally (lingering data). Considering the user-related concerns, various threats can endanger users' privacy. These threats and concerns can be a disclosure of private information to strangers, inability to hide information from a certain group of friends or a friend and other users' posts about an individual [28,29]. Another form of threat is related to the social network provider. In this case, users do not have control to preserve their privacy or shared information, specifically with other parties. Several authors investigate related threats and concerns, which can include issues with data retention, private information browsing by online social network internal employees and sell users' data to other parties [30,31]. Although the companies apply anonymization processes to the data before selling or sharing them with other parties, there are still other risks like reidentification that is often ignored or discounted [12]. Table 12.3 categorizes users' privacy concerns in online social networks.

Though social network users gain advantages from their online presence, they are often incapable of evaluating the risks to privacy which are imposed by sharing information. Even privacy-aware individuals, who care about confidentiality, seem to be eager to compromise their confidentiality to develop their digital attendance in the cybernetic environment. Users realize that control loss on private data of them results in a continuing risk. However, they are not able to analyze and evaluate the whole and

Table 12.3   Users' information privacy concerns in online social networks

Privacy perspective	Related concerns
User related	• Disclosure of private information for the strangers • Inability to hide information from a certain group of friends or a friend • Other users' posts about an individual
Provider related	• Issues with data retention • Private information browsing by online social networks internal employees • Selling the users data to other parties

long-standing threat precisely. Worse, setting privacy preferences in online services are often a complex and laborious duty that numerous individuals feel confused about and typically ignore or skip [32].

On the other hand, users share their information with others while they do not intend to. For example, it has been reported that nearly 32% of users on the Internet have experienced privacy attacks due to various types of unintentional disclosure, like private materials distributed in an unwilling manner or being tagged in a discomforting photo, reluctantly [33].

The other point is that historical research on privacy has frequently concentrated on clarifying privacy matters related to information disclosure that may have tangible significance for affected users, such as financial information. Although publishing and disclosure of this type of information bring privacy risks in online social networks, the revelation of such data is less usual, if not uncommon [34]. In fact, there is evidence that revelation of such private embarrassing information, could disturb users' social position and their relationships [35], establish the key source of risks to users' privacy in online social networks [36].

12.3.3   Measuring privacy in online social networks

One of the significant tasks that should be considered in online social networks is privacy scoring and measurement. It is not inherently clear which information can result in a significant loss such as identity theft. Other risks are even harder to measure: comments and pictures of a user, which is risk-free for a number of individuals, can be detrimental to others. One case is a criticism against a religion or government. In some countries and cultures such criticism is broadly accepted, whereas, in other countries, an individual can get in severe difficulties for performing such an action [37,38]. Another risk of using online social networks is posting vacation information when users are abroad. Therefore, intruders could decide when to rob the house based on the information they gather. There are several techniques and methods for calculating the privacy and information sharing in a public manner [38]. Different authors have proposed various techniques and methods from the algorithmic approach to statistical ones to score and measure the privacy. The main two approaches for measuring the privacy are dichotomous and polytomous. For each approach, several models have been proposed to measure the privacy of users in online social networks. The most well-known methods related to these approaches has been discussed in this study.

12.3.3.1   Dichotomous approach

In this part, first, we discuss a privacy risk formula proposed by Renner [37]. Then we explain a quantifying privacy approach proposed by Becker *et al.* [39]. Next, we introduce privacy awareness enhancement that was proposed by Petkos *et al.* [40]. It is worth noting that all current privacy-scoring methods focus on the single source of data of individuals, while users share their information in different sources of online social networks. Finally, other models and techniques for calculating and measuring privacy risk are introduced.

Renner privacy risk formula

Renner [37] discusses a common approach for defining privacy risk by considering two privacy metrics including negative consequence information leakage and the likelihood of information leakage. This is given by

$$Risk = Negative\ consequence \times Likelihood \tag{12.1}$$

Using such a formula in the context of an online social network will come with a problem: both consequences and likelihood are unknown. As a case in point, it is not easy to define the consequences of leaking an embarrassing picture, which could vary from mere embarrassment in front of friends through to job termination [41]. An even plainer metric to assess privacy is the number of individuals who can access information at a certain time. Of course, this metric can merely guarantee a definite privacy level when the number of individuals with access is adequately small. In this case, a user share the information to whom he/she recognizes and trusts. Nevertheless, this metric is regularly used in the real world. Most individuals discuss private information while on public transport as they assume that only the people in the same compartment will hear them talking, while they would never discuss the same subjects when talking into a microphone such that everyone in the public transport could hear them. In addition to the size, the arrangement of the group, likewise, needs to be taken into account. However, the simple metric of the group size still conveys a sense for how "private" or "public" some piece of information is [37].

Privacy risk score

Maximilien *et al.* [42] proposed a privacy score model to compute the risk of users who participate in online social networks considering the dichotomous approach. For creating the model, they considered visibility and sensitivity of users' information. By considering β_k as the sensitivity of an attribute and $v(k, l)$ as the visibility of attribute k of user l, the final scoring model is described as $PR(k, l)$, which is any combination of visibility multiple in sensitivity. The final equation is given by

$$PR(k, l) = \beta_k \bigotimes v(k, l) \tag{12.2}$$

From the privacy score equation, it can be seen that there is a need to compute the visibility and sensitivity for the final measurement of users' privacy score. Hence, Maximilien *et al.* [42] provided formulas for sensitivity and visibility:

Maximilien *et al.* [42] mentioned that the sensitivity shows the difficulty of sharing an attribute to other users freely accessible. Based on his formula, Sensitivity of an attribute can be calculated given by

$$\beta_k = \frac{(M - |R_k|)}{M} \tag{12.3}$$

where $|R_k|$ is the number of individuals that make their attributes publicly available. As Maximilien *et al.* use a dichotomous approach, the final computed value for sensitivity is between [0,1], where the more sensitive attributes of a user have higher sensitivity score.

The other factor that has an impact on users' privacy is visibility, which Maximilien *et al.* calculate according to (12.4), which measure the probability that user l's kth attribute is public.

$$P_{kl} = Prob[R(k, l) = 1] \tag{12.4}$$

Privacy quotient using a naive approach
One of the models for calculating a privacy score is proposed by Srivastava [43]. In order to model his datasets, by focusing on text messages, they deploy a naive privacy quotient. With M individuals and m attributes, they formed a response matrix $(M \times m)$, which comes with a different range of attributes and users. They listed the profile items as follows: contact number, email, address, birth date, hometown, current town, job details, relationship status, interest, religious views and finally political views. Srivastava [43] dealt with a response matrix by assigning values 0 and 1 for shared information and unshared information about the profile, respectively. Their privacy quotient is capable of measuring sensitivity and visibility of the information as the main parameters of measuring the privacy. In their formula, they measure sensitivity for one user in relation to how much the other users share. For sensitivity calculation, the following formula has been proposed as

$$\beta_k = \frac{(M - |R_k|)}{M} \tag{12.5}$$

where $|R_k| = \sum_l R(k, l)$ is the sum of all public values k of a column of a profile. On the other hand, visibility has been defined by the following steps:

(1) $V(k, l) = Pr[R(k, l) = 1] \times 1 + Pr[R(k, l) = 0] \times 0$;

(2) $V(k, l) = Pr[R(k, l) = 1] \times 1 + 0$;

(3) $V(k, l) = Pr[R(k, l) = 1] \times 1$

where $Pr[R(k, l) = 1]$ shows the probability that an attribute of a user is public, while $Pr[R(k, l) = 0]$ indicates that the attribute is private (by applying these steps, it can be identified which cell will be equal to 1 and which cell will have a zero value). The final equation for calculating the visibility is as follows:

$$V(k,l) = \frac{|R_k|}{M} \times \frac{|R_l|}{m} \tag{12.6}$$

The final privacy score based on Srivastava is given by

$$PQ(j) = \sum_k \beta_k V(k,l) \tag{12.7}$$

where the range of attributes can be between [1,*m*]. The final privacy score gained from the calculation indicates the potential privacy risks of the texts which have been shared and published by users in online social networks.

Privacy-functionality score
Domingo-Ferrer *et al.* [44] proposed a method for measuring the privacy risk of users in social networking sites. In a more specific manner, they tried to understand the benefits that users may obtain by sharing their information in online social networks, such as LinkedIn. For doing so, they computed the effectiveness that an individual may gain from sharing his/her information in social networks given by

$$PRF(j) = \frac{\sum_{j'=1,j'\neq j}^{N} \sum_{i=1}^{n} \sum_{k=1}^{l} \beta_{ik} V(i,j',k) I(j,j',k)}{1 + PR_j} \tag{12.8}$$

$$PRF(j) = \frac{\sum_{j'=1,j'\neq j}^{N} \sum_{i=1}^{n} \sum_{k=1}^{l} \beta_{ik} V(i,j',k) I(j,j',k)}{1 + \sum_{i=1}^{n} \sum_{k=1}^{l} \beta_{ik} V(i,j,k)} \tag{12.9}$$

With the following conditions:

- $I(j,j',k) = 1$ If j' and j are k links away from each other
- 0 otherwise

where j and j' are the users in the social networks, k indicates the number of links between users and n indicates the number of attributes for a user. By applying this formula, users become able to decide what to share with other users at a specific time while maintaining the effectiveness of shared information in the desired social network.

SONET: privacy monitoring and ranking
Nepali and Wang [45] introduced a monitoring and ranking model for privacy in the online social network. Six components formed their SONET model. These components comprise the model for the social network, browse and deduce data by data aggregation, privacy index (which is known as PIDX) and privacy invasion, privacy-preserving and security protection, and finally, monitoring and countermeasures that can be done regarding privacy breaches. The main component of the model is the PIDX where it computes the privacy exposure of individuals based on sensitivity and visibility. Based on Nepali and Wang, the PIDX is a factor of an entity's privacy

vulnerability based on recognized properties. The final calculated model for the PIDX is between 0 and 100, which is given by

$$PIDX = \left(\frac{W_{L_k}}{W_l} \right) \times 100 \tag{12.10}$$

where W_{L_k} is the summation of visibility of each attribute in its corresponding weight. Nepali and Wang define the privacy invasion as when $PIDX \geq T$, where T indicates the threshold of security and privacy. If the computed index is higher than T, it means that the privacy of the entity is not preserved. Accordingly, the SONET model enables users to monitor their PIDX by the defined threshold for their privacy.

Privometer
Talukder *et al.* [46] developed the Privometer tool to compute the leakage of users' sensitive information. The computed score is shown by a numerical value. After providing the computed score as a numerical value, the tool is able to suggest preventative actions, which are known as self-sanitization actions. One of the main features of Privometer is considering all shared information by users in online social networks rather than just considering publicly available data. In contrast, a drawback of the tool is that it is only applicable to social network sites that permit applications to acquire and retrieve individuals' information.

PScore: privacy awareness enhancement
Petkos *et al.* [40] proposed a framework to increase the understanding and knowledge of individuals who use online social networks, considering privacy and security. Three separate features have been considered for the framework: personal preference of users about the sensitivity of their information, the classified structure of information (attributes, values and number of dimensions) to create a semantic organization and inferred information out of the scope of social networks. These three features cover the prerequisites of the framework and clearly make a distinction of the framework compared with other scoring models.

Beside privacy scoring frameworks, some studies consider privacy settings in the online social network and proposed tools for better privacy configuration. Fang and LeFevre [47] proposed a "privacy wizard" using machine-learning techniques. Mazzia *et al.* [48] proposed a graphical tool that provides options for privacy, called as PViz. Although these scoring frameworks are able to measure and compute the privacy risk of users, the tools for privacy configuration can also help users and individuals to select the best settings for the privacy of information in their profile.

12.3.3.2   Polytomous approach

The other approach for calculation of privacy is polytomous based. The difference of this approach with dichotomous one is in the level of shared information by individuals. As mentioned earlier, in the dichotomous approach, there are only two forms for shared information (the information is public or private), while in polytomous approach, we have more than two status for shared information by individuals. As this approach can obtain more different states for shared information, it can provide a more accurate estimation of calculated privacy for the online social network users.

Liu and Terzi proposed a polytomous approach based on item response theory (IRT). Becker *et al.* [39] discuss the significance of quantifying privacy in the online social network. They mentioned that quantifying privacy becomes even more critical in the case of protecting the huge volume of corresponding personal information, especially in large-scale online social networks. Finally, Aghasian *et al.* [38] proposed a privacy scoring model for multiple online social networks.

IRT-based privacy risk score

The first polytomous model has proposed by Liu and Terzi [41]. They expanded previous privacy score models by considering both the dichotomous and polytomous approaches. In their approach, they use the IRT-based method to compute a user's privacy. The derivation of IRT in psychometrics returns to data analysis of gathered information from tests or questionnaire. In their model, a two-parameter (users and users' attributes) IRT-based model had been considered. In this case, their model can quantify users' concern about their privacy. Finally, their model can calculate and measure privacy score as mentioned in [42]. In their polytomous approach, they defined $R(k, l) = n$, indicates that the kth attribute for user l has been disclosed to n nodes further in a graph. Hence, the privacy score provides an indicator of whether the information of an individual is at risk or not. Considering Liu and Terzi's model for computing the privacy risk score for online social networks users, Sramka [49] extended the model to evaluate and assess the risk of privacy from the users' viewpoint. In their new privacy score, Sramka considered users' background knowledge that was publicly available. The main drawback of this method was that only attribute and identity revelation were measured and only a dichotomous approach was considered.

PrivAware – quantifying privacy model

Becker *et al.* [39] presented a tool called PrivAware that is able to discover and report an accidental loss of information in online social networks. For creating the tool, they defined the problem as follows: friends' association with user x have constituted as a set of data which form a record including type, value and weight. By defining a function which shows the value allocated to the user x's friends, they were able to make the effective use of the outcomes with the support of friends with greater social value. As an example, the term type will contain values such as a university, zip code or age. Similarly, for each type of an attribute, there is a value which comes with the weight of that attribute. The weight here decides the importance of that attribute. It should be noted that the value of term weight has a value between zero and one that is set to the attributes based on the disambiguation process. In order to accomplish such task, they recruited 105 participants who shared their profile information for analysis. After proposing the inference algorithm, [39] they used three measures to assess the efficiency of the algorithm. The measures include inferred attributes, verifiable inference and correct inference.[2] They understood that the structured attributes have

---

[2] Inferred attributes indicate those attributes that are inferred by an algorithm. Verifiable inferences indicate that the inferred attributes by proposed algorithms are also available in the target user's profile. So, accuracy and precision of the inferred attributes can be verified. Correct inferences indicate that the inferred attributes are correct matches of the attribute values in the target user's profile.

Table 12.4 Comparison of historical studies

Focus	No. of sources	Data type	Approach	Reference
Attribute inference	1	Structured	Polytomous	[39]
Obtained utility by sharing information	1	Structured	Dichotomous	[44]
Sensitive information leakage of a profile	1	Structured	Dichotomous	[46]
Privacy risk from individual perspective	1	Structured	Dichotomous and polytomous	[41]
Privacy risk of text messages	1	Unstructured	Dichotomous	[43]
Privacy exposure based on known parameters	–	Web data	Dichotomous	[45]
Privacy disclosure score of user's information	4	Structured	Polytomous	[38]

a tendency to be accurately inferred in a more time-consuming manner—such as country, age, high school graduation year, a state with an exception for zip code. Contrariwise, unstructured and semi-structured data tend to be further challenging to infer correctly.

Scoring users' privacy disclosure across multiple online social networks
Aghasian *et al.* [38] proposed a polytomous scoring framework to calculate a user's privacy disclosure score in multiple online social networks. In this regard, they considered two factors that impact a user's privacy: visibility and sensitivity. For measuring the visibility of information, three factors have been identified, namely, accessibility, difficulty of data extraction and reliability. Accessibility refers to how available a user's piece of information is in online social networks—it indicates whether user information is publicly available, semipublic or completely private. Difficulty of data extraction relates to the amount of effort required to gain that information, while the reliability indicates if the obtained information is valid and reliable or not. After calculating visibility and gaining the value for sensitivity from prior studies, a fuzzy-based mathematical system has been applied to measure the final privacy disclosure score of users.

Table 12.4 summarizes the various privacy scoring frameworks.

12.3.4 Privacy-preserving approaches

Current research on privacy protection can be classified into three groups [50], each category concentrating on an aspect of privacy. Privacy by *policy* considers access models, privacy by *statistics* focuses on analytical and statistical technologies to generate tuned information revelation mechanisms, and privacy by *cryptography* aims to develop systems to guarantee the goal of confidentiality, integrity and availability (CIA). While the information utility in privacy by the policy is high, there is no guarantee of privacy-preservation and the strength of privacy is low. In the second category, privacy by statistics, information utility and the strength of privacy is medium, but its strength can be enhanced by particular patterns for accessing data. The third category, privacy by cryptography, has very high privacy strength and can guarantee the privacy in a theoretical manner which leads to low data and information utility. Beside privacy protection, data anonymization has been broadly studied and commonly implemented for preserving data secrecy in non-collaborating data sharing and publishing scenarios [51]. On the other hand, data distribution with a great amount of individuals must consider several matters, involving efficiency, data integrity and secrecy of the data owner.

12.3.5 Privacy-preserving models

Anonymizing data relies on eliminating or altering the identifying variable(s) contained in the data, also known as personally identifiable information.[3] Anonymizing data keeps the referenced person's privacy as a priority while giving attention to a data analyzer's needs (e.g., an analyst examining the data for identification of trends, patterns) [52]. Moreover, anonymization is one of the common methods of providing sanitized data.[4] In this process, information which is identifiable is detached and other attributes are perturbed. Still, there are no assurances for stopping an attack from an intruder and attacker who has background knowledge of the data. Therefore, there is a need for providing other procedures and methods for data retrieval to preserve the privacy of the published information of user profiles in online social networks [32]. From the personalization perspective, diverse users may have dissimilar privacy preferences. As a case in point, some records are more important for some individuals, while other users may pay attention to other attributes. The focus of current methods in personalized protection is on "personalized access control" (e.g., attribute-based encryption [55]) or sensitivity personalization of a single dimension [56], while no one has explored sensitivity personalization in multidimensional data [57].

A variety of anonymization algorithms with dissimilar anonymization processes have been proposed by different authors [51,56,58–63]. Models like k-anonymity, l-diversity and t-closeness are the most approved and accepted methods that deliver appropriate outcomes in anonymization. k-Anonymity [63] and l-diversity [61] are the main accepted models on privacy to quantify the degree of privacy, for sensitive information revelation against record linkage attack and attribute linkage attacks, respectively. Supplementary secrecy models such as t-closeness [64] and m-invariance [65] are also presented for numerous attack in privacy scenarios. Numerous anonymizing processes are applied to maximize the advantage of anonymize datasets, as well as suppression [66], generalization [51,60], anatomization [67], slicing [68] and disassociation [69].

12.3.5.1 k-Anonymity

k-Anonymity is the most common method in privacy-preservation against record linkage attack. If the information for each individual stays undistinguished for the

---

[3]Typically, an identifying variable is one that defines an attribute of an individual that is visible and evident, which is recorded (such as social security number, employee ID, patient ID), or other people can identify.
[4]Data sanitization is the procedure of veiling sensitive data and create datasets by overwriting it with accurate but incorrect information of an identical type [53,54].

Table 12.5   An example of k-anonymized data

Nationality	Zip code	Disease
*	878XX	Acne
*	878XX	Acne
*	878XX	Flu
*	878XX	Flu

Two techniques are applied to achieve k-anonymity and hiding information, the suppression method (applied to the nationality attribute), which does not publish any value, and the generalization method (applied to the zip code attribute), which uses consistent but less specific values to perform anonymization.

other k-1 individuals in a dataset, the k-anonymity is fulfilled. This can be done by two different methods:

- Suppression: Removing the value of an attribute from the perturbed data.
- Generalization: Substitution of an attribute with a less detailed but semantically reliable value.

Moreover, different classifications of attributes in k-anonymity should be considered [63]:

- Key attribute: A user can be identified directly by this attribute.
- Quasi-identifier (QI): Provides capability to recognize a user by a set of parameters and attributes.
- Sensitive attribute.

This method can guarantee that users are safe from linking attacks while they may not be secured and safeguarded against attribute revelation. For example, in order to perform a generalization of a value with suppression for ethnicity, three different levels may exist. At the first level, three different ethnics may appear including Asian, European and South American. At the second level of generalization, only person class exists for all three ethnic groups, and at the last level, every record is anonymized and nothing is available to other users or an adversary. Table 12.5 shows an example of anonymized data using k-anonymity method.

Till now, we have discussed how k-anonymity methods work for preventing the privacy. Like other methods, k-anonymity has some drawbacks, and potential attacks may still occur on the anonymized data, including [61] the following:

- Homogeneity attack, when there is insufficient diversity for the sensitive parameters in a quotient space (equivalence class)[5] of the dataset.
- Background knowledge attack, when the adversary has contextual information and facts.

A privacy breach on the anonymized data can happen if one of the mentioned attacks occur. In order to protect the information against these attacks, other methods have been proposed which are discussed in the next section.

---

[5]A equivalence class is a set of clusters.

274 Big data recommender systems, volume 1

12.3.5.2 *l*-Diversity

l-Diversity is a method that can lessen the risks in k-anonymity regarding the revelation of sensitive information [61]. It guarantees that the values of sensitive parameters are dissimilar in each equivalence class. While *l*-diversity enhances the privacy preservation compared with k-anonymity and helps to mitigate the risks that may occur when using k-anonymity, it is still likely that an adversary infers sensitive information. This can happen if the distribution of a sensitive record in a cluster is very different from the distribution of identical attributes in that class.

Li *et al.* [70] showed two possible attacks on *l*-diversity including skewness attack and similarity attack and indicated that the *l*-diversity method cannot safeguard against these sorts of attacks. Table 12.6 shows that sensitive information needs to be "diverse" in each *QI* equivalence class. As each sensitive attribute (disease) is diverse within each quotient space, no individual may be reidentified.

Machanavajjhala *et al.* [61] describes a variety of *l*-diversity techniques, including the following:

1. Distinct *l*-diversity: Bounding the occurrence of the most frequent value by $1/l$ in an equivalence class.
2. Entropy *l*-diversity: $\log(l)$ is the least acceptable entropy of the sensitive information distribution in each equivalence class.
3. Recursive (c, l)-diversity: The most common value does not appear regularly.

12.3.5.3 *T*-Closeness

In order to solve the problems of previous methods for preventing the privacy, Li *et al.* [64,70] proposed an intuitive privacy preserving model named *t*-closeness. They indicate that the sensitive information distribution within each *QI* compared with its distribution in the original dataset should be close. They also proposed an (n, t)-closeness privacy method which is more flexible [64]. In this case, the method bounds the number of released sensitive attributes that an adversary or an observer can gain from the table.

Table 12.6 An example of l-diversity table

Nationality	Zip code	Disease
Asian	878XX	Acne
Asian	878XX	Flu
Asian	878XX	Acne
Asian	878XX	Shingles
Asian	878XX	Flu
Asian	878XX	Flu
American	878XX	Flu
American	878XX	Acne
American	878XX	Flu
American	878XX	Flu
American	878XX	Acne
American	878XX	Shingles

12.3.5.4 Differential privacy

The concept of differential privacy was initially proposed by Dwork [71] which safeguards private distinguishable data at the severest probable level. It addresses the situation when a reliable data custodian desires to publish some statistics over its data, devoid of disclosing information about a specific value itself. This is done by adding noise to a small sample of user's usage pattern. Dwork defined differential privacy as "A randomized algorithm M is ε-differentially private if for all pairs of adjacent databases x,y, and for all sets $S \subset Range(M(x)) \cup Range(M(y))$":

$$Pr[M(x) \in S] \leq e^{\varepsilon} \cdot Pr[M(y) \in S]$$

where the probabilities are over algorithm M's coins, e stands for exp and "·" indicates that the transformation is stable in at most ε-times of the hamming distance between two datasets.

Table 12.7 summarizes the most common methods of preserving privacy for data publishing.

Table 12.7   An overview of common privacy preserving techniques

Presented model	Applied technique	Author(s)	Year
k-Minimal generalization	Domain generalization hierarchies of the QI	Samarati [72]	2001
Simple k-anonymity model	Mapping information to no, k or incorrect entities	Sweeney [63]	2002
Bottom-up generalization	Masking and hiding information instead of learn patterns	Wang *et al.* [73]	2004
Top-down specialization	Specifying the level of information in a top-down way till the least privacy condition is disrupted	Fung *et al.* [74]	2005
Enhanced k-anonymity model	Protecting both identifications and relationships to sensitive information in data	Wong *et al.* [75]	2006
k-Anonymity in classification issues	Suppression and progressive disclosure algorithm	Fung *et al.* [58]	2007
Differential privacy	Adding properly random noise in data	Dwork [71]	2008
p-Sensitive k-anonymity privacy model	Modifying the initial QI attributes values	Sun *et al.* [76]	2008
Enhanced (L, α)-diversity	Controlling the weight of sensitive information in a in a given quasi identifier cluster	Sun *et al.* [77]	2011
Slicing	Slicing the dataset in a vertical and horizontal manner	Li *et al.* [68]	2012
Concentrated differential privacy	Adding properly random noise in data	Dwork and Rothblum [78]	2016

12.4   Privacy preservation in recommender systems

Different methods have been proposed for preserving the privacy of users in recommender systems. Badsha *et al.* [79] presented a pragmatic privacy-preserving content-based filtering recommender system which works based on homomorphic encryption. To achieve this, they calculate item-to-item similarity of one user and then generate secure recommendations (provide recommendations without revealing sensitive information of users). Nikolaenko *et al.* [80] proposed a new method to leverage sparsity of data to achieve security in recommender systems, which works based on matrix factorization. Shokri *et al.* [81] developed a distributed aggregation mechanism for individuals to obscure the connection between item and user in data sent to a server that is not trusted in a collaborative-filtering-based recommender system. They guarantee that the privacy of users will be kept while the least information loss occurs for individuals. Machanavajjhala *et al.* [82] proposed a differential based privacy-preserving method for graph-based social networks to increase the trade-off between data utility and privacy. In their model, they have considered all edges of the graph as sensitive and proposed an algorithm that was able to recommend a single node for a few target nodes. Hofmann *et al.* [83] proposed a privacy scheme for collaborative filtering recommender systems by factor analysis. They also make use of a peer-to-peer protocol to meet the privacy of individuals' information in their model. The authors in [84–88] developed and proposed privacy-preserving algorithms and models for recommender systems. In their models, they tried to increase the efficiency of algorithms or increase the effectiveness of accuracy versus privacy in such systems. Table 12.8 presents an overview of common recommender-based systems privacy preservation models.

Table 12.8   An overview of common recommender-based systems privacy preservation models

Applied technique	Author(s)	Year
Probabilistic factor (correlation and regression) analysis	Hofmann *et al.* [83]	2005
Distributed aggregation method by modeling a bipartite graph	Shokri *et al.* [81]	2009
Link analysis of graph based on the differential privacy and Laplace and exponential smoothing algorithms	Machanavajjhala *et al.* [82]	2011
Matrix factorization (collaborative filtering)	Nikolaenko *et al.* [80]	2013
Data perturbation by micro-aggregation	Casino *et al.* [86]	2015
Homomorphic encryption based on ElGamal cryptosystem	Badsha *et al.* [79]	2016

12.5 Conclusion and future directions

The growing use of recommender systems in online social networks presents a privacy risk for the many users of these networks. The risks can be considered from two different perspectives: measuring a user's risk of unintended information disclosure and techniques to preserve users' privacy when sharing large datasets. The general objective of the first perspective is to understand both dichotomous and polytomous approaches and the differences between them for measuring privacy. From the privacy-preservation perspective, the challenges in protecting the privacy of online social networks users and recommender systems are to propose real-time methods which can support a high volume of data with data types. Then, we discussed the privacy-preservation models (anonymization techniques and encryption-based methods) for the users in these two systems which all provide information sanitization and data obfuscation to assure data anonymity of individuals.

As users' participation in different types of online social media and recommender systems are increasing rapidly, privacy-preservation of individuals is becoming more challenging. Hence, there is a need to propose new privacy preservation models in the near future that can deal with different data types, and for privacy-preservation systems to take into account dependencies between data. Another consideration is resource consumption. As providing privacy requires substantial computation, factors that impact on computation time should be studied to identify whether new mechanisms are required that are less computationally intensive. Modeling attacks is another significant issue that should be taken into account. While different types of attacks occur on anonymized datasets, modeling attacks on datasets with more complicated features should be a priority so that vulnerabilities can be uncovered before they are exploited. Finally, there is a need to propose novel methods to help organizations to preserve the privacy of users while these organizations are storing, analyzing and mining individuals' data within their organizations.

References

[1] Gross R, Acquisti A. Information revelation and privacy in online social networks. In: Proceedings of the 2005 ACM Workshop on Privacy in the Electronic Society. ACM; 2005. p. 71–80.

[2] Ahmadizadeh E, Aghasian E, Taheri HP, *et al.* An automated model to detect fake profiles and botnets in online social networks using steganography technique. IOSR Journal of Computer Engineering (IOSR-JCE). 2015;17:65–71.

[3] Jeckmans AJ, Beye M, Erkin Z, *et al. Privacy in Recommender Systems. In: Social Media Retrieval.* Twente, NL: Springer; 2013. p. 263–281.

[4] Backstrom L, Dwork C, Kleinberg J. Wherefore art thou r3579x?: Anonymized social networks, hidden patterns, and structural steganography. In: Proceedings of the 16th International Conference on World Wide Web. ACM; 2007. p. 181–190.

[5] Ricci F, Rokach L, Shapira B. *Introduction to recommender systems hand-book. In: Recommender Systems Handbook.* Boston, MA: Springer; 2011. p. 1–35.

[6] Resnick P, Varian HR. Recommender systems. Communications of the ACM. 1997;40(3):56–58. Available from: http://doi.acm.org/10.1145/245108. 245121.

[7] Billsus D, Pazzani MJ. User modeling for adaptive news access. User Modeling and User-Adapted Interaction. 2000;10(2–3):147–180.

[8] Burke R. Hybrid recommender systems: Survey and experiments. User Modeling and User-Adapted Interaction. 2002;12(4):331–370.

[9] Rich E. User modeling via stereotypes. Cognitive Science. 1979;3(4):329–354.

[10] Trewin S. Knowledge-based recommender systems. Encyclopedia of Library and Information Science. 2000;69(Supplement 32):180.

[11] Aldhafferi N, Watson C, Sajeev AS. Personal information privacy settings of online social networks and their suitability for mobile internet devices. International Journal of Security, Privacy and Trust Management (IJSPTM). 2013;2(2):1–17.

[12] Beye M, Jeckmans AJP, Erkin Z, *et al. Privacy in Online Social Networks.* London: Springer; 2012. p. 87–113.

[13] Bünnig C, Cap CH. Ad hoc privacy management in ubiquitous computing environments. In: Advances in Human-oriented and Personalized Mechanisms, Technologies, and Services, 2009. CENTRIC'09. Second International Conference on. IEEE; 2009. p. 85–90.

[14] Kang J. Information privacy in cyberspace transactions. Stanford Law Review. 1998:50:1193–1294.

[15] Ni Q, Bertino E, Lobo J, *et al.* Privacy-aware role-based access control. ACM Transactions on Information and System Security (TISSEC). 2010;13(3):24.

[16] Solove DJ. A taxonomy of privacy. University of Pennsylvania Law Review. 2006:154(3):477–564.

[17] Stone EF, Gueutal HG, Gardner DG, *et al.* A field experiment comparing information-privacy values, beliefs, and attitudes across several types of organizations. Journal of Applied Psychology. 1983;68(3):459.

[18] Taheri S, Hartung S, Hogrefe D. Achieving receiver location privacy in mobile ad hoc networks. In: Social Computing (SocialCom), 2010 IEEE Second International Conference on. IEEE; 2010. p. 800–807.

[19] Smith HJ, Dinev T, Xu H. Information privacy research: An interdisciplinary review. MIS Quarterly. 2011;35(4):989–1016.

[20] Whitman ME, Mattord HJ. Principles of Information Security. Cengage Learning; 2011.

[21] Cherdantseva Y, Hilton J. A reference model of information assurance & security. In: Availability, Reliability and Security (ARES), 2013 Eighth International Conference on. IEEE; 2013. p. 546–555.

[22] Kaplan AM, Haenlein M. Users of the world, unite! The challenges and opportunities of Social Media. Business Horizons. 2010;53(1):59–68.

[23] Boyd D, Ellison N. social network sites: Definition, history, scholarship: Department of Telecommunication. Information Studies, and Media. 2007;13(1):210–230.

[24] Stan J, Muhlenbach F, Largeron C. Recommender systems using social network analysis: Challenges and future trends. In: Encyclopedia of Social Network Analysis and Mining. New York, NY: Springer; 2014. p. 1522–1532.

[25] Zeadally S, Badra M. Privacy in a digital, networked world. In: Computer Communications and Networks. Cham: Springer; 2015. pp. 1–418.

[26] Raynes-Goldie KS. Privacy in the Age of Facebook: Discourse, Architecture, Consequences. Perth, WA: Curtin University; 2012.

[27] Palen L, Dourish P. Unpacking privacy for a networked world. In: Proceedings of the SIGCHI Conference on Human Factors in Computing Systems. ACM; 2003. p. 129–136.

[28] Leenes R. Context is everything sociality and privacy in online social network sites. In: IFIP PrimeLife International Summer School on Privacy and Identity Management for Life. Springer; 2009. p. 48–65.

[29] Rosenblum D. What anyone can know: The privacy risks of social networking sites. IEEE Security and Privacy. 2007;5(3):40–49.

[30] Bonneau J. Attack of the zombie photos. Light Blue Touchpaper. 2009. http://www lightbluetouchpaper org/2009/05/20/attackof-the-zombie-photos.

[31] Walters C. Facebook's new terms of service: "We can do anything we want with your content. Forever." The Consumerist. 2009;15:1–4.

[32] Zheleva E, Terzi E, Getoor L. Privacy in social networks. Synthesis Lectures on Data Mining and Knowledge Discovery. 2012;3(1):1–85.

[33] Lenhart A. Teens, Online Stranger Contact & Cyberbullying: What the Research is Telling Us. Pew Internet & American Life Project; 2008.

[34] Madden M, Lenhart A, Cortesi S, *et al*. Teens, social media, and privacy. Pew Research Center. 2013;21:1–107.

[35] Kowalski RM. I was only kidding Victims and perpetrators perceptions of teasing. Personality and Social Psychology Bulletin. 2000;26(2):231–241.

[36] Madden M, Smith A. Reputation management and social media. 2010.

[37] Renner C. Privacy in Online Social Networks [Thesis]; Social Capital Gateway, Report. Swiss Federal Institute of Tech. 2010.

[38] Aghasian E, Garg S, Gao L, *et al*. Scoring users' privacy disclosure across multiple online social networks. IEEE Access. 2017;5:13118–13130.

[39] Becker JL, Chen H. Measuring Privacy Risk in Online Social Networks [Thesis]; University of California, Davis. 2009.

[40] Petkos G, Papadopoulos S, Kompatsiaris Y. PScore: A framework for enhancing privacy awareness in online social networks. In: Availability, Reliability and Security (ARES), 2015 10th International Conference on. IEEE; 2015. p. 592–600.

[41] Liu K, Terzi E. A framework for computing the privacy scores of users in online social networks. ACM Transactions on Knowledge Discovery from Data (TKDD). 2010;5(1):6.

[42]　Maximilien EM, Grandison T, Liu K, *et al.* Enabling privacy as a fundamental construct for social networks. In: Computational Science and Engineering, 2009. CSE'09. International Conference on. vol. 4. IEEE; 2009. p. 1015–1020.

[43]　Srivastava A, Geethakumari G. Measuring privacy leaks in online social networks. In: Advances in Computing, Communications and Informatics (ICACCI), 2013 International Conference on. IEEE; 2013. p. 2095–2100.

[44]　Domingo-Ferrer J. Rational privacy disclosure in social networks. In: International Conference on Modeling Decisions for Artificial Intelligence. Springer; 2010. p. 255–265.

[45]　Nepali RK, Wang Y. SONET: A social network model for privacy monitoring and ranking. In: IEEE 33rd International Conference on Distributed Computing Systems Workshops. IEEE; 2013. p. 162–166.

[46]　Talukder N, Ouzzani M, Elmagarmid AK, *et al.* Privometer: Privacy protection in social networks. In: Data Engineering Workshops (ICDEW), 2010 IEEE 26th International Conference on. IEEE; 2010. p. 266–269.

[47]　Fang L, LeFevre K. Privacy wizards for social networking sites. In: Proceedings of the 19th International Conference on World Wide Web. ACM; 2010. p. 351–360.

[48]　Mazzia A, LeFevre K, Adar E. The PViz comprehension tool for social network privacy settings. In: Proceedings of the Eighth Symposium on Usable Privacy and Security. ACM; 2012. p. 13.

[49]　Sramka M. Evaluating Privacy Risks in Social Networks from the User's Perspective. Cham: Springer; 2015. p. 251–267.

[50]　Zhang L, Li XY, Lei J, *et al.* Mechanism design for finding experts using locally constructed social referral web. IEEE Transactions on Parallel and Distributed Systems. 2015;26(8):2316–2326.

[51]　Fung B, Wang K, Chen R, *et al.* Privacy-preserving data publishing: A survey of recent developments. ACM Computing Surveys (CSUR). 2010; 42(4):14.

[52]　Abuelsaad TE, Hoyos C. Data Perturbation and Anonymization Using One Way Hash [Generic]. Google Patents; 2011.

[53]　Tambe P, Vora D. Data sanitization for privacy preservation on social network. In: Automatic Control and Dynamic Optimization Techniques (ICACDOT), International Conference on. IEEE; 2016. p. 972–976.

[54]　Edgar D. Data sanitization techniques. A Net Ltd. White Paper. 2000; p. 2003–2004.

[55]　Li M, Yu S, Zheng Y, *et al.* Scalable and secure sharing of personal health records in cloud computing using attribute-based encryption. IEEE Transactions on Parallel and Distributed Systems. 2013;24(1):131–143.

[56]　Xiao X, Tao Y. Personalized privacy preservation. In: Proceedings of the 2006 ACM SIGMOD International Conference on Management of Data. ACM; 2006. p. 229–240.

[57]　Wang W, Chen L, Zhang Q. Outsourcing high-dimensional healthcare data to cloud with personalized privacy preservation. Computer Networks. 2015;88:136–148.

[58] Fung B, Wang K, Yu PS. Anonymizing classification data for privacy preservation. IEEE Transactions on Knowledge and Data Engineering. 2007;19(5):711–725.

[59] LeFevre K, DeWitt DJ, Ramakrishnan R. Incognito: Efficient full-domain k-anonymity. In: Proceedings of the 2005 ACM SIGMOD International Conference on Management of Data. ACM, 2005. p. 49–60.

[60] LeFevre K, DeWitt DJ, Ramakrishnan R. Mondrian multidimensional *k*-anonymity. In: Data Engineering, 2006. ICDE'06. Proceedings of the 22nd International Conference on. IEEE, 2006; p. 25–25.

[61] Machanavajjhala A, Kifer D, Gehrke J, *et al.* *l*-Diversity: Privacy beyond *k*-anonymity. ACM Transactions on Knowledge Discovery from Data (TKDD). 2007;1(1):3.

[62] Samarati P, Sweeney L. Protecting privacy when disclosing information: *k*-anonymity and its enforcement through generalization and suppression. Technical Report, SRI International; 1998.

[63] Sweeney L. *k*-Anonymity: A model for protecting privacy. International Journal of Uncertainty, Fuzziness and Knowledge-Based Systems. 2002;10(05):557–570.

[64] Li N, Li T, Venkatasubramanian S. Closeness: A new privacy measure for data publishing. IEEE Transactions on Knowledge and Data Engineering. 2010;22(7):943–956.

[65] Xiao X, Tao Y. M-invariance: Towards privacy preserving re-publication of dynamic datasets. In: Proceedings of the 2007 ACM SIGMOD International Conference on Management of Data. ACM; 2007. p. 689–700.

[66] Wang K, Fung BCM, Philip SY. Handicapping attacker's confidence: An alternative to *k*-anonymization. Knowledge and Information Systems. 2007;11(3):345–368.

[67] Xiao X, Tao Y. Anatomy: Simple and effective privacy preservation. In: Proceedings of the 32nd International Conference on Very Large Data Bases. VLDB Endowment; 2006. p. 139–150.

[68] Li T, Li N, Zhang J, *et al.* Slicing: A new approach for privacy preserving data publishing. IEEE Transactions on Knowledge and Data Engineering. 2012;24(3):561–574.

[69] Terrovitis M, Mamoulis N, Liagouris J, *et al.* Privacy preservation by disassociation. Proceedings of the VLDB Endowment. 2012;5(10):944–955.

[70] Li N, Li T, Venkatasubramanian S. *t*-Closeness: Privacy beyond *k*-anonymity and *l*-diversity. In: Data Engineering, 2007. ICDE 2007. IEEE 23rd International Conference on. IEEE; 2007. p. 106–115.

[71] Dwork C. An ad omnia approach to defining and achieving private data analysis. In: Privacy, Security, and Trust in KDD. Berlin, Heidelberg: Springer; 2008. p. 1–13.

[72] Samarati P. Protecting respondents identities in microdata release. IEEE Transactions on Knowledge and Data Engineering. 2001;13(6):1010–1027.

[73] Wang K, Yu PS, Chakraborty S. Bottom-up generalization: A data mining solution to privacy protection. In: Data Mining, 2004. ICDM'04. Fourth IEEE International Conference on. IEEE; 2004. p. 249–256.

[74] Fung BCM, Wang K, Yu PS. Top-down specialization for information and privacy preservation. In: 21st International Conference on Data Engineering (ICDE'05). IEEE; 2005. p. 205–216.

[75] Wong RCW, Li J, Fu AWC, *et al.* (α, k)-Anonymity: An enhanced k-anonymity model for privacy preserving data publishing. In: Proceedings of the 12th ACM SIGKDD International Conference on Knowledge Discovery and Data Mining. ACM; 2006. p. 754–759.

[76] Sun X, Wang H, Li J, *et al.* Enhanced p-sensitive k-anonymity models for privacy preserving data publishing. Transactions on Data Privacy. 2008;1(2):53–66.

[77] Sun X, Li M, Wang H. A family of enhanced (L, α)-diversity models for privacy preserving data publishing. Future Generation Computer Systems. 2011;27(3):348–356.

[78] Dwork C, Rothblum GN. Concentrated differential privacy. arXiv preprint arXiv:160301887. 2016:1–28.

[79] Badsha S, Yi X, Khalil I. A practical privacy-preserving recommender system. Data Science and Engineering. 2016;1(3):161–177.

[80] Nikolaenko V, Ioannidis S, Weinsberg U, *et al.* Privacy-preserving matrix factorization. In: Proceedings of the 2013 ACM SIGSAC Conference on Computer & Communications Security. ACM; 2013. p. 801–812.

[81] Shokri R, Pedarsani P, Theodorakopoulos G, *et al.* Preserving privacy in collaborative filtering through distributed aggregation of offline profiles. In: Proceedings of the third ACM Conference on Recommender Systems. ACM; 2009. p. 157–164.

[82] Machanavajjhala A, Korolova A, Sarma AD. Personalized social recommendations: Accurate or private. Proceedings of the VLDB Endowment. 2011;4(7):440–450.

[83] Hofmann T, Hartmann D. Collaborative filtering with privacy via factor analysis. In: Proceedings of the 2005 ACM Symposium on Applied Computing; 2005. p. 791–795.

[84] Li D, Chen C, Lv Q, *et al.* An algorithm for efficient privacy-preserving item-based collaborative filtering. Future Generation Computer Systems. 2016;55:311–320.

[85] Boutet A, Frey D, Guerraoui R, *et al.* Privacy-preserving distributed collaborative filtering. Computing. 2016;98(8):827–846.

[86] Casino F, Domingo-Ferrer J, Patsakis C, *et al.* A k-anonymous approach to privacy preserving collaborative filtering. Journal of Computer and System Sciences. 2015;81(6):1000–1011.

[87] Jorgensen Z, Yu T. A privacy-preserving framework for personalized, social recommendations. In: EDBT; 2014. p. 571–582.

[88] Shang S, Hui Y, Hui P, *et al.* Beyond personalization and anonymity: Towards a group-based recommender system. In: Proceedings of the 29th Annual ACM Symposium on Applied Computing. ACM; 2014. p. 266–273.

Chapter 13

Private entity resolution for big data on Apache Spark using multiple phonetic codes

Alexandros Karakasidis[1] and Georgia Koloniari[1]

13.1 Introduction

Recommender systems are nowadays experiencing a significant boost due to the availability of big data which supply an abundance of user data such as past purchases and browsing history. The benefits are increased when a recommender system can use and combine data that come from multiple sites and illustrate a more complete picture of the user's preferences and interests. However, such data often originate from dispersed, heterogeneous sources, and before processing and analyzing them, it is required to integrate or link them. The problem of linking such data consists of identifying data that refer to the same real-world entity across the heterogeneous sources and is known as *record linkage* or *entity resolution*. As these data also concern human activities, privacy issues arise when linking data across different sources. The problem is known as *privacy preserving record linkage* (PPRL).

In PPRL, two or more dataholders attempt to identify common entities stored in their records, without revealing to each other any additional information. As the data are from heterogeneous sources, they may adhere to different schemas. No common unique identifiers can be found and, as such, the record-linking methods rely on attributes that describe these records and are common to all data sources, such as names, surnames and addresses when identifying the same individual. Thus, to determine whether two records match, all their respective common fields must be compared. The complexity of matching methods is high, as all records belonging to the two dataholders need to be compared against each other so as to determine the matching records. To this end, blocking methods have been introduced [1] to reduce matching complexity by pruning out unlikely to match candidate pairs of records. In addition, data is usually dirty, containing spelling and typographical errors, thus complicating the linkage process further. Exact matching cannot be performed and more expensive approximate matching methods are required.

Different approaches have been applied for approximate matching in the context of record linkage. Most methods rely on hashing, combinations of bigrams and

[1]Department of Applied Informatics, University of Macedonia, Greece

n-grams as well as similarity or appropriate distance measures. A popular approach is based on the use of phonetic codes. A phonetic code is a hash of a string, based on its pronunciation. Phonetic codes are being used on names for almost a century [2] for duplicate detection and record linkage, due to their inherent information suppression properties, which make them tolerant to spelling errors. The use of phonetic codes reduces the problem of approximate matching of dirty data to a problem of exact matching of phonetic codes, leading to faster processing and rendering the use of distance measures redundant. However, this often comes with a cost in quality with regards to precision or recall.

In this chapter, we propose a parallel protocol for PPRL based on phonetic encodings that exploits novel big data processing engines to provide results of high quality in an efficient manner. Our phonetics encoding scheme extends the work presented in [3] that is based on the use of the Soundex phonetic algorithm [2]. This protocol also features noise generation to prevent frequency attacks and encryption of both actual and fake data to enable processing by an untrusted party. However, to cope with the low recall that the existence of a big percentage of dirty data may incur, we propose using Soundex combined with another popular phonetic algorithm, and particularly NYSIIS [4]. By combining two phonetic encodings, our protocol becomes more robust and more tolerant to errors in the matching fields, as it introduces redundancy. Furthermore, as Soundex is particularly vulnerable to errors that occur in the beginning of the encoded text; our protocol deploys another optimization by encoding the reverse of the original text with the second phonetic algorithm.

To cope with the additional processing cost caused by the multiple encodings, we rely on the use of novel parallel-processing platforms. In particular, we implement our protocol using Apache Spark [5]. Apache Spark, a general-purpose cluster computing platform, has evolved as the de-facto standard for big data analytics, providing efficient solutions for a variety of analytics problems dealing with both structured and unstructured as well as with streaming data. Apache Spark is also used in [6] that parallelizes privacy preserving matching (PPM) using a single phonetic encoding, thus inheriting the low recall that the serial approach exhibits. Our protocol is a three party protocol that relies on the use of a third, cloud-based party which is not necessarily required to be trusted as it handles only encrypted data, and no private information is leaked. Our experimental results show that the proposed protocol is both efficient and effective, with higher recall compared to approaches using only a single phonetic algorithm for encoding.

The rest of the chapter is organized as follows. Section 13.2 summarizes related work. In Section 13.3, we formulate the problem we address and briefly present the basic components of our approach. Section 13.4 details the proposed technique, while Section 13.5 contains our empirical evaluation. Finally, Section 13.6 sums up with conclusions and some thoughts for future work.

13.2   Related work

The problem of record linkage has attracted much attention due to the importance and variety of its applications. Useful reviews of the most representative traditional methods for record linkage can be found in [7,8]. However, the classical record linkage problem ignored any privacy concerns and focused only on efficiency and result quality. Privacy issues are first addressed in [9], which presents the challenges and specific requirements of the problem of PPRL. Latest challenges and current research directions are summarized in [10], including techniques providing efficient indexing, real-time matching, dynamic data handling, application of graph-based classification techniques on the privacy-preserving paradigm, interactive assessment of linked records and techniques for privacy-preserving data fusion. In our work, we address the problem of efficient approximate matching deploying phonetic codes and the novel available parallel-processing architectures to deal with big data volumes and real-time processing.

For PPM, Van Eycken *et al.* [11] propose the creation of a single hash string for an entire record, combining the linkage fields, i.e., name, surname, address. However, this method is not tolerant to spelling and other errors and is only appropriate for exact matching. Churches *et al.* [12] propose a method that combines hashing with powersets of bigrams. The method aims at de-identifying the Dice coefficient of n-grams by using hashing. The approach suffers from very high complexity, and as shown in [13], privacy preservation of distance-based methods performed well only in cases of non-encrypted data. Another computationally intensive method is presented in [14], where so as to capture the different typographical errors which may occur within a string, various permutations of the linkage attributes are computed and then encrypted. Du *et al.* [15] propose precomputing all the linkage attributes possible matches, an approach that requires an extreme amount of storage space. Schnell *et al.* [16] have used Bloom filters, which they combine with n-grams to take advantage of their approximate matching properties. However, as indicated in [17], under certain conditions, this method is susceptible to constraint satisfaction cryptanalysis. Homomorphic encryption [18] may be used for privately matching numerical fields [19] and is also not very efficient.

Our matching approach is based on [3] that deploys phonetic codes and then hashing. While the original work proposes using Soundex [2], we extend it by combining another phonetic encoding algorithm NYSIIS [4]. Our approach is more robust to typos and spelling errors as using two encodings with different characteristics introduces redundancy and provides higher recall. Phonetic encoding schemes have been often used for name matching and linkage so as to deal with spelling and other errors giving results with high quality [20]. Other well-known phonetic algorithms that are used for name matching include Metaphone [21], which assumes English phonetics. We selected to combine Soundex with NYSIIS since they are both very popular algorithms with many available fast implementations and their characteristics work complementary in order to achieve a higher recall as was our goal.

To move toward real-time matching and deal with big data, the novel platforms such as Hadoop and Spark that offer parallel processing capabilities have been recently deployed for record linkage [22] and particularly supporting methods for private blocking (indexing) [23,24] and private matching [6,25–27]. In [22], Hadoop is deployed to apply record-linkage using the MapReduce programming model and a tool for defining linkage workflows, which include both matching and blocking (indexing) steps is provided. In [23], a parallel privacy preserving blocking technique based on locality sensitive hashing (LSH) is presented. LSH is used for blocking as it provides the means of a fast approximate comparison functionality by separating bit vectors in chunks that contain similar items. The authors combine LSH with Bloom filters over a MapReduce framework. Similarly, Franke *et al.* [24] also use LSH over Spark for blocking. These works can be viewed as complementary to ours, since we focus on the matching part of the PPRL process, and deploying an efficient blocking technique would further improve the overall PPRL performance. In [25], Hadoop with MapReduce is used for performing a one-to-many matching process for data of different types. Given the fact that Spark offers many advantages against Hadoop [26], it is evident that utilizing Spark comprises a new promising research direction. Pita *et al.* [27] present a first approach that exploits the Spark platform so as to create data marts for the Brazilian Public Health System using large databases from the Ministry of Health and the Ministry of Social Development and Hunger Alleviation. They use the bloom-based method of Schnell *et al.* [16] for privacy preservation inheriting the weaknesses we outlined above.

A first approach to parallelizing the original work of [3] is presented in [6]. However, in this chapter, we propose using two different encoding algorithms so as to improve the quality of the matching results, while exploiting the Spark architecture so as not to compromise performance.

13.3   Problem formulation and background

In this section, we formally define the problem we are solving and present the details of the building blocks that comprise our solution.

13.3.1   Problem formulation and notation used

Without loss of generality, let us consider two data sources, called Alice (A) and Bob (B), who, respectively, hold r^A and r^B records each. We denote as r_i^A and r_i^B the ith record of Alice and Bob, respectively. We represent the jth attribute of these records as $r_i^A.j$ and $r_i^B.j$.

PPRL is the problem of identifying (linking) all pairs of r^A and r^B records that refer to the same real-world entity, so that no more information is disclosed to either A, B or any third party involved in the process besides the identifiers of the linked r^As and r^Bs.

Alice and Bob will most probably use different schemas in their databases. As such, they will have different attributes. Let R^A be Alice's schema and R^B be Bob's schema, and let us assume that in these schemas, m of the attributes are common between the two sources forming a composite key. These attributes might be names, surnames, addresses, birth dates. As such, none of these on its own may comprise a unique identifier that can be used to identify a record. We refer to these attributes as *matching attributes* or *matching fields*. The composite key is used to determine when two records *match*, i.e., when they refer to the same entity. To determine when two records match, the respective attributes forming the composite key need to be compared. Considering that our data is often dirty, matching should rely on a similarity or distance function.

Let us consider a similarity function $sim_j() \rightarrow [0..1]$ and a threshold $t_j > 0$. Given the records r_i^A and r_i^B with matching attributes $r_i.1 \ldots r_i.m$ for both Alice and Bob, we define the following matching function $M \rightarrow \{0, 1\}$:

$$M(r_i^A, r_i^B) = \begin{cases} 1, & \text{iff } sim_j(r_i^A.j, r_i^B.j) \geq t_j, \ \forall j \in [1, m] \\ 0, & \text{otherwise.} \end{cases} \qquad (13.1)$$

If $M(r_i^A, r_i^B) = 1$, then the pair (r_i^A, r_i^B) is considered a possible match. Appropriately tuning the threshold yields an accurate match function with a low false positive rate.

This process is the *matching process*. To preserve privacy, i.e., ensure *PPM*, after the completion of this process, the only information revealed is the identifiers of the matched records.

13.3.2 *Phonetic algorithms for privacy preserving matching*

A phonetic algorithm is an algorithm which maps a word to its phonetic equivalent. Such methods have been broadly used in the past for supporting approximate matching on names [28]. Their operation is quite straightforward: for each word to be encoded, certain rules for grouping similar sounds are applied, resulting in a reduced character string which stands for the pronunciation of the respective word. For instance, for the Soundex algorithm, this reduction consists of a capital letter followed by three digits. For example, the word "Cooper," in Soundex is converted into C160.

An interesting property of all phonetic codes is that of information suppression. That is, a phonetic code comprises a lossy representation of its input. This lossy representation usually consists of a string of a smaller length compared to the input string and a more limited alphabet. As a result, the same output string may be derived from different input strings. For instance, the string "Copper" also has the same Soundex code with "Cooper," i.e., C160. Thus, phonetic encoding algorithms do not provide one-to-one mappings, and it is impossible to determine the input of the encoding algorithm from its output.

This information suppression property makes phonetic algorithms appropriate for approximate matching as it provides them fault tolerance against typographical errors. As we mentioned with our example above, "Copper" that could be the result of an error when typing "Cooper" yields the same phonetic code. Thus, a matching process comparing the phonetic codes instead of the original strings would yield a match. Note that in this case, no distance or similarity measure is required. The problem of approximate matching between the original strings is reduced to performing exact matching between their corresponding phonetic encodings. An advantage of this property is that one does not have to calibrate a distance measure by setting appropriate thresholds.

Table 13.1 Soundex mapping table

a, e, h, i, o, u, w, y	→	0
b, f, p, v	→	1
c, g, j, k, q, s, x, z	→	2
d, t	→	3
l	→	4
m, n	→	5
r	→	6

Regarding processing cost, phonetic encoding algorithms exhibit low complexity. A further advantage is that, traditional database indexes can be deployed over phonetic codes to speed up the matching process even further.

All these properties indicate why phonetic algorithms are appropriate for the PPM process. They are efficient, they can handle dirty data, they provide privacy through information suppression and they reduce the problem of approximate matching to one of exact matching, unlike the approaches usually followed in the literature [16], where transformations are designed in a way that chunks of encoded words are compared to assess similarity using a metric.

In our approach, the common fields are encoded using phonetic codes. As the matching problem is reduced to exact matching, a secure hash function is applied on the outputs of the phonetic algorithms so as to further improve privacy. Finally, to determine whether two records consist a match, the outputs of the hash functions for all their common fields are compared, and if they are identical, the matching process indicates a match. More formally, (13.1), when using phonetic algorithms for matching, is substituted by (13.2). The similarity function sim_j used in the formula has as input the hashes H of a phonetic code PC applied on input strings $r_i^A.j$, $r_i^B.j$ and examines their absolute similarity, returning 1 when the two codes are identical or 0 otherwise.

$$M(r_i^A, r_i^B) = \begin{cases} 1, & \text{iff } H(PC_j(r_i^A.j)) = H(PC_j(r_i^B.j)), \ \forall j \in [1, m] \\ 0, & \text{otherwise.} \end{cases} \tag{13.2}$$

13.3.3 The Soundex algorithm

Soundex [28], based on English language pronunciation, is the oldest (patented in 1918 [2]) and best known phonetic encoding algorithm. It keeps the first letter of a string and converts the rest into numbers according to Table 13.1 [8].

All zeros (vowels and "h," "w" and "y") are then removed and sequences of the same number are merged to a single one (e.g., "333" is replaced with "3"). The final code is the original first letter and three numbers (longer codes are stripped-off and shorter codes are padded with zeros). As an example, the Soundex code for "Alan" is "A450," while the code for "Turing" is "T652." A major drawback of Soundex is that it maintains the first letter of the encoded word intact; thus, any error or variation at the beginning of a name will result in a different Soundex code. To overcome this problem, a common solution would be to reverse the words and use Soundex on the resulting strings.

13.3.4 The NYSIIS algorithm

As described in [8], NYSIIS, the New York State Identification and Intelligence System phonetic encoding algorithm [4], follows another approach for phonetic encodings. In particular, it maintains information regarding the position of vowels in the encoded word by converting all of them to the letter A.

It provides an encoding consisting exclusively of letters, as a result of a series of transformations:

1. The following name prefix conversions take place:
   i.   "mac" → "mcc"
   ii. "kn" → "n"
   iii. "k" → "c"
   iv. { "ph" | "pf" } → "ff"
   v.   "sch" → "sss"
2. The following name suffix conversions take place:
   i.   { "ee" | "ie" } → "y"
   ii. { "dt" | "rt" | "rd" | "nt" | "nd" } → "d"
3. The first character of the resulting string is the first letter of the encoding.
4. The rest of the letters are transformed as following:
   i.   "ev" → "af"
   ii.   { "e" | "i" | "o" | "u" } → "a"
   iii. "q" → "g"
   iv.   "z" → "s"
   v.   "m" → "n"
   vi.   "kn" → "n"
   vii. "k" → "c"
   viii. "sch" → "sss"
   ix.   "ph" → "ff"
   x.   Letter before or after an "h" not a vowel → "h" replaced by letter before it
   xi.   Letter before "w" is a vowel → "w" replaced by "a"
   xii. A letter is added to the NYSIIS encoding only if it is different from the previous letter in the encoding
5. If the last letter of the resulting code is "a" or "s," it is removed
6. If the encoding ends with "ay," it is replaced by "y"
7. The final transformation dictates truncating the encoding so as to be limited to six characters only.

13.3.5 Apache Spark

Apache Spark [5] is an open source, memory-based data-processing framework, suitable for big data. It is considered as the next generation big data processing engine, overtaking Hadoop MapReduce. Spark extends MapReduce in many ways [26]: it is faster, easier to program and it goes far beyond batch applications to support a variety of compute-intensive tasks. Also, it supports rich application programming interfaces (APIs) in several languages (Scala, Java, Python, SQL and R) for performing complex operations on distributed data. Furthermore, Spark's memory model leverages the use of main memory, thus outperforming Hadoop's MapReduce [29].

Its main data abstraction, Resilient Distributed Dataset (RDD), offers the ability of lazy processing in parallel across a cluster. Users create RDDs by applying transformations (such as map, filter and groupBy) to their data. Spark's lazy evaluation of RDDs allows it to find an efficient computation plan. Transformations return a new RDD object representing the result of a computation but do not immediately compute it. When an action is called, Spark looks at the whole graph of transformations, allowing users to build up programs modularly without losing performance, with RDDs providing explicit support for data sharing among computations. A typical Spark cluster setup consists of a master machine directing tasks of a program to be executed, referred to as driver, to worker machines.

The execution of a Spark application involves the following key entities [29]. First, there is the driver. This is a program that considers Spark as a library and describes the computation steps to be taken. The driver program connects to a computing cluster through a SparkContext. Then, there are the workers, which provide resources to the Spark application, namely CPU, memory and storage. An executor, on the other hand, is a distinct Java Virtual Machine process created by Spark for each worker running the respective application. A set of computations is referred to as a job. This is launched in a cluster by Spark and concludes with the results, which are returned to the driver program. A Spark application may consist of multiple jobs. Each time a job is provided to Spark, it forms a directed acyclic graph of stages. Each stage, in its turn is a collection of tasks, each of which comprises the smallest unit of work that Spark sends to an executor.

13.4   A parallel privacy preserving phonetics matching protocol

In our protocol, we consider two parties, Alice and Bob, holding their own data and a third party, Carol, who performs the join operation between the data of the two sources, using the phonetic codes produced by Alice and Bob. We also consider that all three participants have a Spark cluster at their disposal, thus performing computations in parallel.

13.4.1   Multiple algorithms for phonetic matching

Our protocol for performing PPM on textual data relies on phonetic codes and exploits the properties phonetic encoding algorithms exhibit. The facts that phonetic codes exhibit information suppression and that they are not one-to-one mappings are the key features for both ensuring privacy preservation and performing approximate string matching. As we have detailed in Section 13.3.2, their blend of properties is ideal for performing PPRL. However, they also exhibit some weakness.

The intuition behind their use is that since these codes are lossy representations of the original strings, words with similar spellings or misspellings map to the same phonetic code. Indeed, using Soundex for illustration, words with similar spelling such as "Copper" and "Cooper" do yield the same code C160. However, the word "Choufoer" also corresponds to the same phonetic code of C160. This last word seems significantly different from the two others. Unfortunately, there is no upper bound on the edit distance between two words that may yield the same phonetic code. On the other hand, the word "Dooper" corresponds to a different phonetic code (D160) despite its small distance to "Cooper."

To address this issue, we propose using multiple phonetic encodings for the input records, instead of a single one. Our approach is based on the very simple observation that, since different rules are followed by each phonetic algorithm, resulting into different conversions, there should be cases where some phonetic algorithm would work better than some other, being, thus, able to capture different discrepancies and vice versa. To this end, we apply more than one algorithm to the same dataset and consider the union of the results.

In our work, we selected to use Soundex and NYSIIS, as they are both very popular and they have many efficient implementations available. We believe that their characteristics and the transformations they perform work complementary. This fact is confirmed by our experimental evaluation since recall is significantly increased when Soundex is performed on the original string in combination with NYSIIS to its reverse. The use of the reverse of the original string is to counter the sensitivity phonetic-encoding algorithms usually exhibit to errors that occur in the beginning of the string, as demonstrated by the example of "Dooper" vs "Cooper."

It is evident that the use of multiple phonetic algorithms produces an excess of encoded records. The number of produced records raises even higher, considering that we also use fake records in terms of noise to further enhance privacy. We employ noise injection, so that information is hidden by the uncertainty produced for the entire dataset.

In particular, given a set of different phonetic algorithms F, a dataset of size r and inserting f fake records, the size r' of the resulting dataset is equal to

$$r' = r \times F + f \tag{13.3}$$

As our approach significantly increases the dataset size, it also requires increased processing power. To address this issue, we employ a parallel engine suitable for big data processing, and, as we show in Section 13.5, using a small cluster we result in an improved performance in terms of matching quality and time. The processing framework of our choice is Apache Spark [5].

The procedure described thereafter may be used with other PPM methods.

Algorithm 1: Actions taken by Alice and Bob to encode their data

---

   Input:
   - **r:** Plaintext dataset
   Output:
   - **d:** De-identified dataset
1 $d_0 \leftarrow \emptyset$;
2 **foreach** *phonetic_algorithm* P_i **do**
3 | $d_1 \leftarrow$ Map $(P_i$ (r));
4 | $d_0 \leftarrow$ Union (d_0, d_1);
5 **end**
6 $d_2 \leftarrow$ Parallelize (RandomPhonetic ());
7 $d_3 \leftarrow$ Union (d_0, d_2);
8 $d_4 \leftarrow$ Map (SHA1 (d_3));
9 $d \leftarrow d_4$.orderBy (rand ());
10 Collect (d)

13.4.2 Protocol operation

At the beginning of the linkage process, it is sufficient for Alice and Bob to agree on a set of common fields appearing in both their data that are to be used as matching fields. Alice and Bob's data do not have to conform to the exact same schema and usually exhibit heterogeneity. No prior knowledge is required by either party, and appropriate privacy preserving schema matching algorithms [30,31] may be deployed to determine these matching attributes without compromising the privacy of either party.

Next, each party prepares separately its own data for matching following Algorithm 1. First, using a *Map* operation, each of the matching fields is converted to its phonetic equivalent using each of the phonetic algorithms employed (lines 1–5). Afterwards, random fake phonetic codes using a *parallelize* operation are generated (line 6). Then, these two volumes of data are merged using a *Union* operation (line 7). Next, all codes are encrypted through a secure hash function, e.g., SHA1 using again a *Map* operation (line 8). Finally, the entire dataset is randomly sorted to ensure that Carol cannot infer which phonetic codes refer to actual real-world entities (line 9).

At this point, we will discuss some details over the fake generation procedure. As previous work shows [32], the time for on-the-fly fake generation in a parallel environment overwhelms the total execution time of the procedure. This is because parallel engines for big data, Spark included, consider that instead of moving data, which is expensive due to its voluminous nature, computations should be moved instead. The fake generation procedure in our algorithm opposes this principle, as data is generated in parallel at each node and then they are merged with the corpus of the real data. However, this is the cost to be paid for increased security. A computationally cheaper alternative would be to precompute fakes and distribute them before computation by

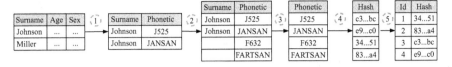

Figure 13.1 Data preparations by Alice

storing them, for instance, in Hadoop-distributed file system (HDFS), so as to avoid transfer in real time. However, this could impose security risks.

To further clarify the preparations at Alice and Bob, we use the following example.

Example 13.1. *As illustrated in Figure 13.1, let us assume that Alice holds two rows in her database and that she has agreed to privately match them with Bob's data using the phonetic-based PPM method we propose using the "Surname" field as the single matching field. We also consider that Alice uses NYSIIS and Soundex as her phonetic algorithms. To this end, the following will occur:*

1. *Alice generates the Soundex and NYSIIS encodings for the matching field (Figure 13.1(1)), thus transforming ,e.g., "Johnson" into "J525" and "JANSAN."*
2. *Then, she generates a number of random fake codes which, in our example, are "F632" and "FARTSAN" (Figure 13.1(2)).*
3. *All codes are encrypted through a secure hash function, i.e., SHA1 (Figure 13.1(3)).*
4. *The created table is randomly sorted to ensure that Carol cannot infer which cipher codes refer to actual records (Figure 13.1(4)).*
5. *A unique identifier in the domain [1..4] is assigned to both actual and fake encoded fields. At this point, Alice maintains two tables. One, where each row consists of two fields: the unique identifier and the cipher (Figure 13.1(5)), and a second one, mapping the multiple encodings of original records to the real ones.*

The protocol proceeds with the data exchanges between parties and matching, which is carried out by Carol, as illustrated in Figure 13.2.

1. Alice and Bob send their encrypted data through a secure channel to Carol.
2. Carol performs the join operation on the encrypted phonetic codes each party has send. Carol's role is important in this setup, since it refrains either Alice or Bob from acquiring information from each other's dataset. Neither of the two dataholders is aware of the others dataset size nor of the data transmitted to Carol. On the other hand, neither Carol has full access to information, since she only collects and joins encrypted phonetic codes.
3. Carol returns the source's identifiers for the encrypted phonetic codes which succeeded at the matching operation, through a secure channel.

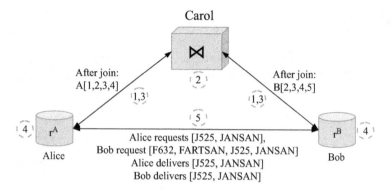

Figure 13.2   Overview of the phonetic matching protocol

4. Each source determines which of these identifiers belong to its own set of actual records. This is an important step, because a party omits from the results the codes which reflect to fake records and those which are highly distinctive.
5. Sources contact directly each other asking for rows the fields of which have the resulting identifiers. Finally, each source delivers to the other the rows that are not tagged as descriptive and that exist in their actual datasets.

13.4.3 Privacy discussion

In this protocol, we assume that all participants exhibit an honest but curious behavior without collusion. This means that they do not try to deviate from the protocol, but they try to learn as much as possible based on the information they gather following the protocol's steps, without cooperating with each other. Using a third party, each source is unable to determine data held by other sources. It is only aware of its own private data. Carol is neither aware of the actual data nor of the amount of data residing in each source, thus becoming unable to perform a frequency attack on these data. This is mainly due to two reasons. First, data reaching Carol are encrypted. Second, not all data represents actual records in the source due to the fake Soundex records injected. The additional records inserted may burden the transmission channel and the participating parties. However, this serves our purpose of providing privacy. The comparison of the encrypted phonetic codes takes place at Carol in order to prevent either source from inferring information upon the size of the dataset of the other party. Furthermore, no information may be leaked from intermediate data, since no such data are generated.

Example 13.2. *Let us continue Example 13.1. Based on their data, each of Alice and Bob creates a table which consists of the matching attribute and its Soundex code. The procedure for Alice is illustrated in Figure 13.1, while Table 13.2 illustrates Bob's data. Bob wishes to match data with ids 2–5, since row 1 holds a fake Soundex code.*

According to our protocol, Bob and Alice send to Carol columns "Id" and "Hash" of their datasets. Carol receives the tables from both sources and joins them. If Carol

Table 13.2   *Bob's data*

Id	Phonetic	Surname	Hash
1	A100		bb...12
2	F632	Fortson	34...51
3	FARTSAN	Fortson	83...a4
4	J525	Johnsen	c3...bc
5	JANSAN	JANSAN	e9...c0

attempted to disclose some information, she would fail, since she would not know which records reflect real-world entities and which are fake. Thus, she would not be able to infer the size of either party's record set. Even in the case she assumed that all entities were real, she would not be able to infer the actual data either due to both the secure encryption used and also the inherent information suppression properties of the phonetic encodings.

After Carol performs a JOIN operation over the encrypted phonetic codes, she returns the ids of the matching codes to their corresponding owners, i.e., A[1, 2, 3, 4] for Alice and B[2, 3, 4, 5] for Bob, as shown in Figure 13.2. Bob recognizes ids B[2, 3, 4, 5] as correct matches, while Alice recognizes A[1, 2] as correct matches, which eventually correspond to a single real-world record, and A[3, 4] as false positives, since its phonetic code resulted from fake data.

Then, both Alice and Bob ask each other for the data represented by the matching codes. At this point, Bob asks Alice for data represented by the hashes "34...51," "83...a4," "c3...bc," "e9...c0" which correspond to phonetic codes "F632," "FARTSAN," "J525" and "JANSAN," respectively. Similarly, Alice asks for "e9...c0" and "2f...e5" that correspond to "J525" and "JANSAN." Finally, the two sources exchange the records based on the intersection of common hash codes, which in this case is "e9...c0" and "2f...e5," i.e., records "Johnson" of Alice and "Johnsen" of Bob.

13.5   Empirical evaluation

In this section, we present the experimental evaluation of our approach. We aim at assessing the increase in matching performance, using multiple phonetic codes and to compare the time consumed to perform the same tasks using both a sequential algorithm and its parallelized approach.

13.5.1   Experimental setup

We have implemented simulations of both the parallel approach we propose and the original sequential algorithm using Anaconda Python 4.3. We tested both implementations using the Okeanos IaaS academic service.[1] Our infrastructure comprises four virtual machines, each of them having one core. For the parallel algorithm we use one machine, having 6 GB of RAM and two cores, as the Spark cluster master. The four other machines operate as workers. These are identical, featuring 4 GB of RAM, but we deploy the default setup that allocates only 1 GB per worker. We tested three different Spark clusters, with 1, 2, 3 and all 4 worker machines. In all parallel setups, data are read directly from the file system and no indexes are used. For the sequential version, we use one of the worker machines which we equipped with MariaDB for holding and joining data, indexed to further increase performance.

We use a dataset originating from the North Carolina voters database.[2] The attributes—last name, first name, middle name, city of residence and precinct description—were chosen as matching attributes. We assume that the attributes chosen comprise a candidate key and deduplicate the dataset using the respective attribute combination. After deduplication, we generated samples, forming two databases so that 25% of their records is common.

We assume that the first generated database of each pair belongs to Alice, while the second one to Bob. Our samples resulted in databases comprising 50, 100, 200, 400, 800, 1,600 and 3,200 thousand records each. Since we are interested in linking low quality data, we corrupted Bob's common records [33]. The corrupted records contain one error per row. With equal probability, the error may be either a character insertion, deletion or substitution.

13.5.2   Experimental results

We will now discuss the performance of the proposed methodology with respect to matching accuracy and time performance. To assess matching accuracy, we consider precision and recall as used by the information retrieval community. Precision is defined as the proportion of the number of relevant records retrieved, to the total number of matched records. Recall refers to the number of relevant records retrieved divided by the total number of existing relevant records. With respect to time performance, we include a comparison with the sequential counterpart of our algorithm implemented as outlined above.

13.5.2.1   Algorithm combination selection

The first set of experiments is targeted toward selecting the most suitable phonetic encoding algorithm combination, which elevates matching performance. For this purpose, we examine the behavior of the two most widely used phonetic encoding algorithms [8], namely, Soundex and NYSIIS. A common issue of these algorithms is the fact that, alterations in the first letter of the encoded string have an impact on the resulting encoding. To this end, we consider various configurations of both forward and reversed inputs for Soundex and NYSIIS. For this case, we do not consider the injection of fake records; since these are randomly generated, a fact that could refrain

---

[1] Available at https://okeanos.grnet.gr/home/
[2] Available at http://dl.ncsbe.gov/index.html?prefix=data/

us from resulting into safe conclusions. The reported experiments were run on the 200K records dataset.

The results of this evaluation are illustrated in Figure 13.3(a). The horizontal axis hosts the evaluated method, with SNDX indicating Soundex and NYS standing for NYSIIS. An "R." prefix means that the input string has been reversed. The vertical axis is linearly scaled and stands for precision and recall. The highest performance is achieved when using classical Soundex in combination with reverse NYSIIS. This way errors occurring in the first letter of a word do not affect the phonetic algorithm with the reversed input, compensating the failure of the normal input. In all cases, precision is very high, reaching 1. Based on the matching quality superiority of Soundex and reverse input NYSIIS, we use this combination for the rest of our evaluation.

13.5.2.2 Matching accuracy

We have measured matching precision and recall for two different cases: (i) without any noise addition and (ii) with the addition of noise. In this first case, we use all available datasets, while in the second, we measure precision for various noise configurations for the 200K dataset. For simplicity in the second case, we have only employed Soundex like fake records.

The results for the first case are illustrated in Figure 13.3(b). The horizontal axis holds the size of each dataset, while the vertical one is scaled from zero to one and stands for precision and recall. We can easily see in this case that the drop in precision and recall are minimal, as the dataset size increases. In particular, precision is in the area of 0.99, while recall ranges between 0.72 for the smallest dataset to 0.708 for the largest one. Thus, we deduce that the dataset size has a minimal impact on our method's matching accuracy.

Figure 13.3(c) illustrates the effect of injecting fake records on matching performance. The horizontal axis designates the percentage of fake records inserted in the 200K, where, for example, 100% means that another 200K records were inserted by each party. The vertical axis, again, stands for precision and recall. It is evident that the addition of noise does not affect either precision or recall at all. Both measures maintain stable values regardless of the amount of injected noise.

13.5.2.3 Time performance

Let us now examine the behavior of the sequential and parallel algorithms in terms of time performance starting with a setup where there is no generation of fake records. We measure the performance of the private matching method with respect to different dataset sizes, while excluding the overhead of generating the infused fake records. We measure the speedup achieved by each parallel setup, defined as the ratio of the sequential execution time to the parallel execution time for the 50K–400K datasets (Figure 13.3(d)) and execution times for the parallel setup for all datasets (Figure 13.3(e)). In both cases, the vertical axis is linearly scaled.

As we may see in Figure 13.3(d), an increase in the input dataset sizes leads to an increasing speedup when the parallel version is employed. Sequential execution time, in this case, starts at 176.27 s for matching 50K against 50K records and reaches 1,040.35 s, when matching 400K against 400K records. The corresponding times for

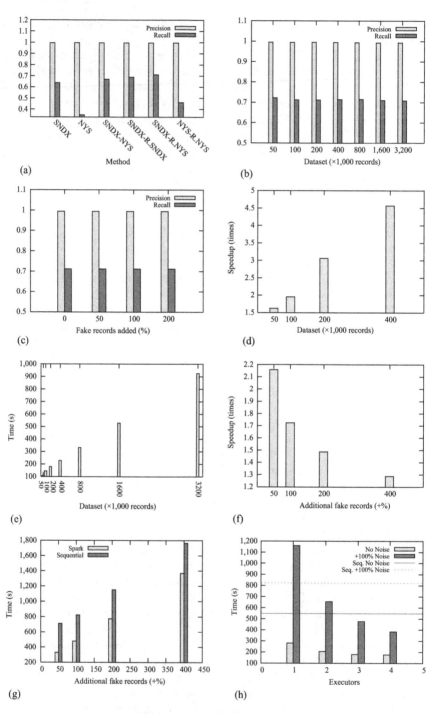

*Figure 13.3   Evaluation of time and matching performance: (a) prec./rec.–method,
(b) prec./rec.–dataset, (c) prec./rec.–noise, (d) no noise–speedup, (e)
no noise–execution time, (f) noise–speedup, (g) noise–execution time,
(h) number of executors vs time*

the parallel implementation are illustrated in Figure 13.3(e). Both the parallelized algorithms, and its sequential version, which exploits the use of the databases index, exhibit linear behavior with respect to the dataset size. However, the sequential algorithm has a steeper gradient, a fact that explains the speedup achieved by the parallel framework.

In the next set of experiments, we study the behavior of the parallel algorithm when fake records are injected. For illustration purposes, Figure 13.3(f) and 13.3(g) includes the results, with the 200K dataset and three workers, for speedup and execution times, respectively. The horizontal axis stands for the percentage of fake records generated with respect to the dataset size. The vertical axes represent speedup and time, respectively. The parallel algorithm outperforms the sequential one in this case as well. However, we can also see that the speedup decreases as the amount of fake records inserted increases. This is due to the fact that new records are generated and have to be transferred within the cluster nodes, which is an inherently expensive operation. To address this issue and improve performance, as we said earlier, the fake datasets could be precomputed and distributed through a distributed file system. However, here, to illustrate the worst case scenario in terms of performance, we have decided to exhibit a scenario where all calculations take place on-the-fly.

Finally, we have performed a third set of experiments to further investigate the behavior of our parallel method with respect to the employed workers in the cluster (Figure 13.3(h)). For this purpose, we have also employed an additional, fourth node. We again use the 200K records dataset and examine how the number of nodes used in our cluster affects execution time in both cases where there is no noise and with the injection of 100% fake records. We employ four setups for each of these settings: first, we utilize only a single worker, then two, then three and finally four workers, comparing with the behavior of the sequential versions, which are illustrated as a light gray bar line for the case of no fake additions and as a dark gray bar for the case of noise addition. The horizontal axis holds the number of nodes used in each case, while the vertical axis represents execution time in seconds. As we may see, utilizing more workers infers a clearly positive impact to the PPRL process in terms of execution time. Furthermore, in the case of noise absence, there is a greater speedup, even when a single worker is used. When noise is injected, more than two workers are required to achieve reduced execution time due to the transfer of the generated noise datasets within the cluster.

13.6 Conclusions and future work

In this chapter, we have presented a cost-efficient parallel protocol for performing qualitative approximate PPM based on the use of multiple phonetic encodings, combining the Soundex and the NYSIIS phonetic algorithms. Furthermore, we proposed using the first algorithm to encode the original text and the second for its reverse. As we have experimentally shown using the Apache Spark platform, our algorithm efficiently handles large volumes of data while improving the quality of the matching process results compared to approaches using a single encoding algorithm.

As a next step, we plan at parallelizing a privacy preserving blocking method [34], which will quickly prune out unlikely to match candidate pairs of records, and incorporating it into our workflow so as to further improve the efficiency of the whole privacy-preserving linkage process.

References

[1]   Christen P. A survey of indexing techniques for scalable record linkage and deduplication. IEEE Transactions on Knowledge and Data Engineering. 2012;24(9):1537–1555.

[2]   Odell M, Russell R. The Soundex coding system. US Patents. 1918;1261167.

[3]   Karakasidis A, Verykios VS. Privacy Preserving Record Linkage Using Phonetic Codes. In: BCI; 2009. p. 101–106.

[4]   Taft RL. Name Search Techniques. Issue 1 of Special report. New York, NY: State Identification and Intelligence System; 1970.

[5]   Zaharia M, Chowdhury M, Franklin MJ, *et al.* Spark: Cluster Computing with Working Sets. In: HotCloud'10; 2010. p. 95.

[6]   Karakasidis A, Koloniari G. Phonetics-Based Parallel Privacy Preserving Record Linkage. In: Advances on P2P, Parallel, Grid, Cloud and Internet Computing. Cham: Springer International Publishing; 2018. p. 179–190.

[7]   Elmagarmid AK, Ipeirotis PG, Verykios VS. Duplicate Record Detection: A Survey. IEEE Transactions on Knowledge and Data Engineering. 2007; 19(1):1–16.

[8]   Christen P. Data Matching. Data-Centric Systems and Applications. Berlin, Heidelberg: Springer-Verlag; 2012.

[9]   Clifton C, Kantarcioglu M, Doan A, *et al.* Privacy-Preserving Data Integration and Sharing. In: ACM DMKD; 2004. p. 19–26.

[10] Christen P, Vatsalan D, Verykios VS. Challenges for Privacy Preservation in Data Integration. Journal of Data and Information Quality. 2014;5(1–2):4: 1–4:3.

[11] Van Eycken E, Haustermans K, Buntinx F, *et al.* Evaluation of the encryption procedure and record linkage in the Belgian National Cancer Registry. Archives of Public Health. 2000;58(6):281–294.

[12] Churches T, Christen P. Blind Data Linkage Using n-Gram Similarity Comparisons. In: PAKDD; 2004. p. 121–126.

[13] Verykios VS, Karakasidis A, Mitrogiannis VK. Privacy preserving record linkage approaches. International Journal of Data Mining, Modelling and Management. 2009;1(2):206–221.

[14] Song DX, Wagner D, Perrig A. Practical Techniques for Searches on Encrypted Data. In: IEEE Symposium on Security and Privacy; 2000. p. 44–55.

[15] Du W, Atallah MJ. Protocols for Secure Remote Database Access with Approximate Matching. In: E-Commerce Security and Privacy; 2001. p. 87–111.

[16] Schnell R, Bachteler T, Reiher J. Privacy preserving record linkage using Bloom filters. BMC Medical Informatics and Decision Making. 2009;9(41):1–11.

[17] Kuzu M, Kantarcioglu M, Durham E, *et al.* A Constraint Satisfaction Cryptanalysis of Bloom Filters in Private Record Linkage. In: PETS; 2011. p. 226–245.
[18] Kissner L, Song D. Privacy-Preserving Set Perations. In: In Advances in Cryptology – CRYPTO 2005, LNCS. Springer; 2005. p. 241–257.
[19] Inan A, Kantarcioglu M, Ghinita G, *et al.* Private Record Matching Using Differential Privacy. In: ACM EDBT; 2010. p. 123–134.
[20] Snae C, Diaz B. An interface for mining genealogical nominal data using the concept of linkage and a hybrid name matching algorithm. Journal of 3D-Forum Society. 2002;16(1):142–147.
[21] Philips L. Hanging on the metaphone. Computer Language. 1990;7(12):235–256.
[22] Kolb L, Thor A, Rahm E. Dedoop: Efficient deduplication with Hadoop. Proceedings of the VLDB Endowment. 2012;5(12):1878–1881.
[23] Karapiperis D, Verykios VS. A distributed near-optimal LSH-based framework for privacy-preserving record linkage. Computer Science and Information Systems. 2014;11(2):745–763.
[24] Franke M, Sehili Z, Rahm E. Parallel Privacy Preserving Record Linkage Using LSH-based Blocking. In: IoTBDS; 2018. p. 195–203.
[25] Bargavi C, Blessa BPM. Data linkage for BigData using Hadoop MapReduce. International Journal of Computer Science and Technology (IJCST). 2015;6(1):93–95.
[26] Shanahan JG, Dai L. Large Scale Distributed Data Science Using Apache Spark. In: ACM SIGKDD; 2015. p. 2323–2324.
[27] Pita R, Pinto C, Melo P, *et al.* A Spark-based Workflow for Probabilistic Record Linkage of Healthcare Data. In: EDBT/ICDT Workshops; 2015. p. 17–26.
[28] Christen P. A Comparison of Personal Name Matching: Techniques and Practical Issues. In: Workshop on Mining Complex Data, held at IEEE ICDM'06. Hong Kong; 2006. p. 290–294.
[29] Salloum S, Dautov R, Chen X, *et al.* Big data analytics on Apache Spark. International Journal of Data Science and Analytics. 2016;1(3–4):145–164.
[30] Cruz IF, Tamassia R, Yao D. Privacy-Preserving Schema Matching Using Mutual Information. In: Data and Applications Security XXI. Springer; 2007. p. 93–94.
[31] Scannapieco M, Figotin I, Bertino E, *et al.* Privacy Preserving Schema and Data Matching. In: ACM SIGMOD; 2007. p. 653–664.
[32] Karakasidis A, Koloniari G. Phonetics-Based Parallel Privacy Preserving Record Linkage. In: International Conference on P2P, Parallel, Grid, Cloud and Internet Computing. Springer; 2017. p. 179–190.
[33] Bachteler T, Reiher J. A Test Data Generator for Evaluating Record Linkage Methods. German RLC Work. Paper No. wp-grlc-2012-01; 2012.
[34] Karakasidis A, Koloniari G, Verykios VS. Scalable Blocking for Privacy Preserving Record Linkage. In: ACM SIGKDD; 2015. p. 527–536.

Chapter 14

Deep learning architecture for big data analytics in detecting intrusions and malicious URL

N.B. Harikrishnan[1], R. Vinayakumar[1], K.P. Soman[1], Prabaharan Poornachandran[2], B. Annappa[3], and Mamoun Alazab[4]

Security attacks are one of the major threats in today's world. These attacks exploit the vulnerabilities in a system or online sites for financial gain. By doing so, there arises a huge loss in revenue and reputation for both government and private firms. These attacks are generally carried out through malware interception, intrusions, phishing uniform resource locator (URL). There are techniques like signature-based detection, anomaly detection, state full protocol to detect intrusions, blacklisting for detecting phishing URL. Even though these techniques claim to thwart cyberattacks, they often fail to detect new attacks or variants of existing attacks. The second reason why these techniques fail is the dynamic nature of attacks and lack of annotated data. In such a situation, we need to propose a system which can capture the changing trends of cyberattacks to some extent. For this, we used supervised and unsupervised learning techniques. The growing problem of intrusions and phishing URLs generates a need for a reliable architectural-based solution that can efficiently identify intrusions and phishing URLs. This chapter aims to provide a comprehensive survey of intrusion and phishing URL detection techniques and deep learning. It presents and evaluates a highly effective deep learning architecture to automat intrusion and phishing URL Detection. The proposed method is an artificial intelligence (AI)-based hybrid architecture for an organization which provides supervised and unsupervised-based solutions to tackle intrusions, and phishing URL detection. The prototype model uses various classical machine learning (ML) classifiers and deep learning architectures. The research specifically focuses on detecting and classifying intrusions and phishing URL detection.

[1]Center for Computational Engineering and Networking (CEN), Amrita School of Engineering, Amrita Vishwa Vidyapeetham, India
[2]Centre for Cyber Security Systems and Networks, Amrita School of Engineering, Amritapuri, Amrita Vishwa Vidyapeetham, India
[3]Department of Computer Science and Engineering, National Institute of Technology Karnataka, India
[4]College of Engineering, IT & Environment, Charles Darwin University, Australia

14.1   Introduction

Over the years, the internet has served as a powerful medium for communication. In today's world in order to hold a successful venture, it is mandatory to have a web presence and proper space to manage the files and the data. The proper management of data and files is inevitable without computers. Despite these advantages of the systems that we use, there is always an attempt to access, modify and misuse the data of an organization/institution/individual. Data is the vital part of any organization, institution or individual. So there arises the question—Is there any unauthorized access to the system? If yes, what are the possible ways to detect and prevent the unauthorized entries? Intrusion detection (ID) is the approach to detect the unauthorized access, abuse and misuse of computer systems by both external and insider intruders. The proliferation of heterogeneous computer network resulted from the task of detecting the intruders very challenging. Several prototypes of ID and phishing URL detection have been deployed in organizations on an experimental basis. But none of them provides an absolute solution to tackle the problem of detecting intruders. The fundamental assumption in an ID system (IDS) is that the behavior of an intruder is notably different from that of a legitimate user. The conventional techniques used to detect intrusions are the statistical anomaly and rule-based misuse models. However, the conventional techniques easily fail in detecting new attacks.

The commercial tools existing in the market are based on statistical measures or threshold computing approaches that use traffic parameters such as packet length, inter-arrival time and flow size as features to learn the network traffic patterns in a particular time window. The commercial system may limit the performance in detecting the complex attacks mainly because the statistical measures are computed based on packet header and packet length.

In recent days, to detect and classify the phishing activities from benign characteristics, self-learning systems are being used. In recent days, to detect and classify the phishing activities from benign characteristics, self-learning systems are being used. Self-learning systems is an ML method that is either supervised or unsupervised. Both supervised and unsupervised approaches use a large corpus of phishing and benign connection records to learn the network traffic behaviors with the aim to distinguish between the benign and attack connections in a network. Self-learning system has the capability to detect the unknown intrusions that help in taking the necessary countermeasures in a timely manner. ML methods are current prominent methods used largely for IDS. These ML-based solutions to real-time IDS are not effective mainly due to the model's outputs in a high false positive rate (FPR) and ineffective in identifying the novel intrusions [1]. The main reason is that the ML models learn the attack patterns of simple features of transmission control protocol (TCP)/internet protocol (IP) packets locally. However, the recent development of ML models resulted in a deep model of ML called deep learning. Deep learning models have achieved significant results in various long-standing AI tasks in the fields of natural language processing (NLP), image processing and speech recognition [2]. It has two essential characteristics: (1) ability to learn the complex hierarchical feature representation of TCP/IP packets globally. (2) Ability to memorize the past information in large sequences of TCP/IP packets. The performance of deep learning methods are transferred to various tasks in cybersecurity; ID [3–7], traffic identification [8–11], binary analysis [12], domain generation algorithms analysis [13–16], URL analysis [17] and malware classification [18–21]. Moreover, recently [22] outlined the taxonomies of shallow and deep learning algorithms to ID. Deep learning which is a subset of ML does not require the feature engineering part which is mandatory in the classical ML technique. Deep learning learns from the raw data. This can be seen as an advantage of deep learning because in most of the cases, choosing the right features plays a crucial role in the problem.

Considering the effectiveness of supervised and unsupervised learning techniques, in this paper, the authors highlight the efficiency of ML-based methods and unsupervised learning technique in detecting and classifying intrusions and phishing URLs. The paper is ordered as follows: Section 14.2 deals with the related works, Section 14.3 highlights the background of classical ML technique and deep learning technique used in the work. Section 14.4 discusses ID using supervised algorithms, Section 14.5 discusses ID using unsupervised algorithms, Section 14.7 includes details about the proposed architecture, and conclusion and future work directions are placed in Section 14.8.

14.2 Related works

14.2.1 Network intrusion detection systems (NIDSs)

Network intrusion detection systems (NIDSs) play an important part of any network security architecture with the rise of fraudulent activities like spam emails and malware attack. There is a huge amount of network traffic data accumulated day by day. A manual way of monitoring the connection records has become impossible. The inefficiency of conventional methods in monitoring the network records resulted in several cyberattacks. Cyberattacks are launched by a computer or group of computers against a network, a computer or multiple computers. The goal of these attacks is either to disable the target computer or to get admin privileges so as to control the system. Attackers achieve these goals by the malicious software, phishing URL, denial of service and even by which fooling the target computer into joining a compromised network which is often called as man-in-the-middle-attack. The solution to this situation is to develop a strong IDS. An IDS continuously monitors the network connection records and alerts the system administrator or network administrator of malicious activities. But the conventional methods like signature-based detection system rely on human intervention to thwart the different kinds of attacks.

Signature-based detection systems compare the network traffic features with the set of existing signatures in the database. If the signature matches then those connection records are blocked. The main drawback of the signature-based detection system is its inefficiency in detecting new kinds of attacks. Other means of detecting intrusions follows anomaly-based detection. Even though these can detect new kinds of attacks but often result in high FPRs. This situation calls for an automatic detection of malicious connection records and prevents them from affecting the system. Wherever there is automation, the research turns in the direction of ML. But the performance of ML techniques heavily depends on the training dataset. But in the case of cybersecurity, there is no data set which generalizes the behavior of all the attacks. This is because attacks are dynamic, and its pattern changes continuously. In such a situation, the supervised learning techniques are not viable in the practical scenario. Other approaches depend on training a large volume of network data. The issue here is, there is no unified data set that captures the generalities of all the malicious connections. At the same time, graph-based methods have shown promising results especially in detecting anomalies. The perspective of sub-dense graph detection has widely used for fake review identification, anomaly detection, etc. In the case of fake review identification, detecting fake review is formulated as a dense sub-graph identification problem. Based on the motivation from dense sub-graph detection problem, researchers have come up with a framework called multidimensional zoom (M-ZOOM) which detects the sub-dense tensor/graph from a higher order tensor. The highlights of M-ZOOM framework are scalability, provably accurate, flexible, effective as mentioned in the base paper [23]. We make use of this framework to model ID as an unsupervised learning problem.

Researchers have introduced various ML-based solutions to NIDS. Applying ML for the enhancement of improvement in detecting the attacks is largely studied in recent days. This section delves into the detailed studies of ML-based solutions to IDS till date and disclosed with the issues of the KDD-Cup-99 data set.

Most research studies considered IDS—a classification task that finds a separating plane for the behaviors of normal and attacks in network traffic data. A large number of methods introduced following the first paper about IDS. In that, ML and data-mining techniques appeared as prominent methods that are largely used toward IDS. However, their performance is less in comparison to other areas as IDS is an evolving problem with new types of attacks. Due to this, IDS has been a vivid area of research for the past 50 years.

The openly available data set for creating an effective ML model for ID is very little. A few data sets exist, but each suffers from its own issues. A most commonly occurred issue is that the data set have failed to represent the real-time network traffic characteristics. KDD-Cup-99 is the most commonly used standard IDS data set for benchmarking the performance of ML models. KDD-Cup-99 data set was used as part of the ID challenge conducted by third International Knowledge Discovery and Data-Mining Tools Competition. The aim of the challenge was to classify the connection records as either benign or attack. Totally, 24 entries were participated and submitted their results. Most of the best performed entries used decision tree and its variants. After the challenge, the KDD-Cup-99 data set was most commonly used data set for evaluation of various ML. Most of the research studies used 10% data set for ID in the case of feature reduction. Other few studies have used their own custom-built data sets. These custom-built in the data set were constructed using the random selection of connection records from 10% train and test connection records.

After the KDD-Cup-99 challenge, many research studies have used KDD-Cup-99 for ID. These studies are not directly comparable to winning entries of KDD-Cup-99 challenge mainly due to the reason that the research studies have used variations of

KDD-Cup-99. With misuse detection context, Sabhnani and Serpen [24] analyzed the effectiveness of various ML algorithms for the same KDD-Cup-99 challenge data set. In addition, the authors proposed the multi-expert classifier and achieved the enhancement in false alarm rate in comparison to the KDD-Cup-99 winning entries. They claimed with various experiments using any ML classifiers achieving acceptable detection rate for low-frequency attacks (U2R nearly 30% and R2L nearly 10%) may not be possible in the context of the misuse detection. The following published results are not directly comparable. Sinclair *et al.* [25] used domain knowledge with ML approaches particularly genetic algorithms and DTs to create the rule for expert systems that classify the network connections as benign and phishing in expert systems.

The task of detecting intrusions is modeled as a classification task in most of the research papers. The goal is to find a separating plane that separates the normal and phishing behavior in the traffic data. ID has been a challenging problem and Denning [26] paved a way for several research papers. In most of the research papers, data mining and ML-related methods are widely used. However, the performance of these methods is less compared to other techniques due to the dynamic and changing nature of intrusion data sets. At the same time, modeling ID as a graph-based problem has shown promising results. Graph partition problems have wide applications like clustering and detection of a dense graph in social and biological networks. There are rich resources in graph-partition problems. Andersen *et al.* [27] have presented a variation of PageRank with a specified starting for local partitioning algorithm. Leskovec and Mcauley [28] have formulated the task of detecting social circles in a network as a node clustering problem on a user's ego network. Subgraph-based fraud detection in the area of telecommunications has been used in [29]. Akoglu *et al.* [30] have proposed an algorithm named Oddball for detecting anomalies in a weighted graph. The study in [30] focused mainly on undirected graphs and can be extended to directed graphs. The study by Beutel *et al.* [31] proposed an efficient method called CopyCatch that analyzes the social graph between users and pages and also the time at which likes are created. By identifying the lockstep page like patterns in the graph, the illegal page likes to different pages can be identified. Researchers in [32] have used the concept of SMR co-clustering for detecting the suspicious network connection records in the KDD-Cup-99 data set. Research has also moved in the direction of tensor decomposition based methods. Tensor decomposition opens a new way of analyzing the network traffic data and overcomes the shortcomings of the existing methods in the field of security [23]. Tensor is a multidimensional array and tensor decomposition breaks down a tensor such as a log file into a set of components. Shin *et al.* [23] proposed a framework called M-ZOOM to identify the dense blocks in a tensor. In this work, we use the framework provided by [23] for classifying intrusions as either benign or phishing.

14.2.2 *Related works on phishing URL detection*

Phishing websites "seem" like genuine, but they direct to malicious contents and trick the users by fraudulent activities [33]. The most commonly used method to carry out different attack is rogue website. In this attack, unsolicited contents are displayed in the form of SQL injection, malware interception, phishing, etc. This leads to losing sensitive information in the hands of fraudsters. World Wide Web is the largest platforms that attackers use. Attackers implement phishing code and broadcast it across the web [34].

This highlights the need of an efficient algorithm to circumvent these phishing activities. So developing an effective phishing URL detection system will abate the increasing cyber threat. The common method used to detect the phishing URL is blacklisting. Blacklists are database of phishing URL's. The database has to be updated continuously in order to handle new phishing URLs. Attackers modify the phishing URL through obfuscation so that it "seems" legitimate and thereby fools users. Garera *et al.* [35] have mentioned four types obfuscation. They are IP-based obfuscation of host, domain-based obfuscation of host, obfuscating the host with misspelling and large host names. These obfuscation technique acts as a layer to hide the phishing nature of URL. Blacklisting methods are easy to implement and at the same time easy to fail for new variants of phishing URL attacks and also require human involvement to update phishing URL repository.

The advance in ML techniques brought a new outlook to tackle the problem [35–38]. ML techniques learn the behavior of phishing URL's from the training data. In addition to this, it learns a prediction function to classify a new URL as phishing or benign. The advantage of ML-based method over blacklisting is the ability to generalize for new URLs. In ML-based methods, choosing the right features is the tedious task. Some of the featured engineering techniques is to extract host based or lexical features for classifying URL as either benign or phishing. Kan and Thi [39] have used ML techniques for URL classification. The strength of deep learning over classical ML techniques is the ability to learn from the raw data. Feature engineering part is not necessary in deep learning. Researchers have highlighted the effectiveness of artificial neural network over classical ML technique for the detection of phishing URL.

14.3 Background

14.3.1 Deep neural network

Deep learning is a subset of ML. The conventional ML technique requires feature engineering technique, i.e., we have to choose right features in order to obtain appropriate results and this purely depends on domain knowledge, whereas deep learning does not require feature engineering part. It learns from the raw data.

Deep neural networks (DNNs) are distinguished from the shallow networks by their depth, that is, the number of hidden layers a neural network has. A shallow network is composed of one input and one output layer, whereas DNN contains input layer, several hidden layers and an output layer. These hidden layers help to recognize more complex features. The main highlight in deep learning networks compared to

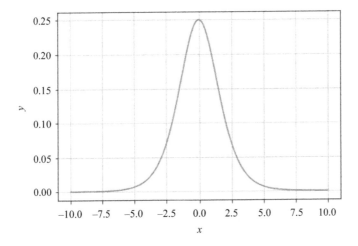

Figure 14.1   Derivative of sigmoid function

classical ML is the ability of DNN to learn the features by itself. In any deep learning architecture, there is a forward propagation, backward propagation and minimizing the loss function with respect to its parameters. These parameters are weights and bias. The activation function used plays a key role in training a neural network. One of the difficulty when activation function like *sigmoid* (σ) is used is the problem of vanishing gradient.

As a result, when the number of layers increases, it becomes difficult to tune the parameters of different layers in neural network, and the problem of vanishing gradient becomes more significant. In Figure 14.1, the derivative of *sigmoid* function (σ) is almost zero for high positive and negative values in the domain. This leads to vanishing gradient.

This problem is overcome by using *ReLU* activation function. The mathematical representation of *ReLU* is given below:

$$f(x) = \max(0, x) \tag{14.1}$$

The derivative of *ReLU* function is 1 if $x > 0$ and 0 if $x < 0$. The gradient has a constant value for $x > 0$; this reduces the chance of the gradient to vanish. Since the gradient of *ReLU* is constant, it boosts the learning during training the neural network. In *ReLU* for $x <= 0$ the gradient is 0, the zero gradient is an advantage since it allows sparsity. In the case of *sigmoid* function, the chance of generating nonzero values is more which makes the connection representation in neural network dense while training. Sparsity always has an advantage over dense representations. A three-layer neural network is represented in Figure 14.2.

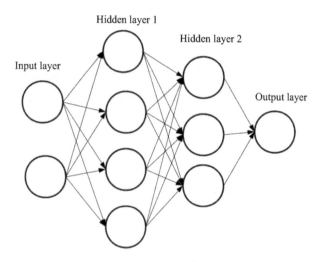

Figure 14.2   Three-layer neural network

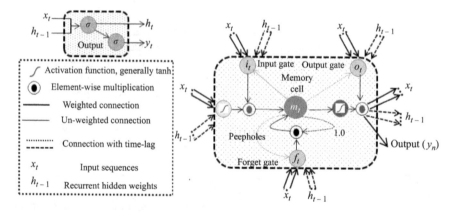

Figure 14.3   Architecture of RNN unit (left) and LSTM memory block (right)

14.3.2   Recurrent neural network

Unlike classical feedforward networks [40], recurrent neural network (RNN) contains a self-recurrent connection unit which helps in sequence modeling by carrying out time-related information from one time-step to another. The architecture of simple RNN unit is shown in Figure 14.3. The self-recurrent connection in RNN helps in learning the temporal dependencies across time-steps. This nature of the RNN network has been very useful in capturing dependencies in the data set.

In general, RNN accepts the unique id which is transformed [2] as a vector as input $x = (x_1, x_2, \ldots, x_T)$ (where $x_t \in R^d$) and maps to hidden input sequence

$h = (h_1, h_2, \ldots, h_T)$ and output sequence $o = (o_1, o_2, \ldots, o_t)$ from $t = 1$ to T by iterating the following equations recursively.

$$h_t = SG(w_{xh}x_t + w_{hh}h_{t-1} + b_h) \qquad (14.2)$$

$$o_t = SF(w_{ho}h_t + b_o) \qquad (14.3)$$

where w represents weight matrices, b terms represents bias vectors, SG is element-wise nonlinear *sigmoid* activation function, SF is element-wise nonlinear *softmax* or *sigmoid* activation function and h acts as a short-term memory to the RNN network. Training an RNN network faces two main problems. They are vanishing and error gradient [41]. This problem of vanishing and error gradient in RNN is solved by long short-term memory (LSTM). LSTM has a memory block which handles vanishing and exploding gradient problem by forcing the constant error flow. A memory block is a complex processing unit which can contain more than one memory cell and a set of adaptive multiplicative gates such as input, output and forget gate, as shown in Figure 14.3. A memory cell has an inbuilt recurrent connection with a value 1 called as constant error carousel. The computation of recurrent hidden layer function at time step t can be generally defined as follows:

$$i_t = \sigma(w_{xi}x_t + w_{hi}h_{t-1} + w_{mi}m_{t-1} + b_i) \qquad (14.4)$$

$$f_t = \sigma(w_{xfg}x_t + w_{hfg}h_{t-1} + w_{mfg}m_{t-1} + b_{fg}) \qquad (14.5)$$

$$m_t = f_t \odot m_{t-1} + i_t \odot \tanh(w_{xm}x_t + w_{hm}h_{t-1} + b_m) \qquad (14.6)$$

$$o_t = \sigma(w_{xo}x_t + w_{ho}h_{t-1} + w_{mo}m_t + b_o) \qquad (14.7)$$

$$h_t = o_t \odot \tanh(m_t) \qquad (14.8)$$

where σ represents the *sigmoid* function; i, f, o and m are input, forget, output gate and memory cell, respectively; h is the hidden layer vector; w and b terms denote the weights and biases, respectively.

To alleviate vanishing and error gradient issue, research on RNN progressed on the three significant directions. One is toward improving optimization methods in algorithms such as Hessian-free optimization methods belong to this category. Second one is toward introducing complex components in recurrent hidden layer of network structure such as LSTM [42], a variant of LSTM network with reduced parameters set, gated recurrent unit (GRU) [43] and third one is toward the appropriate weight initialization with an identity matrix typically called identity-RNN [44,45].

14.3.3   Convolutional neural network

Convolutional neural network (CNN) had shown promising results in the field of computer vision and image processing [46]. CNN has also shown its application in the field of NLP-like sentimental classification [47]. The general architecture of CNN is composed of convolution 1D layer, pooling 1D layer and fully connected layer including nonlinear activation function as *ReLU*. The unique id which is transformed as a vector is given as input features $x = (x_1, x_2, \ldots, x_{n-1}, x_n)$ to CNN. CNN uses convolution 1D operation and estimates feature map *fp* from a set of features *f* and are obtained as

$$h_i^{fp} = \tanh(w^{fp} x_{i:i+f-1} + b) \tag{14.9}$$

where *b* denotes a bias term. The filter *h* is employed to each set of features *f* in connection records $\{x_{1:f}, x_{2:f+1}, \ldots, x_{n-f+1}\}$ as to generate a feature map as

$$h = [h_1, h_2, \ldots, h_{n-f+1}] \tag{14.10}$$

where $h \in R^{n-f+1}$ and after we apply the max pooling on each feature map as $\vec{h} = \max\{h\}$. This obtains the most significant features in which a feature with the highest value is selected. However, multiple features obtain more than one features, and those new features are passed to a fully connected layer. A fully connected layer contains the *softmax* function that gives the probability distribution over each class. A fully connected layer is defined mathematically as

$$o_t = soft \max(w_{ho} h + b_o) \tag{14.11}$$

Instead of passing the newly constructed feature map $FP = CNN(x_t)$ to *softmax* layer, we pass it into LSTM to extract time domain information.

14.4   Intrusion detection

Recent advancement and impressive results of deep learning techniques in the area of computer vision, NLP and speech recognition for various longstanding AI tasks has motivated in applying deep learning techniques toward security tasks too. This paper focuses to apply these deep taxonomy techniques to the network-based intrusion detection (NIDS) with the aim to enhance the performance in classifying the network connections as either good or bad. To substantiate, we model network traffic as time series, specifically TCP/IP packets with a supervised deep learning method such as a DNN, and classical ML techniques using connection records of KDD-Cup-99[1] challenge data set. The main interest is given to evaluate the performance of DNN over classical ML techniques such as support vector machine (SVM), random forest (RF), AdaBoost (AB) and decision tree (DT), naive Bayes (NB), *k*-nearest neighbors (*K*-NN) and logistic regression (LR). The efficient network architecture for all deep models is chosen based on comparing the performance of various network topologies and network parameters. The experiments of such chosen efficient configurations of deep models are run up to 1,000 epochs with learning rate set in the range [0.01–0.5].

14.4.1   Description of KDD-Cup-99 data set

With the sponsorship from DARPA and Air Force Research Laboratory, the DARPA ID Evaluation Group has used 1,000s of UNIX machines and 100s of user's access at a time continuously for 9 weeks, raw tcpdump data was collected and distributed in

---

[1]KDD-Cup-99.

Table 14.1 Description of data set

Attack	Train	Test
Normal	97,278	60,593
DOS	391,458	229,853
Probe	4,107	4,166
R2L	1,126	16,189
U2R	52	228
Total	494,021	311,029

KDD-Cup challenge. The 9-week-collected tcpdump data was composed of 7 weeks of training and 2 weeks of testing. The attacks were ingested to UNIX machines from outside perimeter of its area using Solaris, UNIX, Linux, Windows NT and SunOS environments. Later, to enhance the detection rate, the same raw tcpdump data was preprocessed and converted to a set of connection records with features and a corresponding class label using the MADMAID[2] data mining feature construction framework. The detailed evaluation of KDD-Cup-98 and KDD-Cup-99 was published in [48,49]. The KDD-Cup-99 data set has been made available to further research and the data set is available in two forms (1) full data set (2) 10% of the full data set. The comprehensive description of 10% of KDD-Cup-99 is displayed in Table 14.1. The data set consists of 494,021 train vectors and 311,029 test vectors. A vector in each connection record is defined as

$$V = [fe1, fe2, \ldots fe41, cl] \tag{14.12}$$

where $V = [fe1, fe2, \ldots, fe41, cl]$ denotes a set of features of length 41, cl denotes class label of the features belonging to the particular class. The 41 features were from the following.

- **Simple basic features:** Using the Bro IDS, the contents of packet headers, TCP segments and UDP datagram was extracted in each packet.
- **Content features:** Using the domain knowledge, the content features were extracted from the payload section of each connection. Identifying important features from payload has been a research study for the past years and recently wang [8] has introduced the traffic identification based on the entire payload without using the feature extraction step. Content features are useful in identifying the attacks of R2L and U2R category since R2L and U2R attacks have only a single connection.
- **Time-window of traffic features:** "same host" and "same service" are a family of time-window of traffic features. They are also called connection-based features. These are extracted with a time-window of 2 seconds. Mostly, the probe attacks

---

[2]Mining Audit data for automated models for ID.

Table 14.2   Description of data set

Class	Training data	Testing data
Normal	794,512	157,914
Malicious (Intrusion detected)	1,103,728	262,694

happen in more than 2 seconds, for example, nearly around 1 minute. To mitigate, the first 100 connections were considered for connection-based traffic features. The detailed description is placed in Table 14.1. Table 14.1 shows that both the normal and DOS have a number of records in comparison to the other attacks in 10% KDD-Cup-99. As a result, the detection rate related to normal, DOS and probe connection will be higher in comparison to the other such as U2R and R2L by the IDS model. In order to prevent it, we ideally formed a new set of training data set by adding 400 connection records to R2L and 100 connection records to U2R. Moreover, we randomly removed 250 connection records from both the normal and DOS connection records.

14.4.2   Description of Kyoto network intrusion detection (ID) data set

The data set used for training and testing is the network traffic data from the honeypot systems of Kyoto University [50]. The data set used for classification consists of logs of 360 days. In the data set, the logs of the following dates do not exist. They are (1) 2, 3, 4 March and (2) 13, 14 October. The whole data set has a size of 16.1 GB, but for the experiments, only 25% of the entire data set is used. This 25% data is further divided into 80% for training and 20% for testing. In the data preprocessing step, the categorical features like service, flag and protocol are mapped to $[0$ to $n-1]$, n is the number of symbols in a feature. The data set were normalized as a part of the preprocessing step. The details of Kyoto data set is given in Table 14.2.

14.4.3   Experiments on KDD-Cup-99

This section deals with the effectiveness of various DNN architecture based on the rate at which attack is detected on KDD-Cup-99 data set. All the experiments are run on GPU-enabled TensorFlow[3] in single Nvidia GK110BGL Tesla K40 in order to speed up the performance. The work evaluates the performance comparison of classical ML algorithms such as SVM, RF, NB, AB, DT and K-NN and deep learning technique like DNN. The test results summary in terms of accuracy, precision, recall, F-score, true positive rate (TPR), FPR are provided in Tables 14.3–14.8. The obtained results

---

[3]https://www.tensorflow.org/

Table 14.3   Results for KDD-Cup-99 data set for binary classification using classical machine learning techniques

Methodology	Accuracy	Precision	Recall	F-score	FPR	TPR
Naive Bayes	0.929	0.988	0.923	0.955	0.923	0.955
K-NN	0.929	0.998	0.913	0.954	0.913	0.994
Decision tree	0.927	0.999	0.910	0.952	0.910	0.995
AdaBoost	0.925	0.995	0.911	0.951	0.911	0.982
Random forest	0.927	0.999	0.910	0.952	0.910	0.995
SVM (Linear)	0.828	0.998	0.787	0.880	0.787	0.993
SVM (RBF)	0.811	0.994	0.770	0.868	0.770	0.982

Table 14.4   Results for KDD-Cup-99 data set for binary classification using DNN

Parameters	KDD-Cup-99 data set
Accuracy	0.943
Precision	1.0
Recall	0.929
F-score	0.963

Table 14.5   Results for KDD-Cup-99 data set for multi-class classification using DNN

	DNN		
Class	FPR	TPR	Class-wise accuracy
Normal	0.076	0.997	0.937
DOS	0.003	0.940	0.953
Probe	0.0008	0.830	0.996
U2R	0.0	0.0	0.999
R2L	0.001	0.395	0.981
Accuracy		0.934	

show that the deep learning based DNN has performed better than the classical ML technique. Using DNN architecture gave the highest accuracy of 93.4, whereas classical ML techniques gave the highest accuracy of 92.6 when a DT is used. In this work, we have used the following libraries: sklearn learn which is an open-source ML library and Keras[4] which is written in python is a neural networks API, runs as a front

---

[4]https://keras.io/

Table 14.6   Results for KDD-Cup-99 multi-class classification using classical machine learning technique

	Naive Bayes		Decision tree	
Class	FPR	TPR	FPR	TPR
Normal	0.0769	0.711	0.0850	0.99
DOS	0.022	0.847	0.004	0.941
Probe	0.076	0.963	0.001	0.745
U2R	0.052	0.8	0.002	0.385
R2L	0.001	0.151	0.0002	0.131
Accuracy	**0.803**		**0.926**	

Table 14.7   Results for KDD-Cup-99 multi-class classification using classical machine learning technique

	K-NN		AdaBoost		Random forest	
Class	FPR	TPR	FPR	TPR	FPR	TPR
Normal	0.087	0.99	0.625	0.989	0.093	0.995
DOS	0.012	0.938	0.029	0.383	0.003	0.939
Probe	0.004	0.693	0.002	0.115	0.002	0.751
U2R	0.0004	0.228	0	0	0.000009	0.271
R2L	0.0008	0.0628	0.00007	0.0034	0.00002	0.0004
Accuracy	**0.9219**		**0.4871**		**0.922**	

Table 14.8   Results for KDD-Cup-99 multi-class classification using classical machine learning technique

	SVM (Linear)		SVM (RBF)	
Class	FPR	TPR	FPR	TPR
Normal	0.228	0.984	0.222	0.991
DOS	0.011	0.796	0.012	0.803
Probe	0.0009	0.7510	0.001	0.694
U2R	0	0	0	0
R2L	0.00002	0.051	0.00009	0.0001
Accuracy	**0.811**		**0.816**	

end and which is built on top of Theano, TensorFlow or CNTK. Keras focuses on fast experimentation. For choosing the right parameters like a number of hidden layers, neurons in a layer, the learning rate can be obtained by hyper-parameter tuning. It has been found that a two-layer neural network showed better performance in detecting the connection records belong to Normal, DoS and Probe. For improving the performance, the number of hidden layers has been increased from two to five. It has been empirically found that a six-layer neural network (five hidden and one output layer) and with the following number of neurons: 1,024, 768, 512, 256, 128, 5 in the first, second, third, fourth, fifth and output layer, respectively, gave the best performance. A learning rate of 0.01 was used for the experiments, and a lower learning rate demands more epochs. We have used adam as the optimizer, categorical cross entropy as the loss function. Using a six-layer neural network has improved the detection rate of R2L and U2R.

DNN network structures We have used the following network structures for our experiments:

- Two-layer DNN
- Three-layer DNN
- Four-layer DNN
- Five-layer DNN
- Six-layer DNN

14.4.4 Proposed architecture for KDD-Cup-99 data set

It was empirically found through the experiments that six-layer neural network gave the best performance. By six-layer neural network, we mean five hidden layers and one output layers. The number of neurons in the proposed architecture is the following: 1,024, 768, 512, 256, 128 and 5 in first, second, third, fourth, fifth and the output layer, respectively. A default learning rate of 0.01 was used for the experiments. We have used adam as the optimizer and categorical cross entropy as the loss function. The activation function used is *ReLU* since *ReLU* overcomes the problem of vanishing gradient in DNNs.

1. **Fully connected layers**
   There is a connection from the neurons in the current layer to the neurons in the succeeding layer. That is why it is called fully connected layers. These hidden layers help to learn the complex features. All the hidden layer uses *ReLU* as the activation function.
2. **Batch normalization and regularization**
   The problem of overfitting the model is avoided by introducing a dropout of 0.01 between the fully connected layers. Dropout removes the connections randomly so that the model does not overfit the training samples. We used batch normalization to speed up the training of DNN.
3. **Classification**
   We have framed two problems, one for binary classification and the other for multi-class classification. In the binary classification problems, all attack connections are grouped as one-connection record and benign as the other connection

record. Since it is a binary classification problem, we have used one neuron in the last layer. The loss function used is given below.

$$loss = -\frac{1}{N} \times \sum_{1}^{m} (yt_i \times \log(yp_i) + (1 - yt_i) \times \log(1 - yp_i)) \qquad (14.13)$$

where yp is the predicted probability and yt is the true label, m is the total training examples. Categorical cross entropy is the loss function for the proposed multi-class problem. The mathematical formula of the loss function is below:

$$loss(pt, pp) = -\sum pt(x) \times \log(pp(x)) \qquad (14.14)$$

where $pt(x)$ is the true probability distribution and $pp(x)$ is the predicted probability distribution.

14.4.5 Experiments on Kyoto network intrusion detection (ID) data set

The deep learning experiments are trained using the backpropagation through time (BPTT)–approach. The performance of deep learning models RNN, LSTM and CNN implicitly depends on the hyper-parameters. So in order to reach the optimum parameters, we need to go for hyper-parameter tuning. The experiments were run for 200 epochs with learning rate 0.01 and batch size 128.

The experiments were run for one-layer, two-layer, three-layer, four-layer LSTM networks. The architecture of a basic LSTM contains a single LSTM/RNN layer. These are followed by dropout 0.1 and fully connected layer with 1 neuron (since it is a binary classification problem). For the above trials, 64 memory blocks/units are used. It was found that the performance of two, three, four-layer LSTM gave the same performance. In CNN, we used a single convolution 1D layer, max-pooling 1D layer and followed by 2 fully connected layers. The first fully connected layer contains 32 neurons and a second fully connected layer contains a single neuron. In the case of DNN, we have used a five-layer DNN with 512, 256, 126, 64, 1 in the first, second, third, fourth hidden layer and output layer, respectively.

14.4.6 Proposed architecture for Kyoto

1. **RNN**
   The recurrent layers used have 64 blocks/units. This is followed by a dropout of 0.1 while training. This is followed by a fully connected layer with one neuron with *sigmoid* activation function.
2. **LSTM**
   We have used two-layer LSTM. The first layer LSTM has 64 blocks/units. This is followed by a dropout of 0.1 while training. This is followed by second layer LSTM with 64 units which in turn is followed by a dropout of 0.1 while training. The two LSTM layers are followed by a fully connected layer with one neuron with *sigmoid* activation.

3. **Convolution layers**

   CNN architecture captures the spatial dependencies. The CNN architecture includes convolutional layers followed by max-pooling layers. The architecture of CNN we propose has a convolution 1D layer containing 32 filters with filter length 3. The output of the convolution 1D layer is passed to the max-pooling 1D layer. The max-pooling 1D layer contains a pool length of 2. The max-pooling 1D output is flattened to a vector and passed to a fully connected layer with 1 neuron with *sigmoid* activation function (since it is a binary classification problem).

4. **DNN**

   The architecture for DNN used in the experiments consists of a five-layer DNN with 512, 256, 126, 64, 1 in the first, second, third, fourth hidden layer and output layer, respectively.

5. **Regularization**

   Dropout plays a crucial role by avoiding overfitting. The dropout removes the neurons randomly while training deep learning model. In the proposed architecture, a dropout of 0.1 is placed between deep layers and fully connected layers. The same dropout of 0.1 is used while training RNN, CNN, LSTM. The experiments when carried excluding dropout resulted in overfitting.

6. **Classification**

   The probability that whether a URL is malicious or not is found out using the *sigmoid* function. The *sigmoid* function has values in the range [0,1]. The equation for the *sigmoid* function is as follows:

$$a = \frac{1}{(1 + \exp(-x))} \tag{14.15}$$

The loss function used is binary cross entropy function.

$$loss = -\frac{1}{N} \times \sum_{1}^{m} (y_i \times \log(a_i) + (1 - y_i) \times \log(1 - a_i)) \tag{14.16}$$

where a is the predicted probability and y is the true label, m is the total training examples. To minimize the binary cross entropy, we use adam optimizer.

14.4.7 Evaluation results for KDD-Cup-99

From the experiments, it was empirically found that deep learning has outperformed the classical ML techniques. In the work, two problems were framed: (1) a binary classification problem—this will ensure the efficiency of the ML and DL techniques in detecting intrusions. (2) A multi-class classification problem—this will make sure the efficiency of classifying the connection records into their respective classes. In all the experiments, it was found that DL-based methods, DNN, outperformed the classical

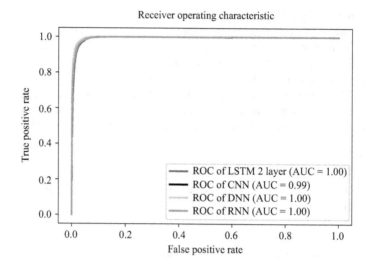

Figure 14.4   ROC curve for DL methods

ML techniques. Due to the computational constraints, more complex architecture cannot be incorporated. The results obtained can be improved by incorporating more complex architectures. Five-layer DNN gave the highest accuracy in both the formulated problem. The DNN architecture gave the highest accuracy of 93.4% and 94.3% in the formulated multi-class and binary class problem, respectively. The experiments support the influence of deep learning techniques in security.

14.4.8   Evaluation results for Kyoto

From the experiments conducted, deep learning architectures such as five-layer DNN and two-layer LSTM is outperforming the classical ML techniques. In classical ML techniques, RF is providing the highest accuracy of 97.4%, whereas in DL techniques, five-layer DNN and two-layer LSTM is giving the highest accuracy of 97.7%. The receiver operating characteristic (ROC) curve for deep learning architectures and classical ML classifiers is shown in Figures 14.4 and 14.5, respectively. The AUC from the ROC curve is highest for DNN, RNN, LSTM in DL techniques, whereas AUC for RF is highest among classical ML techniques. In our experiments due to computational constraints, we have used only 25% of the 16.1 GB data. If more data can be used, the significant performance difference can be achieved between classical ML and DL techniques. The detailed results are reported in Tables 14.9 and 14.10 for deep learning architectures and classical ML algorithms, respectively.

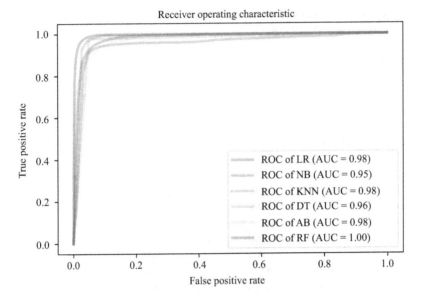

Figure 14.5   ROC curve for classical ML methods

Table 14.9   Results for deep learning based methods

Architecture	Accuracy	Precision	Recall	*F*-score
DNN	0.977	0.975	0.988	0.982
RNN	0.971	0.969	0.986	0.977
LSTM	0.977	0.974	0.989	0.981
CNN	0.971	0.965	0.990	0.977

Table 14.10   Results for machine learning based methods

Methodology	Accuracy	Precision	Recall	*F*-score
Naive Bayes	0.899	0.974	0.861	0.914
K-NN	0.965	0.965	0.979	0.972
Decision tree	0.964	0.970	0.973	0.971
AdaBoost	0.929	0.928	0.962	0.944
Random forest	0.974	0.970	0.989	0.979
Logistic regression	0.942	0.960	0.947	0.953

14.5   Intrusion detection (ID) using multidimensional zoom (M-ZOOM) framework

The fundamental goal of an M-ZOOM framework is, given a higher order tensor then how can we detect the dense blocks present in the tensor. This problem formulation demands the data to be arranged in the form of a tensor. Each feature represents each dimension of the tensor. The following example helps to understand the key idea behind M-ZOOM framework.

The table depicted in Table 14.11 refers to the grade of a student. The fundamental question here is how do we convert this data into a tensor? Let us depict Table 14.11 as R = Grade (student, subject, marks, count). Each tuple (st, s, m, c) represents the student "st" has obtained "c" times' marks in subject "s." Here we refer student as Z1, subject as Z2, marks as Z3 and count as Y. Z1, Z2, Z3 represent the dimension attributes and Y represents measure attribute. When comparing with original data, Z1, Z2, Z3 are the features from original data and Y represents the count of number of times a particular tuple has occurred in the original data set, i.e., if in the original data set the tuple (P, Marks, 30) have occurred seven times, then the Y value for that corresponding tuple is 7. The next step is to define mass. Let C1 = R, P, C2 = Computer science, Maths, C3 = 30,40 represents the set of tuples related to students R or P having marks "30" or "40" in subjects Computer Science or Maths. The Mass of C given by MC is $7 + 5 = 12$. Similarly the $M_{C('R')} = Mass(C('R')) = 5$ and $M_{C('P')} = Mass(C('P')) = 7$. Figure 14.6 represents the tensor representation of data.

The aim of M-ZOOM framework is to find the "k" dense distinct subtensors from R. The detailed algorithm and terminology definitions are provided in [23]. We make use of the methodology provided in [23] for the analysis.

14.5.1   Density measures

This work uses three density measures. Out of the three two-density measures are an extension of classical density measures and are commonly used in sub-graphs [51,52].

Definition 14.1. *(Arithmetic average mass [51]). The arithmetic average mass of a block B of a relation R is defined as* $\rho_{ari}(B,R) = M_B/(S_B/N)$.

Table 14.11   Demo example to show the working of M-ZOOM

Student	Subject	Marks	Count
P	Maths	30	7
Q	Maths	30	2
R	Computer science	40	5
S	Computer science	40	3
T	Physics	45	6

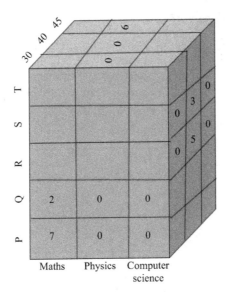

Figure 14.6   Data representation in the form of tensor

Definition 14.2. *(Geometric average mass [32]). The geometric average mass of a block B of a relation R is defined as* $\rho_{geo}(B,R) = M_B/V_B^{(1/N)}$.

The other density measure (Definition 14.3) is the negative log likelihood of MB. The fundamental assumption used is the value on each cell (in the tensor representation) of R follows a Poisson distribution. This has been found useful in fraud detection [53].

Definition 14.3. *(Suspiciousness [53]). The suspiciousness of a block B of a relation R is defined as* $\rho_{susp}(B,R) = M_B(\log(M_B/M_R) - 1) + M_R V_B/V_R - M_B\log(V_B/V_R)$.

The notations used are M_B Mass of B, M_R Mass of R, V_B, Volume of B, V_R Volume of R, N the number of dimension attributes in a relation, S_B is the size of block B and $\rho(B,R)$ is the density of block B in R.

14.5.2   Problem formulation

In this work, the task of detecting intrusions is modeled as a tensor-based unsupervised learning problem. The key part is the arrangement of data in the form of a tensor. We have used 7 features out of 41 features in the KDD-Cup-99 data and count (no of times a particular first 7 features have repeated). These seven features $F = f1, f2, \ldots, f7$ act as the seven dimensions of the tensor. Each location of the tensor is filled with the count value. For connection records that are malicious, the count value will be higher, or in other words, dense connection records represent fraudulent activities. So the task finally boils down to finding k dense subtensors from the original tensor.

14.5.3   Data set description

The data set used is KDD-Cup-99 for the analysis. The data set is released as a part of Third International Knowledge Discovery and Data Mining. The competition is to distinguish between bad connections called as intrusions and good connections named as normal. The data set contains 41 features. The detailed description of the data set is provided in [54]. Instead of using 41 features, we have used 7 features. These features are as follows:

1. Protocol
2. Service
3. Src_bytes
4. Dst_bytes
5. Flag
6. Host_count
7. Src_count
8. No of connections

The first seven features are the dimension attribute, and the no of connections is the measure attribute when the data set is mapped to tensor. The no of connections is obtained by taking the count of the number of times a particular first seven features have occurred in the original data. These seven features act as seven dimensions of the tensor. Also for our experimental analysis, we did not use the full data set. The data set details are reported in Table 14.12. The details of the data set used are given in the following sections.

14.5.4   Experiments and observations

The experiments aim to find the first k dense subblocks. For the experiments, we use k varying from 2 to 5, i.e., $k = 2$ will give the first two dense subblocks whereas $k = 5$ will give the first five dense subblocks. These dense subblocks connections records are assumed to suspicious and assigned a label as attack, whereas the remaining undetected blocks are assumed as normal. By using this information we create the predicted label. This label is compared to the label of the original data set and performance metrics like accuracy, precision, recall, F-score is found out for each k. The detailed results are reported in Table 14.13 for suspiciousness measure, Table 14.14 for geo-measure, Table 14.15 for Ari-measure, Table 14.16 for measures for suspiciousness, Table 14.17 for measures for geo-measure and Table 14.18 for measures for Ari-measure.

Table 14.12   Description of data set

Class	Data samples
Normal	36,691
Intrusion	7,102

Table 14.13 Results for suspiciousness measure

Suspiciousness	Block 2	Block 3	Block 4
Accuracy	96.6	96.4	39.6
Precision	0.987	0.972	0.185
Recall	0.799	0.800	0.801
F-score	0.883	0.877	0.301

Table 14.14 Results for geo-measure

Geo-measure	Block 2	Block 3	Block 4
Accuracy	0.84	0.84	0.965
Precision	0.99	0.991	0.981
Recall	0.013	0.015	0.800
F-score	0.026	0.029	0.881

Table 14.15 Results for Ari-measure

Ari-measure	Block 2	Block 3	Block 4
Accuracy	0.84	0.84	0.841
Precision	0.99	0.991	0.787
Recall	0.013	0.015	0.027
F-score	0.026	0.029	0.051

Table 14.16 Measures for suspiciousness

Block	1
Volume	$1 \times 1 \times 1 \times 1 \times 1 \times 86 \times 86$
Density	3.874955006702407E8
Mass	15041381
Block	2
Volume	$1 \times 3 \times 2 \times 27 \times 28 \times 178 \times 22$
Density	7172032.857548084
Mass	492612
Block	3
Volume	$1 \times 4 \times 2 \times 5 \times 4 \times 6 \times 13$
Density	1902735.4197918875
Mass	94348
Block	4
Volume	$1 \times 4 \times 1 \times 723 \times 3882 \times 24 \times 26$
Density	1091113.6115579782
Mass	147873

Table 14.17   Measures for geo-measure

Block	1
Volume	$1 \times 1 \times 1 \times 1 \times 1 \times 76 \times 76$
Density	4288249.556676802
Mass	14779351
Block	2
Volume	$1 \times 1 \times 1 \times 1 \times 1 \times 1 \times 1$
Density	193190.0
Mass	193190
Block	3
Volume	$1 \times 1 \times 1 \times 1 \times 1 \times 10 \times 10$
Density	135717.77501989543
Mass	262030
Block	4
Volume	$1 \times 3 \times 3 \times 26 \times 25 \times 179 \times 23$
Density	31961.209870425075
Mass	362374

Table 14.18   Measures for Ari-measure

Block	1
Volume	$1 \times 1 \times 1 \times 1 \times 1 \times 76 \times 76$
Density	658951.9554140128
Mass	14779351
Block	2
Volume	$1 \times 1 \times 1 \times 1 \times 1 \times 1 \times 1$
Density	193190.0
Mass	193190
Block	3
Volume	$1 \times 1 \times 1 \times 1 \times 1 \times 10 \times 10$
Density	73368.40000000001
Mass	262030
Block	4
Volume	$2 \times 3 \times 2 \times 3 \times 2 \times 3 \times 7$
Density	21405.045454545456
Mass	67273

From the experimental analysis, suspiciousness acts as the best density measure compared to arithmetic average mass and geometric average mass. With a number of blocks, two in suspicious measure gives the best accuracy in detecting malicious connection records.

14.6 Phishing URL detection

Phishing URL is one of the major threat in cybersecurity. Phishing URL is responsible for various cyberattacks like spamming, identity theft, financial fraud. The growth on the internet increases the rate of fraudulent activities on the web. The traditional methods like blacklisting are inefficient in handling variants of phishing websites and also fails to detect new malicious website. the traditional methods require human intervention to update the database of phishing websites. The ML-based solution has shown promising results in various challenging problems in security. In such a scenario, we propose deep learning which is a subset of ML to detect and classify phishing websites. In this work, we have used various deep learning architecture like CNN, RNN, LSTM, GRU, IRNN. The experiments mentioned in the work were run till 1,000 epochs with a learning rate in the range [0.01–0.05].

14.6.1 Data set description of phishing URL detection

The second task is detecting phishing URL's and classifying it into benign and malicious. The legitimate URLs for the preparing the data are crawled from Alexa and DMOZ directory and phishing URLs are crawled from Phishtank and OpenPhish. The data statistics are described in Table 14.19. The URL which is crawled are randomly grouped into train and test data. These data sets are transformed into a numeric format using text encoding.

14.6.2 URL representation

Data representation in numeric format is very important in any ML tasks. Text encoding converts the raw features into numeric values. There are mainly two types of text representation—sequential and nonsequential representation of texts. Sequential representation retains the word order, whereas nonsequential representation does not retain the word order. We have used a sequential representation of texts. Sequential representation involves tokenizing the sentence into words and words into characters. In the preprocessing stage, the uppercase character is replaced by lowercase characters. The vocabulary is build using lowercase training characters. The second step includes vocabulary creation using the training data. The size of vocabulary creation acts as an equilibrium between the training vectors of each class and the number of parameters to learn for the given task. The input text is converted into a list. A number is assigned to each unique characters in the list. Each unique id is a vector that denotes the size of the vocabulary. These character unique IDS are transformed into feature

Table 14.19 Description of data set

	Malicious URL	Benign URL
Training	27,798	28,101
Testing	14,969	15,132

vectors using the look-up table operation. These continuous vectors are fed as input to RNN, CNN, LSTM, GRU, IRNN and classical ML techniques.

14.6.3 Experiments

This section deals with the performance evaluation of deep learning and ML techniques for detecting and classifying phishing URLs. The preprocessed URLs are passed to RNN, CNN, LSTM, IRNN, GRU, CNN-LSTM and LR with bigrams.

14.6.4 Hyper-parameter tuning

The deep learning experiments are trained using the BPTT approach. The performance of deep learning models like RNN, IRNN, LSTM, GRU, CNN and CNN-LSTM implicitly depends on the hyper-parameters. So in order to reach the optimum parameters, we need to go for hyper-parameter tuning. The experiments were run for 1,000 epochs with learning rate 0.001 and batch size 256.

The experiments were run for three trials for 32, 64, 128, 256, 512 number of units/blocks with a basic LSTM network. The architecture of a basic LSTM contains a single LSTM/RNN/GRU/IRNN layer. These are followed by dropout 0.2 and fully connected layer with 1 neuron (since it is a binary classification problem). The performance with 256 memory blocks/units in LSTM/RNN/IRNN/GRU outperformed the other architectures.

Experiments by passing bigram as input to LR showed lesser performance compared to character level inputs. The experiments were run for three trials for the filters 4, 16, 32, 64, 128, 256 and 512 with filter length 4 in a CNN network. The basic architecture of CNN includes convolution 1D, max-pooling 1D with pool length 2, fully connected layer with one neuron (since it is a binary classification) and *sigmoid* as the activation function. It was found that the performance of CNN with 256 filters outperformed the performance with other filters. Hence, we decided to fix 25 as the number of filters for the remaining experiments. The detailed results are reported in Table 14.20. The ROC curve for both the deep learning architectures and classical ML classifiers for phishing URL detection is shown in Figure 14.7.

Table 14.20 Deep learning based phishing URL

Parameters	GRU	RNN	LSTM	CNN-LSTM	IRNN	CNN	Logistic regression
Accuracy	0.997	0.989	0.997	0.999	0.972	0.981	0.953
Precision	0.996	0.989	0.996	0.999	0.968	0.976	0.960
Recall	0.997	0.990	0.999	0.999	0.977	0.986	0.947
F-score	0.997	0.989	0.997	0.999	0.972	0.981	0.953

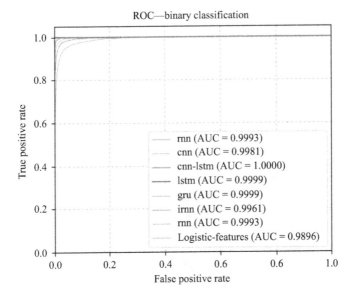

Figure 14.7 ROC curve

14.6.5 *Proposed architecture for URL analysis*

1. **Recurrent layers**
   The high-level architecture of the proposed architecture for URL analysis is shown in Figure 14.8. We have used various recurrent layers. For better performance, we have to tune the hyper-parameters. Based on the result from hyperparameter tuning, 256 number of blocks/units is set. The LSTM memory cell uses hyperbolic tangent as input. The output activation has value in the range $[-1, 1]$. The gates in the LSTM uses *sigmoid* which has values in the range $[0, 1]$.

2. **Convolution layers**
   CNN architecture captures the spatial dependencies. So in order to capture the spatial correlational between characters, the CNN architecture is used. The CNN architecture includes convolutional layers followed by max-pooling layers. The architecture of CNN we propose has a convolutional 1D layer containing 256 filters with filter length 4. The output of the convolution layer is passed to the max-pooling layer. The max-pooling layer contains a pool length of 4. The max-pooling 1D output is flattened to a vector and passed to a fully connected layer. Now, in order to learn the sequential information from the max-pooling layer, we introduce the LSTM layer containing 50 memory blocks.

3. **Regularization**
   Dropout plays a major role by avoiding overfitting. A dropout is an approach to removing the neurons randomly while training deep learning model. In the

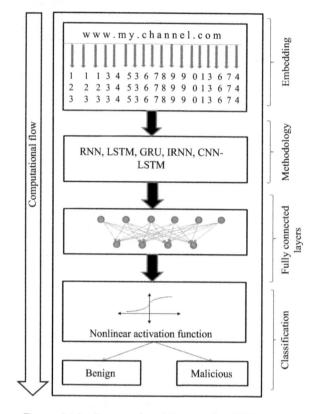

Figure 14.8   Proposed architecture for URL analysis

proposed architecture, a dropout of 0.2 is placed between deep layers and fully connected layers, and for CNN it is 0.3. The experiments when conducted without dropout resulted in overfitting.

4. **Classification**

The probability that whether a URL is malicious or not is found out using the *sigmoid* function. The *sigmoid* function has values in the range [0, 1]. The equation for the *sigmoid* function is as follows:

$$a = \frac{1}{(1 + \exp(-x))} \tag{14.17}$$

The loss function used is binary cross entropy function.

$$loss = -\left(\frac{1}{N}\right) \times \sum_{1}^{m} (y_i \times \log(a_i) + (1 - y_i) \times \log(1 - a_i)) \tag{14.18}$$

where a is the predicted probability and y is the true label, m is the total training examples. To minimize the binary cross entropy, we use adam optimizer.

14.7 Proposed architecture for machine learning based cybersecurity

In computer security, there is an ever-growing use of computer technology, so this makes it important in our society. As per the national statistics 2008, 65% of all households in the United Kingdom were connected to the internet, which is approximately 16 million households (National Statistics 2008). Also, recent years has shown a rapid increase in the amount of computer malware. There is always a risk associated with computer user, even if the system is not connected to the internet. Also, an unattended system is always prone to unauthorized access and misuse of the system. If the computer is connected to a network or internet, the risk of attacks increases to a greater extent. In this situation, any computer can be accessed remotely by any user around the world and attempt to access personal and confidential information. These attacks are commonly carried out by intrusions, phishing URLs. In order to tackle the increase in intrusions, phishing URLs, we propose a cyber threat situational awareness platform for an organization. The high-level architecture of the proposed system is shown in Figure 14.9.

- The prototype model uses distributed deep learning and ML algorithms.
- Due to the difficulty of supervised learning technique for getting annotated data, the prototype also introduces unsupervised learning techniques.

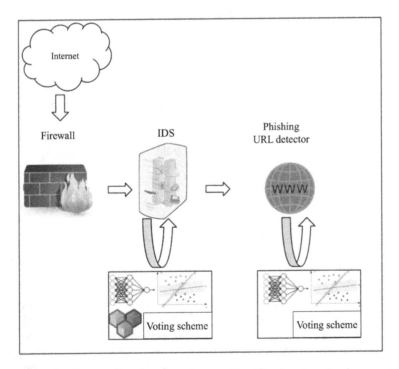

Figure 14.9 Proposed architecture for machine learning based cybersecurity

14.8   Conclusion and future work

This work analyzed the effectiveness of the supervised and unsupervised learning techniques in detecting intrusions and phishing URLs. The detection rates attained for KDD-Cup-99 intrusion data by classical ML classifiers are closely comparable to others. Experiments are evaluated with a full data set and minimal feature sets to understand the importance of each feature. DNN-based classification outperforms all classical ML techniques. This might be improved by promoting training or stacking a few more layer to the existing architectures or adding a new feature to the existing data. In most of the cases, the low-frequency attack categories produce a single connection record. These low-frequency attacks extraction appears to be hard when information of them concealed in other connection records. Overall, the DNN have enhanced the performance in detection rates in comparison to the KDD-Cup-99 challenge-winning entries and other previously published results. Due to the high computational cost in training the deep learning architectures, we could not go for other architectures. So the future work can incorporate the classification using other deep learning architectures like CNN, LSTM, GRU, IRNN and also hybrid networks like CNN-LSTM. When the model is framed as unsupervised learning problem, the detection rates were high. The M-ZOOM framework conveys the potential of unsupervised learning. In the case of phishing URL detection, CNN-LSTM gave the best performance. In this work, we propose an AI-based situational awareness platform to detect intrusions and phishing URL for an organization point of view. The voting schemes in the proposed architecture are a direction toward future work.

Acknowledgments

This research was supported in part by Paramount Computer Systems and Lakhshya Cybersecurity Labs. We are grateful to NVIDIA India, for the GPU hardware support to a research grant. We are also grateful to Computational Engineering and Networking (CEN) department for encouraging the research.

References

[1]   Lee W, Fan W, Miller M, *et al.* Toward cost-sensitive modeling for intrusion detection and response. Journal of Computer Security. 2002;10(1–2):5–22.
[2]   LeCun Y, Bengio Y, Hinton G. Deep learning. Nature. 2015;521(7553): 436–444.
[3]   Staudemeyer RC. Applying long short-term memory recurrent neural networks to intrusion detection. South African Computer Journal. 2015;56(1):136–154.
[4]   Vinayakumar R, Soman K, Poornachandran P. Applying convolutional neural network for network intrusion detection. In: Advances in Computing, Communications and Informatics (ICACCI), 2017 International Conference on. IEEE; 2017. p. 1222–1228.

[5]   Vinayakumar R, Soman K, Poornachandran P. Evaluating effectiveness of shallow and deep networks to intrusion detection system. In: Advances in Computing, Communications and Informatics (ICACCI), 2017 International Conference on. IEEE; 2017. p. 1282–1289.

[6]   Vinayakumar R, Soman K, Poornachandran P. Evaluation of recurrent neural network and its variants for intrusion detection system (IDS). International Journal of Information System Modeling and Design (IJISMD). 2017;8(3): 43–63.

[7]   Vinayakumar R, Soman K, Poornachandran P. Long short-term memory based operation log anomaly detection. In: Advances in Computing, Communications and Informatics (ICACCI), 2017 International Conference on. IEEE; 2017. p. 236–242.

[8]   Wang Z. The applications of deep learning on traffic identification. BlackHat, USA; 2015.

[9]   Vinayakumar R, Soman K, Poornachandran P. Applying deep learning approaches for network traffic prediction. In: Advances in Computing, Communications and Informatics (ICACCI), 2017 International Conference on. IEEE; 2017. p. 2353–2358.

[10] Vinayakumar R, Soman K, Poornachandran P. Secure shell (SSH) traffic analysis with flow based features using shallow and deep networks. In: Advances in Computing, Communications and Informatics (ICACCI), 2017 International Conference on. IEEE; 2017. p. 2026–2032.

[11] Vinayakumar R, Soman K, Poornachandran P. Evaluating shallow and deep networks for secure shell (SSH) traffic analysis. In: Advances in Computing, Communications and Informatics (ICACCI), 2017 International Conference on. IEEE; 2017. p. 266–274.

[12] Shin ECR, Song D, Moazzezi R. Recognizing functions in binaries with neural networks. In: USENIX Security Symposium; 2015. p. 611–626.

[13] Vinayakumar R, Soman K, Poornachandran P. Detecting malicious domain names using deep learning approaches at scale. Journal of Intelligent & Fuzzy Systems. 2018;34(3):1355–1367.

[14] Vinayakumar R, Soman K, Poornachandran P, *et al.* Evaluating deep learning approaches to characterize and classify the DGAs at scale. Journal of Intelligent & Fuzzy Systems. 2018;34(3):1265–1276.

[15] Vinayakumar R, Poornachandran P, Soman K. Scalable framework for cyber threat situational awareness based on domain name systems data analysis. In: Big Data in Engineering Applications. Springer; 2018. p. 113–142.

[16] Mohan VS, Vinayakumar R, Soman K, *et al.* Spoof net: Syntactic patterns for identification of ominous online factors. In: 2018 IEEE Security and Privacy Workshops (SPW). IEEE; 2018. p. 258–263.

[17] Vinayakumar R, Soman K, Poornachandran P. Evaluating deep learning approaches to characterize and classify malicious URLs. Journal of Intelligent & Fuzzy Systems. 2018;34(3):1333–1343.

[18] Pascanu R, Stokes JW, Sanossian H, *et al.* Malware classification with recurrent networks. In: Acoustics, Speech and Signal Processing (ICASSP), 2015 IEEE International Conference on. IEEE; 2015. p. 1916–1920.

[19]   Vinayakumar R, Soman K, Poornachandran P, *et al.* Detecting Android malware using long short-term memory (LSTM). Journal of Intelligent & Fuzzy Systems. 2018;34(3):1277–1288.

[20]   Vinayakumar R, Soman K, Poornachandran P. Deep Android malware detection and classification. In: Advances in Computing, Communications and Informatics (ICACCI), 2017 International Conference on. IEEE; 2017. p. 1677–1683.

[21]   Vinayakumar R, Soman K, Velan KS, *et al.* Evaluating shallow and deep networks for ransomware detection and classification. In: Advances in Computing, Communications and Informatics (ICACCI), 2017 International Conference on. IEEE; 2017. p. 259–265.

[22]   Hodo E, Bellekens X, Hamilton A, *et al.* Shallow and deep networks intrusion detection system: A taxonomy and survey. arXiv preprint arXiv:1701.02145. 2017.

[23]   Shin K, Hooi B, Faloutsos C. M-Zoom: Fast dense-block detection in tensors with quality guarantees. In: Joint European Conference on Machine Learning and Knowledge Discovery in Databases. Cham: Springer; 2016. p. 264–280.

[24]   Sabhnani M, Serpen G. Application of machine learning algorithms to KDD intrusion detection dataset within misuse detection context. In: MLMTA; 2003. p. 209–215.

[25]   Sinclair C, Pierce L, Matzner S. An application of machine learning to network intrusion detection. In: Computer Security Applications Conference, 1999.(ACSAC'99) Proceedings. 15th Annual. IEEE; 1999. p. 371–377.

[26]   Denning DE. An intrusion-detection model. IEEE Transactions on Software Engineering. 1987;(2):222–232.

[27]   Andersen R, Chung F, Lang K. Local graph partitioning using PageRank vectors. In: Foundations of Computer Science, 2006. FOCS'06. 47th Annual IEEE Symposium on. IEEE; 2006. p. 475–486.

[28]   Leskovec J, Mcauley JJ. Learning to discover social circles in ego networks. In: Advances in Neural Information Processing Systems; 2012. p. 539–547.

[29]   Cortes C, Pregibon D, Volinsky C. Communities of interest. In: International Symposium on Intelligent Data Analysis. Springer; 2001. p. 105–114.

[30]   Akoglu L, McGlohon M, Faloutsos C. Oddball: Spotting anomalies in weighted graphs. In: Pacific-Asia Conference on Knowledge Discovery and Data Mining. Springer; 2010. p. 410–421.

[31]   Beutel A, Xu W, Guruswami V, *et al.* CopyCatch: stopping group attacks by spotting lockstep behavior in social networks. In: Proceedings of the 22nd International Conference on World Wide Web. ACM; 2013. p. 119–130.

[32]   Papalexakis EE, Beutel A, Steenkiste P. Network anomaly detection using co-clustering. In: Encyclopedia of Social Network Analysis and Mining. Springer; 2014. p. 1054–1068.

[33]   Heartfield R, Loukas G. A taxonomy of attacks and a survey of defence mechanisms for semantic social engineering attacks. ACM Computing Surveys (CSUR). 2016;48(3):37.

[34] Hong J. The state of phishing attacks. Communications of the ACM. 2012;55(1):74–81.

[35] Garera S, Provos N, Chew M, *et al.* A framework for detection and measurement of phishing attacks. In: Proceedings of the 2007 ACM Workshop on Recurring Malcode. ACM; 2007. p. 1–8.

[36] Patil DR, Patil J. Survey on malicious web pages detection techniques. International Journal of U-and E-service, Science and Technology. 2015;8(5):195–206.

[37] McGrath DK, Gupta M. Behind Phishing: An Examination of Phisher Modi Operandi. LEET. 2008;8:4.

[38] Kuyama M, Kakizaki Y, Sasaki R. Method for detecting a malicious domain by using WHOIS and DNS features. In: The Third International Conference on Digital Security and Forensics (DigitalSec2016); 2016. p. 74.

[39] Kan MY, Thi HON. Fast webpage classification using URL features. In: Proceedings of the 14th ACM International Conference on Information and Knowledge Management. ACM; 2005. p. 325–326.

[40] Elman JL. Finding structure in time. Cognitive Science. 1990;14(2): 179–211.

[41] Bengio Y, Simard P, Frasconi P. Learning long-term dependencies with gradient descent is difficult. IEEE Transactions on Neural Networks. 1994;5(2): 157–166.

[42] Hochreiter S, Schmidhuber J. Long short-term memory. Neural Computation. 1997;9(8):1735–1780.

[43] Cho K, Van Merriënboer B, Gulcehre C, *et al.* Learning phrase representations using RNN encoder-decoder for statistical machine translation. arXiv preprint arXiv:1406.1078. 2014.

[44] Talathi SS, Vartak A. Improving performance of recurrent neural network with ReLU nonlinearity. arXiv preprint arXiv:1511.03771. 2015.

[45] Le QV, Jaitly N, Hinton GE. A simple way to initialize recurrent networks of rectified linear units. arXiv preprint arXiv:1504.00941. 2015.

[46] LeCun Y, *et al.* Generalization and network design strategies. In: Connectionism in Perspective. Zurich, Switzerland: Elsiever; 1989. p. 143–155.

[47] Kim Y. Convolutional neural networks for sentence classification. arXiv preprint arXiv:1408.5882. 2014.

[48] Alshammari R, Lichodzijewski PI, Heywood M, *et al.* Classifying SSH encrypted traffic with minimum packet header features using genetic programming. In: Proceedings of the 11th Annual Conference Companion on Genetic and Evolutionary Computation Conference: Late Breaking Papers. ACM; 2009. p. 2539–2546.

[49] Alshammari R, Zincir-Heywood AN, Farrag AA. Performance comparison of four rule sets: An example for encrypted traffic classification. In: Privacy, Security, Trust and the Management of e-Business, 2009. CONGRESS'09. World Congress on. IEEE; 2009. p. 21–28.

[50] Agarap AF. A neural network architecture combining gated recurrent unit (GRU) and support vector machine (SVM) for intrusion detection in network

traffic data. In: Proceedings of the 2018 10th International Conference on Machine Learning and Computing. ACM; 2018. p. 26–30.

[51]   Charikar M. Greedy approximation algorithms for finding dense components in a graph. In: International Workshop on Approximation Algorithms for Combinatorial Optimization. Springer; 2000. p. 84–95.

[52]   Kannan R, Vinay V. Analyzing the structure of large graphs. Rheinische Friedrich-Wilhelms-Universität Bonn, Bonn; 1999.

[53]   Jiang M, Beutel A, Cui P, *et al.* A general suspiciousness metric for dense blocks in multimodal data. In: Data Mining (ICDM), 2015 IEEE International Conference on. IEEE; 2015. p. 781–786.

[54]   Tavallaee M, Bagheri E, Lu W, *et al.* A detailed analysis of the KDD CUP 99 data set. In: Computational Intelligence for Security and Defense Applications, 2009. CISDA 2009. IEEE Symposium on. IEEE; 2009. p. 1–6.

Index

Accuracy@k 212
activity manager 228
algorithms and theoretical foundations
    of RSs 12
Amazon 1–2, 20–1, 41, 56, 160–1
Ambari architecture 31–2
Android 227
    applications 227–30
    Kernel 229
    libraries 229
    runtime 229
Android Bundle (APK) 226
anonymization 272
Apache Ambari 4, 31–2
Apache Spark 33, 174–5, 284,
    289–90
API Monitor 231
application programming interfaces
    (APIs) 76, 194, 226, 290
applications of RSs 10
Apriori algorithm 245
Arduino UNO 179–80, 189
artificial neural networks (ANN) 34
association rule mining 244–5
attack response and system robustness
    248
    attributes, classification of 248–9
    generic attributes 248
    model-derived attributes 248–9
    detection attributes for profile
        classification 251–4
    detection methods 251
    hybrid recommendation algorithm
        249
    push attacks against enhanced hybrid
        algorithm 249–50

attacks
    average attack detection 248
    Bandwagon attack 242
    defense against profile injection
        attacks 250–3
    dimensions of 240–1
    high knowledge 240
    Love and Hate attack 243
    low knowledge 241
    models of 241–4
    nuke attacks 239, 242–3
    probe attack strategy 239–40
    profile injection 241–2
    push attacks 239, 242
        against enhanced hybrid algorithm
            249
    random and average attack models
        242
    random attack detection 249
    Reverse Bandwagon attack 243–4
    segment attack 242
    vulnerable to 22
audio analytics 143
    dynamic music similarity
        measurement 149–50
    graph-based music recommendation
        challenges 149
    graph-based quality model 148–9
    learning content similarity for music
        recommendation 151
    audio representation 152
    collaborative filters and metric
        learning to rank 151–2
    music feature extraction and indexing
        150–1
    music ranking 151

music recommendation and label
    propagation on song graph 151
personalized tag-based social media
    music recommendation 145
    framework of music
        recommendation 146
    tag-based music recommendation
        challenges 146–7
prediction of genre-based link in a
    two-way graph for music
    recommendation 143
    CORLP method 144–5
    feature extraction 145
    recommendation 145
    preference relation 148
user access patterns music
    recommendation challenges
    151
autoencoder (AE)-based
    recommendation (AutoRec)
    113
autoencoder for recommender systems
    122–3
automated collaborative filtering (ACF)
    algorithm 240
Average and Random attacks 248
average attack detection 248

background knowledge attack 273
backpropagation through time (BPTT)
    318
Bandwagon attack model 242–4
Bayesian classifiers 13, 34, 135–6
Bayesian inference 127–8
belief propagation (BP) approach 51
benchmarking big data recommendation
    algorithms 27, 37–8
    Apache Ambari and Ambari
        architecture 31–2
    Apache Spark 33
    future of Hadoop 32
    Hadoop 28–9
    Hadoop input/output 30–1
    Hadoop works in social networking
        32

MapReduce model, presenting 30
nature-inspired algorithms, systems
    based on 37
recommender systems 33
    collaborative recommendation and
        collaborative filtering 34–5
    content-based recommendation 35
    design of 34
    hybrid recommendation
        approaches 36–7
    reducing sparsity problem 35
    visualization of 36
benefit acceleration 230
big data analysis and integration
    architecture 81–2
    architectural patterns as development
        standards 83
    heterogeneity 82–3
big data analytic 139
    audio analytics: *see* audio analytics
    Hadoop Framework,
        recommendation system with
        163
    image analytics: *see* image analytics
    personalized trip advisor service 162
    text analytics system, steps for 139
    text recommendation using
        angle-based interest model 140
    data structure for calculating the
        angles of interest 140–1
    recommendation mechanism
        141–2
    simulating human reading features
        to emerge interest 140
    video analytics: *see* video analytics
big database management systems
    (DBMS) 72
big DI using HAs based on
    fuzzy-ontology 83
Bloom filters 285–6
BookCrossing 20
Bull Eye algorithm 238–9

C160 287, 291
Carol 290, 292–6
CKNN 210
cold start problem 22, 63, 149
collaborative denoising autoencoders
   (CDAE) 113, 125–7
   generative process of 126
collaborative filtering (CF) 14, 27,
   34–5, 44, 47, 112, 133, 152, 233
collaborative innovation diffusion-aware
   recommendation mechanism 56
collaborative recommendations 135–7
   and collaborative filtering 34–5
collaborative topic models 119–21
collaborative topic regression (CTR)
   model 112
   generative process of 120
   graphical structure of 119
collaborative variational autoencoder
   (CVAE) 113, 127–30
   generative process of 128
commercial organisations (COs) 74
complex representation-based link
   prediction (CORLP) method
   144–5
computational intelligence (CI)
   techniques 60
confidentiality, integrity and availability
   (CIA) 261, 271
content-based (CB) filtering 19, 27–8,
   35
content-based methods 45, 152
content-based recommendation 13, 35,
   134–5, 163
content filtering 34
content providers 228
context-aware recommendation systems
   58–61
   in IoT ecosystem 61
   and social networks 62–4
contextual modeling 59
convolutional neural network (CNN)
   17, 34, 169, 171, 174, 311–12
convolution layer 174, 319, 329
Copper 287, 291

CopyCatch 307
crisp ontology 74, 83
   developing approaches for 84
   identifying appropriate crisp
      ontology elements 95–8
Crowdroid 226
cyberattacks 305
Cypher Query Language 19

Dalvik Virtual Machine (DVM) 229
Darlington pair 182
DARPA 312
database management systems (DBMS)
   71–2
data graph 206–7
data inconsistency (DI) system 71
   approaches to detect and reduce
      77–81
   big DI using HAs based on
      fuzzy-ontology 83
   complexity and issues of big DI 81
data sanitization 272
datasets for recommendations 20–1
data sparsity problem 21, 194, 196,
   204–5
decision support system (DSS)
   technology 81
decision trees 34
deep generative models, for
   recommender systems 125
   collaborative denoising autoencoders
      (CDAE) 125–7
   collaborative variational autoencoder
      127–30
deep learning, for recommender
   systems 121
   autoencoder for recommender
      systems 122–3
   multilayer perceptron based
      recommender systems 124
   restricted Boltzmann-machine-based
      collaborative filtering 121–2
   RNN/LSTM for recommendation
      124–5

deep learning architecture 303
  convolutional neural network (CNN)
    311–12
  deep neural networks (DNNs) 308–9
  future work 332
  intrusion detection (ID) 312
    description of KDD-Cup-99 data
      set 312–14
    description of Kyoto network
      intrusion detection data set 314
    evaluation results for KDD-Cup-99
      319–20
    evaluation results for Kyoto 320–1
    experiments on KDD-Cup-99
      314–17
    experiments on Kyoto network
      intrusion detection data set
      318–19
    proposed architecture for
      KDD-Cup-99 data set 317–18
    proposed architecture for Kyoto
      318–19
    using multidimensional zoom
      (M-ZOOM) framework 322–6
  network intrusion detection systems
    (NIDSs) 305–7
  phishing URL detection 307–8, 327
    data set description of 327
    experiments 328
    hyper-parameter tuning 328
    proposed architecture for 329–30
    URL representation 327–8
  proposed architecture for machine
    learning based cybersecurity
    331
  recurrent neural network (RNN)
    310–11
deep learning-based techniques 3
deep neural networks (DNNs) 308–9,
  320
deep segregation of plastic (DSP) 169
  deep learning 172–4
  experiments and observation 185
    training process 185–7
  future work 188

hardware components used 179
  Arduino UNO 179–80
  stepper motor 181
  switching power supply 181–2
  ULN 2003 182
  webcam 182–3
  windshield wiper motor 181
hardware setup for segregation
  183–5
related work 171–2
scalable architecture 174–6
software and packages 176
  Keras 177
  OpenCV 177–9
  TensorFlow 176–7
software framework 176
definitions of RSs 10
demographic recommendations 138
Denial of Service (DoS) assault 230–1
design of recommender systems 34
DexClassLoader 232
differential privacy 275
Dirichlet distribution 118
diverse heterogeneous sources (DHS)
  71–2
DREBIN 226
DroidBox 231–2
DroidMat 226
DroidScope 226
dynamic music similarity measurement
  149–50

eal-time video recommendation
  challenges 155
e-commerce 1–2, 11
efficient recommendation: *see*
  socio-aware recommendation
  systems
electronic health records (EHRs) 72
enhanced collaborative filtering 247
enhanced hybrid algorithm
  push attacks against 249–50
Erdos–Rényi (ER) model 47

evidence lower bound (ELBO) 118
expectation maximization (EM)
    algorithm 116

Facebook 1–2, 32, 41
feature engineering 173
feature learning 173
feed-forward neural networks 17
filter mean target difference (FMTD)
    attribute 253
Foursquare 1, 194, 209–10, 212–16
fully connected layer 174, 186, 312,
    317
functional dependencies corresponding
    relational variables 78
Fuzzy Description Logics (FuzzyDL)
    syntaxes 93
fuzzy multi-attribute theory 78
Fuzzy-Ontology
    big DI using HAs based on 83
    developing HAs for 84–6
    elements 93–5
    extracting big data key business
        functions for proposed HAs
        based on 86–7
    resources elements 93
    result affirmation 98
Fuzzy-Ontology Generation Framework
    (FOGA) 87

gather – apply – scatter (GAS) model
    206
generative models, for recommender
    systems 113
    collaborative topic models 119–21
    latent Dirichlet allocation (LDA)
        116–19, 118
    probabilistic latent semantic analysis
        (PLSA) 114–16
    probabilistic matrix factorization
        113–14
Gibbs EM algorithm 202, 205, 207
Gibbs sampling-based inference 118
Google 1, 28, 41, 176
Google Play Store 225

graph-based quality model for music
    recommendation 147
    challenges 149
    graph-based quality model 148–9
    preference relation 148
graph databases (GDBs) 9, 17–20
graphical processing units (GPUs) 173
graphical user interface (GUI)-based
    PDA applications 226
GraphLab framework 193, 206, 208,
    212, 216, 219
graph-partition problems 307
GraphQL 19
GroupLens 20

Hadoop 3, 27–9
    future of 32
    input/output 30–1
    recommendation system with 163
    in social networking 32
Hadoop Distributed File System
    (HDFS) 3, 27, 235–6, 393
    architecture 236
    security issues in 237
    security methods 237
        Bull Eye algorithm 238
        Kerberos construction 237–8
        name node algorithm 238–9
    high knowledge attacks 240
    homogeneity attack 273
    homomorphic encryption 276, 285
    Horton mechanism 31
    hybrid approaches (HAs) 3, 71
        analysis of result 104–6
        big data architecture 74–6
        big DI using HAs based on
            fuzzy-ontology 83
        complexity and issues of big DI 81
            big data analysis and integration
                architecture 81–3
        crisp ontology, developing
            approaches for 84
        different approaches to handle big
            data 76–81

extracting big data key business
functions for proposed HAs
based on fuzzy-ontology 86–7
fuzzy-ontology, developing HAs for
84–6
Hybrid Integration Development
Approaches (HIDAs) 87–8
hypertension-specific diagnosis
based on HIDAs 88
crisp ontology elements,
identifying appropriate 95–8
data collection 88–90
determining and ascertaining the
necessity for fuzziness in
hypertension diagnosis 91–2
documentation and notes 99
formalisation 98
Fuzzy-Ontology elements 93–5
Fuzzy-Ontology result affirmation
98
HIDAs contrivance and excellence
90–1
reusing subsisting Fuzzy-Ontology
resources elements 93
reusing the subsisting HIDAs
resources 92
specifying fuzzy-associated
elements in hypertension data 92
mathematical simulation of
hypertension diagnosis 99–104
Hybrid Integration Development
Approaches (HIDAs) 87–8, 105
applicability and interoperability of
105–6
methodological guideline of 105
hybrid PLSA (H-PLSA) 115
hybrid recommendations 36–7, 52,
138–9, 249
hybrid recommenders 16
hyperbolic path-based recommendation
system 48–50
hyperbolic recommendation-known
destination (HRKD) algorithm
49–50
hyperbolic recommendation-unknown
destination (HRUD) 49–50
hyper-parameter tuning 316, 318, 328
hypertension-specific diagnosis based
on HIDAs 88
crisp ontology elements, identifying
appropriate 95–8
data collection 88–90
determining and ascertaining the
necessity for fuzziness 91–2
documentation and notes 99
formalisation 98
Fuzzy-Ontology elements
appropriate subsisting 93
identify appropriate 93–5
result affirmation 98
HIDAs contrivance and excellence
90–1
reusing the subsisting
Fuzzy-Ontology resources
elements 93
reusing the subsisting HIDAs
resources 92
specifying fuzzy-associated elements
in hypertension data 92

image analytics 157
images-textual hybrid
recommendation system 157–8
recommendation system for styles and
substitutes based on image 158
features 161
generating recommendation 161
Mahalanobis transform 159–60
style space 160–1
weighted nearest neighbor 159
image-based recommenders 17
images-textual hybrid recommendation
system 157–8
information communication
terminology (ICT) 72
information diffusion-aware
recommendation approaches
55–8
information filtering system 10, 28, 33

information privacy, defined 261
information systems (ISs) 76
Internet of Things (IoT) 42
intrusion detection (ID) 312
  description of KDD-Cup-99 data set
    312–14
  description of Kyoto network
    intrusion detection data set 314
  evaluation results for KDD-Cup-99
    319–20
  evaluation results for Kyoto 320–1
  experiments on KDD-Cup-99
    314–17
  experiments on Kyoto network
    intrusion detection data set
    318–19
  proposed architecture for
    KDD-Cup-99 data set 317–18
  proposed architecture for Kyoto
    318–19
  using multidimensional zoom
    (M-ZOOM) framework 322
  data set description 324
  density measures 322–3
  experiments and observations
    324–6
  problem formulation 323
intrusion detection system (IDS) 304,
  306
item-based algorithms 235–6, 242,
  249, 254
item-based collaborative filtering 247
item response theory (IRT) 270

Java reflection strategy 226
Java Virtua Machine (JVM) 229
Jensen's inequality 120
Jester 20
JIM 210

k-Anonymity 272–4
KDD-Cup-99 306–7, 313
  evaluation results for 319–20
  experiments on 314–17
  proposed architecture for 317–18

Keras 177
Kerberos 237, 315–16
key distribution center (KDC) 237–8
keyword-aware service
  recommendation (KASR) 136
k-means clustering 246
k-nearest neighbor 34, 54, 245–6
knowledge-based recommendations
  137–8
Kyoto network intrusion detection data
  (ID) set 314
  experiments on 318–19

Lagrange multipliers 115
large-scale databases (LSDB) 72–3,
  76–7, 81
latent Dirichlet allocation (LDA) 112,
  116–19, 118
LCA–LDA 197, 210, 213
l-diversity 272, 274
learner rating matrix 34
length variance (LengthVar) 252
Link Bench 38
Linux kernel 229
local area network (LAN) 72, 239
locality sensitive hashing (LSH) 286
location-aware recommender system
  (LARS) 136
location-based social networks
  (LBSNs) 193–5, 218
long short-term memory (LSTM) 311,
  318, 320
Love and Hate attack 243–4
low knowledge attacks 241

machine learning (ML) 19, 172,
  232, 303
MADMAID 313
Mahalanobis transform 159–60
malignant applications 230
malware applications 230
Mapper stage 157
MapReduce 3, 29–30, 162, 285–6
  slope one algorithm based on 157

Markov chain probability model 99–106
Markov random fields (MRFs) 50–1
Maxpool layer 174
mean absolute error (MAE) 250
memory-based techniques 15
message passing interface (MPI) 3
METAINF 230
Metaphone 285
metric learning to rank (MLR) algorithm 151
micro-video on big data, recommendation system for 155
  content-based recommendation 155–6
  slope one algorithm based on MapReduce 157
  slope one recommendation 156
mobile application risk reduction, proposed recommender system for 231
  dataset 233
  emulation and testing 232
  features extraction 232
  machine learning 232
  preprocessing 231–2
model-based approaches 15–16, 45
MovieLens 20
multi-agent system (MAS) 61
multi-attribute decision-making (MADM) 78–9
multidimensional zoom (M-ZOOM) framework 306–7
  intrusion detection (ID) using 322–6
multilayer perceptron based recommender systems 124
music genre weight-based music recommendation (MGW) model 143
music recommendation 11, 143
  graph-based quality model for 147
    graph-based music recommendation challenges 149
    graph-based quality model 148–9
    preference relation 148

learning content similarity for 151
  audio representation 152
  learning similarity: collaborative filters and metric learning to rank 151–2
  personalized tag-based social media music recommendation 145
    framework 146
    tag-based challenges 146–7
  prediction of genre-based link in a two-way graph for 143
    complex representation-based link prediction (CORLP) method 144–5
    feature extraction 145
    recommendation 145
  using acoustic features and user access patterns 149
    dynamic music similarity measurement 149–50
    music feature extraction and indexing 150–1
    music ranking 151
    music recommendation and label propagation on song graph 151
    user access patterns music recommendation challenges 151

name node algorithm 238–9
Name Node Security Enhance (NNSE) 239
Namespace cv 177
natural language processing (NLP) 112, 173, 304
nature-inspired algorithms, systems based on 37
need for RSs 10
neighborhoodness graph 57
Netflix 2
network-centric privacy 263
network intrusion detection systems (NIDSs) 305–7, 312
neural collaborative filtering (NCF) 113, 123–4

notifications manager 228
not only structured query language
(NoSQL) 18
nuke attacks 241–4
Nvidia GK110BGL Tesla K40 314
NYSIIS algorithm 284, 289

Okeanos IaaS academic service 296
online social networks, measuring
privacy in 265–71
dichotomous approach 266–9
polytomous approach 269–71
online social network services 259
online social network services, privacy
of 260–3
OpenCV 177–9
Open Handset Partnership (OHA) 227
OpenMP 3
ordinal matrix factorization (OMF) 53
ordinal random fields 53–4
ordinal RFs (ORF) 53
overspecialization or diversity problem
22

PageRank 307
pairwise-MRF (PMRF) modeling 51–3
pairwise recommendation MRFs 51–2
Pearson correlation 34, 240
Pearson correlation coefficient (PCC)
46
personalized tag-based social media
music recommendation 145
framework of music recommendation
146
tag-based music recommendation
challenges 146–7
personalized trip advisor service 162
personally identifiable information 272
phases of RSs 12
phishing URL detection 307–8, 327
data set description of 327
experiments 328
hyper-parameter tuning 328
proposed architecture for 329–30
URL representation 327–8

phonetic algorithms for privacy
preserving matching 287–8
phonetic codes 284–5, 287–8, 290–2,
phonetic encoding schemes 285
phonetics matching protocol 290
multiple algorithms for 290–1
operation 292–4
privacy discussion 294–5
possibly undesirable applications
(PUAs) 230
post-filtering 59
precision, defined 296
preference Markov random fields 54–5
preference networks (PNs) 52–3
prefiltering 59
privacy, defined 261
privacy index (PIDX) 268–9
privacy of online social network
services 260–3
privacy preservation 260, 271–2, 276–7
privacy preserving matching (PPM)
284, 290
phonetic algorithms for 287–8
privacy-preserving models 272
differential privacy 275
k-anonymity 272–3
l-diversity 274
t-closeness 274
privacy preserving record linkage
(PPRL) 283–6
privacy quotient 267
private entity resolution for big data on
Apache Spark 283
Apache Spark 289–90
empirical evaluation 295
experimental results 296–9
experimental setup 295–6
future work 299–300
NYSIIS algorithm 289
phonetic algorithms for privacy
preserving matching 287–8
phonetics matching protocol 290
multiple algorithms for 290–1
operation 292–4
privacy discussion 294–5

problem formulation 286–7
related work 284–6
Soundex algorithm 288–9
PrivAware 270–1
Privometer tool 269
probabilistic generative models (PGMs)
    112–13
probabilistic graphical models 50
    ordinal random fields 53–4
    pairwise recommendation MRFs
        51–2
    preference Markov random fields
        54–5
    preference networks (PNs) 52–3
probabilistic latent semantic analysis
    (PLSA) 112, 114–16, 246
probabilistic matrix factorization (PMF)
    112–14
problems related to RSs 21
    cold start problem 22
    data sparsity problem 21
    overspecialization or diversity
        problem 22
    scalability 22
    vulnerable to attacks 22
profile injection attacks 239, 241–2
    defense against 250–4
PScore 269
PSSG (projected scaled sub-gradient)
    202–3, 206
push attacks 241–3
    against enhanced hybrid algorithm
        249–50
PViz 269

radio frequency identification (RFID)
    170
random attack detection 249
random graph (RG) model 47
rating average deviation (RAD) 251–2
real-time video recommendation
    generation 154–5
recall, defined 296
receiver-oriented linear threshold model
    56

recommendation, visualization of 36
recommendation algorithms for
    unstructured big data 133
    big data analytic 139
    audio analytics 143–52
    image analytics 157–61
    personalized trip advisor service
        162
    recommendation system with
        Hadoop Framework 163
    text analytics 139–42
    video analytics 152–7
    recommender methods 134
    collaborative recommendations
        135–7
    content-based recommendations
        134–5
    demographic recommendations
        138
    hybrid recommendations 138–9
    knowledge-based
        recommendations 137–8
    recommender systems: challenges
        and limitations 163–4
recommendation problem 43–4
recommendation systems (RSs) 42–6
recommender algorithms 244
    association rule mining 245
    base algorithms 245
    and evaluation metrics 246
    enhanced collaborative filtering
        247
    item-based collaborative filtering
        247
    user-based collaborative filtering
        246–7
    k-means clustering 246
    k-nearest neighbor 245–6
    probabilistic latent semantic analysis
        (PLSA) 246
    profile classification 247–8
recommender methods 134
    collaborative recommendations
        135–7

content-based recommendations
134–5
demographic recommendations 138
hybrid recommendations 138–9
knowledge-based recommendations
137–8
rectified linear unit (ReLU) 174, 177,
309
recurrent neural network (RNN) 218,
310–11
recurrent recommender network (RRN)
113, 123
Reducer stage 157
remote procedure calls (RPCs) 236
Renner privacy risk formula 266
Resilient Distributed Dataset (RDD)
290
Resnick's algorithm 245
Resource Description Framework
(RDF) 98
resource manager 228
Restricted Boltzmann-machine-based
collaborative filtering
(RBM-CF) 113, 121–2
reverse Bandwagon attack 243–4
RiskRanker 226
RNN/LSTM for recommendation
124–5
rough set theory 77

Sandbox 229, 232
scalability problem 22
scale-free (SF) 47
security spillage/individual data
burglary 230
Segment attack 242–4, 249, 254
self-learning systems 304
self-sanitization actions 369
shilling attacks 64, 239
sigmoid activation function 174, 311
sigmoid function 177, 309, 319
signature-based detection systems 305
similarity degree (DegSim) 252
Simultaneous Extraction of Context and
Community (SECC) model 63

social network analysis 46–8
social networks, privacy concerns in
263–4
social RSs (SRS) 46
socio-aware recommendation systems
48
context-aware recommendation
systems 58–61
in IoT ecosystem 61
and social networks 62–4
hyperbolic path-based
recommendation system 48–50
information diffusion-aware
recommendation approaches
55–8
probabilistic graphical models 50–1
ordinal random fields 53–4
pairwise recommendation MRFs
51–2
preference Markov random fields
54–5
preference networks 52–3
SONET model 268–9
Soundex algorithm 284–5, 287–9
Spark: *see* Apache Spark
SPARQL 19
sparsity problem, reducing 35
spatial item, defined 198
spatial–temporal sparse additive
generative (ST-SAGE) model
193
experimental settings 209
comparative approaches 210–11
datasets 209–10
evaluation methods 211–12
model description 199–202
model inference 202–4
parallel implementation 205–8
preliminaries about 197
problem definitions 197–9
recommendation effectiveness 212
impact of different factors 214–15
results and analysis 212–14
recommendation efficiency 215
model training efficiency 216

online recommendation efficiency
216–17
related work 217–19
spatial item recommendation using
208–9
spatial smoothing 204–5
spot garbage 171
static examination 226, 231
stepper motor 181–2
stochastic gradient descent (SGD),
real-time matrix factorization
model update based on 153–4
STREAM 226
Structured Query Language (SQL) 18,
78
ST-SAGE-LS 216–17
ST-SAGE-TA 216–17
support vector machine (SVM) 17,
152, 171
swarm intelligence 37
switching mode power supply (SMPS)
181–2
switching power supply 181–2

TaintDroid 226
Target Model Focus (TMF) attribute
253
t-closeness 272, 274
TensorFlow 176–7
text analytics system, steps for 139
text recommendation using angle-based
interest model 140
data structure for calculating the
angles of interest 140–1
recommendation mechanism 141–2
simulating human reading features to
emerge interest 140
Ticket Granting Ticket (TGT) 237
time, defined 198
time-aware RSs (TARS) 60
TOPSIS (Technique for Order
Preference by Similarity to Ideal
Solution) approach 79

Torch7 framework for Lua 172
transmission control protocol
(TCP)/internet protocol (IP)
packets 304
Twitter 41, 209
two-phase stepper motor 181
types of RSs 13–20

ULN 2003 182–3
uniform resource locator (URL) 303,
308
UPS-CF 210, 213–14
user access patterns music
recommendation challenges
151
user activity, defined 198–9
user-based algorithms 235–6, 240, 243
user-based collaborative filtering
245–7
user home location, defined 198
user profile, defined 199
user's privacy in recommendation
systems 259
future directions 277
privacy of online social network
services 260–3
privacy preservation 276
taxonomy of privacy 263
measuring privacy in online social
networks 265–71
privacy concerns in social
networks 263–4
privacy-preserving approaches
271–2
privacy-preserving models 272–5
user-specific privacy risks and
invasion 264–5
uses of RSs 11
movie/music recommendation 11
product recommendation 11
scholarly search and news articles 11
services 11
UTE+SE 210

variable order Markov chains (VOMC) 63
variational inference (VI) 118
variety 2
vector quantization (VQ) threshold 152
velocity 2
veracity 2
video analytics 152
    real-time video-recommendation system 152
        challenges 155
        generation 154–5
        real-time matrix factorization model update based on stochastic gradient descent 153–4
    recommendation system for micro-video on big data 155
        content-based recommendation 155–6

slope one algorithm based on MapReduce 157
slope one recommendation 156
view system 229
vindictive applications 230
volume 2

webcam 182–3
Web Ontology Language (OWL) 98
weighted average deviation (WAD) 252
weighted degree of agreement (WDA) 252
weighted nearest neighbor 159
wide-area network (WAN) 72
windshield wiper motor 181

YahooWebscope datasets 21

9 781785 619751